CONRAD: EASTERN AND WESTERN PERSPECTIVES
General Editor: Wiesław Krajka

VOLUME VI

CONRAD, JAMES AND OTHER RELATIONS

EDITED BY KEITH CARABINE AND OWEN KNOWLES
WITH PAUL ARMSTRONG

SOCIAL SCIENCE MONOGRAPHS, BOULDER
MARIA CURIE–SKŁODOWSKA UNIVERSITY, LUBLIN
DISTRIBUTED BY COLUMBIA UNIVERSITY PRESS, NEW YORK

1998

CONRAD: EASTERN AND WESTERN PERSPECTTIVES

General Editor: Wiesław Krajka

VOLUME VI

Copyright © 1998 by Maria Curie-Skłowdowska University, Lublin
ISBN 0-88033-974-8
Library of Congress Catalog Card Number 97-62082

Printed in the United States of America

TABLE OF CONTENTS

PART I: CONRAD AND JAMES

PART II: CONRAD, JAMES AND OTHER RELATIONS

ABBREVIATIONS

I. Conrad's Works

Ch	*Chance*
LJ	*Lord Jim*
N	*Nostromo*
NLL	*Notes on Life and Letters*
NN	*The Nigger of the "Narcissus"*
PR	*A Personal Record*
SA	*The Secret Agent*
SL	*The Shadow-Line*
SS	*A Set of Six*
TLS	*'Twixt Land and Sea*
TU	*Tales of Unrest*
UWE	*Under Western Eyes*
V	*Victory*
WT	*Within the Tides*
YS	*Youth: A Narrative, and Two Other Stories*

All references to Conrad's works in the following essays are to the Dent Collected Edition (1946-55) or Oxford University Press's World's Classics Edition, whose pagination is identical to the Dent.

II. Conrad's Letters

CL *The Collected Letters of Joseph Conrad,*
ed. F. R. Karl and L. Davies (Cambridge: Cambridge U.P., 1983-), 5 vols.
LL *Joseph Conrad: Life and Letters,*
ed. G. Jean-Aubry (London: Heinemann, 1927), 4 vols.

Part I

Conrad and James

Eloise Knapp Hay,
University of California,
Santa Barbara, USA

James, Conrad and the Genealogy
of the Revolutionary Novel

Henry James's importance in the history of the revolutionary novel depends largely on *The Princess Casamassima*. After more than 30 years, I want to retract the words I wrote back in 1963 and repeated in 1981 (Hay, 239). In those years, comparing James's tragic novel with Conrad's grim comedy in *The Secret Agent,* I found *The Princess Casamassima* "frolicsome" and "a little frivolous" when set beside Conrad's "profoundly disturbing" satire. Beside James's precursors among the novelists of revolution – Dickens, Balzac, Hugo, Flaubert, Zola, Dostoevsky, Tolstoy and Turgenev – it did not seem to me that James ranked very high, whereas Conrad's four or five revolutionary novels represented for me the summit or culmination of all the rest. I wish now to make amends for underrating James by offering a new reading of *The Princess Casamassima* and then I hope to reconfigure the place of this novel in the genre of the revolutionary novel. In significant ways, *The Princess Casamassima* prepares the way not only for Conrad but also for such post-colonial novels as the Kenyan Ngugi wa Thiong'o's *A Grain of Wheat* and *Petals of Blood*.

The crux of *The Princess Casamassima* once seemed to me, as it still appears in the best critical essays from those of Lionel Trilling and Irving Howe onwards, to hinge on the hero's tormenting choice between service in the cause of suffering humanity at one extreme and at the other, defence of his cultural heritage as he finds it exemplified in the legacies of high European civilization. Put this way, however, the choice suggests that the novel centers on a false dichotomy. If the chief character were indeed so divided, no wonder that Howe could call him a "sticky little *arriviste*," crying for the moon of beauty, wealth

3

and leisure from which the diminutive Hyacinth Robinson has been disinherited by his cruel father, the murdered seducer Lord Frederick Purvis (*The Princess Casamassima,* 136). Now, after years of reading James, I feel sure that James knew as well as we do that social justice is not incompatible with high culture. The justice with which James is concerned in the novel is indeed alien to "militant socialism" (18) but in ways that I could not see and could not find explained in the essays of Trilling and Howe, or even in the fine later essays that commented on theirs, by Oscar Cargill, Daniel Lerner and W. H. Tilley among others. Evidently there must be more to Hyacinth Robinson's torment than a recoil from poverty and squalor if he – and the novel – are not to be accused of trivial pursuits.

James was the least schematic of writers, though again I learned this only after years of reading. He did not, as I once thought, tear his hero Hyacinth's soul apart through inability to reconcile qualities derived from his aristocratic English father (a rotter) with memories inherited from his proletarian French mother. One of many clues to save us from this misreading is in the derivation of Hyacinth's name. Of course, we quickly and rightly run to mythical associations, although James nowhere mentions the classical Hyacinth: the beautiful youth transformed into a flower after being accidentally killed by Apollo, god of radiant mind and beauty. The novel hints at a mythical reading, but only to point away from the romantic realm to the real conditions of life in late nineteenth-century London. What James does specify is that Hyacinth's mother, Florentine Vivier, named him after his French revolutionary grandfather, who died on the barricades of Paris in 1830. The delicate beauties associated with floral motifs are thus connected most clearly with his French mother, Florentine, and also with her experience of revolutionaries and the injured poor.

At other points in the novel, Hyacinth's aesthetic sensitivities are further associated with his awareness of his French blood and the sorrows of those closest to him – the dressmaker Amanda Pynsent, his impoverished foster-mother and the poor musician Anastasius Vetch. Hyacinth's native delicacies are thus nurtured by two poor artists. Through Pinnie's self-sacrifice, he studies French and other languages at an academy. Through Vetch, he finds employment in a bookbindery and develops an art of his own. The doting ministrations of these surrogate parents ensure that nothing in the world of superior tastes will be lost on him. However, his undemonstrative love for them and their very tender concern for his interests also sink deep roots of bitterness against, and envy of, his father's privileged class, which has subjected them no less than himself to the ignoble conditions in which they live. Vetch, a radical "of the old--fashioned, constitutional sort" (141), along with Pinnie and Hyacinth himself, are all natural aristocrats by virtue of their high valuation of one another and their respective arts.[1] All three reject their inclinations to bitterness and envy as unworthy. James tells us that "morally [Pinnie] had the best taste in the world" (66). She relies on her Christian faith for her trust that, despite her troubles, human society is ultimately indivisible (175). Vetch avoids vindictiveness by falling back on occasional cynicism. He lays blame for their sick society more on his own world of petty bourgeois Philistines than on either the aristocracy or the criminal underworld (39). Thus Pinnie, Vetch and Hyacinth (as I originally failed to see) have a peculiarly Jamesian strength in their awareness of the whole world's poor history and in their resistance to the worst evils, which in James's canon of values, are envy and its associated vice, malicious violence. Theirs are the "fine conscience[s]" which Conrad found so central in his essay on James. In contrast to Pinnie and Vetch, however, Hyacinth must grapple tragically with the demon of envy.

The superbly drawn Pinnie poignantly and absurdly reveres the world of fashion for the best of reasons: her natural taste in furtherance of her dressmaker's art. Paradoxically, it is she – with her addiction to style and beauty, "whose preference for distinguished forms never deserted her" (63) – who excites Hyacinth's fatal attraction to the Princess Casamassima's entourage, to which Pinnie so forgivably thinks he belongs by virtue of his father's blood, related to "half the aristocracy of

England" (138). There is another paradox in the violinist Vetch
– despiser of capital punishment – who with equally good
intentions, takes Hyacinth into the world of violent anarchism
by introducing him to employment in the bookbindery. There
Hyacinth meets yet another artist and strong advocate of
humane values, Eustache Poupin. This radical socialist, exiled to
England after his part in the Paris Commune, could well be at
one extreme a model for Conrad's humane idealist, the Garibal-
dino Viola in *Nostromo,* and at the other extreme a model for the
comfortable anarchists of *The Secret Agent,* whom Conrad
situates so safely at home in London, like the anti-capitalist
Poupins. Poupin disposes Hyacinth more than ever toward the
Paris of Poupin's happier memories, which is also the Paris of
Hyacinth's mother. The influences through whom this Hyacinth
becomes the accidental victim of Apollo are thus largely *the same*
persons as those devoted to social justice.

James identifies his cockney hero very closely with the poet
Keats, in both "Preface" (17) and the novel. Hyacinth's
undersized, rather effeminate stature, combined with tough-
-mindedness and manly good looks, recall the cockney poet's
anomalous five-foot height. Such discordant qualities strikingly
emphasize the real split in Hyacinth's nature, which was also
observed in Keats – his passionate devotion to beauty uniquely
combined with an extraordinary sensitivity to the suffering of
the world. James seems to allude again to Keats in showing how
the tragic illness and death of Hyacinth's mother contribute to
these desperate yearnings, toward poetry on one hand and
toward the relief of human misery on the other. Unlike Keats,
however, with his circle of educated, literary and artistic friends,
Hyacinth must rely on very different allies of a later generation,
met through his work: radical socialists of various stamps, who
further inflame his sense of the world's injuries. Some of these
radicals, like Vetch, Poupin and Schinkel the cabinet-maker, are
like Hyacinth himself, men distinguished by love of their arts and
therefore, in James's gallery, men redeemed from such crimes as
the novel reveals in those who cannot love anything or anyone,
but nurse their ideologies out of cold desire for action and

revenge. Paul Muniment and Diedrich Hoffendahl are such men, treating all things and people simply as so many weapons in their battle against the social order. That men of the kind existed and persist beyond James's time I was all too aware this year, worrying about the Unabomber on my way through Los Angeles International Airport, also remembering the sort of revenge other bombers took recently in the New York World Trade Center and in Oklahoma City. We have seen through the essays of Trilling, Tilley, Baldinger and others how thoroughly James authenticated the wide range of revolutionary types with whom he surrounds his hero.

To satisfy all of Hyacinth's longings, James gives him with equal verisimilitude two women with axes to grind, women from opposite stations in life. The lower-class, saucy fashion-model Millicent Henning and the Princess Casamassima are both able to staunch yearnings for his lost mother, for a sensual lover, and a partner in his quest for social equality. The Princess earns her title role by appearing to belong in all the worlds of his imagination: the enticing world of ideal refinements, along with the wealth on which for the moment these depend, and also the conscientious society of those committed to removing the barriers between classes, which have so impoverished him and those he loves.

The Princess, rejecting the aristocracy she seems to belong to, really belongs in none of these worlds. She comes into Hyacinth's life appearing to offer both preservation of "civilized" values and hope for rescuing "the disinherited," among them himself. One of James's little jokes, however, is that the only blooded aristocrats in the novel are Lady Aurora and the Princess's Italian husband, neither of whom values the high civilization with which Hyacinth associates the great cultural patrons of history. But isn't it just the point that his reverence for beauty is an idealized *dream* of rare qualities, a dream of perfection that seems possible to him only in contemplating the achievements of the past, removed from the imperfections of current life? While dining with the Princess at her country house,

> his other senses were so awake that hunger dropped out and he ate, as it were, without eating – and the grave automatic servant filled his glass with a liquor that reminded him of some lines of Keats in the "Ode to a Nightingale." He wondered if he should hear a nightingale at Medley.... (261)

With the Princess, he longs to escape from the world's misery and forget its pain, like Keats listening to the nightingale. The seductive Princess also awakens his need (as in another poem of Keats) to lie on "fair love's ripening breast." At this point Hyacinth has just committed himself to do the will of Hoffendahl, to serve the anarchist cause even with his life. His two impulses – to engage in social action but also to escape into an ideal world, away from "the fever and the fret" of human misery – are evident during his stay at Medley. He takes refuge with a *belle dame* who herself promises total immersion in the revolutionary cause. While he is infatuated with the Princess, we know very early what Hyacinth discovers too late, that if he cannot satisfy her taste for drama, she will drop him, and she does.

As soon as the Princess dominates the scene, James stresses how doubly unfortunate the late-born romantic Hyacinth is bound to be, and how deceptive the attraction to beauty can become. James's apology in the "Preface" for reviving Christina Light from his early novel, *Roderick Hudson,* stresses her double rôle as *femme fatale,* driving men to suicide, and as one variety of revolutionary. Being the rootless child of an illicit liaison, all the more illicit because she is the child of a mindless Anglo--American adventuress and the equivalent Italian for father, the Princess was thrown into the nineteenth century rather than born into it. In her incarnation as revolutionary, she is one of James's most original and seminal creations, as Louise Bogan has fully explained (472). The Princess is a perfect model of all "radical chic," inspiration of such later creations as Hardy's Sue Bridehead and (less attractively) Conrad's radical upper-class airheads in *The Secret Agent,* "The Informer," and *Under Western Eyes.* She has turned from a life of boredom in the dangerous cities of Italy to thrill-seeking among the slums and revolutionary hideouts of safe old England.

At first she desires only thrills, connection with a great force that will give her entry into history. She wants to be part of a movement that will "set the world on fire" (165). But she is also Hyacinth's sister under the skin and the possible lover for whom he is more than ready. Both are illegitimate children of misalliances; both are vulnerable to abuse, blackmail and disinheritance by reason of their irregular origins. Both will seek out strength in the revolution and be betrayed by it.

When Hyacinth disappoints the Princess because he lacks the single-minded resolution that she, also lacking it, identifies with strength, she turns to Paul Muniment. This Lancashire chemist has been the one character in the novel universally praised by critics as true to the life of radical workers, from the time of Bakunin and Marx to that of Lenin and Stalin. Muniment is praised also as anticipating, in Hyacinth's words, a future prime minister of England (181), though we see him less as an upcoming Ernest Bevan than as a working-class equivalent to Sidney and Beatrice Webb, herself a Lancashire radical. If we stress Muniment's general, humane appeal, we miss the qualities in him that make him one of James's least sympathetic characters, a man reminding me of Isabel Archer's suitor Lord Warburton, who creeps up on her slowly like a handsome snake and in the end is driven away without being fully seen, at least by the reader.

Hyacinth immediately takes Muniment's measure when they meet at Poupin's, surmising that he – Muniment – "would make society bankrupt, but he would be paid." He has qualities that Hyacinth knows he lacks himself, however, and Hyacinth admires him in his generous way. Paul is "tall and fair and good-natured looking" (97), remarkable for the kind of af-fability that comes with complete indifference to persons, something Hyacinth could never have. As Muniment's invalid sister Rosie remarks, "What my brother really cares for – well, one of these days, when you know, you'll tell me" (118). Even poor Rosie is important to Muniment because she is useful to him as a catspaw for sympathizers to the revolutionary cause. Likewise, Muniment regards Hoffendahl in purely functional terms. To him, Hoffendahl's loss of a hand under police torture represents an "economy of material" in view of the expense of other "materials" that might have been lost (251). As Poupin remarks Muniment is concerned with "arithmetic," and such utilitarianisms "fearfully English!" (252).

Ominously, the Princess admires Muniment's hardness, associating him and his name with the cold marble in monuments and the strength of fortresses (284). He wants to save "valuable property," whatever the cost in human lives, because "we shall put the correct sort" into the properties (250-1). When Hyacinth reveals his susceptibility and vulnerability to all things human and lovely, thereby showing his doubts as to the revolutionary destruction for which he has pledged himself to Hoffendahl, the Princess switches her attentions to Muniment. Soon afterwards, however, she learns that she too is only "material" to him. Her husband catches her in the act of taking Muniment to bed and cuts off her funds, upon which Muniment drops her. She is no longer useful.

Some have said that James is inconsistent in allowing Muniment a brief love affair with the Princess, but we do well to trust this author on the many differences between love and manipulation. Whatever Muniment feels or doesn't feel, however, his fling with the Princess is an indiscretion for him, incurring the distrust of Hoffendahl, who cuts off his connection with the movement. The novel's intensely dramatic closing scenes, like those in the best of James's fiction, require us to follow well-motivated but mysterious impulses, sudden changes in rôles like Muniment's and the Princess's, which determine fateful conclusions, like the one seen in Hyacinth's final hours. Muniment has gradually become aware of his sexual power over the Princess, while she has gradually come to recognize Hyacinth's submission to men inferior in quality to himself. When first hearing of the secret meeting where Hyacinth made his self-sacrificing vow to Hoffendahl and Muniment, the Princess had said compassionately to the little bookbinder, "We have a curious way of being fond of you" (292). Now, following her liaison with Muniment, when his heartless manipulations become clear to her, she also becomes clearer about her own treatment of others, and for the first time she questions her relations with the revolutionaries. Muniment sees Hyacinth only as an expendable instrument and describes the duke (whose assassination is meant to provoke a political crisis) not as a man but as "a very bad institution." Thus, belatedly, the Princess is driven to wonder if Muniment's – and Hoffendahl's – disregard for a human life is a strange manifestation of their political values. "However [the duke] falls," she asks, "will it be useful, valuable?" – as if suddenly seeing that "value" may not be the same as "use" (528).

James has told us in his "Preface" that the Princess "had not been...completely recorded" in *Roderick Hudson,* that he found himself now in the later novel named for her, "clothing her chilled and patient nakedness" (19). In rapid changes, she first capriciously asks to substitute herself for Hyacinth as the duke's assassin and then tries feverishly to *save* a life – Hyacinth's – when she realizes he may be dead, thus registering (too late, of course) the "value" of this life, ignored by the "militant socialists."

Though she is the title-figure, the Princess is not the novel's center, only a principal source of light on Hyacinth. As the true center, he turns to her – Christina Light – as even sick flowers turn to a clouded sun. Similarly in Conrad's first three revolutionary novels, the title-figures seem deliberately located off-center, pointing toward the more sentient hero or heroine. Nostromo is the main source of light on the failure of Charles Gould's revolution, dedicated to "material interests." The vapid "secret agent," Verloc, witlessly wakes Winnie Verloc from lethargy into horror. And "the Western eyes" of the later title throw light on the central agony of Razumov, himself like the other novels' focal figures caught from ordinary life under the juggernaut of revolution. The Princess Casamassima similarly appears to be mainly a silly weather vane, but in the end (like Nostromo and the "Western eyes") she is essential in reflecting the full tragedy of the hero. As she throws herself in devastated comprehension on Hyacinth's dead body, James endows her with tragic importance (an Aristotelian uniting of *peripetia* and *anagnorisis*). Implied is the rejection of her romance with revolution at the same moment as she recognizes the role she has played in Hyacinth's suicide.

The great contrast in the novel is not, then, between a "sticky little *arriviste*'s" pining for high society and a complex social upheaval. It is between a wide variety of sympathetic social outcasts and a secret cell that will do anything to change the people in power for other people in power – for purely utilitarian ends. One of England's chief Marxist critics has recently put his finger on the very distinction James is making. Terry Eagleton, in an essay on "Theory in the Space Between Culture and Capitalism," focuses on the way in which many radicals have (like Muniment) separated the means to their ends from what Eagleton calls "the realm of being." This realm, as opposed to the realm of "doing," is for Eagleton the realm where culture lives, and I think it is the realm where Hyacinth Robinson – along with all the other "little" artists in James's novel – lives. "Ever since the Enlightenment [says Eagleton] culture has been the 'other' of political society....If culture split off from society, it was partly because that society, as it fell under the sway of instrumental Reason, had less and less time for the values [that culture] nurtured" (Eagleton, 3). Paul Muniment's incisive mind epitomizes the "instrumental Reason" that Eagleton refers to. At the other extreme, with the gap in between that Eagleton also describes, is the utopian ideal which Hyacinth pursues, a cultural ideal isolated from its "traditional social functions," so that its supporters grow impotent and – in Hyacinth's case – suicidal.

James meticulously traces the steps in Hyacinth's path along the empty space between the things he values and the world of efficient social action. As James had said in "The Art of Fiction," there is nothing so good as "a psychological reason" in writing a novel (61). The psychological reason in Hyacinth's case is his acute consciousness of *envying* the lives of people like the Princess, who have freedom and all the resources of cultivated minds and senses at their disposal. Though not the first critic to focus on this, Trilling has correctly noted that envy lies behind Hyacinth's commitment to abstract justice (89).[2] No-one, however, has sufficiently examined how crucial Hyacinth's experience of envy is, not only in his attraction to the revolutionary cause but later also in his growing disgust with the movement and with himself. It isn't just the envy of have-nots for the haves, as one might think (an envy that justifies "what the police are for," according to Winnie Verloc's simple reasoning in Conrad's *The Secret Agent* – *SA*, 173). Hyacinth is fully aware of how banal such envy can be, and he repeatedly distances himself from it. He reflects with satisfaction that he and his fellow bookbinders at Crook's are immune to "the social jealousy lying at the bottom of the desire for a fresh deal," partly because they are (unlike Muniment) "highly skilled workmen" and artists (*The Princess Casamassima,* 360).

The matter is far from simple. Hyacinth has previously reflected that there is a kind of envy, possessed by the shopgirl Millicent, who merely "env[ies] other people for possessing [things she couldn't have]" – and sets about acquiring them for herself while disparaging those who happen to have them already. By contrast, "the remedy for him was terribly vague and inaccessible." When his "sense of exclusion...settle[s] on him like a pall" he observes that his feelings are "not invidious...not moods of vengeance...they [are] simply states of paralyzing melancholy." In such states, he is especially conscious of the "high human walls, the deep gulfs of tradition, the steep embankments of privilege and dense layers of stupidity fencing the 'likes' of him off from social recognition." Yet, still cross-examining his feelings, he finds they are "not the fruit of morbid vanity on his part, or of a jealousy that couldn't be intelligent; his personal discomfort [is] the result of an intense *admiration* for what he [has] missed" (132-3; my emphasis). What draws him into committing himself to Hoffendahl's terrorist campaign is *admiration* for Muniment, and this protects him from hostile jealousy: "he [has] no envy of the man" trusted by Hoffendahl (246).

On closer acquaintance with Muniment, Hyacinth does make "invidious" comparisons between the two of them, but the contrast is all in Muniment's favor. While Hyacinth is overly sensitive to the poor, he approves Muniment's "cheerful stoicism," the "dry statistical and scientific air" and hard objectivity that make Muniment capable of seeing the failures of the poor as clearly as the injustices of the rich. To Hyacinth, Muniment's "absence of passion" appears "reasonable," for "most enviable of all was the force that enabled [Muniment] to sink personal sentiment where a great public good was to be attempted" (347). Hyacinth is now able to admit envying Muniment because he makes admiration rather than dislike the basis of the emotion, an important difference in the novel and in James's life.

The distinction is one found recurrently in James's autobiography. For instance, in *Autobiography: A Small Boy and Others;...* (1910), recalling with delight long walks he had alone with his father in New York, James stops to observe that his brother William also enjoyed such paternal attentions and that William had later remembered them in some detail. James writes, "I sometimes wished, with a retracing jealousy, or at least envy, that I might also have fallen heir to [these memories]" (*Autobiography: A Small Boy and Others;...*, 41). Envy, as seen here, is psychologically lesser than jealousy because jealousy makes an enemy of one's rival, whereas envy focuses on an advantage that another has gained without offence. (Dictionaries still cite this difference between jealousy and envy.) James makes the distinction again later in his memoir when he finds himself (paradoxically) envying his cousin Gus Barker both for his freedoms from parental pressures as an orphan and for his attendance at a military school, from which together they visit the nearby penitentiary at Sing-Sing. Here they meet a prisoner lounging at ease, and again James remarks on his envy of such unabashed idleness. It was not "jealousy...a sort of spiritual snatching" to the other's detriment, James insists, but rather "the restlessness of envy," which led him to see "'gifts' everywhere" as ones he himself might possess. After the moment's bemusement, he allows himself a small victory: envy "was the effect at least of self-abandonment – I mean to visions" (99-102).

As we have seen, this struggle to find redeeming aspects in envy had already preoccupied James some twenty-five years earlier, while telling Hyacinth's story. The intense concern is curiously reminiscent of Chaucer's analysis of the "deadly sin" of *invidia* in *The Canterbury Tales*. Indeed, in "The Parson's Tale," envy is called "the worst of sins." Citing Aristotle and St. Augustine and including jealousy together with envy under *invidia*, the Parson notes that each of the other deadly sins "may be only against one special virtue" – chastity for instance. But "Envy is against all the virtues and against all goodness. It sorrows in the excellence of its neighbors....Only Envy takes no delight in what it sins against." It also "sorrows in another man's prosperity, which is naturally a matter for joy." It is "truly like the devil in that it ever rejoices in another's harm" (Chaucer, "The Parson's Tale," 288-9; translation mine).

In making envy a continuous anxiety for Hyacinth, James thus revives a cultural emphasis that has been – like many other cultural imperatives – trivialized in the age of "instrumental Reason." At the novel's climax, the envy (which Hyacinth has buried to the point of feeling incapacitating melancholy) confronts him openly – and aptly – when he is finally able to visit the great fountainheads of European culture in Paris, Milan and Venice. Only in these surroundings does he realize that envy has motivated the anarchist movement to which he has pledged his life. He concedes that "the general fabric of civilization as we know it [is] based upon all the despotisms," but thanks to them, he concludes, "the world is less of a 'bloody sell'" than it will be if Hoffendahl and the anarchists have their way. Hoffendahl "would cut up the ceilings of the Veronese into strips, so that everyone might have a little piece...and I've a great horror of that kind of invidious jealousy," he writes to the Princess (*The Princess Casamassima*, 352-3). What we may miss is that Hyacinth also convicts himself at this point, confessing

> a deep distrust of that same grudging attitude – the intolerance of
> positions and fortunes that are higher and brighter than one's own;
> a fear moreover that I may in the past have been actuated by such
> motives, and a devout hope that if I'm to pass away while I'm yet
> young it may not be with that odious stain upon my soul.

In fact, however, the "odious stain" is fated to spread in him through new channels. His Princess rejects him as one of her intimates after hearing the effect the European tour has had on him, leading him to see that she now prefers Lady Aurora's company, and later Paul Muniment's intimacy, to his own. He grows "sad for strange vague reasons that he couldn't have expressed," the old melancholy gripping him as he resists a new jealousy, which can only make him despise those he most admires (389, 468). Compelled by Prince Casamassima to spy on his wife's clandestine affair with Muniment, Hyacinth experiences "the rage of jealousy" for a man he has now learned to distrust, and feels his heart "beat insanely, ignobly" (468). He finds within himself what he had before deplored mostly in others ("Everywhere, everywhere he saw the ulcer of envy – the greed of a party hanging together only that it might despoil another to its advantage" – 361). It was bad enough to find the idealist Poupin hungering to possess Paris by dispossessing those who presently enjoyed that wonderful city. But now, devoured by frustrated hunger for a renewed intimacy with the Princess and by hatred for his rival, Hyacinth despises himself.

Relief comes briefly in one of the novel's most powerful scenes, when love and delight revive on a Sunday spent with Millicent, his alluring childhood friend. In her company, London with its old parks and churches seems once again "the richest expression of the life of man" (430), closing that abyss between cultural value and political ideology which has threatened to engulf him. As token of the trust he now invests in Millicent, a companion so similar in social standing to himself, he lowers his protective mask. For the first time he shares with another the secret of his mother's shame – the murder of her seducer. Millicent responds with "a generous agitation" and returns his kiss "with the full mass of her interest" (481, 483). Like Keats at the same age (twenty-four), Hyacinth loses his suicidal sadness momentarily in the promising arms of a fair woman, loving but unfortunately (like the Princess) erratic.

Hoffendahl's letter promptly follows, demanding fulfilment of his vow – to rid the world of a "humbug" Duke (like Hyacinth's own father) and to shake the complacency of a moribund aristocracy (like the Casamassimas). Having re-lived his mother's agony in describing it to Millicent, though, Hyacinth is now aghast that he will repeat her crime in killing the Duke. The inevitable publicity of his crime will furthermore bring her forgotten shame "again into the eye of the world" (529). The overwhelming memory of his mother's degradation makes the possibility of flight with Millicent his one last hope as he looks for her in the shop where she works. When he finds Millicent, as he fears, playing him false with Captain Sholto, his last support is shattered. All he can do, it seems, is conquer envy with a regard for other lives. In turning the pistol on himself, we are led to conjecture that he keeps his vow to Vetch not to carry out the assassination of the Duke. But rather than live with his broken vow to the anarchists, he surrenders a life made "odious" by the "stain" of jealousy (352-3).

I have traced the central episodes in James's one novel of revolution in order to stress the changes he made in the genre he admittedly received from Turgenev and the other nineteenth-century novelists I have mentioned. These changes, principally in the hero's long struggles of conscience with fundamental values, inherited from centuries of European tradition, focus for Hyacinth Robinson on fidelity, the refusal to despise or betray – through a Keatsian envy of their happier lot – what he has received from others. The changes obviously appealed in powerful ways to Conrad, who took much more from James than is usually allowed. We know from Conrad's autobiography his "conviction that the world...rests on a few very simple ideas;...among others, on the idea of Fidelity" (PR, XXI). Though Conrad speaks of fidelity as an "idea," his revolutionary novels represent it rather as a fundamental cultural value, part of a man or woman's state of "being" (in Eagleton's use of the term), very like the way James represents envy as part of his own and his hero's state of being. T. S. Eliot was right when he observed that neither James nor Conrad wrote novels of "ideas." Eliot's famous point in 1918, that James "had a mind so fine that no idea could violate it" (Eliot, *The Little Review,* 46) was matched the following year when Eliot wrote, "Mr. Conrad has no ideas, but he has a point of view, a world. It can hardly be defined, but it pervades his work and is unmistakable" ("Kipling Redivivus," 298). Eliot would probably agree that what he identifies as "a point of view" and "a world" could be more specifically called a complex cultural tradition and the standpoint from which Conrad personally viewed it.

Such terms, when applied to the novels of James and Conrad, are closely related to some struggle for integrity, the inner "being" of both author and character. Conrad called it "the whole 'sentiment of existence'" in "Author's Note" to *Lord Jim* (*LJ*, VIII). James is more explicit, perhaps, when he writes in his autobiography that all he demanded was "just to *be* somewhere – almost anywhere would do – and somehow receive an impression or an accession, feel a relation or a vibration" (James, *Autobiography: A Small Boy and Others;...,* 17). He connects this sense of being with the importance of the "inward life," as when he considers how little event or action there was in his childhood home and asks why "we yet weren't more inane?" He answers, "This was doubtless by reason of the quantity of our inward life – ours of our father's house in especial, I mean – which made an excellent, in some cases almost an incomparable, *fond* for a thicker civility to mix with when growing experience should begin to take that in. It was also quaint...to have *begun* with the inward life; but we began, after the manner of all men, as we could, and I hold that if it comes to that we might have begun much worse" (34). Without this emphasis in his life and work, we cannot estimate James's contribution to the novel of revolution.

Conrad carried much farther than James his recognition that the modern world was undergoing many revolutions and that it behoved him to write about them – with ferocious animus but not without sympathy – such sympathy as indeed led James's Hyacinth into revolutionary company. After all, Conrad notes in *A Personal Record* that his own father along with his paternal grandfather, an uncle and an aunt "were all deeply involved in the revolutionary work" of freeing Poland from its oppressors (*PR*, 57). Considering the extreme ambivalence that "revolutionary work" excited in Conrad, we would expect treatments far more varied in his novels of revolution than those we find in James. In *Nostromo,* there are five revolutions, starting with the admirable one to free Latin America from colonial rule.[3] In *The Secret Agent,* many motifs that appear in the London of *The Princess Casamassima* are turned from tragedy into farce. The anarchists, on whom both novels center, in Conrad's story have turned from real action to lazy pretences of action. Conrad seems aware of Marx's comment in 1851 that "all facts and personages of great importance in world history occur...twice: the first time as tragedy, the second as farce" (Marx, *The Eighteenth Brumaire...,* 141). In Conrad's third novel of revolution, *Under Western Eyes,* the farcical figures of pretentious frauds are still in evidence, but the hero, Razumov, is as tragic a figure as Hyacinth Robinson and for similar reasons. That is, Razumov is drawn into the revolution by accident and finds that he must become a betrayer or face ruin. He, too, in the end chooses "perdition" rather than go on betraying even his betrayers, as well as the woman he loves (*UWE*, 362). One could go on to Conrad's last finished novel, *The Rover,* and detail the same pattern of accidental involvement in revolution and the hero's final suicide in the service of love – two loves, in fact: love of a woman and love of his homeland, France.

But let me end with what I see as James's greatest legacy to the novel of revolution, I mean his focus on the marginal, or superfluous, man. Turgenev had captured this type of modern man in *The Diary of a Superfluous Man* (1850) and amplified it in his later novels. James was especially affected, as we know, by Turgenev's portrait of the figure, in *Virgin Soil,* as the illegitimate, disinherited and unwanted child of a vain aristocrat. Turgenev's Nezhdanov, like James's Hyacinth, is emblematic of an anarchic, dying world, struggling toward a new, democratic society. But James vastly enlarged this man's inner life and his relations with a wider range of dissident and revolutionary types, achieving (in Trilling's view) "an incomparable representation of the spiritual circumstances of our civilization" (95).

Conrad carried this marginal man still further, to deeper regions of social dislocation and with greater knowledge from his own experience as a marginal man. Without Hyacinth Robinson's subtle sense of betraying and being betrayed by his society, however, we should not be so likely to have Conrad's corrupted Italian sailor, Nostromo; or Winnie Verloc – compelled to endure marriage and life in an alien world with a vacuous secret agent. Most certainly we should not have Conrad's Razumov, fellow countryman of Turgenev's Nezhdanov, but greatly expanded by virtue of Razumov's initial acts of betrayal and imposture – so parallel to Hyacinth's guilty sense of his shameful birth, which compels him to wear a mask from boyhood till his last hours. We could even include Conrad's old pirate Peyrol, self-drafted into serving, and committing suicide for, the French Revolution, despite Peyrol's contempt for its methods and consequences. Though Conrad's personal experience of alienation and exile from his native land unquestionably strengthened his hand in writing these revolutionary novels, we recall that Turgenev and James were also self-exiled, and both also (through Turgenev's acquaintance with Bakunin and Kropotkin) had personal knowledge of revolutionaries. All three novelists shared some of the temptations, doubts and guilt felt by their deracinated heroes and heroines for subversive action (if only in writing) against their homelands.

The literary tradition enriched by these writers can be found in revolutionary novels written in post-colonial Africa, India and Latin America, where Conrad stands very high and James hardly at all. Conrad was the first *globally* conscious novelist of their stature, and this has made him especially important to fellow-writers like the Trinidadian V. S. Naipaul, the Indian R. K. Narayan and the Africans Chinua Achebe and Ngugi wa Thiong'o. Recently reading Ngugi's *Petals of Blood* with one of my classes, I was struck by the way in which marginal, or superfluous, man still dominates the revolutionary novel, now with no reference to his first appearances in Turgenev and James, but with Ngugi's full acknowledgement of a debt to Conrad.

Petals of Blood is the last novel Ngugi wrote before rejecting English in favor of his African language. One of his four chief figures in the novel is a truly dislocated man, Godfrey Munira, who is alienated by reason of his father's rejection (as are the heroes of *Virgin Soil, The Princess Casamassima* and *Under Western Eyes*). But Munira is no tragic figure. He is a hollow man, alienated from the revolutionary movement by his religious fanaticism, which he inherits from a Christianized father and uses finally as a weapon against him; and also against Kenya's Leninist revolution. Gutted by sexual jealousy and by history's contempt for him, this marginal man turns betrayer and finally murders three neo-colonialist entrepreneurs, pursuing his puritanical rage against a fellow African woman's "weakness of the flesh." Ngugi's interest is riveted from first to last on betrayals of the revolutionary movement rather than of persons. He is as concerned as James and Conrad with closing the gap Eagleton discusses, between cultural values and political action. However, Ngugi plainly approves the demolition of all Westernized institutions, calling for a return to the mythical origins of "the people," cultural values evidently disembodied except in folk tales. Left standing is only the ideology constructed by the revolutionaries' "instrumental Reason."

Like the anarchists in James's and Conrad's novels, Ngugi's revolutionaries hope to raze the visible monuments of their history in order to clear space for a new society. But unlike James and Conrad, whose new society would allow for a common language and the community of all existing classes, Ngugi's narrative focuses recurrently on an unbridgeable chasm between social classes and between the author's own and other languages. Indeed, Ngugi's analysis of "culture" seems driven by the dissecting process of "instrumental Reason," which Eagleton sees as hostile to both culture and effective political change: "Culture [Ngugi writes] is a product and a reflection of human beings communicating with one another in the very struggle to create wealth and to control it" (*Decolonizing the Mind,* 15).

   In this light we may better understand Ngugi's qualified praise
of Conrad:

> *Nostromo* was my favorite. I still think it is a great novel, but on the
> whole I found Conrad's vision limited. His ambivalence toward
> imperialism – and it was imperialism that supplied [Conrad] with the
> setting and subject matter of his novels – could never let him go
> beyond the balancing acts of liberal humanism. But the shifting points
> of view in time and space; the multiplicity of narrative voices; the
> narrative-within-a-narration; the delayed information that helps the
> revision of a previous judgment so that only at the end with a full
> assemblage of evidence, information and points of view, can the
> reader make full judgment – these techniques had impressed me. (76)

Petals of Blood demonstrates all these "techniques," these
instances of "instrumental Reason" in the novel's apparatus.
But in paying tribute to Conrad's virtuosity, Ngugi inevitably, if
grudgingly, pays homage also to Conrad's larger capacities and
insights, in fact to his cultural values as revealed in the intense
interiority of his "shifting points of view," which cannot be
subtracted from his "techniques." Ngugi's most powerful hero
in *Petals of Blood,* Abdulla, resembles Conrad's Nostromo and
James's Hyacinth in that Abdulla experiences a "rebirth" from
being the object of other people's wills into being "a complete
man" (137). He alone undergoes the transformation, derived as
it appears to me from Conrad and James, which is likely to be
found at the heart of all great novels of revolution.[5]

NOTES

   1. The sense of natural aristocracy is crucial in reading James, certainly
from his characterizations of men and women from Christopher Newman
(in *The American,* 1875) through that of Adam Verver (in *The Golden Bowl,*
1904). They need not be Americans, however. As his typing of Hyacinth
Robinson indicates, Europeans with no inherited privileges may also
qualify. Ivan Turgenev, whose *Virgin Soil* provided numerous suggestions
for *The Princess Casamassima,* was himself by James's account a natural
aristocrat, though – unlike Hyacinth – provided with a wealthy, middle-
-class Russian family. In James's first essay on Turgenev (1874), he

commends Turgenev for his "impalpable union of an aristocratic temperament with a democratic intellect" (*Literary Criticism,* 992). As the essay proceeds, the features of "an aristocratic temperament" include Turgenev's "devoutly attentive" vision, his "impulse toward universal appreciation" of "every class of society, every type of character, every degree of fortune, every phase of manners," his "deeply sympathetic sense of the wonderful complexity of our souls," and his "apprehension of man's religious impulses" (972-4). What Turgenev nevertheless lacks as "realist" and "elegiast" is "an ideal of joy." This element is also part of "the aristocratic temperament," judging by James's representations. Turgenev's "pessimism," derived from disappointments in Russia, "the land that is dear to him," leads him and his chief figures to "the abuse of irony" and "sarcasm." James's natural aristocrats are "purged of sarcasm" and cling to an "ideal of joy," but still they exemplify his agreement with Turgenev's "temperamental" view, that "evil is insolent and strong; beauty enchanting but rare; goodness very apt to be weak; folly very apt to be defiant; wickedness to carry the day; imbeciles to be in great places, people of sense in small, and mankind generally, unhappy" (996-8).

2. In 1925, Van Wyck Brooks faulted James for having Hyacinth envy the socially advantaged, arguing that "a young man in Hyacinth's position would have...gone to Australia or vanished into the slums, or continued with the utmost indifference at his trade of binding books" (82-3). Hitting from the other end, against Hyacinth's self-reproach for *being* envious, in 1951 F. W. Dupee granted James's emphasis but said that Hyacinth's worries about envy mark him as a "man who is too good for this world....Surely [he] travels far to learn what he could have read any day in the *Times*: that radicals are envious" (157).

3. For the five revolutions in *Nostromo,* see my chapter on the novel in *The Cambridge Companion to Conrad,* ed. J. H. Stape (Cambridge: Cambridge U.P., 1996), 81-99.

4. See D. S. Mirsky's discussion of the *Diary,* in *A History of Russian Literature,* 198.

5. I am grateful to Martha Banta and Millicent Bell for inspired comments on this essay. Both of them, on different points central to my discussion, drew my attention to James's autobiographical treatment of these same subjects: of "Envy" (Professor Banta) and of "being versus doing" (Professor Bell).

WORKS CITED

Baldinger Friedrich. *Vom Faktum zur Fiktion: Eine historische und literarische Untersuchung von Henry James' "The Princess Casamassima" und Joseph Conrad's "Under Western Eyes."* Bern: A. Francke, 1981.

24   Eloise Knapp Hay

Bogan Louise. "James on a Revolutionary Theme," *Nation*, 144 (April 23, 1938).
Brooks Van Wyck. *The Pilgrimage of Henry James*. New York: E. P. Dutton, 1925.
Cargill Oscar. *The Novels of Henry James*. New York: Macmillan, 1961.
Chaucer Geoffrey. "The Parson's Tale," *The Poetical Works of Chaucer*, ed. F. N. Robinson. Boston: Houghton Mifflin, 1933.
Dupee F. W. *Henry James*. London: Methuen, 1951.
Eagleton Terry. "Discourse and Discos: Theory in the Space Between Culture and Capitalism," *Times Literary Supplement*, July 15, 1994.
Eliot Thomas Stearns. "In Memory" [of Henry James], *The Little Review*, 5:4 (August 1918).
Eliot Thomas Stearns. "Kipling Redivivus," *Athenaeum*, 4645 (May 9, 1919).
Hay Eloise Knapp. *The Political Novels of Joseph Conrad*. Chicago: U. of Chicago P., 1981 (1963).
Howe Irving. *Politics and the Novel*. New York: Meridian Books, 1957.
James Henry. "The Art of Fiction," in James Henry *Literary Criticism: Essays on Literature; American Writers; English Writers*. New York: Library of America, 1984.
James Henry. *Autobiography: A Small Boy and Others; Notes of a Son and Brother; The Middle Years*, ed. Frederick W. Dupee. New York: Criterion Books, 1956.
James Henry. "Ivan Turgenev," in James Henry *Literary Criticism: French Writers; Other European Writers; The Prefaces to the New York Edition*. New York: Library of America, 1984.
James Henry. *The Princess Casamassima*. Harmondsworth: Penguin Books, 1977. [Text is from the New York Edition rather than the edition of 1886 upon which the later Penguin edition is based.]
Lerner Daniel. "The Influence of Turgenev on Henry James," *The Slavonic Year-Book*, (American Series 1), 20 (December 1941) (*The Slavonic and East European Review*).
Marx Karl. *The Eighteenth Brumaire of Louis Bonaparte. December 2, 1851: Contemporary Writings on the Coup d'État of Louis Napoléon* [selections from], ed. John B. Halsted. Garden City: Doubleday, 1972.
Mirsky D. S. *A History of Russian Literature from Its Beginnings to 1900*, ed. Francis J. Whitfield. New York: Knopf, 1958.
Ngugi wa Thiong'o. *Decolonising the Mind: The Politics of Language in African Literature*. London: Heinemann, 1986.
Ngugi wa Thiong'o. *Petals of Blood*. New York: Penguin, 1991.
Tilley W. H. *The Background of "The Princess Casamassima."* Gainesville: U. of Florida P., 1960.
Trilling Lionel. *The Liberal Imagination: Essays on Literature and Society*. Garden City: Doubleday, 1948.
Turgenev Ivan. *Virgin Soil*, 2 vols. New York: Macmillan, 1917.

Rodie Sudbury,
York, England

Anarchism and Suicide in *The Princess Casamassima* and *The Secret Agent*

In March 1920, when Conrad had just finished turning *The Secret Agent* into a play for the stage, he said in a letter to Galsworthy: "I've managed to ram everything in there except the actual cab-drive" (*LI,* II, 238). Fifteen months later, after Galsworthy had seen the script and had apparently ruffled Conrad's feelings by suggesting various cuts, Conrad wrote: "I have often felt that not only the Third but the Second Act could come out altogether;" and he added:

> Indeed I was tempted, or I might have been tempted, to begin the play with the three delightful anarchists sitting in the parlour round the fire and Mr. Verloc explaining to them the circumstances which force him to throw a bomb at some building or other, discussing ways and means, and ending the effective scene by taking Stevie by the scruff of the neck. 'Come along, youngster, you carry the bomb,' and Comrade Ossipon blowing a kiss as they all go out at the door to Mrs. Verloc, who stands horrorstruck in the middle of the stage. Curtain. (258)

From there, Conrad says, one could go direct to the third scene of the fourth Act without changing a word.

Despite its deliberate absurdity, this projected removal of all that constitutes the artistic shape of both play and novel does nevertheless show what, for Conrad, are the irreducible bare bones of the drama. The story is a domestic tragedy, triggered by the existence of anarchists. The *Princess Casamassima,* also, is concerned with an intimate personal tragedy which comes about because of the hero's involvement with an anarchist organization. The similarities and the differences between the two books are quite considerable; but I shall try to show that in the end the two are more similar than different.

25

Conrad in his "Author's Note" to *The Secret Agent* described
how the story of Winnie Verloc and her maternal passion came to
stand out complete, for him, "from the days of her childhood to
the end;" and he said: "*This* book is *that* story, reduced to
manageable proportions, its whole course suggested and centred
round the absurd cruelty of the Greenwich Park explosion" (*SA*,
XII). I agree totally with that formulation: the explosion is at the
heart of the book, and the story is elaborately constructed so as to
show how that one terrible event and its aftermath come about
through a kind of cat's-cradle of cross-purposes and secret
motivations, with all the characters moving intently on their own
overlapping circular paths – like the circles drawn by Stevie. (And
one might also say that at the heart of *The Princess Casamassima*
lies the horrific moment when the gun will be fired, although one
doesn't know until the very end who the victim will be.)

Conrad called it Winnie's story; but centering it round the
explosion makes it unavoidably the story of Winnie *and* Stevie.
They are in a sense joint victims of the bomb; Winnie's death is
inextricably bound up with Stevie's, just as her life has been
bound up with his life. Winnie and Stevie together form a kind of
composite figure that can be seen as corresponding to the figure
of Hyacinth in *The Princess Casamassima* – Stevie the innocent
manipulated victim, Winnie who is driven to both murder and
suicide. And their composite view of society forms one of the
central statements of the book: Stevie sees with devastating
clarity that it's a "Bad world for poor people," and Winnie
placidly tells him "Nobody can help that," and the police "are
there so that them as have nothing shouldn't take anything away
from them who have" (171-2). Winnie deals with existence by
not questioning the status quo; she feels life doesn't stand much
looking into. But the book does look into it; it examines the
whole issue of suffering, both the attitude of those who say
"Nobody can help that," and of those who claim that it can be
helped. Conrad said to Galsworthy in 1906, "I had no idea to
consider anarchism politically" (*LL*, II, 37); but through the
anarchists, and through the ironic treatment which he chose
because it was the only way he could say all he felt he would have

to say "in scorn as well as in pity" (*SA,* XIII), he is able to look at the place of compassion in reformist politics. He interrogates the comfortable presuppositions of his readers by opposing the figures of Stevie and the Professor, and by depicting the eventual fate of Comrade Ossipon.

Stevie's compassion is total, and it's totally ineffectual; it's summed up in his wish to take the broken-down cabman and his broken-down horse to bed with him – and he knows that he can't. At the other extreme is the Professor, totally committed to the destruction of society, who can't allow himself any compassion at all, because the society he aims to destroy is built on the needs of the weak. He would exterminate the weak (undeterred by the ironic fact that physically he's quite weak himself); and he yearns for a little madness and despair in the present mediocre state of things, because with madness and despair for a lever, he could move the world.

But Ossipon knows that they are there, and the book ends with the poetic justice of the heartless calculator, the rational believer in science, being driven insane by the unwanted knowledge that he daren't pass on to anyone. The newspaper account of Winnie's suicide refers to the "impenetrable mystery" hanging over "*This act of madness or despair*" (310-11), and Ossipon is the only one who holds the answer to the mystery. He doesn't feel guilt, he doesn't feel pity; but unlike Verloc, and unlike the reporter who wrote this rather facile story, Ossipon can't escape his overwhelming realization of Winnie's agony of mind. He is punished for, and through, a rationality which allows no place for compassion; we leave him marching in the gutter with his ambrosial head bowed, muttering to himself with scientific insight: "I am seriously ill" (311).

Near the end of his "Author's Note" to *The Secret Agent,* Conrad talks about "moments during the writing of the book when I was an extreme revolutionist, I won't say more convinced than they but certainly cherishing a more concentrated purpose than any of them had ever done in the whole course of his life" (XIV). He may mean partly that as a writer he has entered into the minds of his revolutionaries in order to imagine their beliefs,

but I think he means something else as well. He ends "Author's
Note" (written in 1920, when he was working on the stage
version) by saying that he's recently been forced to look on the
bare bones of his tale, and they make a grisly skeleton. But, he
says, in "telling Winnie Verloc's story to its anarchistic end of
utter desolation, madness and despair,...I have not intended to
commit a gratuitous outrage on the feelings of mankind" (XV).
Maybe not; but he has wanted to make people feel the outrage
that is the bony core of his tale. Winnie's story ends in anarchy in
the sense that the whole meaning and structure of her life have
been overturned; and it's an anarchistic story, too, in that it
attacks the peace of mind of the public. In his article "Autocracy
and War," written in 1905, a year before Conrad started on *The
Secret Agent,* he says that "the stimulus of a great art" is
sometimes able to break through "that saving callousness which
reconciles us to the conditions of our existence" and awaken
"our sympathetic imagination, to which alone we can look for
the ultimate triumph of concord and justice" (*NLL,* 84). Conrad
remarks in "Familiar Preface" to *A Personal Record* that he
hasn't been revolutionary in his writings, and that the hard,
absolute optimism of the revolutionary spirit is repulsive to his
mind by the menace of fanaticism and intolerance it contains
(*PR,* XXI-XXII). But when he wrote Winnie's anarchistic story
he was surely cherishing the concentrated revolutionary purpose
of awakening our sympathetic imagination to the terrible
muffled desolation and desperation of her life. He wanted to give
her experience to his readers, in every sense: he, like the
Professor, understood that madness and despair can move the
world. Winnie's original "Nobody could help that" aligned her
far more than she knew with the so-called anarchists (the
Professor excluded), whose bland acceptance of the status quo
allows them to enjoy their histrionic posturings without making
any attempt to translate them into concrete action; and her fate
is to end exactly as the Professor would wish, finding her own
corner of society totally unacceptable, and destroying what
remains of it with her own hands. Conrad wants us to recognize
that it is a bad world for poor people; and his hope is that we will

respond with something between expedient complacence and the fanatical intolerance of the Professor.

James absorbed the atmosphere for *The Princess Casamassima* in solitary walks around London, exactly as Conrad did with *The Secret Agent* (*The Princess Casamassima*, I, V). James says he haunted the great city, and penetrated it, imaginatively, in as many places as possible; and on the basis of the knowledge gathered in this way, he felt able to render the effect "of society's not knowing, but only guessing and suspecting and trying to ignore, what goes on irreconcilably, subversively, beneath the vast smug surface" (XXII). His "Preface" talks also about the presentation of "the suggested nearness (to all our apparently ordered life) of some sinister anarchic underworld, heaving in its pain, its power, and its hate" (XXI). It should be noted that within the book Paul Muniment and his companions are never actually referred to as anarchists; but Lionel Trilling argues that the revolution envisaged by James is anarchist, rather than Marxian, and that *The Princess Casamassima* gives "a very accurate account of anarchism" (66). I think it would perhaps be fair to say that James's revolutionaries are anarchists, just as Conrad's anarchists are revolutionaries.

Conrad admired James for being what he called "the historian of fine consciences" (*NLL*, 17). Winnie can't afford to look into life, and she can't afford a fine conscience; she has had to make the wellbeing of Stevie her only priority. We can see how much life she suppressed for his sake in the sketch of her romance with the butcher's son, cut short when she opted for marrying Verloc instead; and in the strength of the life-wish that makes her incapable of dragging herself through the London streets to the river bridge, even when she knows drowning will be her only way of escaping the gallows. Her suicide is one of wretchedness and terror, and her conscience is not involved at all. But Hyacinth is a different matter; and Hyacinth's conscience must be one of the finest that James ever explored.

In his "Preface" to *The Princess Casamassima* James says, as regards characters in fiction, that "there are degrees of feeling;"

and those with "the power to be finely aware and richly responsible 'get most' out of all that happens to them, and in so doing enable us, as readers of their record...also to get most" (*The Princess...*, I, VIII). He says "the mind of little Hyacinth" is "exquisitely sensitive" and "shiningly clever;" and his "passion of intelligence" is "his highest value for our curiosity and our sympathy" (XIV). Hyacinth owes his education almost entirely to books; "reading was his extravagance," and Mr. Vetch, "as he grew older...lent him every volume he possessed or could pick up for the purpose" (100-1). Hyacinth is also deeply affected by books as well as artefacts: "the delicate, charming character of the work he did at old Crook's...was a kind of education of the taste, trained him in the finest discriminations, in the recognition of the rare and the hatred of the cheap." This sensitivity accentuates his tendency to be "frightened and harrowed" by the "misery and vice" that he sees collected in public-houses in the poorer parts of London; and it makes him "ask himself questions that pierced the deeper because they were met by no answer" (159). Hyacinth looks as deeply into life as he possibly can, both that of others and his own. He is keenly affected by the bitterness of the freakish chance summed up by the Princess (II, 61): "constituted as you're constituted, to be conscious of the capacity you must feel, and yet to look at the good things of life only through the glass of the pastry-cook's window!" At times "his brothers of the people" serve only "to represent in massive shape precisely the grovelling interests which attracted one's contempt" (I, 169); as early as chapter XI, he is aware of the inconsistency of working "underground for the enthronement of the democracy" while feeling an "intense admiration" for "the flower of a high civilisation," and becomes "even rather faint to think that he must choose" (170-1).

On the evening of the gathering in the *Sun and Moon,* he chooses readily enough. Muniment is "as plain as possible on the point that their game must be now to frighten society...to make it believe that the swindled classes were at last fairly in league" (though he is also plain that this is not yet so); and Hyacinth, ever aware of what it is to have been particularly swindled, allows his imagination to launch itself "into the idea of how he might in a given case settle for himself that question of paying for the lot" (355-6). His apprehension of London matches the vision of a "monstrous town" which was one of Conrad's starting points for *The Secret Agent,* "a cruel devourer of the world's light," deep enough for any passion, dark enough to bury five million lives. He is so keenly aware of "the huge tragic city where unmeasured misery lurked beneath the dirty night, ominously, monstrously still," that he wishes "that exalted, deluded company should pour itself forth with Muniment at its head and surge through the sleeping world and gather the myriad miserable out of their slums and burrows, should roll into the selfish squares and lift a tremendous hungry voice and awaken the gorged indifferent to a terror that would bring them down" (*The Princess...,* I, 358). In a fine flush of heroism and with a passionate desire for Muniment's approval, he offers his services as an assassin; and there is a wry sadness to the distress he later feels because Muniment has so readily accepted the offer, without compunction "[putting] forward...for the terrible 'job' a little chap he to all appearance really liked" (II, 136). The latter emotion forms a dark undercurrent during the pregnant visit in chapter XXXV to Greenwich, where "the little brick observatory...sets the time to English history" (209); and Greenwich Park, which in *The Secret Agent* carries such a fatal significance for Stevie, constitutes one of the most curious of the many resonances between the two books. We become throughly aware of Hyacinth's predicament as he sits talking to Muniment on the grass with the distant prospect of London, and all London means, spread below. Hyacinth feels "the sweetness of loafing there...with a chum who was a tremendously fine fellow even if he didn't understand the inexpressible." Muniment believes in the advent of democracy, but he has begun to doubt that Hyacinth shares this belief; Hyacinth, who admits "I don't know what I believe, God help me," can see "the immeasurable misery of the people, and yet he saw all that had been, as it were, rescued and redeemed from it: the treasures, the felicities, the splendours, the successes of the world." Finally he tells Muniment, "I believe

in *you,* and doesn't that come to the same thing?" – and the
chapter ends with him drawing comfort from the "immense deal
of affection between them. He didn't even observe at that
moment that it was preponderantly on his own side" (214-19).
Hyacinth, like Conrad and like the Professor, wants, when
singleminded, to awaken the masses; Stevie is capable of no more
than a vague allegiance to those who appear to him to share his
perception that it's a bad world for poor people. But each is
primarily moved by specific hero-worship of an individual
figure; and their admiration is quite callously exploited by both
Muniment and Verloc.

The more important side of Hyacinth's disillusionment results, of course, from what James called "the complication most
interesting" – that is, that Hyacinth "should fall in love with the
beauty of the world...at the moment of his most feeling and most
hating the famous 'iniquity of its social arrangements;' so that
his position as an irreconcilable pledged enemy to it...becomes
the sharpest of his torments" (I, XVII). In the course of his visit
to Paris, his priorities begin to change: "What was supreme in his
mind today was not the idea of how the society that surrounded
him should be destroyed; it was much more the sense of the
wonderful precious things it had produced, of the fabric of
beauty and power it had raised" (II, 125). He has "a revulsion for
which he had made no allowance" when it comes over him "that
the most brilliant city in the world was also the most blood-
-stained" (121). When he writes his letter from Venice to the
Princess, he tells her how he no longer minds about the "want
and toil and suffering" which are "the constant lot of the
immense majority of the human race," because he has become
struck by "the great achievements of which man has been
capable in spite of them – the splendid accumulations of the
happier few, to which doubtless the miserable many have also in
their degree contributed." He talks about "The monuments and
treasures of art, the great palaces and properties, the conquests
of learning and taste, the general fabric of civilisation as we know
it, based if you will upon all the despotisms, the cruelties, the
exclusions, the monopolies and the rapacities of the past, but

thanks to which, all the same, the world is less of a 'bloody sell' and life more of a lark." He says he feels himself capable of fighting for these things; and it seems to him that the revolutionist Hoffendahl holds them too cheap, and wishes to substitute for them something in which Hyacinth can't believe as he does "in things with which the yearnings and the tears of generations have been mixed" (145).

For Hyacinth, the great achievements of art come to represent a celebration of the best and the worst in the human condition; when he returns from the continent he urges the function of pictures and statues as "ameliorating influences," saying with heroic absurdity "The more the better, whether people are hungry or not" (170). With his "mixed, divided nature, his conflicting sympathies, his eternal habit of swinging from one view to another," his abiding fear is that "the democracy wouldn't care for perfect bindings or for the finer sorts of conversation" (263). The accident of his birth has given him the capacity, but not the real opportunity, to appreciate the finer things of civilization; and the sorry paradox is that a world in which his father couldn't have exploited his mother will also be a world in which there aren't many finer things to be enjoyed. Winnie is forced against her will to look into life, and it kills her; Hyacinth looks readily, and finds it to be irredeemably unfair. But although he ceases to believe in a policy of violence, he is still bound by his sacred vow. He says "I didn't promise to believe; I promised to obey" (371); and what he ultimately obeys is his personal inability to reconcile the opposing claims of art and multiple misery. The Professor feels no qualms at all about destroying the good along with the bad, and himself too if necessary; Hyacinth in the end destroys himself alone, in order to avoid worse. His death unites what his life could not; as Derek Brewer puts it in his introduction to the Penguin Classics edition, it is his symbolic statement, his work of art (17).

Both *The Princess Casamassima* and *The Secret Agent* show a central character driven to suicide because of the harshness and injustice of life; both also show that violent revolution is no kind of answer. Winnie doesn't even look for an answer; in her own unthinking way she quite approves of the society she lives in: "No one need be a slave in this country," she says. But then, she approves partly because she thinks she's got things arranged so that the dreary equilibrium of her life does at least mean security for Stevie. Hyacinth's suicide is a logical and conscious decision; Winnie's is no more than the inexorable conclusion of the eruption of unthinking savagery which begins when she is forced to realize that all her self-sacrifice on her brother's behalf has been mistaken and in vain. The murder of Verloc and Winnie's suicide are indissolubly bound up with the atrocity of the Greenwich Park explosion; the central event of this book is in effect the wiping out of an entire family, and even Verloc is presented in sufficient depth to give him, too, a claim on our pity. Hyacinth's death stands alone as the climax of *The Princess Casamassima,* entirely eclipsing the shadowy murder he refrains from committing; but both books explore the inadequacies of society in acutely personal terms. Both show that political imperatives can weigh cruelly on individuals, and that there is an intimate association between material and psychological needs. Human bonds are what make Winnie's existence worthwhile, and at the end she can even cling to the last resort of a human bond with Ossipon, if it will save her from death. Hyacinth as he approaches his end clings to his human bonds too, but he does it with hopelessness already in his heart. The protective affection that he in his vulnerability has always called forth from his friends and surrogate relatives fails him at the last, and even though Vetch, the Poupins and the Princess know or suspect in varying degrees his agonizing dilemma, none of them is able to keep him from the final disaster. Unlike Winnie, Hyacinth has looked at the political alternative; the revolution is a real possibility to him, even if it isn't to the reader; and his reluctant conclusion is that post-revolutionary society will be a bleak and soulless place. But he has also come to see violence as a cowardly solution, and steady rational confrontation as the way of true courage.

The question of the relationship between art and human suffering is not raised nearly so explicitly in *The Secret Agent*. Nevertheless I want to suggest that Conrad believes in art as a mode of apprehension in very much the same way as does James; and that for both of them the writing of fiction in general, and these two books in particular, is a political act. James is keenly interested in the diametrical oppositions which stand in the way of a perfect society, and in the resultant moral difficulties involved in adopting any kind of political stance. Conrad focuses more on the present state of the world than on the possibility of change, and on the many imponderable accidents which restrict our freedom. Both are aware that although their art can, to some extent, make sense of misery, it also, and inevitably, involves compromise. Spender said of James: "He saw through the political and social life of his time, but he cherished the privilege which enabled him to see through it" (Spender, 109); and Conrad, like the Professor (that "true propagandist"), knows that the employment of language involves the acceptance of a culture, just as the terrorist and the policeman, equally, are players of games who "both come from the same basket." Conrad's answer is a book which shatters the composure of the reader. It is his perfect detonator: in the reverberations of one single explosion he encapsulates a triple tragedy, and our recognition of the human suffering displayed here is a step in the direction of the "ultimate triumph of concord and justice." He wants, before all, to make us see; and the grimmer the life he shows us, the more he insists that we should look.

Conrad's world view at its most pessimistic could perhaps be summed up in his conception of the universe as a huge knitting-machine, included in a letter to Cunninghame Graham of 1898: "It knits us in and it knits us out. It has knitted time, space, pain, death, corruption, despair and all the illusions – and nothing matters" (*CL,* I, 425). But in *A Personal Record* one finds a more positive view – partly, of course, because of the motives out of which it was written: Conrad wanted to define his

personality, and show that it could stand up to the rigors of life in
a knitting-machine.

I give two quotations. The first comes from near the end of the
"Familiar Preface," where Conrad says he is convinced that the
world rests on a few very simple ideas: "It rests notably, among
others, on the idea of Fidelity" (*PR, XXI*). I would suggest that
for Conrad one of the most important aspects of that fidelity was
allegiance to an ideal of artistic truth; and that the discipline of
working for that ideal was truly what stood between him and
suicide, and kept him alive. For James, the temptation to suicide
was probably a lot less real; but I think one can at least wonder
whether his active commitment to art didn't in some degree save
him from feeling driven into a corner like the corner in which
Hyacinth ends up.

My second quotation is from chapter 5 of *A Personal Record,*
where Conrad rejects the ethical view of creation, because it
involves "so many cruel and absurd contradictions." He says: "I
would fondly believe that its object is purely spectacular:
a spectacle for awe, love, adoration, or hate, if you like, but in
this view – and in this view alone – never for despair!...And the
unwearied self-forgetful attention to every phase of the living
universe reflected in our consciousness may be our appointed
task on this earth" (92). Hyacinth's ultimate response to the
living universe is despair; but when Conrad, in accordance with
his appointed task, communicates to us a vision as stark as that
embodied in *The Secret Agent,* our obligation as thinking beings
is fulfilled by the depth of our attention to the presented
spectacle. In the letter to Graham about the universe, Conrad
says: "I feel it ought to embroider – but it goes on knitting."
Maybe, in a brighter mood, Conrad might have said that it's up
to us to supply the embroidery; and that we do supply it, and we
call it art.

WORKS CITED

James Henry. *The Princess Casamassima,* 2 vols [New York Edition]. New Jersey: Augustus M. Kelley (reissue), 1977.

James Henry. *The Princess Casamassima,* ed. and Introduction Derek Brewer. London: Penguin, 1987.

Spender Stephen. "The Contemporary Subject," in *Henry James: A Collection of Critical Essays,* ed. Leon Edel. New Jersey: Prentice-Hall International, 1987.

Trilling Lionel. *"The Princess Casamassima." The Liberal Imagination.* Oxford: Oxford U. P., 1981, 56-88.

Paul B. Armstrong,
University of Oregon,
Eugene, USA

Cultural Differences in Conrad and James: *Under Western Eyes* and *The Ambassadors*

"I don't meanwhile take the smallest interest in their name."
"Nor in their nationality? – American, French, English, Polish?"
"I don't care the least little 'hang'...for their nationality. It would be nice if they're Polish!"...
"So you see you do care."...
"I think I should if they were Polish. Yes," he thought, "there might be joy in that." (*The Ambassadors,* 116)

As writers who made their careers away from their native lands, Henry James and Joseph Conrad were especially self-conscious about the paradoxes and contradictions of cultural identity. "Both at sea and on land my point of view is English," Conrad wrote, "from which the conclusion should not be drawn that I have become an Englishman. That is not the case. Homo duplex has in my case more than one meaning" (Najder, 240). Conrad both is and is not English, just as he both is and is not Polish. James's cultural identity is similarly double and split. Like many of the characters in his international fictions, his identity as an "American" is both confirmed and questioned, cast into bolder relief and blurred, by his prolonged encounter with "Europe." These contradictions suggest that a certain doubleness characterizes cultural identity. One's membership in a community is paradoxically both a necessity and a contingency – defined ineradicably, once and for all, by birth and family, but also susceptible to change by education, migration and declaration of allegiance. As Edward Said points out, cultural belonging is a matter of both "filiation" (with one's natal community) and "affiliation" (with groups to which one is aligned by virtue of social, political or professional practices). These modes of belonging can reinforce or oppose one another: "affiliation sometimes reproduces filiation, sometimes makes its

own forms" (Said, 24). Émigrés or exiles who have experienced
the possibility of discrepancy and even conflict between "filiation" and "affiliation" would be more likely to understand the
contradictions of cultural identity than would someone for
whom the paradoxical contingency and necessity of cultural
belonging have not been exposed by defamiliarizing, denaturalizing displacements.

The paradoxes of cultural identity are a central, recurrent
theme in the works of Conrad and James, perhaps nowhere more
than in *Under Western Eyes* and *The Ambassadors*. As an
orphan, his filiative place uncertain, Razumov is especially open
and vulnerable to be claimed by the various affiliations competing to define "Russian" identity. That the relation between
filiative bonds and affiliative allegiances is an issue of some
urgency for him is evident in the insistence of his claim: "'Russia
can't disown me. She cannot!' Razumov struck his breast with
his fist. 'I am *it!*'" (*UWE*, 209). The tautology here is meaningful
only because the equivalence is not as transparent as he insists.
"Russia" both is and is not who Razumov is, and that
contradiction makes his identity problematic for himself and for
others, a matter of uncertainty, anguish and contestation.
Ambiguity and conflict similarly characterize the identity of
Lambert Strether, the ambivalent American ambassador in
Paris, because he both is and is not Woollett. As Strether's
adventures begin, the narrator explains: "He was burdened,
poor Strether – it had better be confessed at the outset – with the
oddity of a double consciousness. There was detachment in his
zeal and curiosity in his indifference" (*The Ambassadors*, 18).
This doubleness results because he is not identical to the interests
he represents, even as they nevertheless define his mission and to
some degree his very sense of self, so that he is genuinely torn
between the worlds he attempts to mediate and feels at the end
that he must return to America to discover what his adventure
really meant.

The doubleness of cultural identity which Razumov and
Strether dramatize reflects the fundamental duplicity and decen-
teredness of human being which Helmut Plessner captures in the

telling phrase: "*Ich bin, aber ich habe mich nicht* [I am, but I do not have myself]" (quoted in Iser, *Prospecting:...,* 305n). According to Wolfgang Iser's explication, this paradox describes the plasticity of human being, which does not have one essential form, but is only as it stages itself in an ever-changing variety of modes of being (see *Prospecting:...,* 213-14; *The Fictive...,* 79-86, 296-303). Analogously, in a well-known example from *Being and Nothingness,* Sartre argues that a waiter cannot be a waiter but can only play at being one because we are never identical to the roles in which we enact ourselves (see 101-3). These existential and ontological paradoxes are crucially at stake in the formation of cultural identity because membership in a group is a structure of negation.

The role of negation in cultural belonging is evident in Althusser's argument that the cultural subject is formed by "interpellation or hailing," as in "the most commonplace everyday police (or other) hailing: – 'Hey, you there!'" (Althusser, 174). In turning around and recognizing the call, we both are the person named and not it ("does he mean me?") because it could be anyone, different from us. If, as Althusser argues, "Before its birth, the child is therefore always-already a subject, appointed as a subject in and by the specific familiar ideological configuration in which it is 'expected' once it has been conceived" (176), those filiative roles are susceptible in greater or lesser degrees to affiliative confirmation or contestation because they may be experienced by the subject in question as convergent or divergent with who he or she is or desires to be. Razumov is "hailed" by a variety of parties who recognize him as "Russian" and therefore "one of us," and he invariably experiences such recognition as simultaneously a misrecognition because he both is and is not the identities they assign to him. Strether similarly finds his identity in crisis because he recognizes himself when called in different directions whose claims exclude each other, and he can feel ties both to Woollett and Paris, despite their contradiction, because each is and is not who he is.

The role of the negative in cultural subject-formation means that one's belonging to a nation or community is not simply a given, determined once and for all, but (in Homi Bhabha's terms) a "narration" dependent on both "pedagogy" and "performance." In teaching a people the lesson of their belonging, "the scraps, patches, and rags of daily life must be repeatedly turned into the signs of a national culture [Bhabha explains] while the very act of the narrative performance interpellates a growing circle of national subjects. In the performance of the nation as narration there is a split between...the pedagogical, and the...performative," and "this splitting...becomes the site of *writing the nation*" (Bhabha, 297). If a nation, culture or community must be "written" to exist, the negative distance between individual identity and group-belonging is the difference that makes pedagogy both possible and necessary. This negation means that performances of cultural or national identity will be double structures of staging who one is in narrations which are necessarily not who "we" are. Otherwise they wouldn't need to be performed and learned in order to continue to define "us." As structures of difference, nations and cultures are therefore internally heterogeneous and open to variation despite the stories they may tell of their timeless homogeneity.

Under Western Eyes and *The Ambassadors* explore the alternative outcomes which may ensue from the negativity and doubleness of cultural identity in the areas of self-creation and communication. With regard to self-creation, national identity can feel like a trap or a prison, an alienation we experience by producing it, because we are not how we are hailed, even as we sustain its coercive authority by performing the pedagogies through which we have learned the patterns of belonging that define us. Or alternatively, the contingency of cultural belonging can allow the negative to be used for play, transformation or protest – to create "room for maneuver" (in Ross Chambers' phrase) out of the difference between who one is and who one is not. With regard to communication, the gap between one's interpellated role and one's sense of self may mean that one can lie with one's self-presentation or that one's status as a member of a culture can feel like a misrepresentation. Or alternatively, the differences and doubling constituting identity may make possible negotiations, revelations and exchanges which could not occur if both parties were locked in homogeneous, self-identical monads. Razumov's and Strether's stories do not resolve these oppositions. Instead, the disjunctions and ambiguities in the narrative structure of these two novels displace the issues at stake onto the experience of the reader. The narrative indeterminacies of *Under Western Eyes* and *The Ambassadors* stage for the reader the contradictions of cultural identity.

1. *Under Western Eyes*: The Doubleness of Being Russian

Most readers of *Under Western Eyes* wonder what to make of the obtuse narrator, the "teacher of languages," through whose self-avowedly "occidental" perspective we see the story ("this is not [he often reminds us] a story of the West of Europe").[1] His repeated generalizations about Russia call attention to his own incapacity to understand the story he tells:

> I confess that I have no comprehension of the Russian character. The illogicality of their attitude, the arbitrariness of their conclusions, the frequency of the exceptional, should present no difficulty to a student of many grammars; but there must be something else in the way, some special human trait – one of those subtle differences that are beyond the ken of mere professors. (*UWE*, 4)

Despite his plea of ignorance, the narrator offers a veritable catalogue of Russian traits which seems sometimes odd, sometimes profound, and often not justified by the facts of the story.[2] Even here, for example, his own lack of comprehension is quickly translated into a sweeping assertion about the irrationality and fundamental strangeness of the Russian people. Displacing the problem elsewhere, his inability to understand paradoxically becomes the foundation of a claim to knowledge about the peculiar excess of "Russian-ness" in relation to available norms, its sublimity or mostrosity (it could be either) because it transcends ordinary measures.

The narrator's generalizations constitute a kind of Orientalism (to invoke Edward Said's much-discussed idea) which seeks mastery over another culture by claiming to know it as well or even better than it knows itself. The narrator's conversion of his ignorance into a license to generalize is a simultaneously defensive and aggressive gesture which lays bare the contradiction of Orientalism as a claim to epistemological mastery whose authority is based on the very cultural distance which disables it. His disclaimer elsewhere that "one must be a Russian to understand Russian" traits (104) is belied by his assertion that he knows their secrets. Two strategies for seeking power over that otherness are to insist on its homogeneity (each of his formulas implies a uniform Russian essence) and to brand its difference as exotic or excessive (some "special human trait" beyond normal "ken"). The narrator's insistent, repetitive typing of things Russian is based on a fundamental opposition of "us" versus "them" which exaggerates the uniformity and peculiarity of "Russian-ness," making it seem stranger and more unique than our ability to recognize and identify with the hopes, fears and concerns of the story's characters suggests. The narrator's generalizations about Russia suggest that what a culture is for other cultures inevitably entails an element of misrepresentation because it is not what that community is for itself – a difference which can give rise to conflicts over whose representation will prevail – and this raises the question of whether and how a just and fair representation might be attained.

Some readers have been puzzled by the discrepancy between the narrator's obtuseness as an ethnographer of Russia and the intimate knowledge he offers of Razumov's and Nathalie's thoughts, feelings and actions.[3] One effect of this contradiction, however, is to move the reader back and forth between the two sides of identity (as being-for-others and being-for-oneself) in a way that dramatizes its intrinsic doubleness and challenges us to do justice to the characters better than the narrator does. Conrad justifies his use of this narrator in "Author's Note" by citing his need for "scrupulous impartiality" and "absolute fairness" (VIII). It is an odd sort of justice that is created by deploying a mediator incapable of representing justly what he portrays, but this suggests that right representation is not attainable by simple transparent reflection or by finding the correct "grammar." Rather, justice to another person or culture requires negotiation – a to-and-fro exchange – between the competing claims and perspectives of one's own world and the other world one can only enter into from a position outside it.[4] The reader experiences this back-and-forth movement by oscillating between involvement in the stories of the characters and observation of the inadequacy of the narrator's characterizations. Rejecting his generalizations as inadequate leaves open the question of how to do justice to Razumov and Nathalie while calling attention to the problem that any attempt to do so will, like the narrator's stereotypes, involve representations which are not who they are. Representing Russia more adequately than the narrator turns out to be both easy (he is obviously wrong) and elusive (what would a just and fair representation be?) because of the double structure of identity.

Curiously, the Russian characters in the novel repeatedly make pronouncements about Russian cultural identity which often seem just as homogenizing, exoticizing and misleading as the narrator's stereotypes. Peter Ivanovitch proclaims, for example:

> In Russia it is different. In Russia we have no classes to combat each other, one holding the power of wealth, and the other mighty with the strength of numbers. We have only an unclean bureaucracy in the face of a people as great and as incorruptible as the ocean. (119)

Different in function although similar in form to Orientalist typing by an external party, generalizations like these by Russians about Russian character and culture are instruments of pedagogical self-performance – declarative acts which establish cultural identity through the very process of enunciating it.

Instruments of cultural subject-formation, these generalizations are ways in which Russians call on each other and themselves to conform to, or acquire cultural traits. Sometimes the element of coercion in pedagogical hailing is painfully obvious, as when Peter Ivanovitch attempts to bully Nathalie by an appeal to national needs: "You must come out of your reserve. We Russians have no right to be reserved with each other. In our circumstances it is almost a crime against humanity" (127). The disciplinary force of interpellation is harder to see when cultural typing enunciates an ideal, articulating the nation's values by interpreting its destiny, as when Nathalie explains: "We Russians shall find some better form of national freedom than an artificial conflict of parties....It is left for us Russians to discover a better way" (106). Here, too, however, the enunciation of a mission "hails" Russians to an identity which may be described as their fate, and therefore inevitable, but which they must be educated to recognize, accept and perform.

Such statements display the differential structure of cultural identity because their articulation of "Russian-ness" depends for its power and significance on the gap between the image they project and the subjects interpellated to it. These self-descriptions uncannily resemble the Western narrator's misrepresentations of Russian character because of the rôle of the negative in cultural identity. Only because Russian traits do not absolutely and uniformly define who Russians are, is it possible and necessary for Russians to create their community and themselves by talking about who they are. Only because they both are and are not who they say they are, do the definitions they exchange have meaning and force. That difference, the doubleness of cultural identity, is what enables a people to perform themselves and to teach themselves to be who they are.

It also makes their community more heterogeneous than the frequent generalizations in the novel about the homogeneity of the Russian people suggest. Razumov thinks of himself at one point as a "Servant...of the mightiest homogeneous mass of mankind with a capability for logical, guided development in a brotherly solidarity of force and aim such as the world had never dreamt of...the Russian nation" (301-2; second ellipsis original). The revolutionary Peter Ivanovitch declares: "Everything in a people that is not genuine, not its own by origin or development, is – well – dirt!" (211). If a nation is homogeneous, then everything not at one with its essence is an impurity to be eradicated. Both conservatives and revolutionaries use this logic of purification because both envision culture as a unified totality, with a single defining origin and telos, rather than a heterogeneous ensemble of projects with differing beginnings and ends.

Their conflict leaves Razumov caught in the middle of "a furious strife between equally ferocious antagonisms." The uncompromising will-to-power on both sides suggests that homogeneity is not a given or a natural state but an artificial structure that can only be forged through strenuous acts of exclusion and discipline. Such acts employ negation in a self--contradictory attempt to erase differences. This is Razumov's impossible double bind, that he can only establish an identity in either of the communities he is caught between by eradicating the differences which define the self as not the other selves with whom it is affiliated. Both sides can give him what he seeks – an identity within a community – only if he gives up what he needs to achieve it, because identity and community are structures of difference.

Understandably but impossibly, Razumov seeks to evade this dilemma by submerging his sense of difference in a oneness of common origin. He asks the prominent revolutionary, Sophia Antonovna: "don't you think...that you and I come from the same cradle? [...] You mean – Russia?" she asks, before advising him: "The great thing is not to quarrel amongst ourselves about all sorts of conventional trifles. Remember that, Razumov" (253-4). Earlier Razumov gives himself similar advice after arguing with Peter Ivanovitch over whether the Russian people are "children" or "brutes:" "what's the use of disputing about names?" Because filiative bonds do not necessarily determine the affiliative relations which arise out of them, however, names are not decided by birth (hence the question of Razumov's own proper name as the son of the enigmatically designated Prince K–). Disputes about how to name and characterize a community are precisely how a nation and a culture get defined.

This community-building work can create affiliative bonds even if consensus is never reached. As Jean-Loup Amselle argues, "For there to be an identity, society, culture, or ethnicity, it is not necessary for the members to agree on what defines that culture; it is enough that they agree to debate or negotiate the terms of that identity" (quoted in ten Kortenaar, 32). The disagreements among the various Russian characters in *Under Western Eyes* illustrate how contestation about a culture's identity can create that identity through the very act of disputation, even if no agreement is reached about it. This sort of culture-building conflict occurs not only between the conservatives and the revolutionaries but also within each camp, in the numerous and lengthy conversations among the exiles in Geneva, for example, or in the discussion between Razumov and Councillor Mikulin about patriotism, the Russian character ("we Russians are a drunken lot," Razumov declares – *UWE*, 96), and his intriguingly elliptical, five-line "political confession of faith." Russia in the late-nineteenth century was at a moment of crisis in its sense of cultural identity, and at such times the processes of community-formation are exposed to view with special visibility. Fearing the eradication of difference as much as he desires solidarity, Conrad depicts the intent of both sides to homogenize and purify the nation as a dangerous threat to the very conditions of heterogeneity that make identity possible, even as he shows how unsettling and destabilizing to identity disputes about the meaning and destiny of a community can be.

What Razumov needs is reciprocity based on mutual recognition which would disarm the will-to-power in conflicts over cultural identity and enable an uncoerced exchange of differences. In a moment of profundity, the narrator declares: "A man's real life is that accorded to him in the thoughts of other men by reason of respect or natural love" (14). This formulation suggests the double structure of identity inasmuch as we are who we are not, because we are as others see us. Unless made the basis of a to-and-fro exchange through "respect or love," that difference can be disabling because it locates the power of self-definition elsewhere, outside the self, as Razumov feels at one point: "Was it possible that he no longer belonged to himself?" (287). His illusion was to think that he ever did, inasmuch as the doubleness of identity prevents anyone from simply and totally owning themselves. The presumption of Victor Haldin's unsolicited confession shatters that illusion by revealing the extent to which Razumov exists as a being-for--others which he cannot completely understand and control because it is not his alone. Haldin's construction of Razumov as someone who would welcome his confidences – "I understand your silence," he says, "You are a man of few words, but I haven't met anybody who dared to doubt the generosity of your sentiments" (16, 15) – is a misinterpretation which demonstrates the will-to-power in the claim to know, an exercise of power made possible by the doubleness of identity. Razumov's career as a receptor of others' erroneous miscategorizations continues in Geneva where the common perception of him as "an extraordinary person" and "a marked personality" allows him to function as a secret agent but never lets him rest easy because he is once again not who he feels himself to be.

This difference allows the surveillance through which authority exercises its power by oversight which blocks reciprocation. Acting as the agent of surveillance, however, is just as maddening to Razumov as receiving unwanted confidences, because in both cases he is coerced into not being who he is. This difference is maddening to him, not something he can remain indifferent to, because his being in the eyes of others is not merely false. It also nevertheless defines him. He is who he is not, and he wants simply to be. His response is impulsively to confess, whether to the reactionaries or the revolutionaries, in a futile effort to replace his doubleness with a single, self-identical being which would eliminate the gap between who he is for others and who he is for himself. That gap can never be completely erased, however, because of the differential structure of identity, and so Razumov's confessions inevitably displace the problem he seeks to resolve and initiate new conflicts or new attempts to control him.[5] As Mikulin asks when Razumov declares his intention "simply to retire:" "Where to?" (99). There is no place where he can escape the doubleness of identity.

The act of reading *Under Western Eyes* uncannily duplicates the absence of mutual recognition which maddens Razumov even as it offers the only site where the novel suggests reciprocity might be enacted. Razumov angrily declares at one point: "I am not a young man in a novel." Even to us as readers, his identity is double because he is not who he is, even as he is who he is not. We recognize him in a rôle, as a character in a novel, which he explicitly repudiates – even if he does so as a character in a novel. The point of this paradox is both to display once again the doubleness of identity and to call on the reader to recognize Razumov as he is for himself (*not* "a young man in a novel"), even while we simultaneously acknowledge the barriers to perfect recognition because his being-for-others (as a character to the reader) can never coincide with his being-for-himself.

The temporal displacement between the first and second parts of the narrative creates for the reader a double vision of who Razumov is and who he is not in Geneva, which allows us to share his sense of doubleness. The text stages this doubleness by giving the reader parallel discordant perspectives of Razumov as he appears to Nathalie and the other Russians in Geneva – the mysterious, polite young man whom her brother's letters have praised as "unstained, lofty, and solitary,...an intimate friend" – and as we know him from "Part First" as Haldin's betrayer and murderer. We are both inside, sharing his secret, and outside, observing how he is misconstrued. This doubleness may not allow true reciprocity with a character we cannot converse with, but it may nevertheless enable the sort of to-and-fro movement between different perspectives, neither sufficient in and of itself, through which the justice of competing representations can be negotiated. Such an oscillation of perspectives, never stabilizing into a rigid frame, keeps exchange going and prevents the doubleness of identity from reifying into the one-dimensional trap Razumov experiences when others fix him by their definitions.

Conrad cannot imagine social conditions which would establish reciprocity once and for all because such negotiation is a contradictory practice which cannot be automatically determined by political structures. Instead he shapes the social space of reading to create paradoxical, contradictory challenges for the reader which give us practice in negotiating the differences which define identity and culture. Recognizing the difficulties of doing justice to a character in a novel who denies he is a character in a novel constitutes a provocation and appeal to the reader to reflect about the dilemmas of doing justice to other people and cultures who are not what they are, even as they are what they are not.

2. *The Ambassadors*: The Doubleness of Mediation

Strether's role as an "ambassador" between conflicting worlds stages the paradoxes of mediation. Strether's career suggests that representing the claims of different communities to each other is both made possible and thwarted by the doubleness of cultural identity. "Nothing for you will ever come to the same thing as anything else," Maria Gostrey tells him near the beginning (*The Ambassadors*, 53). This attunement to differences is useful equipment for a mediator attempting to orchestrate exchanges between opposing worlds, but it also suggests the impossibility of ever finding perfect equivalences. Newly arrived in Europe, he finds "he was in the presence of new measures, other standards, a different scale of relations:" "However he viewed his job, it was 'types' he should have to tackle. Those before and around him were not as the types of Woollett" (77, 44). Strether needs to learn new "types" and "relations" which have a double structure of difference. They are "not Woollett," because European, and therefore in need of translation to communicate their meaning to a culture with other categories and norms. But the "types" and "relations" he seeks to understand are also not what they represent. They only stand for states of affairs they are not identical to and so themselves require deciphering even when one understands their grammar.[6]

The structure of representation as "standing for" leads Gayatri Spivak to deny that Western intellectuals can adequately represent a subaltern culture because their efforts to portray it are invariably only substitutes or proxies for an identity they can never capture as it is in and for itself. "Two senses of representation are being run together," she argues: "representation as 'speaking-for,' as in politics [*vertreten*], and representation as re-presentation, as in art or philosophy [*darstellen*]" (Spivak, "Can the Subaltern Speak?," 275). Even aesthetic or epistemological "re-presentations" entail the substitution of signs for other signs, however, and so the opposition between *darstellen* and *vertreten* is a distinction without a difference – and that is Spivak's point, I think. In her view, representation invariably entails what she calls "catachresis" because a sign is not what it takes the place of (see "Marginality...").

The necessity of catachresis is suggested by the pervasiveness of metonymic figuration in *The Ambassadors*. "Woollett" and "Paris" are themselves metonymic expressions for "America" and "Europe." Their opposing worlds exhibit themselves to Strether in a series of metonymies, where parts stand for the absent wholes they both designate and defer: the "lemon--covered volumes" of French novels as opposed to "the green covers [of his journal] at home" (*The Ambassadors*, 63); Chad's momentous grey hair which figures for Strether the young man's transformation; the "article produced" at the Newsome factory which expresses more about Woollett for not being specified; and later the Pococks, his replacements, who signify Woollett more effectively than he does ("Jim's the note of home," Strether feels – 245). In each case, the part both is and is not the whole it represents because it is simultaneously a proxy which stands in for the absent totality and a way of making its presence felt.

Spivak argues somewhat flamboyantly that the subaltern cannot "speak," or represent itself in its own terms, because a *Darstellung* is never more than a *Vertretung* in disguise. A more accurate statement of the problem, however, would be that even when a subordinate culture acquires the power to communicate, it can represent itself only in terms which are alien to it.

Deciphering its messages reveals what it is through the epistemologically and politically fraught mediation of what it is not. Mediation can be a political battleground, where the right to decide the meaning and shape of differences is contested, because representation is not epistemologically transparent. The trials of mediation Strether undergoes call attention to the related rôle of differences in the constitution of cultural identity and in acts of mediation between communities. Americans and Europeans simultaneously are and are not what their cultural norms define them as (hence the heterogeneity of the American community in Paris, and hence too the internal differences among the Woollett faction – even Sarah, Mamie and Jim are not all at one). Because their identities are split and discordant, cultures can be represented to one another through signs, metonymies and other figures which similarly both are and are not what they stand for. The doubleness of cultural identity already contains the structure of representation, with one's being-for-others both displaying and deferring one's being-for--oneself. Both cultural identity and representation are double structures defined by "as."

Cultural identity, as a split entity, both welcomes and defies representation. Hence the ambiguity of Strether's perilous situation between worlds which he seeks to represent to one another. On the one hand, this is something he can hope to do not only because proxies can stand for what is not there, but also because finding translations for cultural identity entails seeking signs to stand for a double state of affairs which is already semiotic. On the other hand, this is something he can never perfectly achieve not only because the absent party is never fully and adequately presented by its substitute but also because the split structure of what he seeks to represent means that it can be recognized only by being misrecognized. The negotiation of differences is made possible, then, by the very structures of substitution, deferral, doubleness and splitting which also block and impede it and give rise to conflicts of interpretation.

Not surprisingly, Strether alternates between feeling exhilarated and maddened by the negotiations he conducts.[7] His exhilaration comes in part from the new revelations and the new ways of creating meaning to which encounters between different cultures can give rise. The Paris of *The Ambassadors* is what Mary Louise Pratt calls a "contact zone," "where disparate cultures meet, clash, and grapple with each other, often in highly asymmetrical relations of domination and subordination" (4). Even when one party is clearly more powerful than the other, she argues, neither side alone can control encounters in a "contact zone," and the meetings may have results (including changes in the participants) which neither party by itself could produce or predict. Such meetings are all the more volatile and open-ended when power is relatively equal or still in question, unlike the colonial encounters Pratt studies, but like Strether's Paris. His position of cultural subordination can make him feel like a helpless infant or a bumbling pupil ("Have I passed?" he wonders at Gloriani's party – "for of course I know one has to pass here" – *The Ambassadors,* 121; and cultures are not on equal footing if one has the privilege of testing and ranking its rivals). Other Americans show their sense of power and entitlement, however, by insisting that the encounter will take place on their terms (Waymarsh's "wilfully uncomfortable" resistance to Europe – 29; Sarah's refusal to recognize any change in Chad or any merit in Madame de Vionnet, or her husband Jim's instrumentalizing view of Paris as a playground at his disposal). The excitement and ambiguity of meetings in the "contact zone" is that their outcome is uncertain, beyond the power of either side to manage, despite the force, energy and wit it invests. Strether finds this open-endedness invigorating, but it also frustrates him because his own attempts to orchestrate the encounters enjoy no more success than anyone else's. Although Woollett emerges victorious in one sense because the wayward son returns home, the unpredictable course of events and their somewhat surprising outcome (including the changes in the lead ambassador) suggest that the to-and-fro of cross-cultural inter-action may transcend anyone's agency or designs.

Strether's adventures in the "contact zone" dramatize how such encounters can produce epistemological and semantic gains neither side could manage by itself. James Clifford's notion of "ethnographic surrealism" suggests that the anthropologist comparing different cultures should emulate the surrealist enterprise of juxtaposing discordant entities from incommensurable realms, with an increase in knowledge and meaning--making capacity attributable to neither area alone. A surrealist collage can generate surprise and shock and give rise to new ways of seeing by removing mundane, trivial elements from their familiar settings and combining them in unprecedented ways (Clifford cites "Lautréamont's famous definition of beauty, 'the chance encounter on a dissecting table of a sewing machine and an umbrella'" – 119).[8] "The surrealist moment in ethnography [Clifford argues] is that moment in which the possibility of comparison exists in unmediated tension with sheer incongruity" (146). The epistemological and semantic value of ethnographic juxtaposition is that each culture can make the other strange, exposing its contingency by denaturalizing it, thereby providing a perspective on the other which it would lack by itself.

The juxtapositions and disjunctions he experiences give Strether repeated moments of revelatory disorientation. Finding that events have "taken all his categories by surprise" (*The Ambassadors,* 161), he again and again feels the tonic shock of defamiliarization, "sweeping away, as by a last brave brush, his usual landmarks and terms" (119).[9] The discord between the "types" of Paris and Woollett exposes for view the artificiality and constructedness of a world whose naturalness he had never previously questioned. The juxtaposition of opposing worlds displays the difference of his community's categories from other possible norms, and this disjunction reveals the status of both worlds as contingent structures of differences. The revelatory power of the incongruities generated when cultures meet explains why Strether's discoveries about Paris tell him as much, if not more about Woollett.

One result of such collisions is that new possibilities for meaning-making become available not contained in the repertoire of either world. Hybrid forms abound in Strether's Paris, including the many European-Americans like Little Bilham and

Maria Gostrey who bear traces of their home-culture but who
have gone beyond its boundaries by combining it with foreign
elements. Madame de Vionnet, of French and English parent-
age, is herself a hybrid whose combination of cultural styles
leaves Strether intrigued and baffled. "It would doubtless be
difficult to-day, as between French and English, to name her and
place her," he thinks – "You might confess to her with
confidence in Roumelian, and even Roumelian sins" (139). The
intermingling of cultures opens up possibilities for creation and
criticism beyond the resources of any single community. If
meaning is a construction of differences, encounters in the
"contact zone" create more differences. Strether reports that
"the way [being abroad] boldly took him was to make him want
more wants" (37). Desire is a lack, an absence calling to be filled,
and the multiplication of differences feeds Strether's imagination of possible "wants" by producing more empty spaces to
play with. Encounters between cultures can be semantically
expansive because they enlarge the realm of negativity which
sustains imagination, innovation and desire.

This constructive, revelatory interpretation of the produc-
tivity of cultural exchange is not the whole story, however. The
contact zone is also a site of conflict and power. The exchanges
Strether attempts to mediate are not only playful explorations
and negotiations of difference but also combative assertions of
will which seek victory and domination. Negation can under-
write imagination and desire, but it can also be used for exclusion
or registration, banishing otherness or controlling it by setting
up strict structures to contain it.

Strether's invitation to revel in the possibilities of meaning-
-making opened up by cultural differences is refused by those
who lack a sense of play and instead employ doubleness to
dominate, coerce or exclude. Sarah denies the contingency of her
categories and values insisting on the solidity and naturalness of
her identity – she is "a decent woman" (278) with a clear sense of
duty – and she is willing to sacrifice Strether to preserve moral
and cultural purity: "what is your conduct but an outrage to
women like *us*?" (276). The very form of her question exhibits

a doubleness which belies her insistence on moral and ontological singleness. She and others like her (such as Mrs.
Newsome) are what they are only by being *as* they are, and the
"as-structure" of identity suggests that one could always be
otherwise. This contingency of identity is precisely what Sarah
vehemently denies. Her self-contradiction, of course, is that she
uses this as-structure to play games with Strether and to mislead
him, to act as if she is other than she is, to accomplish her ends.
Her singleness requires the duplicity it repudiates. Sarah plays
the game of representation, however, not to negotiate differences
and expand possibilities of meaning but to achieve a victory
which would fix clear boundaries between inside and outside
(who is "decent" and who is not) and which would reaffirm
a rigid hierarchy of values.

   Her style of mediation, different from Strether's, is non-
-reciprocal and refuses mutual recognition. Through Sarah,
Strether feels, Mrs. Newsome "was reaching him somehow by the
lengthened arm of the spirit, and he was having to that extent to
take her into account; but he wasn't reaching her in turn, not
making her take *him*; he was only reaching Sarah, who appeared
to take so little of him" (276). Mrs. Newsome requires mediators
to get her message across, but the action is all one-way. She
withdraws behind the screen her representatives provide and uses
it to establish her ascendancy as acting without being acted upon
in return. Mrs. Newsome plays to win and thus refuses to put
herself or her values at risk, whereas Strether, more uncertain of
his ends and more aware of the contingency of his commitments
and categories, plays to keep meaning-making in motion, ever
expanding and transforming itself.[10] His willingness to put his
beliefs at risk makes him vulnerable but opens up to him
possibilities of self-creation and self-understanding which Sarah
and her mother close off. Mrs. Newsome's weakness but also her
strength, Strether thinks, is "that she doesn't admit surprises:"

> She had, to her own mind, worked the whole thing out in advance, and
> worked it out for me as well as for herself. Whenever she has done that,
> you see, there's no room left, no margin, as it were, for any alteration.
> (297-8)

There is no room for play, in the sense of a possibly transformative exchange of differences, but only for a game of dominance and submission, with the single difference that counts the one between winning and losing.

Strether and Sarah dramatize two alternative models of mediation. Because mediation between different worlds is not just a matter of reflection or the clear passage of messages through a transparent screen, it requires an exchange between participants which can be either reciprocal or asymmetrical, mutually transformative or a uni-directional assertion of power. Each side may try to do the other justice by imagining that a case might be made for different beliefs and values, or one culture can seek hegemony over its rivals by asserting the right to rank and judge them. The real issue in mediation, then, is not who owns the signs (no one does) but how they are used – whether in reciprocity, with both sides making themselves vulnerable by acknowledging the contingency of their values and the possible justice of other norms (Strether's model), or with the goal of victory, pursued by refusing to recognize the dignity and worth of the other world and by using doubleness and duplicity for a single, unyielding set of ends (the Newsome-Pocock model).

The choice between these models would seem clear, but the problem is that it is not simply a matter of choice. Strether cannot by himself choose that reciprocal modes of mediation will prevail if others will not play the same game. The Newsome--Pocock model is less vulnerable because, as a one-way assertion of power, it does not depend on the other's recognition and response, but the unpredictability of the contact zone suggests that even its will-to-power cannot call all the shots. Mediation is an ethical matter because it is a question about the relative merits of different sorts of conduct toward others, but it is also a political issue because it depends on how social relations are structured beyond any individual's agency.

James cannot resolve this dilemma, and so he transfers it to the reader. Our relation with Strether is simultaneously reciprocal and asymmetrical in a manner that stages the opposition between the novel's two models of mediation. James plays in different ways with the double structure of identification in reading – how it entails a duplication of the "real me" of the reader with the "alien me" of the various perspectives in the text the reader occupies even as we are not identical with any of them. For example, the intrusive narrator repeatedly refers to Strether as "our friend" in a double gesture which simultaneously asserts intimacy and creates distance. We are with him, aligned with his point of view, but his perspective is also not ours (he is only "our friend"), and we observe him from a distance through the very act of narratorial commentary. James's handling of point of view is similarly double. We see through Strether's eyes even as we see him seeing, critically examining the gaps, limits and leaps of faith which characterize his perspective. The reader thereby has an experience of double vision – observing the world through Strether's point of view even as we observe his manner of understanding – analogous to the double vision through which his own impressions are typically rendered as memories which recreate them at the same time as they analyze and ponder them.[11]

One effect of this doubleness is to appeal to the reader to undertake a reciprocal relation with Strether even while pointing out that this is impossible. The act of identification with his perspective calls for acknowledgement of the equal dignity and worth of his way of seeing and judging, but this recognition cannot be mutual because the return is blocked. The ambiguity of the ending of *The Ambassadors* makes this impasse especially acute. Is Strether right or wrong to return to Woollett? By making this controversial decision plausible, James asks us to do justice to Strether's choice by recognizing that there may be a case to be made for his unique, peculiar act which combines renunciation and engagement. But the justice of his choice is debatable, and no individual reader can decide it on his or her own. The ambiguity of the ending foregrounds the paradox that reading is simultaneously an ethical act for whose conduct the reader is responsible and a social process through which the reader participates in a history of reception transcending his or her interpretation of the text. Whether and how Strether's claims receive the justice they deserve both depend on the reader's conduct (will we rise to the challenge of the kind of mediation he models?) and transcend it because it depends on social structures and interactions which no individual can control (how criticism of the novel has made Strether's choice a nub of controversy). This paradox recapitulates in the experience of reading the dilemma faced by Strether: that the question of which model of mediation will prevail in his world both depends on, and goes beyond his acts.

What is to be done about this dilemma cannot be settled by the act of reading alone. What reading can do is to educate the reader, through practice and reflection, about the sorts of behavior and social structures which might produce various desirable or undesirable patterns of mediation. Like Conrad in *Under Western Eyes,* James in *The Ambassadors* leaves it to the reader to go beyond the limits of his work in imagining alternatives to the dilemmas of cultural difference he dramatizes. This does not mean that their works simply replicate the dominant ideologies of their time or, at best, offer unconscious compensations for them. Instead, James and Conrad transform the deficiencies in their worlds into negative spaces which stage possibilities of play and criticism for the reader. These gaps and blanks allow their works to speak across historical distance by leaving open how we might respond to dilemmas of identity, representation and mediation which, however, they may have changed, have not lost their urgency.

NOTES

1. Among the most interesting analyses of the narrator's obtuseness are Lothe (263-93), Berthoud and Erdinast-Vulcan (120-4).
2. For example: "I suppose one must be a Russian to understand Russian simplicity, a terrible corroding simplicity in which mystic phrases clothe a naïve and hopeless cynicism" (104); "they detest life, the irremediable life of the earth as it is, whereas we westerners cherish it with perhaps an equal exaggeration of its sentimental value" (104), and so on with an ultimately tedious and even annoying repetitiveness.

3. Erdinast-Vulcan, for example, complains about the "disturbing duality in the position of the narrator – the incompatibility of his pose as 'a dense occidental' with his virtual omniscience" (120).

4. See my "The Politics of Reading."

5. The ending of the novel is consequently, to my mind, not entirely satisfactory. Its images of harmony and care – Nathalie departing for Russia to do good deeds ("I shall never give up looking forward to the day when all discord shall be silenced," she tells the narrator – 376, and the ailing Razumov tended by Tekla "with the pure joy of unselfish devotion" ("There was nothing in that task to become disillusioned about" – 379) – seem wishful thinking about the possibility of oneness rather than a genuine resolution of the problems dramatized in Razumov's history. The doubleness of identity prevents the oneness Razumov longs for, as his story shows until the very last pages, where his desire for unity seems to infect the text too, and its insight into the inevitability of difference and deferral becomes occluded.

6. On the workings of signs and representation in *The Ambassadors,* see also my *The Challenge of Bewilderment:...,* 66-95 as well as Rivkin, Rowe (190-217), Griffin (33-56) and Williams (49-89).

7. Although useful correctives to the still-persistent vision of James as a disengaged aesthete whose defining gesture is renunciation, the recent insistence of Posnock and Walton on his life-affirming openness to multiplicity and transformation is one-sided because they neglect his sense of how difference and play can tip over into violence and battles for power.

8. For a more extensive analysis of the innovative semantic powers of acts of "selection" and "combination," see Iser, *The Fictive and the Imaginary:...,* 1-21.

9. For a more extensive analysis of Strether's epistemological revelations, see my *The Challenge of Bewilderment:...,* 66-96.

10. In "The Play of the Text," Iser distinguishes usefully between two kinds of play: that "directed toward winning something, thereby ending itself at the same time as it removes difference" by "establishing meaning," and that which "refutes any such removal of difference,...an ever-decentering movement" that resists closure (*Prospecting:...,* 252). See also my "Play and Cultural Differences."

11. For more extensive analyses of these aspects of James's novelistic technique, see my *The Challenge of Bewilderment:...,* 74-7, 86-8, 94 and "Reading James's Prefaces and Reading James."

WORKS CITED

Althusser Louis. *Lenin and Philosophy and Other Essays,* trans. Ben Brewster. London: New Left Books, 1971.

Armstrong Paul B. *The Challenge of Bewilderment: Understanding and Representation in James, Conrad, and Ford*. Ithaca, NY: Cornell U. P., 1987.

Armstrong Paul B. "Play and Cultural Differences," *The Kenyon Review*, 13:1 (Winter 1991), 157-71.

Armstrong Paul B. "The Politics of Reading," in *Culture and the Imagination*, ed. Heide Ziegler. Stuttgart: M. and P. Verlag, 1995, 117-45.

Armstrong Paul B. "Reading James's Prefaces and Reading James," in *Henry James's New York Edition: The Construction of Authorship*, ed. David McWhirter. Stanford: Stanford U. P., 1995, 125-37.

Berthoud Jacques. "Anxiety in *Under Western Eyes*," *The Conradian*, 18:1 (Autumn 1993), 1-13.

Bhabha Homi K. "DissemiNation: Time, Narrative, and the Margins of the Modern Nation," in *Nation and Narration*, ed. H. K. Bhabha. London: Routledge, 1990, 291-322.

Chambers Ross. *Room for Maneuver: Reading (the) Oppositional (in) Narrative*. Chicago: U. of Chicago P., 1991.

Clifford James. *The Predicament of Culture*. Cambridge, MA: Harvard U. P., 1988.

Conrad's Polish Background: Letters to and from Polish Friends, ed. Zdzisław Najder, trans. Halina Carroll. London: Oxford U. P., 1964.

Erdinast-Vulcan Daphne. *Joseph Conrad and the Modern Temper*. Oxford: Clarendon P., 1991.

Griffin Susan M. *The Historical Eye: The Texture of the Visual in Late James*. Boston: Northeastern U. P., 1991.

Iser Wolfgang. *The Fictive and the Imaginary: Charting Literary Anthropology*. Baltimore: Johns Hopkins U. P., 1993.

Iser Wolfgang. *Prospecting: From Reader Response to Literary Anthropology*. Baltimore: Johns Hopkins U. P., 1989.

James Henry. *The Ambassadors* (1903), ed. S. P. Rosenbaum. New York: W. W. Norton, 1964.

Lothe Jakob. *Conrad's Narrative Method*. Oxford: Clarendon P., 1989.

Posnock Ross. *The Trial of Curiosity: Henry James, William James, and the Challenge of Modernity*. New York: Oxford U. P., 1991.

Pratt Mary Louise. *Imperial Eyes: Travel Writing and Transculturation*. London: Routledge, 1992.

Rivkin Julie. "The Logic of Delegation in *The Ambassadors*," *PMLA*, 101 (1986), 819-31.

Rowe John Carlos. *The Theoretical Dimensions of Henry James*. Madison: U. of Wisconsin P., 1984.

Said Edward. *Orientalism*. New York: Vintage, 1979.

Said Edward. *The World, the Text, and the Critic*. Cambridge, MA: Harvard U. P., 1983.

Sartre Jean-Paul. *Being and Nothingness* (1943), trans. Hazel E. Barnes. New York: Washington Square, 1966.

Spivak Gayatri Chakravorty. "Can the Subaltern Speak?," in *Marxism and the Interpretation of Culture,* ed. Cary Nelson and Lawrence Grossberg. Urbana: U. of Illinois P., 1988, 271-313.

Spivak Gayatri Chakravorty. "Marginality in the Teaching Machine," in Spivak Gayatri Chakravorty, *Outside in the Teaching Machine.* New York: Routledge, 1993, 53-76.

ten Kortenaar Neil. "Beyond Authenticity and Creolization: Reading Achebe and Writing Culture," *PMLA,* 110 (1995), 30-42.

Walton Priscilla L. *The Disruption of the Feminine in Henry James.* Toronto: U. of Toronto P., 1992.

Williams Merle A. *Henry James and the Philosophical Novel.* Cambridge: Cambridge U. P., 1993.

Elsa Nettels,
College of William and Mary,
Williamsburg, USA

Unread Words: The Power of Letters in the Fiction of Henry James and Joseph Conrad

James and Conrad were voluminous letter writers all their lives. More than twenty-five volumes of their correspondence have been published, and more volumes are projected. Thousands of their letters in librairies have been read by countless readers. In effect, they wrote for posterity, but like other letter-writers, famous and obscure, they wrote to communicate to another person – to express feelings, convey or request information, extend and answer invitations, and sustain friendships. With some correspondents, the exchange of letters continued for decades.

The fiction of James and Conrad represents a different situation. Many characters in their novels write letters; but more often than not, the transaction is not completed, the circuit remains unclosed. That is, we seldom see a letter being written, read the text of the letter, and see the reaction of the recipient. Almost always, when the text of a letter is given, we never know how the addressee responded, or even whether the letter was ever received or posted.

There are, of course, important exceptions in the fiction of both writers.[1] But Conrad and James are more concerned to show the effects upon their characters of letters they are *not* able to read or choose not to read. In the fiction of both novelists, the power of unread words is greater than the power of words the characters actually read. It is the *unread* words that stimulate the imagination, create desire and induce anxiety and fear.

This essay deals with two kinds of letters: first, the texts within texts – letters written by central characters and reproduced in the body of the narrative; and second, letters that the protagonist receives or hears about but never reads – letters that powerfully

65

effect him precisely because he never reads them. The functions
of letters in the fiction of James and Conrad help to distinguish
them from their Victorian predecessors and to define them as
modernists. At the same time, the effects of unread words and
the desires they create are different in the fiction of the two
novelists. Comparison thus illuminates differences in the modernism of James and Conrad.

Among the most important inserted letters are the following
texts within texts. In *Roderick Hudson,* Rowland Mallett writes
a long guilt-ridden letter from Rome to his cousin Cecilia in
Massachusetts, detailing alarming signs of the degeneration of
the title-character, a sculptor whom Rowland has taken to
Europe to advance his career. In *The Princess Casamassima,*
Hyacinth Robinson in a letter from Venice to the Princess in
London, confesses his loss of faith in the anarchist cause to
which he had pledged his life; he also affirms his resolve to fight
to preserve the treasures of civilization from the anarchists' acts
of violence. Marlow's long reflective letter to the "privileged
man," the member of Marlow's audience who refused to believe
that Jim had "mastered his fate," accompanies the manuscript
that constitutes the last nine chapters of *Lord Jim.* In *Nostromo,*
the journalist Decoud, in a twenty-page letter to his sister in
Paris, narrates the events in Sulaco in the throes of revolution.[2]

The situations of the four letter-writers are very different.
James's protagonists are preoccupied with their own private
dilemmas. Conrad's letter-writers picture an entire community
on the verge of destruction. But the differences make similarities
all the more striking.

All the letter-writers are men. Three of them are writing to
women, but none is writing a love letter. Each addresses the
intended recipient as *you* and recalls something in their past
association, but each writes to set forth his impressions about
a situation in which he, but not the addressee, is deeply
implicated. For the letter-writer, the addressee exists primarily
as a listener within his own mind, to whom he can unburden
himself. That the addressee lives far away – in another country or

on another continent – heightens the sense of the writer's isolation.

Rowland and Hyacinth will later see the women to whom they write but none of the addressees replies, nor do we know that Decoud's sister or Rowland's cousin or the Princess Casamassima ever received their letters. Marlow's addressee, the "privileged man," is portrayed as he sits down to read the contents of Marlow's packet, but he then disappears from the novel, his reaction to Marlow's narrative never disclosed. In the absence of a response, the reader of the novel assumes the role of the addressee. We are invited to interpret actions, evaluate character and predict the outcome – in short, we become participants like the "privileged man" in *Lord Jim,* to whom Marlow writes: "I affirm nothing. Perhaps you may pronounce – after you've read."

Each of the four letters appears after the midpoint of the novel, at a crucial turning-point, beyond which lie the denouement and the catastrophe – the suicide of either the letter-writer (Hyacinth and Decoud) or the person to whom the writer is most deeply bound (Roderick Hudson and Jim). Each of the letter-writers has helped to bring about the situation that moves him to compose his letter, but the letter does not cause the catastrophe, or indeed, have any apparent consequences within the novel. Each letter, however, creates expectations of answers to questions raised by the text. Will Roderick Hudson recover himself or continue to degenerate? When Hyacinth Robinson returns to London, how will his conversion affect his actions and his relations with other characters? How will the outcome of the Monterist revolt in Sulaco affect all the characters in *Nostromo*? Only Marlow knows the conclusion of his story when he writes to the "privileged man;" but he stimulates his reader's curiosity by hinting at, but not revealing, the nature of Jim's fate. The other three writers, whose letters are part of an ongoing narrative, can recollect the past but cannot know the future; thus, they participate in the uncertainty and suspense their letters are designed to arouse in the reader.

The motives of the four letter-writers are different; but for all four of them, writing is an assertion of will, a form of control in the face of events beyond their control. Significantly, three of them address a person who they know has expressed or will express scepticism or disapproval of the writer's attitude or purpose. Rowland Mallett's cousin had advised him against taking Roderick to Rome and warned Rowland of the kinds of problems he would encounter. The Princess Casamassima has ardently embraced the cause which Hyacinth is repudiating. The "privileged man," the one addressee who is pictured reading a letter, had denied the possibility of Jim's redemption in Patusan. Writing a letter is thus not only an assertion of will; it satisfies the writer's need both to confess and to defend himself against hostile judgement. In each novel, the letter, addressed to a possible opponent, underscores the morally ambiguous or controversial nature of the writer's purpose. But in each novel, I believe, the author's intention is to create sympathy for the letter-writer and his point of view, to encourage in the reader an attitude similar to Ralph Touchett's towards Isabel Archer: "though it was contemplative and critical, it was not judicial" (*The Novels and Tales of Henry James*, III, 86-7).

The inclusion of letters in narratives connects Conrad and James to literary conventions well established by the eighteenth century. But the inserted letters in *Roderick Hudson, The Princess Casamassima, Lord Jim* and *Nostromo* differ essentially from the kinds of letters of earlier novelists. Consider Trollope, for instance, of whom James wrote: "No contemporary story--teller deals so much in letters...the modern English epistle...is his unfailing resource" (*Partial Portraits*, 122). Take a single example, one of Trollope's shortest novels, *Sir Harry Hotspur of Humblethwaite* (1871) (with striking resemblances to *Washington Square*, as John Halperin has pointed out). Trollope's novel contains the text of fourteen letters and references to many others. All the characters write with a definite purpose – to ask for a loan or refuse it, to seek an invitation or extend it, to utter threats and make conditions.[3] Victorian fiction is full of such letters that convey information crucial to the resolution of the plot. A letter reveals that Jane Eyre is heir to a family fortune. A letter exonerates the Reverend Mr. Crawley from the charge of theft in *The Last Chronicle of Barset*. Mr. Micawber reveals Uriah Heep's villainy in a letter heard by several characters in *David Copperfield*.

In contrast, Rowland, Hyacinth, Marlow and Decoud write of situations the addressee can do nothing about. Their letters solve neither mysteries nor change the course of anyone's life. The writers make no requests, although implicit in their letters is the longing to be understood or justified in the eyes of another person. Above all, they write to express their sense of their situations and thus to preserve something of themselves, as the narrator says of Decoud, who desires "to leave a correct impression of the feelings, like a light by which the action may be seen when personality is gone" (230).

James and Conrad were always interested in the psychology of letter-writers. They were equally preoccupied with the *effects* of letters, particularly those that are never seen by the protagonist or the reader of the novel. The presence of letters withheld or unopened contributes to the sense of anxiety, doubt, dislocation or isolation that assails characters of both novelists.

From the beginning in Conrad's fiction, letters sealed or withheld heighten the character's sense of a world baffling, dangerous, ruled by invisible, indefinable powers. In "Heart of Darkness," as Marlow travels up the river into "this strange world of plants and water and silence," he feels himself bewitched, "cut off for ever" from the reality of his past life. But human actions and artifacts do as much as nature to render Marlow's world absurd, inscrutable, dream-like. The letters delivered to the French man-of-war where men are dying of fever every day; letters sent from the Central Station requesting rivets that never come; a board with an incomprehensible message and an illegible signature; "bits of absurd sentences" from letters about Kurtz that Marlow overhears – all contribute to his sense of uneasiness, of being kept "away from the truth of things." An agent at the Central Station speaks portentously to Marlow of letters which informed the Company that "the same people who

sent [Kurtz] specially also recommended you," but Marlow
never sees these letters from unknown agencies. Among the litter
of pages and torn envelopes in Kurtz's cabin is a letter about
Marlow from an unknown source, which he never reads.[4]
Marlow is not only the subject of unseen letters. Here, as in
Lord Jim, he is also the receptacle of letters addressed to others.
Before Kurtz dies, he gives to Marlow a bundle of papers
containing letters, which Marlow later refuses to give to
a company official and a journalist. By his own account, Marlow
does not read the letters. When he gives the "slim packet" to
Kurtz's Intended, he wonders whether Kurtz gave him the right
letters. If the letters are those the Intended wrote to Kurtz, it is
fitting that Marlow return them, unread, to her. As he withholds
from her the dark knowledge of Kurtz's end, so in returning her
letters he gives her the mirror which reflects back to her the
image of herself and Kurtz as emissaries of light and noble
purpose.
Marlow is thus complicit in maintaining the webs of secrecy
and deception that had bound him, and he knows this. In
Conrad's world, the subjects of unseen letters of mysterious
origin are themselves implicated in the work of agencies that
foster secrecy. Characters may be writing or withholding letters
that compromise others; all the while they are aware of letters
that may incriminate them.
This double-edged situation is most powerfully dramatized in
Under Western Eyes, in the ordeal of the Russian student
Razumov. When he betrays to the police his fellow-student
Haldin, the assassin of a Czarist minister, Razumov betrays
himself as well, putting himself under the surveillance of every
political faction he is forced to serve, knowing that "[t]he eye of
the social revolution was on him" (*UWE,* 301). After he informs
the police and three weeks pass with no sign to him of the
"written communications" (296) the State Councillor had led
him to expect, he succumbs to "an unnamed and despairing
dread" (301), wondering "What did it mean? Was he forgotten?"
(301).

When Razumov goes to Geneva as a police spy masquerading as the accomplice of Haldin, instructed to infiltrate a revolutionary group and report back to Moscow, he lives in a state of perpetual unease, feeling severed from his own identity. His apprehension is intensified by repeated references to letters about him that others have received but will not show to him. The narrator of the novel, a teacher of languages and the tutor of Haldin's sister in Geneva, where he meets Razumov, tells him that he is "the only man" mentioned in Haldin's letters to his mother and sister. But when Razumov demands, "What could he have written of me?" the teacher replies: "Only a few words. It is not for me to repeat them to you" (190).

More disturbing to Razumov is his encounter at the Chateau Bôrel with the leader of the revolutionaries, Peter Ivanovitch, who tells Razumov: "You don't suppose...that I have not heard of you from various points where you made yourself known on your way here? I have had letters" (206). Moments later he adds: "People you have met imparted their impressions to me; one wrote this, another that, but I form my own opinions" (207-8). The unsettling effect of these words is intensified by the dark-blue glasses that conceal the eyes of Razumov's surveillant.

The arrival of Sophia Antonovna, another of the revolutionaries, again forces Razumov to measure the effect of his own words as he tries to read the thoughts of a potential adversary. Sophia Antonovna does not wear dark glasses but he feels that "It was impossible to guess what she had in her mind" (244). Their conversation centers on a letter she had received from a student in St. Petersburg who saw Razumov on the day of the assassination, attending lectures at the university. Razumov wonders: "Who could have written about him in that letter from Petersburg?" (258) and feels he must "get at the bottom of what that St. Petersburg letter might have contained" (259). She tells him that she has shown the letter at a meeting of "several men of action," and adds tantalizingly: "I have it in my pocket now" (276). Razumov says to himself: "'She won't offer to show the letter to me. Not likely. Has she told me everything that correspondent of hers has found out?' He longed to see the letter, but he felt he must not ask" (277).

These unseen letters intensify Razumov's sense of struggling in the dark for a foothold on slippery ground. The fact that the letter-writers have misjudged his character and misinterpreted events, thereby leading the readers in Geneva to false conclusions, compounds irony and multiplies the sources of confusion. But Razumov is not doomed by letters. In fact, he is cleared of any suspicion by a letter that seems to prove that Ziemianitch is guilty of Haldin's capture and death. Moreover, although Razumov feels himself forced into acts that have no reality for him, he takes effective measures to conceal his identity as a secret agent.[5] To draft "his first communication for Councillor Mikulin" in St. Petersburg, he seeks the absolute security of a small island, reachable only by a single bridge, where no one can approach him unseen. He posts the report to "a certain person living in Vienna," where, at the Embassy, it will be "copied in cypher, by somebody trustworthy, and sent on to its destination" (317) – a circuitous route that apparently works successfully "to make him safe – absolutely safe" (317).

But the very release from the perpetual fear of exposure, from the "constant necessity of prudence" (205) allows the moral horror of his false position to overwhelm him. Only when he feels relieved of the mental strain of fabricating a convincing account of himself – "No more need of lies" (284) – only then do "the choking fumes of falsehood" (269) become unbearable. He is driven to confession – first to Haldin's sister, then to the revolutionaries – by "the moral consequences of his act" (299), by his intolerable sense of isolation, guilt and self-betrayal.

The characters of Henry James also suffer profound effects of letters withheld from them, but the nature of the letters and their effects are different. Unlike the letters in Conrad that pass from faceless officials to inscrutable agents, letters in James are typically written by one central character to a second and withheld from a third.[6] In *The Bostonians,* for instance, Olive Chancellor receives an unpleasant shock when she learns that her beloved friend and colleague, Verena Tarrant, has received a letter from Basil Ransom, Olive's adversary, who will fight her for possession of Verena until he wins. The revelation that Verena has kept the existence of the letter a secret from Olive intensifies Olive's jealous fears and urgent desire to secure Verena for herself. As in so many Victorian novels, the letter conveys information vital to the progress of the plot, namely Ransom's address, which enables Verena to secure him an invitation to her speech on women's rights which she gives in New York. There he engages her in hours of conversation that assure his eventual victory over Olive.

In his late fiction, James uses letters in a highly distinctive way that sets him apart from Conrad as well as their predecessors. These memorable letters are seen but never read, never even opened. Such letters, like the crucial facts, conversations and scenes withheld from characters and readers, illustrate the power of the blanks or gaps, so common in James's late fiction, "tense emotional vacuums," as John Auchard terms them (8), which may become "charged expression and the major force of human action" (89).[7] These sealed letters affect the minds of characters more powerfully than the letters they actually read, as Mrs. Newsome's letter to her daughter Sarah Pocock in *The Ambassadors*, for Strether, "drew from the fact of its being unopened a sudden queer power to intensify the reach of the author" (*The Novels and Tales of Henry James,* XXII, 143).

The most complex effects of unopened letters are dramatized in the closing chapters of *The Wings of the Dove,* after Merton Densher has returned to London from Venice, where Milly Theale, the American heiress stricken by mortal illness, lies close to death. In the eyes of Kate Croy, in love with Densher, the plot she has induced him to enact with her will now succeed. Milly, who has loved Densher, will bequeath to him part of her large fortune and Kate and Densher will then be able to marry. A letter from Milly, presumably announcing her bequest to him, reaches Densher on Christmas Eve, shortly after her death. The next day he takes the letter, unopened, to Kate, declaring that "it is a symbol of my attitude" (XX, 386). Why Densher refuses to open the letter, why he prefers to "*think* of, rather than to know,

what [Milly] has written" (Cameron, 148) is left to the reader to
imagine. Densher may fear what it will reveal of Milly's
knowledge of his relations with Kate. He may simply be
protecting himself from the shame induced by sight of the actual
words – visible proof that the plot has succeeded. Kate declines
to break the seal and casts the letter into the fire – perhaps to
refuse responsibility for a symbolic act of violation, perhaps
because she reads in Densher's refusal his fear of his own feelings
– "Your attitude, my dear, is that you're afraid of yourself" (*The
Novels and Tales of Henry James,* XX, 386), she tells him – and
will not allow him to deny it. In any case, she knows that in
a short time official notification of the bequest will arrive from
Milly's law firm in New York.

Once Milly's letter is gone, it assumes over Densher a kind of
power the words themselves could never exert. The lost letter
becomes for him like a living presence which he keeps in
a "sacred corner" of his room and tenderly removes from its
"soft wrappings," "handling *it,* as a father, baffled and tender,
might handle a maimed child" (396). The startling image of the
maimed child may convey his sense of what he and Kate, by their
deception, have done to Milly.[8] But guilt and remorse are not
what determine his mental state. The unread words of Milly's
letter, which he has lost forever, hold "possibilities that,
somehow, by wondering about them, his imagination had
extraordinarily filled out and refined" (396).

The passage does not show Densher imagining the words
Milly might have written, but seeks the precise image to express
his awareness that the loss of her words has enabled his
imagination to give them their supreme value. His imagination

> had made of them a revelation the loss of which was like the sight of
> a priceless pearl cast before his eyes...into the fathomless sea, or rather
> even it was like the sacrifice of something sentient and throbbing,
> something that, for the spiritual ear, might have been audible as a faint
> far wail. This was the sound he cherished when alone in the stillness of
> his rooms. (396)

The "priceless pearl" reinforces the contrast between Densher
and Kate, who has valued Milly above all for her material

wealth, represented for Kate in Venice by "the long, priceless chain" of Milly's pearls, "heavy and pure" (217). For Densher what is priceless is created by the absence of words and things. The effect of Milly's letter suggests the paradox of Emily Dickinson's poems: possession comes only through loss; one knows the value of something only in the absence of it. "Water is taught by thirst." "To comprehend a nectar requires sorest need." The "priceless pearl" does not exist until the imagination creates it.

The power of an unopened letter to act on the mind of the recipient is again dramatized in the unfinished novel, *The Ivory Tower,* which James laid aside in August 1914, after completing three of the projected ten books. In some ways, the situation James outlined in his scenario for the novel resembles that in *The Wings of the Dove.* As Densher in refusing to open Milly's letter signals his renunciation of her bequest, so Gray Fielding's refusal to accuse or expose the friend who defrauds him of his uncle's bequest is foreshadowed when he receives and leaves unopened a letter written to him by his uncle's one-time business associate.

Like Milly's words to Densher, the contents of the letter to Gray are apparently known to no living person. The author of the letter has died; his daughter, who delivers the letter to Gray, declares she knows "nothing whatever of what he has written you" (XXV, 145). Because Gray fears that the sealed letter will reveal the source of his inheritance in nefarious deeds of his uncle – "black and merciless things that are behind the great possessions" (295) – he refuses to open the letter. Because he fears to act out of fear, he refuses to destroy the letter, as his opportunistic friend proposes. Instead, he keeps the sealed letter locked in a miniature cabinet, wondrously fashioned of "pale rich ivory" (147) in the shape of a tower. Gray himself accepts the traditional symbolism of the ivory tower when he identifies it with isolation and detachment, "the most distinguished retirement" (147) that so attracts him by its promise of escape from painful knowledge and fateful act. So long as the letter remains sealed in the tower, it moves him to wonder – not what it says

– but what he will eventually do with it. The letter, representing a choice still to be made, comes to signify for the reader Gray's unknown future (destined never to be written) which Gray figures as "an extraordinary blank cheque" to be filled out by his own capacities, "according to his judgement, his courage and his faith" (239).

Both Densher and Gray typify those of James's characters – most of them male – who instinctively prefer the role of spectator to actor, the consciousness of desire to the satisfaction of it. This is true even of characters obsessed with attaining a particular end. The overmastering desire of the narrator of "The Aspern Papers" is to wrest the poet Jeffrey Aspern's love-letters from the woman to whom they were written decades ago. And yet the intensity of his desire raises expectations that possession of the letters could never satisfy. The narrator seems to sense this near the end when he is finally offered the chance to secure and read the letters, by marrying the elderly niece of Juliana Bordereau. This unappealing prospect turns the coveted letters into "a bundle of tattered papers" (XII, 137); the narrator wonders at "the importance I had attached to Juliana's crumpled scraps" (138). The reader easily perceives that the quest impelled by desire is the narrator's defining experience. It is the quest for the letters, not possession of them, that gives the narrator his best hours in Venice – his exhilarating sense of being in the company of the great poet, of walking and conversing with him. "I had invoked him and he had come....I felt even a mystic companionship, a moral fraternity with all those who in the past had been in the service of art" (42-3). Without desire, without the quest for the hidden letters, there would be no "mystic companionship," but desire inspirits the imagination only as the object of desire remains unobtainable.

In most instances in James's fiction, letters are unread because characters choose not to read them. Densher and Gray Fielding deliberately refrain from opening letters. In *The Turn of the Screw,* the children's guardian refuses to read the headmaster's letter dismissing Miles from school and thus allows the letter to generate unprovable assumptions in the mind of the governess, who, denied recourse to authority, becomes the author of a situation. Adam Verver in *The Golden Bowl* declines Charlotte's offer to show him the incriminating telegram to her from the Prince and so is not deterred from his resolution to marry her.

We can hardly imagine Conrad's characters such as Marlow or Razumov or Decoud refusing to read letters addressed to them, not wanting to know what they contain. In "Heart of Darkness," Marlow struggles to keep "[his] hold on the redeeming facts of life" and longs to live in "a world of straightforward facts." He knows or learns that no such world exists, that "the language of facts" can be more "enigmatic than the craftiest arrangement of words" (*Lord Jim*). Nevertheless, his desire is to reach some kind of truth, to penetrate darkness, to look behind the veil of appearances, to catch "glimpses through the shifting rents in a thick fog," as he says of his efforts to discover the meaning of Jim's life. Marlow is not satisfied, as Densher is, in the presence of absence and silence, to retreat to an inner world of the imagination. When Marlow reads the words of Jim's abortive letter – "an awful thing has happened....I must now at once," he surmises that Jim despaired of writing, that he "had seen a broad gulf that neither eye nor voice could span." But Marlow will try to span the gulf, to give Jim a voice, to see what Jim saw, to connect Jim to readers he could not reach. Marlow in his imagination turns outward, not inward, to convey what he imagines to be the reality of Jim's last days in Patusan.

Unlike Marlow, James's characters do not tell stories to an audience. Characters such as Densher, Gray Fielding and the narrator of "The Aspern Papers" ultimately seek to commune with another presence through the power of the imagination, "the beautiful circuit and subterfuge of our thought and our desire" as James expressed it in "Preface" to *The American* (*The Novels and Tales of Henry James,* II, XVI). Conrad's characters such as Marlow and Decoud undertake to be historians, to "get at the truth of things." But the truths they seek – the springs of emotion, the meaning of actions – cannot be known through observation alone. In aiming for "the fundamental why" and not merely "the superficial how" of Jim's desertion of the *Patna*

(*Lord Jim*), Marlow lives as intensely in his imagination as any of James's characters do.

James and Conrad are modernists who are also realists: they represent realities familiar to the reader in their portrayal of characters barred from the consciousness of other persons, groping for comprehension of situations destined to remain obscure. In the fiction of both novelists, the presence of unread letters intensifies the effect of worlds where mysteries are not solved, where moral dilemmas cannot be resolved by written words. Whether the letter is written by a character or withheld from him, the effect is to isolate him in his burdened consciousness from other characters. At the same time, letters bind character to readers when we are the only readers of his letters and when we confront with him the unread letter pregnant with undisclosed meaning.

NOTES

1. For instance, in *Roderick Hudson,* the text of Mary Garland's letter to Rowland Mallett is reproduced and his response is described. In *The Portrait of a Lady,* the text of Isabel Archer's letter to Lord Warburton refusing his proposal of marriage is followed by the painful conversation between them precipitated by her letter. In *Lord Jim,* Marlow reads parts of two letters from the owner of a rice mill who befriends Jim and a passage from a letter to Jim from his father, which Marlow discovers among Jim's belongings after his death.

2. These inserted letters have received relatively little critical attention. Marlow's letter to the "privileged man" has been given the most detailed analysis. Of the four addressees, he alone is pictured reading the letter and his attitude is the most controversial. For different evaluations of his judgement of Jim, see Ambrosini (180-2) and Batchelor (140-2).

3. The many functions of letters in *Sir Harry Hotspur* are discussed by David Pearson (403-18).

4. In "Heart of Darkness," Marlow does not mention sending letters from Africa, unlike Conrad, who wrote a number of letters to relatives and friends from the Congo. See "Congo Diary." Volume I of *The Collected Letters of Joseph Conrad (CL)* contains four letters to Marguerite Poradowska and one letter each to Karol Zagórski and Maria Tyszkowa (49-63) written during the journey.

5. For discussion of Razumov's mental state, see Carabine (19-21) and Fogel (208-11).

6. An important exception in *The Princess Casamassima* is Hoffendahl's letter to Hyacinth Robinson, contained in an unaddressed letter delivered by an intermediary to a German worker, Schinkel, who gives the letter to Hyacinth (Chapter 44). Even this letter, however, concentrates attention on personal relationships and the feelings of affection and concern expressed by Hyacinth's friends.

7. Many critics have emphasized the importance of blanks, gaps and silences in James's later fiction. See Armstrong (17-19, 48, 72-3), Auchard (7-16), Bradbury (13-35) and Brooks (173-92). An interesting variation on the idea of the blank created by the unopened letter is the figure of the blank page on which writing appears when the letter is exposed to fire. In "The Diary of a Man of Fifty," forgotten impressions are "like the lines of a letter written in sympathetic ink; hold the letter to the fire for a while and the grateful warmth brings out the invisible words" (389). In *The Golden Bowl*, Maggie moves her father to speak the words she needs to hear, "as if she had held a blank letter to the fire and the writing had come out still larger than she hoped" (James, *The Novels and Tales...*, XXIV, 272).

8. In "Preface" to *The Tragic Muse,* James compares to a maimed child the novel he imagined "having launched...in a great grey void from which no echo or message whatever would come back" (VII, VI)).

WORKS CITED

Ambrosini Richard. *Conrad's Fiction as Critical Discourse*. Cambridge: Cambridge U. P., 1991.

Armstrong Paul B. *The Challenge of Bewilderment: Understanding and Representation in James, Conrad, and Ford*. Ithaca: Cornell U. P., 1987.

Auchard John. *Silence in Henry James: The Heritage of Symbolism and Decadence*. University Park: The Pennsylvania State U. P., 1986.

Batchelor John. *"Lord Jim."* London: Unwin Hyman, 1988.

Bradbury Nicola. *Henry James: The Later Novels*. Oxford: Clarendon P., 1979.

Brooks Peter. *The Melodramatic Imagination: Balzac, Henry James, Melodrama, and the Mode of Excess*. New Haven: Yale U. P., 1976.

Cameron Sharon. *Thinking in Henry James*. Chicago: U. of Chicago P., 1989.

Carabine Keith. "The Figure Behind the Veil: Conrad and Razumov in *Under Western Eyes*," in *Joseph Conrad's "Under Western Eyes:" Beginnings, Revisions, Final Forms,* ed. David R. Smith. Hamden, CT: Archon Books, 1991, 1-37.

Fogel Aaron. *Coercion to Speak: Conrad's Poetics of Dialogue.* Cambridge: Harvard U. P., 1985.

Halperin John. "Trollope, James, and 'The Retribution of Time'," presented at the Modern Language Association Convention, Washington D. C., 1984.

James Henry. "The Diary of a Man of Fifty," in *Collected Tales of Henry James,* vol. 4, ed. Leon Edel. Philadelphia: J. B. Lippincott, 1962.

James Henry. *The Novels and Tales of Henry James,* New York Edition, 26 vols. New York: Charles Scribner's Sons, 1907-1909, 1925. [Vols. I, II, III, VI, VII, XII, XX, XXII, XXIV, XXV.]

James Henry. *Partial Portraits.* London: Macmillan, 1911.

Pearson David. "'The Letter Killeth:' Epistolary Purposes and Techniques in *Sir Henry Hotspur of Humblethwaite,*" *Nineteenth Century Fiction,* 37 (1982), 396-418.

Millicent Bell,
Boston University,
Boston, USA

James and Conrad: The Fictions of Autobiography

In *Lord Jim* Conrad suggested that the true self was not invariably expressed in life. This is Jim's plea after his jump from the *Patna*. For Jim, that jump introduces a fatal fissure between what he feels he is and what he has done. It is a fissure between essence and existence, once assumed to be united. And Marlow discovers the impossibility of talking about Jim either by reference to "a fixed standard of conduct" or by seeking a coherent relation between a man and some community of recognizable types – as society and story-tellers understand them – by which he can be identified as "one of us."

Of all his works, moreover, this is the one in which Conrad experiments most flagrantly with the manipulation of his story's time-sequence by the use of a distractable narrator who seems to break his tale into pieces that are disordered non-logically in his casual telling. The effect, as one reads, is an annihilation of the causal sequences understood as plot – above all the sequence that connects character and action. For a prolonged time, we share Marlow's sense of Jim's personal quality without understanding the blemish action has placed upon it. Though the reader gradually restores the temporal order of events in his mind, the scepticism this disruption has aroused does not completely disappear, and we continue to share Marlow's baffled sense of the disjunction of man and deed.

James's similar doubts about the linkage of character and destiny were expressed in *The Ambassadors,* begun that same year. Lambert Strether could not be more unlike Jim except for one thing – his sense that life has not afforded him an opportunity to exhibit or enact some personal essence, that, in the life preceding his middle-aged adventure in Europe, he has not really "lived." Jim, of course, had had a seaman's outward career culminating in the *Patna* experience. But it is his romantic conviction that he requires and deserves "a second chance" to disprove the significance of his failure to act rightly at the testing moment, to prove this failure an irrelevant accident of fate, a narrative discrepancy not to be accounted for, or counted a false evidence of his true self. So, Strether, who has simply failed to seize any visible adventure at all, is detected by Gloriani to be a man who might have been someone else, "if everything had been different" (James, *The Novels and Tales*..., XXI, 197-8). So James in his "Preface" later wondered on behalf of his hero, in words that suit Jim after the *Patna* trial, "*Would* there yet perhaps be time for reparation? – reparation, that is, for injury done his character; for the affront, he is quite ready to say, so stupidly put upon it?" (*Literary Criticism:*..., 1305).

Patusan does not, perhaps, provide an altogether conclusive answer, though Jim, as he vanishes "in a mist" in Marlow's memory, may have been satisfied that he has proved himself the hero of his own romantic narrative, despite what might look like a second failure. Strether's opportunity to realize himself more fully seems hardly evident in the collapse of his original mission and the more important defeat of his discovered one. His friends, Chad and Madame de Vionnet, end up as they were going to, despite his attempt to influence them first one way and then another. He, himself, does not realize in any active fashion his personal capacity for passion. And yet, here, too, the conclusion is ambiguous, and Strether may, after all, have had his self--realizing adventure of feeling and perception. Like Jim, he seems to claim this himself in his last conversation with his baffled friend, Maria Gostrey. She admits to him, "but with your wonderful impressions you'll have got a great deal" (*The Novels and Tales*..., XXI, 478).

When they came to writing their autobiographies, however, Conrad and James took opposite views. James's project, like Conrad's, was an attempt to deal with the emergence of the writer-self now made manifest in the novelist's books, his already established fame, his sense that this and nothing else is what he is. But for James the self that was the grown man and the accomplished artist had been present within the infant personality like the homunculus crouched, according to the early embryologists, in the human germ cell. What would happen to him was what was bound to happen because he was the person he had been from the beginning. Looking back at the small boy of his title, *A Small Boy and Others,* he indulges in a conscious anachronism, a suggestion that even at his smallest the child felt in himself the sensibility that would animate the mature writer" though he had as yet so little to "show" for it. By adolescence, James's conviction that he must write had long been established. When only a schoolboy in Bonn, he relates in *Notes of a Son and Brother,* he had long felt himself "attuned to the life of letters." His "impressions...had begun...to scratch quite audibly at the door of liberation, of extension, of projection," finding "a unity, a character and a tone...that *was* positively to face the aesthetic, the creative, even, quite wondrously, the critical life and almost on the spot to commence author" (James, *Autobiography,* 253). He had, as yet, not really anything to show for his conviction, but at Harvard Law School two years later, when the banner of self was still hidden like a rolled pocket-handkerchief in his pocket, "what I 'wanted to want to be'," he remembered, "was, all intimately, just *literary*" (413). He "gathered as from one day to another that fortune had in store some response to my deeply reserved but quite unabashed design of becoming as 'literary' as might be" (439).

Conrad's midlife impulse to write after twenty years as a seaman seemed to him a sudden eruption from the deep, a conversion experience which could not be explained by anything he had been before. He insists, in *A Personal Record,* that his turn to the writer's role was not the result of any native propensity, derived from a knowable inner center. In 1889, waiting in London lodgings for a new shipboard berth, he suddenly, as he famously recounts, pushed aside his breakfast dishes and began writing *Almayer's Folly.* It was an unpremeditated action he describes as impelled not by any conscious need for self-expression – the usual idea of literary motive – but by "a hidden obscure necessity, a completely masked and unaccountable phenomenon." Until that moment, he said, he had

> written nothing but letters, and not very many of these. I never made
> a note of the fact, of an impression or of an anecdote in my life. The
> conception of a planned book was entirely outside my mental range
> when I sat down to write; the ambition of being an author had never
> turned up amongst these gracious imaginary existences one creates
> fondly for oneself at times in the stillness and immobility of
> a day-dream:... (*PR*, 68)

Even then, he "was not thinking in the least of being a writer."
He was, he says, "very far from thinking of writing a story,
though it is possible and even likely that [he] was thinking of the
man Almayer" (74). And yet, after he had written the first page
of the manuscript, about 200 words, the die was cast.

If Conrad saw himself as Jim, the man to whom things
inexplicably happened, James did not see himself as Strether, for
he felt that he had fulfilled his own character in the life he led.
And yet, in a formal sense, Conrad and James's autobiographical enterprises are closer than the novels they wrote on the
theme of personal development. Though it is also the history of
a man whose life, like Jim's, failed to express what he was, *The
Ambassadors,* steadily progressive in its time-sequence, does not
use Conrad's method of disordering the narrative to obscure the
connection of his hero and his deeds. Only when he came to write
his autobiography did James follow Conrad's structural model.
A Personal Record, published in the *English Review* from
December 1908 to June 1909, where James must have read it,
follows the form Conrad had used eight years earlier – the
first-person narrative which digressively meshes the disordered
fragments of the hero's tale with that of other persons – in the
case of the novel, a crowd of victims or survivors of the trials of
courage, in the case of *A Personal Record* members of Conrad's
own family. Coming after both in 1913 and 1914, perhaps
influenced by them, *A Small Boy and Others* and *Notes of a Son
and Brother* mingle personal recollections with family history
and give over the telling to a wandering first-person consciousness like that of Conrad's Marlow.

Similar artistic form may serve opposite motives – or may
suggest a resemblance less obvious. Marlow's digressions and

doubts keep us from identifying the hero as an ignoble failure, and perhaps, as I shall suggest, the veerings and reversals of *A Personal Record* function similarly. Conrad's claim that chance governed his life helped him to conceal connections and explanations he did not want to explore, choices whose origins he would rather call unknowable. The effect of James's meander among youthful memory is to relate everything, without regard to time, to the writer's inalienable personality as though there had not been any moment when he deliberately rejected alternatives to the life he would lead. He does not identify any particular moment of cataclysmic change. Yet even for him, I believe, there may have been a crisis of choice he preferred to obscure; James may hide doubts and halts along a course not nearly so obviously directed by unchanging character as he claimed. Both writers' theories of self-development are alike in denying the act of choice; James's destiny had been long foreseen, and Conrad's discovery of art had been sudden and surprising, but perhaps each equally felt a need to deny responsibility for the way life had turned out. For the ends of partial, evasive self-disclosure a similar autobiographical form served them both.

A Personal Record begins in 1893 with the writing of the tenth chapter of *Almayer's Folly* on board the *Adowa* anchored in Rouen, goes back to Conrad's signing on for that non-voyage, then plunges back to the young boy who resolved in 1868 to go to a blank spot on the map of Africa, and comes forward to the trip to Stanley Falls in 1890 with seven chapters of the novel in his baggage, followed by his illness in Geneva during which the eighth was written. He recalls the 1892 trip on the *Torrens* during which he showed nine chapters to a passenger. He remembers that he almost lost the manuscript in Berlin earlier in 1890 on the way to revisit Poland, and recalls the visit made in 1864 with his dying mother to her brother in the Ukraine. At his uncle's in 1890, he saw the desk given her by great-uncle Nicholas Bobrowski, and this brings to mind the story of how this ancestor served in Napoleon's army and ate the flesh of a dog on the retreat from Moscow. At the end of the second chapter, the narrator is fifteen, travelling in Switzerland in 1873 with the tutor who tried to cure him of his notion of going to sea.

All of the third chapter is devoted to the history of Nicholas Bobrowski and returns only at the end to mention the young Conrad's return to exile with his mother; but the fourth chapter brings up, at last, the moment when *Almayer's Folly* was begun by the thirty-two-year-old Conrad, reverting for just a moment to his first reading of Shakespeare in his father's translation in 1870. He then recounts his meeting with the real Almayer in Borneo in 1887. The philosophical fifth chapter hardly includes any past reminiscences at all and this is true of the sixth except for its humorous description of his examinations for promotion in the Merchant Service, after which we hear something about the start of his sea careeer in Marseille, and in the last chapter of his acquaintances there among the harbor pilots, and his first sight of the English flag.

It is, as he admits, a very unchronological, fragmentary, discursive story, and it is not altogether frank. No Rousseauian tell-all, Conrad omits any sexual history and never mentions his marriage at the age of thirty-nine; the Marseille love-affair, recounted in *The Arrow of Gold* and *The Mirror of the Sea* and probably invented, is not mentioned either nor is his proposal to a girl he met on the island of Mauritius. Perhaps his preference for the all-male society of ships had a homosexual ingredient, as was also the case with James. We do not know. The unavowable is one explanation for elliptic form.

But even the statement that he had never thought of being a writer before that morning in the Belgravia lodging-house – and not even then – may not be quite true. Three years earlier, just as he got his Master's certificate, he had made a bid, as he does not relate, for a literary career by entering a short-story contest. It *was* true that his recent history had been full of turns he did not understand, but most of these *A Personal Record* does not describe, though some had already emerged in his fiction. We know that he did not win the story contest, but neither did he get the captaincy he was expecting, and he signed on as first mate on the *Highland Forest* bound from Amsterdam to Java. During a gale at sea a flying spar struck him down. In hospital and on the beach in Singapore he passed a period of irresolution like Jim's before signing on the *Patna,* loafing among those who avoided the strenuous "home service" with its "severer view of duty" until suddenly, giving up the idea of going home, he became mate of a local steamer and went into Borneo. He soon threw over this berth as described in *The Shadow-Line*: "one day I was perfectly right and the next everything was gone, glamour, flavour, interest, contentment – everything."[1] Then in 1888 he was offered a command, his first and last. The *Otago* seemed cursed by mishap, and again impulse struck, as from behind a blind, and during a brief stop at Mauritius he impulsively asked a girl to marry him – and was, perhaps fortunately, rejected. In Australia, he resigned his command and went back to London as a steam-boat passenger.

Then, in 1889, he began his first novel, but the commitment to writing was by no means as decisive as he claims. Only after Poland, the Congo, the last engagement with the sea aboard the *Torrens* and the *Adowa,* did he finish *Almayer's Folly.* He married soon after and wrote Edward Garnett the same day:

> When once the truth is grasped that one's own possibility is only a ridiculous masquerade of something hopelessly unknown the attainment of serenity is not far off. Then there remains nothing but the surrender to one's impulses, the fidelity to passing emotion which is perhaps a nearer approach to truth than any other philosophy of life. And why not? If we are "ever becoming – never being" then I would be a fool if I tried to become this thing rather than that. (*CL,* I, 267-8)

Conrad himself appears not to have had any *conscious* sense of self-direction a good deal of the time, and there is a truth to his own experience in the way *A Personal Record* makes no effort at all to explain or connect the events of what does seem a curiously spasmodic history, his years from 1889 to 1894. His narrative – if it can be called that – merely picks up dispersed moments associated with the wanderings of the uncompleted novel packed and

packed up again and once nearly lost. The manuscript traveling
in his baggage – now and then added to, now and then forgotten
– is like a part of the self sometimes remembered sometimes
repressed – though if it represented a constant inner dream,
Conrad seems to deprecate the suggestion. And yet, the suspicion remains that true biography might discover more reasons
and connections than the liver of this life was fully aware of.

Above all, was there not, along the way, a key event that more
than anything else made it necessary for the remembering
Conrad to suppress the idea that choice had been exercised? This
was his deliberate decision to exile himself forever from Poland.
It was his *choice* – which he could hardly bear to recognize as
choice and which (as Jocelyn Baines was the first to assert) he
was still trying to come to terms with after many years, even as he
wrote *A Personal Record*. In its loops and leaps the autobiography turns back only in momentary references to this early
disruptive change as though it forms a precedent for the act of
becoming a writer. The "jump" from Poland to the seaman's
career under a foreign flag was a step, he declares, that remained
"totally unintelligible" to his family and himself. Why was this
Polish boy set upon going to sea and attracted to the service of
a nation whose language he did not yet know? In "A Familiar
Preface" signed "J. C. K." as though he had not yet surrendered
his Korzeniowski identity, he writes:

> Having broken away from my origins under a storm of blame from
> every quarter which had the merest shadow of right to voice an
> opinion, removed by great distances from such natural affections as
> were still left to me, and even estranged, in a measure, from them by
> the totally unintelligible character of the life which had seduced me so
> mysteriously from my allegiance, I may safely say that through the
> blind force of circumstances the sea was to be all my world and the
> merchant service my only home for a long succession of years. (*PR*,
> XVI)

It was the same as the jump to writing would be, and Conrad
deliberately connects the two: "I dare say I am compelled,
unconsciously compelled, now, to write volume after volume, as
in past years I was compelled to go to sea voyage after voyage....I

do not know which of the two impulses has appeared more mysterious and more wonderful to me."

The fact is that *A Personal Record* is curiously haunted by a subject other than its narrowly autobiographical one. This is the autobiographer's homeland and family, and the need to assert his enduring attachment to these. His early intention seems to have been to respond to the charge that he was a man without a country. In August 1908, a few weeks before he first wrote to his agent, Pinker, about the idea of writing something directly autobiographical, he had been attacked by an English critic for writing in English; the critic had written, "Mr. Conrad, without either country or language, may be thought to have found a new patriotism for himself in the sea. His vision of men, however, is the vision of a cosmopolitan, a homeless person."[2] Conrad reacted by resolving to compose something that, like *Under Western Eyes* (on which he was then engaged) would bring the Polish world before the English reader. In his autobiographical memoir, he wrote to Pinker, he proposed to "make Polish life enter English literature." His chief source would be his uncle Bobrowski's two-volume memoir. But his agent and his publisher were not encouraging, and Conrad seems to have resolved to follow their advice to concentrate on "himself and about how he came to write."[3]

His original intention, the defensive evocation of his abandoned national inheritance, seems to have been partially suppressed. In "Author's Note" appended seven years after the first publication of *A Personal Record* (signed now simply "J. C."), Conrad expressed pleasure in having discovered that his father's writings, including a memoir concerning the initiation of a Polish nationalist underground, had not all been destroyed, as he had supposed, and that Apollo Korzeniowski had not been altogether forgotten in Poland. But when *A Personal Record* was written in 1908-9 he had had no such confidence and yet he had not felt obliged to describe his father and his sacrifices. He had included *nothing* about his father's and mother's exile, except for recording his memory of the visit with his mother to his uncle during this period. He had not even mentioned the tragic early deaths of both of his parents, nor evoked his father's funeral when he, a twelve-year-old, walked alone behind his father's coffin through the streets of Cracow. The subject of Polish patriotism erupts in *A Personal Record* only in the oddly incongruous emphasis on the privations and valor of the great-uncle who had "eaten dog."

As with Conrad, James's elliptic form may permit omissions he may have required for unavowable reasons. He, too, gives no history of his sexual development but offers only his posthumous idealized and fraternal feeling for Minny Temple as a doubtful instance of heterosexual love. He tells nothing about the issues of sexual identity that must have preoccupied his adolescence and early manhood. But concerning vocational commitment, his main subject about which he speaks constantly, he is more evasive than he seems. Among memories of childhood, the "I" of *A Small Boy* also wanders digressively to include the lives of the "others," his family and their society in the American world from which he had also long separated himself. He returns again and again to the theme of exile from these others, an exile seen as an inevitable destiny. James is determined also to show that there had never been a possibility of any alternative to the life of the detached and expatriated artist. The small boy was already an observer:

> Just to *be* somewhere – almost anywhere would do – and somehow to receive an impression or an accession, feel a relation or a vibration. He was to go without many things, ever so many – as all persons do in whom contemplation takes so much the place of action; but everywhere, in the years that came soon after, and that in fact continued long, in the streets of great towns, in New York still for some time, and then for a while in London, in Paris, in Geneva, wherever it might be, he was to enjoy more than anything the so far from showy practice of wondering and dawdling and gaping. (James, *Autobiography*:..., 17)

From this beginning, as James's narrative bends itself to show, the path to the role of detached witness of life – and consequent novelist – was undeviating. He describes the little Albany "gaper" – receptive of every impression. If he was always behind his brother William in outward exhibitions, it was a case of someone "whose faculty for application is all and only in their imagination and their sensibility" (8). Even his family's traveling propensities that condemned him to being a "hotel child" a good deal of the time "must have" made him feel "the charm of the world seen in a larger way...incomparably...the chance to dawdle and gape...measured almost by miles; it was even as if I had become positively conscious that the social scene so peopled would pretty well always say to me than anything else" (19-20). The future novelist of manners dares to ask, "What was my incipient sense of persons and things, what were my first stirred observant and imaginative reactions, discriminations and categories, but a vague grouping [for the 'value' each presented]?" (21). Nearly a fourth of *A Small Boy* is devoted to recollections of plays he saw as a child, a foretaste not only of his liking for drama but of his spectatorial role in life. The "scene," he whimsically claims, became important when a "spoiled" girl cousin was told not to "make" one, though it would be a long time before he could distinguish between such a scene and "those producible on another [literary] basis." Scenes were something one could "make" as one chose – "which should involve detachment, involve presence of mind....The passage...had been itself a scene, quite enough of one, and I had become aware with it of a rich accession of possibilities" (107).

He already feels the inevitability of expatriation. He sees again aunts and uncles doomed to early death, and their orphaned children whose homelessness gave him his "first assured conception of true richness...that [one] should be sent separately off among cold or even cruel aliens in order to be there thrillingly homesick" (11) – a fate of enviable but unsought separation. It was the condition the adult James would hardly seek and yet would find. James's most extravagant claim for a career determined at the time of earliest consciousness is a forecasting glimpse of the Place Vendôme from a carriage window during his family visit to Paris when he was five. But his interest in Europe was soon awakened in New York by a teacher who was "personal France" (13): "I was later on to feel – that is I was to learn – how many impressions and appearances, how large a sense of things, her type and tone prefigured." And by an "incorruptibly French" (21) schoolmate: "If I drop on his memory this apology for a bayleaf it is from the fact of his having given the earliest, or at least the most personal tap to that pointed prefigurement of the manners of 'Europe,' which, inserted wedge-like, if not to say peg-like, into my young allegiance, was to split the tender organ into such equal halves" (22). Even his later attachment to England is predicted when he sniffs the "English smell" in a New York bookstore: "What else can have happened but that, having taken over, under suggestion and with singular infant promptitude, a particular throbbing consciousness, I had become aware of the source at which it could best be refreshed" (48). His family's anglophile talk affected him "quite as if my infant divination proceeded by the light of nature" (49).

When, at twelve, he finds himself again in Europe he is full of "stores of preconception," ready for an epiphany – the sight, one day, travelling in the alps, of a ruined castle and a peasant woman – which "made a bridge over to more things than I then knew" (161). And in the Louvre there was the "foretaste (as determined by that instant as if the hour had struck from a clock) of all the fun...one was going to have and the kind of life, always of the queer so-called inward sort...one was going to lead" (198). The lesson of Europe and the lesson of Art were always to be joined. *A Small Boy and Others* gathers many strains of recollection into its fabric but none so prominent as this theme of preparation. *Notes of a Son and Brother* exhibits the young man, no longer a child, returning to Europe in 1859 with a character already formed.

But James's predestined progress, like Conrad's succession of unforseeable jumps, may gloss the truth. His autobiographical musings reveal, without admitting it, that there may have been a climactic turning-point when a choice was made, though *choice* was precisely what he had been urged since childhood to deprecate. Along with his brother William – the other of the elder Henry's two geniuses among his five offspring – he had been confronted throughout his growing up with a gospel of deceptive permissiveness. Henry senior did not urge these clever boys to attach themselves, practically and promptly, to professions. On the contrary, he met their shy stirrings of ambition with a prohibition of choice disguised as a tolerance of inaction which had a transcendental sound. "Just to *be* something, something unconnected with specific doing," was quite enough, the parent urged. His own disinclination towards the occupations of their schoolmates' fathers had been a source of embarassment. His children were not relieved by his "Say I'm a philosopher, say I'm a seeker after truth, say I'm a lover of my kind, say I'm an author of books if you like, best of all, just say I'm a Student" (278).

This idealist philosopher (who had the means to carry off his rejection without discomfort) rejected the vulgar materialist goals of mid-nineteenth century American society. But he also opposed the commitment of William and Henry to refined ends, and when William wanted to study painting, wondered whether art might not be "narrowing" (269). He professed distaste for "literary men:" "When a man *lives,* that is, lives enough, he can scarcely write" (352). He even regarded the idea of college with "extreme tepidity" (302), since it might open the way to a "career." Perhaps they heard unuttered messages in his constant dissuasions. This man with ideas on innumerable subjects had failed, himself, to make any mark upon his world. Was he sincere – or did he understand himself sufficiently when he insisted to his children that there was "scant measure of...difference, after all, for the life of the soul, between the marked achievement and the marked shortcoming?" (301). All benignity, he positively urged failure. His father's message affected William most severely; his struggle to discover a vocation would be prolonged for years. Henry promptly agreed with John Lafarge that his talent was for literature, but he had to contrive a way of reconciling this with his father's distaste for active doing and even choosing. The life of art was a condition of being that might be held superior to mere vulgar doing.

Of course, he had been *fated* to be a mere spectator of the Civil War. When he was a small boy, a teacher who put out a candle between finger and thumb illustrated a courage he doubted, predictively, to find in himself. A walk in the New York streets where excavation and demolition were taking place forecast the battlefields of the war he would "witness" only through the accounts of others. That his parents allowed him to wander freely in the dangerous city must mean that he seemed to them neither "reckless nor adventurous;" it was already clear that "the only form of riot or revel ever known to [him] would be that of the visiting mind" (16). At that later moment in Cambridge when he felt that "to be literary" was all he wanted to be while his classmates were all rushing to sign up as soldiers, he claims an ineluctible call that superceded the call to arms – and he began seriously to write stories, to woo "the muse of prose fiction" (439). All the while, as the autobiography notes, Harvard classmates were leaving to enlist. Soon, he would hear of the deaths of cousins Will Temple, Gus Barker, and Vernon King, of Cabot Russell, killed at Fort Wagner where his father found and rescued the wounded Wilky, and – closest of all – of the battlefield sufferings of his other younger brother, Bob.

James makes the bizarre claim that his famous "obscure hurt" – so private that it could not be described – had at once prevented more active participation and *become* participation in the "huge, comprehensive ache." It had, he says, treated him to "the honour of a sort of tragic fellowship" with the "interest of the extending War...the hurrying troops, the transfigured scene" (415). The foredoomed spectator had to content himself with knowing the Civil War "in view of that indirectness of its play which my conditions confined me, with such private, though I must add, alas, such helplessly unapplied resentment, to knowing it by" (276). But knowing the war, thus, in an "indirect and muffled" fashion, it was yet "intensified through all lapses of occasion and frustrations of contact," so that it remained "a more constituted and sustained act of living, in proportion to my powers and opportunities than any other homogeneous stretch of experience that my memory now recovers" (383).

The father had always urged the principle of "conversion" – a sort of Emersonian compensation – but this conversion which made him a writer instead of a soldier may not have been easy. A domestic struggle with the elder Henry James may be concealed by his son's account. Garth Wilkinson and Robertson James were allowed to be soldiers, though they were younger than William and Henry. The willful parent had, as he told a friend, held on tightly "to the coat tails" of his elder sons to keep them from enlisting. Alfred Habegger argues that the head of the James family – convinced of the special gifts of these two – "chose to sacrifice the expendable sons to action so that the favored sons could be dedicated to thought."[4]

The son blames only his own innate bias for the reflective, literary life, and blames the accidental injury which removed any lingering remnant of other possibility. He would rather have us believe that an "obscure" destiny had kept him from joining his younger brothers, three cousins and so many friends in the efforts and sacrifice of war, though one may wonder about the true state of mind of this young man at the threshold of maturity. Maybe he *had* wanted to join the army. But, held by the coat-tails, he turned from the defining act of those peers among classmates and cousins whom he most admired – and committed himself once and for all to the role of bystander. It might later seem the right and inevitable decision – or a defection from an ideal of manhood it was impossible to ignore.

James does not describe such a crisis any more than Conrad represents the real challenges with which, at the same youthful age of seventeen, *he* struggled before going to Marseille. How strange it is that the "record" which fails to describe his parents' careers as political partisans or tell how both died before he was twelve also does not mention his attempted suicide in Marseille at 20. Yet this suicide attempt may have been, as Frederick Karl thinks, an attempt to cut himself off, finally, from the claims of Poland. Only, after recounting the story of great uncle Bobrowski, he asks, "Why should I, the son of a land which such men as these have turned up with their ploughshares and bedewed with their blood, undertake the pursuit of fantastic meals of salt junk and hard-tack upon the wide seas?"

There is ground for suspecting that the seeds of lasting guilt had been planted in both James and Conrad's moments of youthful crisis and defection, though this is not expressed in their autobiographies. There may not be much difference between James's intimation that there had never been any question of participation in the Civil War – since non-participating witness he had always been destined to be – and Conrad's depiction of his unpremeditated and inexplicable need to leave Poland for a life at sea – an instance of the general inexplicableness of a life ruled by mysterious impulse. Both may be defensive fictions of the autobiographical imagination. Out of both defections, however, sprang the compensatory participations of art.

NOTES

1. *Joseph Conrad: Selected Literary Criticism and "The Shadow-Line,"* ed. Allan Ingram (London: Methuen, 1986), 117.
2. Zdzisław Najder, "Introduction," in Joseph Conrad, *"The Mirror of the Sea" and "A Personal Record"* (New York: Oxford U. P., 1988), XIV-XV.
3. *Ibid.*, XVI.
4. Alfred Habegger, *The Father: A Life of Henry James, Sr.* (New York: Farrar, Straus and Giroux, 1994), 420.

WORKS CITED

Habegger Alfred. *The Father: A Life of Henry James, Sr.* New York: Farrar, Straus and Giroux, 1994.
James Henry. *Autobiography,* ed. Frederick W. Dupee. New York: Criterion Books, 1956.
James Henry. *Literary Criticism: French Writers, Other European Writers.* New York: Library of America, 1984.
The Novels and Tales of Henry James, New York Edition. New York: Charles Scribner's Sons, 1907-1909. [vol. XXI]
Najder Zdzisław. "Introduction," in Joseph Conrad *"The Mirror of the Sea" and "A Personal Record."* New York: Oxford U. P., 1988.

Allan Simmons,
St. Mary's University College,
Twickenham, England

Conrad on James: Open-endedness
and Artistic Affiliation

Conrad's essay "Henry James: An Appreciation" (1905) focuses mainly on the related subjects of endings and the possibility of completeness. The essay commences with Conrad bemoaning the fact that there is no complete collection of James's novels, and concludes with the claim that his tales "end as an episode in life ends. You remain with the sense of the life still going on;" (*NLL,* 19). Along the way, Conrad notes that the absence of a Collected Edition of James's work is symbolic of the quality of the work itself, which contains "no suggestion of finality" (11); we learn that "the spring of [James's] benevolence will never run dry" (12), and that it is associated with "inextinguishable youth" (13); the artist invests his subject matter with "permanence in this world of relative values" whilst the reader demands to be "taken" from "perishable activity into the light of imperishable consciousness" (13); there is an anecdote which imagines the end of the world (13-14). And all of this, and more, occurs within an essay of nine pages. In one sense, the lack of "finality" claimed for James's work is no more than the quality which makes us return to all great art: we don't come to the end of knowing it. But Conrad's general concern with endings and closure in this essay – and, in particular, with the role of the artist in refuting such closure – has resonances for the "modern" quality of the fiction of both writers. More subtly, though, in his "Appreciation" Conrad identifies himself artistically with James by invoking the master's style. My examination of Conrad's essay on James will, thus, be in two parts: first, I shall consider the open-endedness in the modern novel to which both Conrad and James contribute, and which provides the major theme of the "Appreciation," and, second, I shall analyze the style of

Conrad's essay to show how it provides an indicator of his
artistic affiliation with James.[1]

Open-endedness

One of the definitive features of the modern novel is its
open-endedness; it rejects the tidy ending of its Victorian
counterpart, described by James as "a distribution at the last of
prizes, pensions, husbands, wives, babies, millions, appended
paragraphs and cheerful remarks."[2] Not that the Victorian
novelist was unaware of the artificiality of such attempts at
closure. George Eliot said that "Conclusions are the weak points
of most authors, but some of the fault lies in the very nature of
a conclusion, which is at best a negation."[3] It is this idea of
negation which the modern novel seeks to address: rather than
simply destroying the illusion of constructed, on-going reality,
negating it by means of some imposed end-point, the modern
novel tries to preserve that sense of "life still going on." In her
essay, "Modern Fiction," Virginia Woolf, pointing to the
Russian influence on English fiction, identifies the sense that "if
honestly examined life presents question after question which
must be left to sound on and on after the story is over in hopeless
interrogation." In the same essay, she offers a description of the
"uncircumscribed" quality of life that the modern novelist must
needs convey: "life is a luminous halo, a semi-transparent
envelope surrounding us from the beginning of consciousness to
the end."[4] Woolf's description of the subject of fiction uses
imagery which echoes that used to describe Marlow's approach
to story-telling in "Heart of Darkness:"

> to him the meaning of an episode was not inside like a kernel but
> outside, enveloping the tale which brought it out only as a glow brings
> out a haze, in the likeness of one of these misty halos that sometimes
> are made visible by the spectral illumination of moonshine. (*YS*, 48)

But, paradoxically, in being more truthful to the sense of created
reality, the modern novel's open-ending denies its readers access

to a point of interpretative reference, to the magnetic north which enables one to recognize the direction of the meaning. To put this another way: one of the reasons why we go to art is that it offers completeness, judgement and certainty, a pattern that is missing from the minute-by-minute subjective experience of life; in its attempt to render the experience of life, the modern novel challenges this very sense of completeness, of pattern. Ian Watt argues that:

> Both Conrad and James were very much aware that the way a novel ended reflected a general view of life, and they broke with the traditional closed form of ending which attempted a complete resolution of the main problems of the novel's plot and characters.[5]

Critics have tended to place this absence of closure within the broader context of modern man's predicament as he confronts the possibility of a Godless universe. In the absence of a transcendental signified, *the* source and home of all meaning, the truth to life of the modern novel lies in its refusal to countenance one single overarching meaning, which would simply be to set up an alternative God, and its portrayal instead of the myriad, subjective centers of consciousness, each with its own (perhaps incommunicable) truth.[6] Two forces are at work here: the absence of an ending and the subjective nature of truth. (The death of God doesn't eliminate truth or meaning; instead, it removes the all-embracing, shared context of this truth, leaving in its place a truth that is individual and subjective.) As Wallace Stevens suggests, art's transcendence is subjective, but it is transcendence:

> The world about us would be desolate except for the world within us. The major poetic idea in the world is and has always been the idea of God. After one has abandoned a belief in God, poetry is the essence which takes its place as life's redemption.[7]

Flaubert wanted the novel to strike its reader as "an aesthetic object rather than a communicative act."[8] Yet this immediately challenges the reader's expectations. As Frank Kermode argues:

To read a novel expecting the satisfactions of closure and the receipt of a message is what most people find enough to do; they are easier with this method because it resembles the one that works for ordinary acts of communication. In this way the gap is closed between what is sent and what is received.[9]

In his essay on *Chance,* James claims that Conrad's method was to "glory" in precisely such a gap, delaying what Kermode calls "the satisfactions of closure."[10] It would be going too far to claim that either novelist eschews meaning or communication in his work, but I would want to argue that both eschew *single* meaning. This is demonstrated in their repeated reliance upon an intradiegetic narrator (or narrators): not only does the technique of presenting the narrative through the perceiving consciousness of one of the characters remove at a stroke any claim to omniscience, but this expressed viewpoint must needs call attention to the suppressed viewpoints of other characters, and hence the limitations and vulnerability of single meaning.

James's story "The Figure in the Carpet" dramatizes the limitations of first-person perspective. In effect, the plot dynamics of the story might be said to mirror the dynamics of Jamesian fiction generally: James's "weak specifications" make one constantly aware of meanings which remain, tantalizingly, elusive. As he claims in his "Preface" to *The Princess Casamassima*: "It seems probable that if we were never bewildered there would never be a story to tell about us" (IX). In "The Figure in the Carpet," the reader's sense of anticipation and frustration mirrors the experience of the narrator himself. First, the discovery of Vereker's secret lies beyond the narrator – who, nonetheless, confirms the existence of this secret. Then, Corvick takes over and his impending marriage to Gwendolyn Orme is suggested as a possible reason for the narrator's failure: success, it is implied, is linked, at least in part, to knowledge outside his experience. Corvick succeeds where the narrator failed, but dies leaving his widow the only heir to his discovery. She in turn, despite remarrying, preserves the secret out of respect for her first husband's memory. The mystery around which the "action" is structured is solved only for the solution to be lost. The reader, like the narrator, is left with the curious sense of having been denied closure even though such closure has been achieved.

Conrad was stung by James's criticism of his narratorial method in *Chance*. In his essay, James refers to "Marlow's omniscience" as "a prolonged hovering flight of the subjective over the outstretched ground of the case exposed."[11] In retrospect, this criticism seems to stem from James's sense that Conrad's narratorial method in *Chance* is uncomfortably close to his own. Both authors tend to employ narrative techniques which often render meaning as an unfinished process. In this, they might be said to be responding to a modern impulse towards inconclusivity. As the deracinated Birkin says in *Women in Love*: "You have to be like Rodin, Michael Angelo, and leave a piece of raw rock unfinished to your figure."[12] In *Chance* by advertizing the fact that he's searching for the precise word to convey his meaning, Marlow reveals just this "piece of raw rock unfinished." For instance, describing Flora's impending torment at the hands of the Governess, he says:

> She went bored to bed, and being tired with her long ride slept soundly all night. Her last sleep, I won't say of innocence – that word would not render my exact meaning, because it has a special meaning of its own – but I will say: of that ignorance, or better still, of that unconsciousness of the world's ways, the unconsciousness of danger, of pain, of humiliation, of bitterness, of falsehood. (*Ch*, 99)

Marlow rejects successive terms in his search for precise meaning: "innocence" is deemed less exact than "ignorance," and "ignorance" in its turn is altered to "unconsciousness." The narrative is revealed to be less a finished product than a text in the process of composition, and reading thus becomes not so much a quest for final meaning as an invitation to view the processes by which meaning is constituted.

Both James and Conrad comment upon the openness of experience in their non-fictional prose. James's claim that "Experience is never limited, and it is never complete" finds an echo in Conrad's comment upon *The Nigger of the "Narcissus*:" "As to the lack of incident well – it's life. The incomplete joy, the incomplete sorrow, the incomplete rascality or heroism – the incomplete suffering" (*CL*, I, 321). Such inconclusivity leads Alan Friedman to discover in Conrad's fiction "the progressive emergence of a finally open experience as normative for fiction."[13] Such openness can be traced in the form of the modern novel which might be said to offer as a substitute for what George Eliot called "the arrangement of events or feigned correspondences according to predominant feeling,"[14] the juxtaposition of incidents and of interpretations of them, leaving the reader to provide the connecting logic. How else do we find a place for, say, the "pink toads" incident in *Lord Jim* or the Corvick marriage in "The Figure in the Carpet?" Indeed, as Roger Shattuck argues: "The twentieth century has addressed itself to arts of juxtaposition as opposed to earlier arts of transition."[15]

The sense of relativism which replaces objective truth is conveyed by both novelists through various techniques we now consider "Modern." For example, the texture of Jamesian prose, with its proliferation of subordinate clauses, perfectly reflects the difficulties of communication in an age of uncertain truth, whilst Conrad's penchant for modalizing locutions such as the "as if" and "as though" constructions simultaneously promises and delays the revelation of meaning.

In his essay on James, Conrad claims that, "in this world of relative values" and "perishable activity," the reader turns to the novelist for something "imperishable." This in turn issues from the idea that the permanence associated with art is "the permanence of memory" (*NLL,* 13). In a weak sense this says no more than the obvious: we live in the past because we have no other known place in which to live. But, in another, stronger sense, to find permanence in memory, as we do in Proust, reflects a new way of inhabiting time and this is mirrored in the Modern composition of the novel where the interpreting consciousness cuts across time, working to link epiphanic moments through memory. In Proust, as Charles Taylor argues, "The recovery of the past stops the wasting of time." This strategy of looking to the past for some sense of permanence and pattern with which to oppose the flux lies behind such works as "The Waste Land" and *Ulysses*.[16]

In his explanation of James's methods, therefore, Conrad is associating the two of them with defining features of the modern experience. His comment upon the artist's role extends this. Whilst echoing James's comment upon the reader's paradoxical demand on the author for "this sham of Divine Omnipotence" in the "desire for finality for which our hearts yearn" (18), Conrad's essay nonetheless pulls in two directions: on the one hand, he argues, as T. S. Eliot would do in *Four Quartets,* that the realm of possibility is itself influential in the impossibility of endings, whilst on the other he equates endings with death and, by extension, openness with life. Conrad addresses the unavoidable problem behind all narrative conclusions thus: first, he argues that, whilst most people live their lives by compromise between truth and falsity, James's characters derive their sense of integrity from being more absolute. They reject what they deem to be false. But, Conrad then argues, this sense of finality is itself deceptive as, in his words, "a solution by rejection must always present a certain lack of finality" (18) precisely because of the unexplored alternative. As Eliot says in "Burnt Norton:"

> What might have been and what has been
> Point to one end which is always present.

For Conrad then, the existence of possibility renders a narrative unfinishable (as, indeed, must the alternative "compromise" which strands its subject between possibilities). But in such openness, we discover, lies salvation of a sort. Conrad claims that "The artist in his calling of interpreter creates...because he must. He is so much a voice that, for him, silence is like death" (14). In other words, like Sheherezade, the author is driven by the need to narrate without end. If the silence of ending is "like death" to the author, the discourse that is the tale must continue, and the way that this can be achieved is to commit the reader to the process of fiction and its open-endedness.

The structure of *Lord Jim* suggests to the reader that the conclusion will offer a key to the tale. As the omniscient

third-person narrator gives way to the first-person narration of
Marlow in Chapter 5, we sense that the enigma in this tale is the
psychology of Jim and to unravel this secret the sympathy of
a fellow seaman is required. We soon learn, though, that a single
viewpoint will not suffice as Marlow's narrative quickly embeds
the views on Jim of a host of other narrators like the French
Lieutenant. This multiple perspective then gives way to Stein's
experiment in the second half of the novel, a structural
development which in itself promises that this will provide the
answer to the riddle posed by Jim's character. Yet the narrative
concludes with Marlow's inability to effect closure: "Is he
satisfied – quite, now, I wonder?" (*LJ*, 417). As the observations
of the "privileged man" on Jim serve to demonstrate, the tale's
structure suggests a resolution which its transmission frustrates.
By the end of the novel, the reader's question as to whether Jim is
finally a hero or a coward has been shown to be too narrow: *Lord
Jim* questions the very certainties which enable us to think of
heroism in terms of such a dualism and forces us to ask instead
whether heroism itself is possible. The narrative design thus
suggests that the frustrations of closure are deliberate. Far from
challenging artistic unity, this multiple meaning actually reflects
Conrad's concern with the "wholeness" of meaning by refusing
to exclude potential interpretations.

James's desire for this wholeness of meaning is expressed in his
"Preface" to *The Ambassadors*, the novel which offered him "the
opportunity to 'do' a man of imagination:" "to account for
Strether and for his 'peculiar tone,' was to possess myself of the
entire fabric" (VIII, XI). In *The Ambassadors*, Lambert Strether,
the editor of a cultural review in Woollett, Massachusetts, is sent
to Paris by his fiancée, Mrs. Newsome, a wealthy widow. His
mission is to rescue her son, Chad, from the enticements of
old-world Europe. The simple opposition between American
and European values collapses as Strether, the ambassador of
Woollett morality, gradually falls under the spell of the unhap-
pily married Madame de Vionnet, whose relations with Chad
pose the puzzle that occupies Strether for most of the novel.
Confessing himself to be "a reaction against a mistake," Strether

urges one of Chad's friends, Little Bilham, to "Live all you can; it's a mistake not to" (218, 217). As Jacques Berthoud puts it: "the fascination that Madame de Vionnet exerts over Strether is that in everything she does she seems to hold out the promise of life-as-art."[17] Selecting Strether as the focus of perception has two important consequences: firstly, it ensures that the reader's interpretative process is restricted to Strether's own attempt to understand the relationship between Chad and Madame de Vionnet; and, secondly, it makes Strether's vision the locus for narrative unity and coherence.

Lily Briscoe's painting in *To the Lighthouse* or the articulation of the "broken images" that compose "The Waste Land" demonstrate how art alone seems to offer coherence and form to the fractured modern experience. It is therefore fitting that the climactic scene in *The Ambassadors* should concern the relationship between art and life. In Book 11, Chapters 3 and 4, Strether journeys into the French countryside in search of the original landscape depicted in a painting he once failed to buy. Although Strether discovers his landscape, his ideal mental picture of it is not complete. That evening, however, as he is about to dine at a riverside restaurant, a rowing-boat comes into view: "It was suddenly as if these figures, or something like them, had been wanted in the picture, had been wanted more or less all day, and had now drifted into sight, with the slow current, on purpose to fill up the measure" (256). The couple turn out to be Chad and Madame de Vionnet, and the upshot of the ensuing encounter is that Strether becomes aware of their adulterous liaison. Strether's painting is thus completed in such a way as to compromise its sense of unity. Neither Strether's artistic ideal nor the reality he inhabits survives the encounter intact. *The Ambassadors,* thus, depends for its sense of unity on Strether's vision, yet he is unable to reconcile the aesthetic claims of Europe with the ethical demands of Woollett.

Artistic affiliation

Stylistically, "Henry James: An Appreciation" is striking for its
self-conscious artistry, on the one hand, and its echoes of the
master himself, on the other. The essay's rhetorical flourish soon
becomes apparent. It begins on a note of mock deference: "The
critical faculty hesitates before the magnitude of Mr. Henry
James's work" (*NLL,* 11). We know that this is *mock* deference
both because the essay has already advertized the "critical
faculty" of its author in its sub-title: "An Appreciation" – and,
after all, it was Conrad himself who said: "there is nothing more
exasperating than an ignorant appreciation" (*CL,* II, 35) – and
because there is little that is "hesitant" in what follows: the
sentences (and the paragraphs) of the essay lenghten as the essay
develops and the impersonality of "the critical faculty" gives
way to the first-person. Only two paragraphs later, for example,
Conrad is emphatically present in the first-person: "I do not
know into what brand of ink Mr. Henry James dips his pen;
indeed, I heard that of late he had been dictating; but I know that
his mind is steeped in the water flowing from the fountain of
intellectual youth" (12). The artful balance between denial and
assertion ("I do not know...but I know that"), which itself
suggests argument and authority, facilitates the development of
the "ink"-image into "waters...from the fountain of intellectual
youth" and the practical act of composing ("brand of ink,"
"dips his pen") into the mystery of inspiration. Conrad's
self-conscious artistry becomes evident in the same paragraph as
these ink/fountain images generate references to the "spring of
[James's] benevolence," "The stream of inspiration" and, finally, "It is, in fact, a magic spring" (12). In this paragraph, too,
Conrad refers to *The Ambassadors* (1903), as "the latest of his
works" (12). In the references to "fountains" and "magic
springs," however, the reader is also likely to hear a buried
reference to the novel James published two years earlier, *The
Sacred Fount.*
    With the assertion that "It is, in fact, a magic spring" (12), the
developing fountain-images reach the conclusion towards which

they have been leading, whereupon the voice of Conrad the critic blends with and comments upon the virtuosity of Conrad the artist:

> With this phrase the metaphor of the perennial spring, of the inextinguishable youth, of running waters, as applied to Mr. Henry James's inspiration, may be dropped. In its volume and force the body of his work may be compared rather to a majestic river. All creative art is magic, is evocation of the unseen in forms persuasive, enlightening, familiar and surprising, for the edification of mankind, pinned down by the conditions of its existence to the earnest consideration of the most insignificant tides of reality. (12-13)

The deliquescent metaphor is "dropped" only to be replaced by the comparison of James's work to a "majestic river," an image which, in turn, is given added weight by the contrast with "insignificant tides of reality," advancing the claims of art over life. More pertinently, once the issue of artistic technique is introduced (via the reference to "metaphor"), the essay offers an explanation of creative art as "magic...evocation of the unseen in forms persuasive," an explanation, in other words, of precisely the process whereby "ink" has just been transmuted into "magic spring." In his essay, then, Conrad celebrates James's creative powers via his own creative flourish and, simultaneously, offers his own explanation of the process of artistic creation.

Conrad's essay might also be said to offer an appreciation of James's fiction at a more subtle level: both in their syntactic complexity and in the profusion of their qualifying clauses, Conrad's sentences mimic James's own mannerist style. As such labyrinthine sentences as the following demonstrate, it is as if Conrad believed that the sincerest form of tribute was affectionate parody:

> In a world such as ours, so painful with all sorts of wonders, one would not exhaust oneself in barren marvelling over mere bindings, had not the fact, or rather the absence of the material fact, prominent in the case of other men whose writing counts (for good or evil) – had it not been, I say, expressive of a direct truth, spiritual and intellectual; an accident of – I suppose – the publishing business acquiring a symbolic meaning from its negative nature. (11)

According to Conrad, the lack of finality in James's writings is symbolically reflected in the failure of the publishing business to provide a collected (and, thus, "final") edition. In other words, the negligence of publishers is, in a paradoxical and unintended sense, a fitting tribute to James. To convey this sense of paradox, Conrad's sentence includes a range of counterbalanced elements: hesitancy in the speaking voice is balanced by authority ("I suppose"/"I say"); abstract nouns coexist with concrete nouns ("wonders"/"world"); and vastly different scales of magnitude are juxtaposed ("world"/"mere bindings"). The true sense of convolution, though, exists within the sentence-structure itself, as the parenthetic observations and subordinate clauses serve to create the impression of an intellectual struggle towards finer and subtler shades of meaning. In so doing, the style conveys that sense of "something both intensely understood and supremely inexpressible" that is the hallmark of James's fiction.[18]

Although Conrad sub-titled his essay on James "An Appreciation," it is really a testament to the shared working practice of the two writers. As James later wrote in his "Preface" (1907) to *Roderick Hudson*:

> Up to what point is such and such a development *indispensible* to the interest? What is the point beyond which it ceases to be rigorously so? Where, for the complete expression of one's subject, does a particular relation stop – giving way to some other not concerned in that expression?
> Really, universally, relations stop nowhere, and the exquisite pattern of the artist is eternally but to draw, by a geometry of his own, the circle within which they shall happily *appear* to do so. (VII)

In its emphasis upon the role and function of the artist, Conrad's "appreciation" of James is simultaneously his personal testament to his own status as a writer. Perhaps reflecting the *fin de siècle* mood, Conrad recounts how the artist will respond to the end of the world, "on the eve of that day without tomorrow" (*NLL*, 14).[19] In doing so, Conrad self-consciously locates himself within the Western tradition of narrative by evoking the Biblical paradigm, which begins with Creation and ends with

Apocalypse. But he evokes this framework only to reject it. In Conrad's version of the last day, as Creation withers "against the feeble glow of the sun" (13), the artist, usurping the role of the Creator, will continue to create:

> The artistic faculty, of which each of us has a minute grain, may find its voice in some individual of that last group, gifted with the power of expression and courageous enough to interpret the ultimate experience of mankind in terms of his temperament, in terms of art. I do not mean to say that he would attempt to beguile the last moments of humanity by an ingenious tale. It would be too much to expect – from humanity. I doubt the heroism of the hearers. As to the heroism of the artist, no doubt is necessary. There would be on his part no heroism. The artist in his calling of interpreter creates (the clearest form of demonstration) because he must. (13-14)

In Conrad's scenario, the artist does not falter before the inevitable; he has the last word before life ends, creating as Creation itself ceases. The motivation behind this extreme moment of creation is identified as the force behind art generally: a combination of communal responsibility and the artist's coercion to speak. For Conrad, the artist as the interpreter of man's experience has no choice but to create. This sense of the artist as, in some sense, possessed has obvious implications for the Romantic figure of the artist that Conrad intends: the artist-hero continuing to fulfil his function of interpreter as life dies around him.

Conrad's parenthetic observation in the above quotation, that "each of us has a minute grain" of the artistic faculty, highlights the creative role of the addressee in narrative. Both Conrad and James emphasize the place of the reader in the production of meaning in their fiction. At its simplest, this is evident in the relationship between the narrator and the reader: for instance, in *Lord Jim,* whilst Marlow's "confounded democratic quality of vision" (*LJ,* 94) may not communicate itself to characters such as the privileged man, it is certainly shared with the reader. More pertinently, though, the reader's collaborative role is urged by both authors.[20] In his essay "The Novels of George Eliot"

(1866), James argues that the reader is "made" by the author expressly for this purpose:

> In every novel the work is divided between the writer and the reader; but the writer makes the reader very much as he makes his characters. When he makes him ill, that is, makes him indifferent, he does no work; the writer does all. When he makes him well, that is, makes him interested, then the reader does quite half the labour.[21]

Conrad voices these sentiments in his letters. Writing to R. B. Cunninghame Graham on 5 August 1897, Conrad concludes: "one writes only half the book; the other half is with the reader" (*CL*, I, 370). Similarly, in his letter to Harriet Mary Capes of 22 March 1902, Conrad says: "the reader collaborates with the author" (II, 394).

Conrad's portrait of the artist as poet-hero is fused with the Classical image of the poet through the essay's frequent references to springs and fountains, which conjure up images of the Castilian spring of Greek legend with its twin connotations of poetry and prophecy. Thus, James's mind is "steeped in the waters flowing from the fountain of intellectual youth...the spring of [his] benevolence will never run dry....It is in fact a magic spring" (*NLL*, 12). Within the context of an essay which is a testament to the shared working practices of Conrad and James, such references to an already established artistic pantheon serve to locate not only James but also Conrad himself within this tradition. In "Henry James: An Appreciation" Conrad identifies himself with his chosen career. To paraphrase him, the essay bears witness to the fellowship of another craft.

NOTES

1. Unless otherwise stated, all references to James's works are to *The New York Edition of Henry James*, 26 vols. (New York: Charles Scribner's; re-issued by Augustus M. Kelley, 1971-76).

2. Henry James, "The Art of Fiction," in *Selected Literary Criticism*, ed. Morris Shapira (Cambridge: Cambridge U. P., 1981), 52-3.

3. George Eliot to John Blackwood, letter of 1 May 1857, in *The George Eliot Letters,* ed. Gordon S. Haight, vol. 2: 1852-1858 (New Haven: Yale U. P., 1954), 324.

4. Virginia Woolf, *The Common Reader,* First Series (London: The Hogarth Press, 1942), 194, 189.

5. Ian Watt, *Conrad in the Nineteenth Century* (London: Chatto and Windus, 1980), 207.

6. In September 1898, Conrad saw the recently invented Röntgen X-ray machine, demonstrated by Dr John McIntyre, in Glasgow. Recounting the experience to Edward Garnett, in a letter dated 29 September 1898, Conrad relates X-rays to states of consciousness: "The secret of the universe is in the existence of horizontal waves whose varied vibrations are at the bottom of all states of consciousness. If the waves were vertical the universe would be different. This is a truism. But, don't you see, there is nothing in the world to prevent the simultaneous existence of vertical waves at any angles; in fact, there are mathematical reasons for believing that such waves do exist. Therefore it follows that two universes may exist in the same place and in the same time – and not only two universes but an infinity of different universes – if by universe we mean a set of states of consciousness" (*CL,* II, 94-5).

7. Wallace Stevens, *Opus Posthumous,* ed. Samuel French Morse (New York: Vantage Books, 1982). It seems true to say of Modernism that it is self-conscious in spirit. It is the age in which, to quote Matthew Arnold, "the mind's dialogue with itself has begun." T. S. Eliot's Prufrock dramatizes this, being both "you and I," whilst Hamlet, to whom he refers, surely derives his "Modern" status from just this dialogue. This self--reflexivity is advertized most obviously in the techniques whereby modern art proclaims its status as art (and is one reason why we tend to think of *Tristram Shandy* as a modern novel) and, again paradoxically, the open-endedness of the modern novel addresses this: in attempting to replicate the open-endedness of life, it frustrates "closure" of the definitive pattern of stories. Interestingly, the archetypal ending to story, "And they lived happily *ever after*" itself resists closure – but does offer certainty.

8 Jonathan Culler, *Flaubert: The Uses of Uncertainty* (London: Paul Elek, 1974), 15.

9. Frank Kermode, *Essays on Fiction 1971-82* (London: Routledge and Kegan Paul, 1983), 138.

10. Henry James, "The New Novel," in *Selected Literary Criticism...,* 311-42.

11. In a letter to John Quinn, 24 May 1916, Conrad recalled James's comments as "the only time a criticism affected me painfully" (cited in Jocelyn Baines, *Joseph Conrad: A Critical Biography* [Harmondsworth: Penguin, 1986], 383).

12. D. H. Lawrence, *Women in Love* (Phoenix Edition), 349.

13. Alan Friedman, *The Turn of the Novel* (New York: Oxford U. P., 1966), 99.

14. George Eliot, *Selected Essays, Poems and Other Writings* (London: Penguin, 1990), 233.

15. Quoted in Charles Taylor, *Sources of the Self: The Making of the Modern Identity* (Cambridge: Cambridge U. P., 1989), 466.

16. Taylor, 464-5. Taylor goes on to argue: "We in our time need to recover the past in order to attain fulness. But this is not so much because history has meant decline, as because the fulness of meaning isn't available with the resources of a single age....The modernist retrieval of experience involves a profound breach in the received sense of identity and time, and a series of reorderings of a strange and unfamiliar kind. These images of life have reshaped our ideas in this century of what it is to be a human being. As a result of this, the epiphanic centre of gravity begins to be displaced from the self to the flow of experience, to new forms of unity, to language conceived in a variety of ways – eventually even as a 'structure'."

17. Jacques Berthoud, in *The Cambridge Cultural History: Early 20th Century Britain,* ed. Boris Ford, vol. 8 (Cambridge: Cambridge U. P., 1992), 53.

18. *Makers of Nineteenth Century Culture,* ed. Justin Wintle (London: Routledge and Kegan Paul, 1982), 320.

19. In his "Speech of Acceptance upon the Award of the Nobel Prize for Literature," William Faulkner's vision of the artist at the end of the world seems to owe a debt to Conrad: "when the last ding-dong of doom has clanged and faded from the worthless rock hanging tideless in the last red and dying evening [...] even then there will still be one more sound: that of his puny, inexhaustible voice, still talking," in *The Best of Faulkner* (London: Chatto and Windus, 1955).

20. For a counter-argument to this, see Vivienne Rundle's essay "Defining Frames: The Prefaces of Henry James and Joseph Conrad," *Henry James Review,* 16: 1 (Winter 1995), 66-92. Rundle argues that whereas Conrad grants the reader a place and a role, James tends to be overly determined and exclusive.

21. Henry James, *Literary Criticism: Essays on Literature; American Writers; English Writers* (New York: Viking, Library of America, 1984), 922.

Anthony Fothergill,
University of Exeter,
Exeter, England

Memory and Experience Lost: Conrad's "Karain: A Memory," and James's "The Beast in the Jungle"

I

Two rock songs of the late 60's, in which some of us may take solace in our more nostalgically uncritical moments, offer radically different ways of expressing or rather imagining our personal relationship to time and lived experience. Inspired by Ecclesiastes 3: 1, "To every thing there is a season and a time to every purpose under heaven," the Byrds sang, "There is a time, turn turn turn, to every season, turn turn turn." In stark contrast to this lyricism came stuttering, protective mock-cynicism from The Who, in their throwaway refrain to "My Generation:" "Hope I die before I get old." Theirs is the voice of radical modernity, of disenchanted time, of the fear of optimism disappointed, of a life always ready unfulfilled. Whereas the first song promises completion, experiential meaning and justification in the fullness of time, the second – romantic in its gesture of protest against the emptiness of time passing – anticipates and tries to fend off failure by means of anachronism, of dying before my time.

II

The conclusion of Henry James's "The Beast in the Jungle" and Joseph Conrad's "Karain: A Memory" carry a sense of endings which do not quite happen.[1] Both tales structurally conjure the promise that the life-experiences of the protagonists, John Marcher and the white gun-traders respectively, will be somehow redeemed: they conjure the promise that in the fullness of

113

time events and their meanings will be reconciled. Yet both tales
thematize the belated; they suffer anachronism. The real end has
already happened elsewhere, "in another country," to someone
else. That fullness of time of which Ecclesiastes speaks is
conspicuous only through its absence. The tales offer powerful
images for the impossibility of dying, or at least the impossibility
of living the full life and dying the good death. In both stories, the
endings – John Marcher falling face down on to the grave of May
Bertram in "The Beast of the Jungle," and, in "Karain," the
narrator meeting up with Jackson in all the hectic business of the
Strand in London – the endings gesture towards a life that has
not been lived, and that therefore cannot be relinquished and
mourned. The end, as a meaningful culmination, as the transformation of accident (or happening) into Fate, is displaced onto
another. The end is seen, sensed, by the chief protagonists in
a refracted way through another person, not directly experienced. As James puts it of Marcher, but it applies to both tales,
"he had been the man of his time, *the* man, to whom nothing on
earth was to have happened" ("The Beast in the Jungle," 401;
original emphasis). James and Conrad thus anticipate in their
works the theoretical expression of modern experience which
Walter Benjamin later offers us (and to which I will return).
Benjamin distinguishes between two concepts of experience and
their associated forms of memory: lived-through experience
(*Erfahrung*) and mere occurrence (*Erlebnis*). In the disenchanted
time of the modern man, things occur, of course, but in a double
sense they remain issueless.

Interestingly, in both stories, the figure for "real" experience,
for those events that would transform sheer passage of time into
a shaped life (whether fraught or fulfilled), is the image of the
beast pouncing. In Conrad's story, Karain describes the haunting, dangerous presence of Matara thus: "He waits for me on
the paths, under the trees, in the place where I sleep – everywhere
but here" (*TU*, 25). The "here" in this context is the European
space, symbolized by and embodied in the ship, the space of
"power, of endeavour, of unbelief – the strong life of white men
which rolls on irresistible and hard on the edge of outer

darkness" (26). The "here" is the space of modernity, of capital progress unhampered by remembrance of things past: measured by the "firm, pulsating beat of the two ship's chronometers ticking off steadily the seconds of Greenwich Time [which seemed to the narrator] a protection and a relief" (40) from the life that Karain represented. One sort of temporality erases another. Though Karain's other temporality is called by the disenchanted narrator a life of "illusions," they are illusions "that give joy, that give sorrow, that give pain, that give peace." They are "invincible illusions that can make life and death appear serene, inspiring, tormented or ignoble" (40). They are, in other words, illusions which sound suspiciously like the full life lived. And against the threat and trauma but also the energizing pleasure of these illusions, modernity offers the scepticism of disenchanted instrumental rationality in the guise of colonial, capitalist progress. We could put it this way, following the distinctions between token and totem which Daphna Erdinast-Vulcan offers us: what from a modern disenchanted viewpoint is merely a *token* – the Queen Victoria sixpence which Hollis theatrically gives to Karain – is transformed in the giving into a *totem*.[2] The sixpence functions, that is, as an authoritative embodiment of belief, enabling Karain to act, to accomodate and remember (rather than to deny) past experience. The simple, cynical, view of this gift is that its acceptance signals the naïveté of the native. But that very view, with its patronizing and racist tendency, is confounded by another. We remember that Hollis himself has kept the coin and a bit of silk ribbon among other "gifts of heaven – things of the earth" as "amulets...charms and talismans" (48). Within this alternative frame of reference – which Hollis, and, by the end of the story, Johnson, recognize – this magical gift establishes an understanding and implicit cross-racial solidarity between Hollis and Karain. And the gift is the accidental occurrence through which Karain resolves his fear of Matara into remembrance.

Henry James's tale dramatizes experience denied. The possibility of the leap of the beast in the jungle is self-evidently, structurally, stated, John Marcher's doubled (or, in Eve Kosofsky Sedgwick's terminology, closeted[3]) secret is his secret belief, indeed his life-narrative, that some (secret) form of unmediated experience will encounter him, leap upon him as his fate. What May Bartram comes to recognize, but of course Marcher does not, is that, for Marcher, this beast of experience has always already sprung. Indeed May recognizes this precisely *because* Marcher does not.

> It had sprung as he didn't guess; it had sprung as she hopelessly turned from him, and the mark, by the time he left her, had fallen where it *was* to fall. He had justified his fear and achieved his fate; he had failed, with the last exactitude, of all he was to fail of; and a moan now rose to his lips as he remembered she had prayed he mightn't know. ("The Beast in the Jungle," 402)

A profoundly anachronistic sense of destiny thus ghosts Marcher's progress. The fullness of Marcher's time has passed him by, or rather, has been by-passed by him. That Sedgwick, calling it "homosexual panic," and Stanley Cavell, calling it "castration anxiety,"[4] try to put a name to this secret beast seems to me reductively misplaced. It is not a *particular* experience, or trauma, which is avoided or denied, but rather the possibility of there being *any such quality of experience* for Marcher.

Only once, with a wonderfully equivocal use of the past preterite tense precisely in the middle of the tale, does James hint at things having the possibility of turning out otherwise: "Since it was in Time that he was to have met his fate, so it was in Time that his fate was to have acted" (379). Read one way (his fate was to have acted; to act was his fate) the sentence might imply his redemption as creator of his own future. It is this possibility which is only gestured towards in its non-fulfillment. Read another way, the sentence implies that Fate is the actor. Thus, experience lost, he falls victim to what James calls the law of "common doom" (388).

For John Marcher, this sort of ending – which we might term a death by default – is prefigured at the tale's very beginning, which appropriately enough is not a beginning. While Marcher's name allegorically signals "will" or "intentional progress," and hence has a symbolic potential for springtime generation, the opening of the story promises us no future because it secures us no past. Marcher's meeting with May Bartram, on an October afternoon, at Weathersend, carries, in James's rendering, an overdetermined sense of temporality (season, cycle), any fulfilment of which is immediately undercut. May's face, in its separateness, is a kind of flawed or lost narrative: "a reminder, yet not quite a remembrance." Marcher's meeting with her repeats the figure of an unremembered past, "a sequel of something of which he had lost the beginning" (352). Even the weather has no future.

III

For Walter Benjamin, being subject to this law of common doom is a condition of modernity.[5] The very possibility of experiencing our own history is in jeopardy under modern capitalist conditions, defined by industrial reproduction, information – and sensory-overload, and redundance. The idea that the subject can achieve self-understanding through the transformation and remembrance of life events is precarious. Benjamin views this hope as a nostalgic specter haunting our empty days.

What for Benjamin contests the order and complacency of time passing is the shock which momentary encounters and impressions can produce. But their potentiality for conversion into remembrance is fragile:

> The greater the share of the shock factor in particular impressions, the more consciousness has to be alert as a screen against stimuli; the more efficiently it does so, the less do these impressions enter experience (*Erfahrung*), tending to remain in the sphere of a certain hour in one's life (*Erlebnis*). Perhaps the special achievement of shock defense may be seen in its function of assigning to an incident a precise point in time in consciousness at the cost of the integrity of its content. This would be a peak achievement of the intellect (Rationality); it would turn the incident into a moment that had been lived (*Erlebnis*). (Benjamin, *Illuminations,* 165)

The distinction which Benjamin makes here between two notions of experience – *Erfahrung* and *Erlebnis* – is crucial, and to them are attached two modalities of memory, *Gedächtnis* and *Erinnerung*, or remembrance and recall as we could translate them, Benjamin's categories echoing James's opening phrase of "The Beast in the Jungle."

The conscious ordering of events into a temporal sequence is a strategy of defense against the shock-effects of experience.[6] The transformation of impressions into *Erlebnis* – merely that which has consciously happened at a particular time and place, as something accounted for, over and done with, its impossibilities of return occurring only through conscious factual recall – *Erlebnis* signals a withering of experience, *Erfahrung*. Factual remembering and forms of narration which accompany it insulate the present and the future from the trouble and shock, but also the weight and integrity of past events. These are no longer sites of promise or despair, possibilities to be chosen or renounced. They are merely what happened once.

The closing paragraphs of "Karain," present such a view of disenchanted modernity. It is a view offered up by the narrator to Jackson as evidence, self-evidence, of the Real:

> Our ears were filled by a headlong shuffle and beat of rapid footsteps and an underlying rumour – a rumour vast, faint, pulsating, as of panting breaths, of beating hearts, of gasping voices. Innumerable eyes stared straight in front, feet moved hurriedly, blank faces flowed, arms swung. (*TU*, 54)

The scene, the crowd, is not quite in the mythological Limbo of Eliot's Wasteland flowing over London Bridge. But it nevertheless, and contradictorily, represents both "home" for the narrator and spiritual negativity, an endless Endgame. This is activity without meaning, time passing and accumulating without being redeemed as experience, the march of relentless time. It falls under different guises and we may choose to call it progress, capitalism, modernity, success.

Both figuratively and literally halting this flow are the narrator and, differentiated from him and the crowd, Jackson, lately returned from the East. For Jackson, the real exists elsewhere, more in a story, more in the memory of Karain than in the here and now of modernity as it is embodied in civilized London. Its form is uncannily like a beast.

> It is there; it pants, it runs, it rolls; it is strong and alive; it would smash you if you didn't look out; but I'll be hanged if it is yet as real to me as...as the other thing...say, Karain's story. (55)

Against the grain of the narrator's fully confident assertion that this is "home," and that this home is "the real," the story challenges us to question these normative claims for modernity. Though they cannot share in them, except vicariously in Karain's story, Jackson and Hollis recognize that alternative realities offer fuller experiential possibilities.

On the other hand, the narrator's dismissive final comment – "decidedly he [Jackson] had been too long away from home" (55) – rebounds ironically to highlight his own unacknowledged alienation. From Jackson's perspective, life experience has been more fully accessible in a story he has heard, that is, through art, than in the actualities of gun-running, colonial power and multi-national political intrigue.

IV

Succor for Benjamin, as for James and (if I can put it this way) Jackson, is to be found in a second and secondary order of experience, that of story. In his essay on Leskov, Benjamin says:

> The novel is significant not because it presents someone else's fate to us, perhaps didactically, but because this stranger's fate by virtue of the flame which consumes it yields us the warmth which we never draw from our own fate. What draws the reader to the novel is the hope of warming his shivering life with a death he reads about. (Benjamin, *Illuminations,* 101)

There is a sense in which in both "The Beast in the Jungle" and "Karain" the protagonists are spectators on another's life at

precisely the moment they are imagining they are most powerfully living out their own. For Marcher this is of course the moment
when he encounters at May's grave, in what Benjamin would call
a moment of profane illumination, the man mourning the loss of
his wife. The chance (not willed) encounter with the man, the
look of the man's face, interrupts Marcher's habitual performance of grave visitation which had lapsed into the settled
"sense that he once *had* lived" ("The Beast in the Jungle," 398;
original emphasis).

Experience lost can be recognized, once removed, through the
aesthetics of storytelling: the experience is written on the body of
those pushed to the margins by virtue of their gender or race, in
the unfulfilled potentialities of May, and more optimistically in
the figure of Karain. Karain can reinvest an empty token, the
coin, with belief, which enables him to act – not in the merely
theatrical sense in which he has been described, but in the
existentially authorized sense in which he takes control of his
own history. As Kafka puts it, yes, there is hope, infinite hope
– only not for us.

As I re-read the opening exchanges between May and Marcher
at Weathersend, another song springs to mind. Marcher is
confidently mis-recollecting their first meeting seven years
before. No, not seven, more like ten, corrects May. And not in
Rome but Naples. And not with the Pembles but the Boyers. As
someone else sang: "Ah, Yes! I remember it well!" (Ah! My
Chevalier! as Hopkins once put it.)

In a chivalric age such forgetting produces forgiveness,
forgiveness evokes remembrance, and remembrance forges love.
In a Jamesian, Conradian age of disenchantment, when May
points out that he really didn't remember the least thing about
her, we have Marcher's own acknowledgement that "when all
was made conformable to the truth, there didn't appear much of
anything left" (354).

NOTES

1. References are to Henry James, "The Beast in the Jungle," in *The Complete Tales of Henry James,* ed. Leon Edel (London: Rupert Hart--Davis, 1964), vol. 11.

2. Daphna Erdinast-Vulcan, *Joseph Conrad and the Modern Temper* (Oxford: Clarendon, 1991), 31 ff.

3. Eve Kosofsky Sedgwick, *Epistemology of the Closet* (Berkeley: U. of California P., 1990), Chapter 4.

4. Stanley Cavell, "Postscript (1989): To Whom It May Concern," *Critical Inquiry,* 16 (1990), 248-89.

5. Walter Benjamin's essays, "The Storyteller," "On Some Motifs in Baudelaire" and "The Image of Proust," which provide a good starting--point for his discussions of modes of experience and memory, are available in *Illuminations* (London: Fontana, 1973), to which edition my subsequent references refer.

6. I am indebted here to a discussion of Benjamin and James in an as yet unpublished paper given by Jay Bernstein, at a conference on "Anachronism," University of Exeter, December 1994.

Robert Hampson,
Royal Holloway and Bedford New College, University of London,
London, England

Storytellers and Storytelling in "The Partner," "The Informer," "The Lesson of the Master" and *The Sacred Fount*

This essay examines fictional self-consciousness in certain stories by Conrad and James which feature storytellers or storytelling. Conrad's stories "The Partner" and "The Informer," in their different ways, present a storyteller and engage with storytelling.[1] In "The Partner," as in James's "The Lesson of the Master," a professional storyteller is involved. In "The Informer," as in *The Sacred Fount,* it is the process of storytelling that is the focus. In both cases, as I will show, the titles themselves play a part in the stories' fictional self-consciousness, drawing attention to relations and mediations which ultimately involve the reader as well.

As Cedric Watts has noted, the development of periodicals in the mid-to-late nineteenth century in both Britain and America meant that there was a huge market for shorter narratives.[2] This is the context for the self-conscious engagement with storytellers and storytelling in the shorter fiction of Conrad and James. This essay considers Conrad's exploration of the relation between "raw material" and the genres of magazine fiction in "The Partner," and his exploration of the relations between storyteller and audience in both "The Partner" and "The Informer." James's "The Lesson of the Master" was one of a series of his works that explores the position of the artist, the relationship between life and art, the demands of art and the demands of the market.[3] This essay focuses, in particular, on the relationship between "raw material" and final product as thematized in Conrad's fiction and as exemplified in James's story, exploring the way in which the "germ" (as outlined in the *Notebooks*) is handled in the published story and arguing that, in "The Lesson

123

of the Master," the original idea is not so much demonstrated as objectified and problematized. This reading of the relationship between "raw material" and final product is then further explored through *The Sacred Fount*. In the latter as in "The Informer," the process of storytelling itself becomes the subject, and James presents the process of storytelling self-reflexively with self-conscious reference to his own techniques and aesthetic of narrative elaboration.

I. Partners

"The Partner" (1910) is probably the most neglected of Conrad's stories.[4] However, attention to storytelling as the leading theme of the story (and exploration of the ambiguous reference of the title) reveals a more interesting work than has previously been suspected. The frame-story involves a smoking-room encounter between a stevedore and a magazine-story writer. The stevedore is curious about "the process by which stories – stories for periodicals – were produced" (*WT*, 90). He asks the almost unanswerable question that writers regularly encounter about their fictions, "How do they ever come into your head?," and the writer answers, in his casually superior way, that "one generally got a hint" (90). The writer then instances a story he has been told locally about a wreck, which he says could be "used as a hint for a mainly descriptive bit of a story with some such title as 'In the Channel'" (90). The stevedore then tells him the true story of the wreck, and the tale he tells is very far from being "a descriptive bit of a story." It is a tale of an insurance scam and a murder, and the writer comments at the end that it is "too startling even to think of such things happening in our respectable Channel" (128). Where the magazine-story writer is interested in the comforting and comfortable, the stevedore's story is dark and disturbing. At the same time, the magazine-story writer's casual assumption of superiority over what he sees as "this statuesque ruffian" (91) is similarly set against and subverted by the stevedore's concern for truth, experience and responsibility.[5]

In the end, the stevedore's narrative exploration of "how far people who were out after money would go" (92), includes in its critique the practice of the professional writer. At the center of the stevedore's story is the partnership between two businessmen, George Dunbar and a Dutchman called Cloete, but the story generates a whole chain of partnerships: George Dunbar and his brother Harry; George and Cloete; Cloete and Stafford. In each case, the partnership is unequal – with one of the pair being simultaneously shadier and more knowing than the other – so that there is a moral spectrum running from the honest sea-captain, Harry Dunbar, through this chain of secret sharers, down to the crooked mate, Stafford – and the climax to the story comes from the first fully--represented meeting between the first term in the series, the captain, and the last term, the mate.[6] As the story proceeds, we are also conscious that what we are reading is itself the product of another partnership – between the writer and the stevedore. The stevedore tells his story in a kind of telegraphese: it is merely the raw material for a story. And there is repeated attention to the way in which this raw material could be handled to turn it into a magazine story. For example, when the stevedore observes "You'll mind that this was long before Cloete came into it at all," the writer re-assures him "We generally say: some years passed" (96). Similarly, a moment later, the writer notes:

> I discerned his intention to point out to me...the influence on George Dunbar of long association with Cloete's easy moral standards, unscrupulously persuasive gift of humour (funny fellow), and adventurously reckless disposition. He desired me anxiously to elaborate this view, and I assured him it was quite within my powers. (96-7)

The stevedore's story is presented explicitly as "raw" material for a story, but, of course, there is no elaboration of his material by the writer, no fully realized version. Instead, there is a dual presentation of story and displayed devices, which has obvious ironic and self-subversive possibilities. In particular, the story-teller's assumption of superiority repeatedly exposes him to the stevedore's criticism. For instance, on the topic of invention, the

storyteller observes: "Sometimes it pays to put in a lot out of
one's head, and sometimes it doesn't. I mean the story isn't
worth it" (92). What the storyteller tries to present as an aesthetic
decision, the stevedore immediately sees as economic. Later,
when they return to the same issue, the stevedore warns the
writer again: "Don't you think that there will be any sea-life in
this, because there ain't. If you're going to put in any out of your
own head, now's your chance." This time, he offers a different
challenge to the storyteller: "I suppose you know what ten days
of bad weather in the Channel are like? I don't. Anyway, ten
whole days go by" (109). He casts doubt on the adequacy of the
storyteller's invention, while cheekily responding to the storyteller's earlier advice on the handling of time in narrative ("some
years passed" – 96).

At the end, the writer decides that the "material" he has been
given by the stevedore "was not worth many thanks." He
explains why: "This story to be acceptable should have been
transposed to somewhere in the South Seas. But it would have
been too much trouble to cook it for the consumption of
magazine readers" (128). "The Partner" thus gestures towards
various genres of magazine fiction: the "descriptive" story, the
story of "sea life," the story of the South Seas, but, in doing so, it
also gestures towards another kind of unequal partnership
– between writer and reader, with the writer this time as the
shadier, more knowing partner, cooking his material to make it
"acceptable," palatable, for the magazine reader. The magazine-
-story writer is thus aligned with the boatmen who tell silly yarns
to summer visitors, who "must be told something to pass the
time away" (89); or with the advertizers of patent-medicine, who
"live by [their] wits" (92) and "don't care what they say" (116) to
promote specious products that promise comfort and relief;
perhaps even with Cloete, whose amusing "little tales" (93) seem
part of his *modus operandi* as a "business man." However, one
aspect of Cloete's storytelling more closely resembles the
stevedore's: the stevedore observes that some of Cloete's stories
"must have opened George Dunbar's eyes a bit as to what
business means" (94); the stevedore's own story seems designed

to have a similar effect upon the magazine-story writer, just as Conrad's storytelling in this instance seems designed to open the reader's eyes to various aspects of the "business" of magazine--fiction.[7] It is tempting, therefore, to align the stevedore's storytelling impulse with the most famous expression of Conrad's conception of his "task:" "by the power of the written word to make you hear, to make you feel...before all, to make you *see*" (*NN*, X). The stevedore's concern for "truth" – "Would truth be any good to you?" (*WT*, 91) is the aggressive question he addresses to the "writer of stories" (90) at the outset – goes beyond a demand for factual accuracy to an interrogation of the writer's whole way of seeing. In the same way, Conrad's storytelling in "The Partner" forces the reader to examine the nature of their involvement and investment in the reading of fiction. Elsa Nettels has commented on the difficulty of explaining what Conrad means by "the glimpse of truth" which the writer gives to the reader, even though the reader might have "forgotten to ask" for it (*NN*, X). As she observes, Conrad "makes clear in the preface that the truth to be unveiled is not one of the laws of nature; nor, it seems apparent, is the underlying truth a kind of transcendent reality of which the surface or object is a symbol or an emanation."[8] In "The Partner," the "glimpse of truth" granted to the reader derives from Conrad's engagement with the relation between reality and fiction, given the fictional devices and genres through which reality is mediated, combined with the reader's own truthful and responsible engagement with her own relation with fiction.

II. Wives

With James, I want to begin at the most obvious starting-place, the first of his stories to deal with writers and writing, "The Lesson of the Master" (1888), and I want to focus particularly on how James begins with a certain amount of "raw material," the "germ" of the story, and how he then "cooks" that material for his readers. The "germ" for "The Lesson of the Master" is given in James's *Notebooks* under 5 January 1888:

> Another [idea] came to me last night as I was talking with Theodore
> Child about the effect of marriage on the artist, the man of letters, etc.
> He mentioned the cases he had seen in Paris in which this effect had
> been fatal to the quality of the work, etc. – through overproduction,
> need to meet expenses, make a figure, etc....So it occurred to me that
> a very interesting situation would be that of an elder artist or writer,
> who has been ruined (in his own sight) by his marriage and its forcing
> him to produce promiscuously and cheaply – his position in regard to
> a younger *confrère* whom he sees on the brink of the same disaster and
> whom he endeavours to save, to rescue, by some act of bold
> interference – breaking off the marriage, annihilating the wife, making
> trouble between the parties.[9]

The editors of the *Notebooks,* after outlining the plot of "The
Lesson of the Master," comment that St George's marriage at
the end to Marian Fancourt "adds an ironic twist to the story"
but "possibly blurs the main point by raising an ambiguity"
(*Notebooks,* 87). What their conception of "the main point"
might be is made clear in a paraphrase of the master's lesson
offered by Wagenknecht:

> The artist's only concern is with the absolute; the relative does not
> matter; and since the passion that possesses him is enough to subsume
> all others, he has no right to be deflected by other interests. Wives are
> even more dangerous when they think they sympathise and under-
> stand then when they do not. A writer who means to do something has
> no right to have a family.[10]

However, as Wagenknecht suggests, James does not just "blur
the main point" by giving an "ironic twist" to the story, he
produces "a masterpiece of irony and ambiguity" (Wagenknecht, 50-1).

The story very quickly sets us up with Paul Overt, the literary
aspirant, "a student of fine prose...with the artist's general
disposition to vibrate;" the master, Henry St George, "a high
literary figure;" although his later production has not main-
tained the quality of "his first three great successes" ("The
Lesson of the Master," 5); and the master's wife, who makes her
first appearance as "the important little woman in the aggres-
sively Parisian dress" (9). As this description suggests, Overt is

inclined to see, in the master's wife, the explanation for the master's decline. Thus, when she mentions how she once made the master "burn up a bad book," Overt is immediately convinced that "the burnt book...would have been one of her husband's finest things" (11).

The story then presents, through the figure of St George, a series of lessons. The first is in line with Overt's reading of the master's wife and corresponds to the "germ" with which James started. In the smoking room at Summersoft, St George presents himself explicitly as a lesson to the younger man: "take my lesson to heart...the deplorable illustration of the worship of false gods....The idols of the market; money and luxury and 'the world;' placing one's children and dressing one's wife; everything that drives one to the short and easy way" (36). The second lesson is more ambiguous. This is the image of St George in his study "a room without windows," standing at his desk "in the erect posture of a clerk in a counting-house" (62). St George presents the room as teaching "a fine lesson in concentration" (63), and Overt himself responds professionally to the room as the ideal place in which to write: "Lord, what good things I should do if I had such a charming place as this to do them in!" (64).[11] Overt, significantly, is appreciative of the windowless room, precisely because "The outer world, the world of accident and ugliness, was so successfully excluded" (64). However, the image of the "clerk in a counting-house" and St George's description of himself as "walled in" to his "trade" (63) present a counter-evaluation in support of the first lesson: the artist who has whored after false gods, "the idols of the market," and whose literary production has been damaged as a result. In this reading, the fact that the room was invented by the master's wife and that she locks him up there every morning only offers further confirmation of her role in his decline. Indeed, St George goes on to present himself again as a lesson in precisely these terms: he has led "the mercenary muse" to "the altar of literature" (67), and he has led "the life of the world...the clumsy conventional expensive materialised vulgarised brutalised life of London" (72). He has, as he puts it, "got everything in fact but the great thing" (69): "The sense of having done the best – the sense which is the real life of the artist...of having drawn from his intellectual instrument the finest music that nature had hidden in it" (79).

So far, then, we have St George, who presents himself as a terrible warning to the younger writer, as in James's first conception of the story, and we have, in Paul Overt, an aspirant writer, who believes that the master's work has declined and is predisposed to see in the master's marriage the reason for that decline. James's particular technical addition is the focalizing of the story largely through Overt. An important aspect of James's handling of this focalization is the way in which Overt's perceptions and interpretations are, at various points, subtly questioned. Thus, for example, Overt's first impression of St George is at odds with his expectations: St George is described as "beautifully correct in his tall black hat and his superior frock coat" (14), and Overt finds this dress "disconcerting," implying that St George is wearing the conventional uniform of worldly success rather than something more artistic – perhaps the velvet jacket and loose shirt-collar of "the author of 'Beltraffio'." However, Overt's response is undermined by the narratorial comment that he "forgot for the moment that the head of the profession was not a bit better dressed than himself" (14). Similarly, Overt's first impression of Mrs St George ("he himself would never have imagined [her]...the partner for life, the *alter ego,* of a man of letters" – 9) has to be set against his later surprise, when he finds that he "got on" with her "better than he expected" (29), and against St George's comments, after her death, that "She took everything off my hands – off my mind. She carried on our life with the greatest art, the rarest devotion, and I was free, as few men can have been, to drive my pen, to shut myself up with my trade. This was a rare service – the highest she could have rendered me" (82). Obviously, St George's comments are also open to question: his view of his wife could well be conditioned by his emotional and psychological responses to her death. Nevertheless, the narrative repeatedly and explicitly questions the degree and nature of Overt's perceptiveness. For example, when Mrs St George announces herself "faint with fatigue," the narrator observes: "She professed that she hadn't the strength of a kitten...a character he had been too preoccupied to discern in her while he wondered in what sense she could be held to have been the making of her husband" (29). Here the particular problem with which the central character is engaged seems to have blinded him to other issues and questions. This is an issue which is, of course, central to *The Sacred Fount*.

James's major elaboration of the "germ" relates to the figure of Marian Fancourt. Overt's first impression is of a "conventionally unconventional" young woman in "aesthetic toggery" (20). Her grey eyes, "magnificent red hair," and "dress of a pretty grey-green tint and of a limp silken texture" (12) certainly suggest a familiar type of Pre-Raphaelite beauty. With her interest in – and apparent responsiveness to – "art and music and literature" (8), she also seems to stand in contrast to the more worldly figure of Mrs St George.[12] However, the lesson she embodies for Overt actually places her in opposition to "art and music and literature:"

> The feeling she appealed to, or at any rate, the feeling she excited...was responsive admiration of the life she embodied, the young purity and richness of which appeared to imply that real success was to resemble *that*, to live, to bloom, to present the perfection of a fine type, not to have hammered out headachy fancies with a bent back at an ink-stained table. (19)

For Overt, she embodies a temptation towards life, which is at odds with what he conceives of as the role of the artist. This opposition surfaces again in Overt's discussion with St George in his study, when "the full rich masculine human general life, with all the responsibilities and duties and burdens and sorrows and joys – all the domestic and social initiations and complications" (72), which St George has experienced, are set against the artistic success, which he claims to have missed.

The master thus gives – and Overt receives and accepts – the lesson about "the effect of marriage on the artist" which was James's original idea for the story. However, when the master praises his wife, after her death, for arranging their life so that he was free to write, Overt is bewildered by the sense of contradiction. And, when the master subsequently marries Marian Fancourt, Overt can't help feeling that he has been "duped, sold, swindled" (88). The figure that the master presents, seems to Overt his final lesson and is not so much disturbingly ambiguous as diabolically mocking:

> Somehow, standing there in the ripeness of his successful manhood, he didn't suggest that any of his veins were exhausted. "Don't you remember the moral I offered myself to you that night as pointing?" St George continued. "Consider at any rate the warning I am at present." (95)

However, Overt's attempt to blame St George is not supported by the text. In his first encounter with Marian Fancourt, there is a deficiency in his response which the narrator points up: "Paul Overt met her eyes, which had a cool morning light that would have half-broken his heart if he hadn't been so young" (21). A different kind of deficiency is suggested by the very different responses of Overt and St George to their contemplation of her "form:" "One would like to represent such a girl as that" (41) is Paul's response. By contrast, St George affirms "there's nothing like life!," and then continues, with equal ambiguity but with a series of striking metaphors that surely tease Overt with their entwining of writerly and sexual impotence: "When you're finished, squeezed dry and used up and you think the sack's empty, you're still appealed to, you still get touches and thrills, the idea springs up – out of the lap of the actual" (41). Overt sees her as "a fine subject," "part of the glory of a novel" (42); St George, by contrast, sees that she would "make a splendid wife" (77). It is also true that Overt could have returned two years earlier to Marian Fancourt, but he was restrained from "rushing back to London" (83) by his sense of the "promise" glimpsed in certain pages of his manuscript. In other words, he chooses to give priority to the novel, and, as Barry has noted, this choice is made when the "prohibition against marriage" would seem to have been withdrawn by the master's praise of his dead wife and the arrangements she made for him (Barry, 389). The effect of this, as Barry suggests, is that "the life and art debate is left entirely open: we are given no guarantees that the married and vigorous St George will not produce good work, or that the celibate Overt will" (389).

One reading strategy often adopted in relation to this story, perhaps prompted by the editorial gloss in the *Notebooks*, is to recuperate its contradictions by reference to the sincerity or insincerity of the master; the approach undertaken here, so far, has been to recuperate the contradictions in the story by reference to the character of Paul Overt; a third approach would subsume these first two in a sense of the staging of the original idea. In other words, by the end of the story, the idea that was the "germ" has not so much been demonstrated and asserted as objectified and problematized. The idea of the damaging effect of marriage on the artist is asserted by the master and accepted by the aspirant, but questioned by the story itself. I want to consider briefly how something similar happens in *The Sacred Fount*.

III. Detectives

On 17 February 1894, James wrote the "germ" of that novel in his *Notebooks*:

> The notion of the young man who marries an older woman and who has the effect on her of making her younger and still younger, while he himself becomes her age....Mightn't this be altered (perhaps) to the idea of cleverness and stupidity? A clever woman marries a deadly dull man, and loses and loses her wit as he shows more and more. Or the idea of a *liaison*, suspected, but of which there is no proof but this transfusion of some idiosyncrasy of one party to the being of the other – this exchange or conversion? The fact, the secret, of the *liaison* might be revealed in that way. The two things – the two elements – beauty and 'mind,' might be correspondingly, concomitantly exhibited as in the history of two related couples – with the opposition, in each case, that would help the thing to be dramatic. (*Notebooks*, 150-1)

The Sacred Fount (1901) plays with both of these ideas: the young man married to the older woman and the suspicion of a *liaison* between a clever woman and a dull man, unequal partnerships marked by the unidirectional flow of youth or cleverness from one partner to the other.[13] These form the crossed narrative threads, while the curiously vampiric idea of closed systems of exchange between couples undergoes various discussions and thematic variations.[14] *The Sacred Fount* is a novel of gossip – it takes place among the Edwardian leisure-class during a country-house weekend. It is also a kind of detective novel. Unusually for James, it is a first-person narrative; and the unnamed narrator, having seen the remarkable change for the better in Gilbert Long (he is no longer merely "a fine piece of human furniture" used to make "a small party seem more numerous" – *The Sacred Fount,* 2), sets out to discover, in line with his theory of "the sacred fount," who the clever woman is with whom Gilbert Long must be having a *liaison.* The novel consists of various encounters and a series of interrogations, but above all it consists of the narrator's steadily developed narrative explanation of his weekend companions.[15] It is a directed interpretation of varied impressions in line with a particular theory. The narrator's investigation into Long's putative affair, however, is hampered by the problem identified by Mrs Brissenden at the outset: "such people...cultivate, to cover their game, the appearance of other little friendships. It puts outsiders off the scent" (10). The narrator's interpretations are, accordingly, obliged to negotiate the simultaneous need to distinguish and the impossibility of distinguishing between deliberate performance and accidental self-betrayal, between what is put up as a screen and what is "real." Thus, for example, he notices "at luncheon:"

> Gilbert Long, watching the chance given him by the loose order in which we moved to it, slipped, to the visible defeat of somebody else, into the chair of conspicuity beside clever Lady John....Mrs Server then occupied a place as remote as possible from this couple, but not from Guy Brissenden, who had found means to seat himself next her while my notice was engaged by the others. (91)

The difficulty, here, is that two opposed principles of interpretation are in operation simultaneously: spatial contiguity or spatial remoteness can both be read as signs of emotional closeness, depending on whether the couple is assumed to be concealing or betraying their relationship. The difficulty of interpretation and the ambiguity of signs is emblematized by the painting of "the Man with the Mask:"

> The figure represented is a young man in black – a quaint, tight black dress, fashioned in years long past; with a pale, lean, livid face and a stare, from eyes without eyebrows, like that of some whitened old-world clown. In his hand he holds an object that strikes the spectator at first simply as some obscure, some ambiguous work of art, but that on a second view becomes a representation of a human face, modelled and coloured, in wax, in enamelled metal, in some substance not human. The object thus appears a complete mask, such as might have been fantastically fitted and worn. (55)

The picture demands to be construed: the narrator describes it as "the picture, of all pictures, that most needs an interpreter" (55). At the same time, its ambiguities prevent any confident attribution of meaning. In the discussion that follows between Mrs Server, Overt and the narrator, it is suggested that the mask represents Death – or perhaps Life; that the young man is about to put it on, "unless indeed he has just taken it off;" that the mask is "charmingly pretty" and resembles "a lovely lady" (56) – or "bad" (57) and resembles one of the men of the party. For the reader seeking, like the narrator, for clues, this enigmatic mask is explicitly identified with Mrs Server, the "lovely lady," and with Brissenden. A further frustration, for both narrator and reader, is lack of access to what seems to have been an earlier discussion of the painting: "The distinguished painter listened while – to all appearance – Gilbert Long did, in the presence of the picture, the explaining" (52). The implication here is that Long is presenting an extensive and impressive reading of the picture and, further, that this is additional evidence of the great change that has taken place in him. Overt's assertion that Long is "perfectly amazing" (54) is apparently confirmation of both these readings; however, Overt's words are susceptible of other interpretations. Finally, we might notice that the painting of "the Man with the Mask" (59) is an enigmatic art-work which represents within it a second enigmatic, "ambiguous work of art" that, "on second view," becomes "a representation of a human face" modelled "in some substance not human" (55).

In the final chapters, the jigsaw that the narrator has carefully put together, the "crystal palace" (205) of narrative he has monomaniacally erected, is destroyed by Mrs Brissenden. Not only does she sketch out an opposed narrative to explain the series of relations, but she also repeatedly casts doubt on the narrator's sanity. In "The Lesson of the Master," as I suggested, one method by which the contradictions of the story could be recuperated is through the character of the central consciousness. In *The Sacred Fount,* there are various places in the narrative at which the narrator's interpretation reflects back upon his character, and threatens to undermine itself by doing so. As Sara Chapman says, "because there are no perceptions except the narrator's, there are no referents against which any of the novel's observations may be checked;" and, as a result, "since all of the perceptions in the novel belong to this comically monomaniacal character, all are functions of our assessment of his reliability."[16] Mrs Brissenden's characterization of the narrator as "crazy" (278), however, while it momentarily has the effect of reinforcing the reader's doubts about him, almost immediately, by being explicit, merely sets itself up as a competing narrative. Furthermore, once we begin to think of Mrs Brissenden's narrative, the same questions about the character and motives of the narrator apply to her also. It is one of the curious features of the narrator's story that he accepts from the outset as a given the love between Mr and Mrs Brissenden; he never allows himself to consider that Mrs Brissenden might be involved with Gilbert Long; or that, when they joined him in his carriage at Paddington, he was being used as a "screen" (36). Mrs Brissenden's observation that "such people" (10) cover their game could be seen as just one of the many masks and screens in the story. If Mrs Brissenden is involved with Gilbert Long, then this solution to the mystery he sets out to solve is like the "purloined letter" in Poe's tale, which remains hidden by being displayed. Equally, although he registers her evasiveness under his remorseless interrogation in the final chapters, the narrator never stops to ask what exactly she might have to hide. Nor does he seem to register that, if there has been an affair between Briss and Mrs Server, as Mrs Brissenden claims, then he needs to look elsewhere than Briss (according to his theory) for the source of Mrs Brissenden's youthfulness.

In his essay, "The Typology of Detective Fiction," Todorov describes how the detective story consists of two stories, "the story of the crime and the story of the investigation:"

> The first, that of the crime, is in fact the story of an absence: its most accurate characteristic is that it cannot be immediately present in the book....The status of the second story is, as we have seen, just as excessive; it is a story which has no importance in itself, which serves only as a mediator between the reader and the story of the crime.[17]

In *The Sacred Fount,* we have a story of investigation that fails to produce the story of the crime. The story of the investigation is even more *"excessive"* than in the detective novel, since *The Sacred Fount* offers, to use the comparison that Todorov makes, a *subject* (plot) without a determinate *fable* (story).[18] As R. P. Blackmur put it long ago:

> What is prodigious about *The Sacred Fount* is in the mystery that the book encompasses and acknowledges, lucidly and luminously, but which it never reveals, as novels are expected to reveal mysteries, in terms of a plot or a series of actions.[19]

IV. Informers

Conrad's story, "The Informer," provides a useful comparison. Conrad's narrator is a collector of "Chinese bronzes and porcelain." His friend, "a collector of curiosities," who, like James in his *Notebooks,* collects "rare and interesting" acquaintances ("The Informer," 73), sends to him "Mr X."[20] Mr X is a notorious revolutionary writer and conspirator, who is also a connoisseur of "bronzes and china" (74). The narrator initially defends himself from Mr X by creating a set of oppositions between the two of them:

> I don't understand anarchists. Does a man of that – of that
> – persuasion still remain an anarchist when alone, quite alone and
> going to bed, for instance?...I am sure that if such a faith (or such
> a fanaticism) once mastered my thoughts I would never be able to
> compose myself sufficiently to sleep or eat or perform any of the
> routine acts of daily life. I would want no wife, no children;...and as to
> collecting bronzes or china, that, I should say,would be quite out of
> the question. (75)

However, the apparent contradiction between being a revolutionary and being a connoisseur provides the basis for a challenge
to these oppositions. Accordingly, the narrator's contemplation
of Mr X leads him to a merging of categories, as he associates
him with the exquisitely monstrous quality of certain Chinese
bronzes. He then exposes the strategy of "othering" involved in
this comparison to Chinese bronzes: "But then he was not of
bronze. He was not even Chinese, which would have enabled one
to contemplate him calmly across the gulf of racial difference"
(76).[21] Instead, he finds himself confronted with an "other,"
who is disturbingly the same: "He was alive and European; he
had the manner of good society, wore a coat and hat like mine,
and had pretty near the same taste in cooking. It was too
frightful to think of."[22] The question of taste, in relation to both
food and connoisseurship, is crucial: the narrator is particularly
shocked that a mouth which shares his taste in cooking also
emits revolutionary utterances. Significantly, he describes what
he sees as Mr X's "cynicism" as "distasteful" (78-9).

Nevertheless, the narrator does want to meet and hear from
Mr X. He notes, for example, how "there was some excitement in
talking quietly across the dinner-table with a man whose
venomous pen-stabs had sapped the vitality of at least one
monarchy," and he has a particular "curiosity" regarding Mr
X's "underground life" (76). Mr X observes that his writings
were, at one time, "the fashion – the thing to read with wonder
and horror" among "the well-fed bourgeois" and criticizes this
"idle and selfish class" that "loves to see mischief being made,
even if it is made at its own expense" (78). This attack on
"amateurs of emotion" (78) is the prelude to the story he tells of

Sevrin, the Lady Amateur and the Hermione Street anarchists. The story responds to the narrator's particular curiosity ("I became all expectation" – 79), but the narrator doesn't recognize the extent to which he is implicated by this very curiosity in the category "amateurs of emotion." The reader, of course, is also implicated through sharing the narrator's curiosity and expectation.

Mr X's story is a story of plot and counter-plot, and it is, also, a story of performers: the Lady Amateur with her "gestures" (81) and "consummate art" (85); the Variety Agency, which provides a cover for the coming and going of anarchists; the police-spy, Sevrin, who has "the air of a taciturn actor" (85); and the dénouement involving the "theatrical expedient" (86) of a fake raid by sham police. The narrator's responses indicate an appalled fascination, but the description of his responses also sets him up as an object for our criticism. For example, when he is told that the Lady Amateur's "usual task" (89) was to correct the proofs of the *Alarm Bell* and the *Firebrand,* he observes: "To think of a young girl calmly tracking printers' errors along the sort of abominable sentences I remembered was intolerable to my sentiment of womanhood" (89-90). Near the end of the story, he again tries to distance himself from the story by asserting "that anarchists in general were simply inconceivable to me mentally, morally, logically, sentimentally, and even physically" (97). However, it is too late, and the story leaves its mark on him: he gives up dining in the "very good restaurant" (75) and takes to "dining in [his] club" (101). This retreat, after hearing Mr X's story, echoes the withdrawal made by the Lady Amateur after receiving Sevrin's diary from Mr X: "She went into retirement; then she went to Florence; then she went into retreat in a convent" (101). She has been "exposed to such a terrible experience" (99); arguably, the narrator feels the same.

However, there is a final twist to the story. In the brief coda, the narrator describes meeting his friend in Paris. His friend is "all impatience to hear of the effect produced" on the narrator by Mr X. When the narrator comments on the "abominable" (101) cynicism of Mr X, the friend confides "he likes to have his

little joke sometimes" (102). Conrad's story ends with the
bewilderment of the narrator: "I have been utterly unable to
discover where in all this the joke comes in" (102). One
possibility is that the entire story of Sevrin and the Lady
Amateur has been invented by Mr X as an attack on the
narrator. Conrad has carefully set the narrator's concern with
safety against his imaginative indulgence in "a disturbing vision
of darkness" (77): he keeps his "treasures" in "three large rooms
without carpets and curtains," where no fires are lit "for fear of
accidents" and "a fire-proof door separates them from the rest of
the house" (74); but, despite his protestation, in dining with Mr
X he does "play with fire." Mr X, for his part, has admitted to
"malice" (101) in sending the Lady Amateur Sevrin's diary; and
giving the manager of the Variety Artists' Agency the name
'Bomm,' while eating a *bombe glacé*" (82), is perhaps over-
-playing his hand against the narrator.[23] However, if the entire
story has not been a malicious invention of Mr X's, then it is
impossible to determine what might be true and what might be
false. This clearly constitutes an attack on the reader as well. The
reader has shared the narrator's curiosity and the narrator's
trust in the storyteller; in the end, reader and narrator face the
possibility that they might have been the victim of the story.

   "The Partner," as a title, referred to a chain of partnerships:
"The Informer" similarly has more than one referent. Mr X's
story is about the unmasking of Sevrin, the police spy, as the
informer within the group of anarchists; but, in telling his story
to the narrator, Mr X is himself acting as an informer about the
"underground life" (76) of subversion and surveillance; and, in
re-telling the story, the narrator is, in turn, an informer not only
about this "underground life" but also about bourgeois "amateurs of emotion" (78), a group which includes both himself and
the reader. As in "The Partner," the title is part of the literary
self-consciousness of the story. As in *The Sacred Fount,* the
narrative ends with the assertion of a "joke," that is difficult to
comprehend but, nevertheless, has the effect of subverting the
entire narration. Mrs Briss's tactical move of asserting the
narrator's madness in Chapter 13 is the prelude to the "joke"

(*The Sacred Fount,* 317) in Chapter 14 with which their dialogue concludes. Having asserted a relationship between Long and Lady John (using her husband as her authority), she then produces a second "revelation" on the same authority: her husband's relationship with Mrs Server. She speaks of this "as a broad joke" (317), but how this confession could be a joke is not clear, unless it is her joke at the narrator's expense. Certainly, he is the joke's immediate victim: "everything, within a minute, had somehow so given way under the touch of her supreme assurance, the presentation of her own now finished system" (318). Like *The Sacred Fount,* "The Informer" entertains or engages its reader with a narrative that cancels itself at the end. In both cases, the process of storytelling replaces the product of "a story told:" James's narrator constructs an elaborate fiction which finally collapses; Conrad's narrator is revealed to have been the victim of a "joke."[24]

V. Conclusion

In conclusion, I want to connect this, briefly, with another feature of *The Sacred Fount.* I have already suggested that, in both "The Lesson of the Master" and *The Sacred Fount,* James objectifies the original idea for the story. In *The Sacred Fount,* he also objectifies his own ways of fabulation, of narrative elaboration of the "germ," and his own conception of the novel as a form. As Joseph Wiesenfarth observes, *The Sacred Fount* is "basically, a novel which represents the process of imaginative fabrication of a 'structure' from a 'germ' that has been conceived as a 'subject'."[25] Or, as Jean Frantz Blackall puts it, "the development of the *donnée,*" which usually occurred in James's *Notebooks,* has in this instance occurred to an uncommon degree during the composition of the book."[26] Moreover, the development of the *donnée* has itself become the novel's subject.

There was a hint of such self-consciousness in "The Lesson of the Master," when Overt reflected on St George's face "not having told its whole story in the first three minutes:"

> That story came out as one read, in short instalments – it was
> excusable that one's analogies should be somewhat professional – and
> the text was a style considerably involved, a language not easy to
> translate at sight. ("The Lesson of the Master," 18)

Given that "The Lesson of the Master" itself came out in two
installments in the *Universal Review* in July and August 1888,
there is a distinct sense of *mise en abîme* at this moment.
Similarly, in "The Informer," Mr X describes how Stone's Dried
Soup was "put up in large square tins, of which six went to
a case" (*SS*, 82). Since "The Informer" was itself collected in
A Set of Six, it is tempting to ask whether this volume is the
container for "unappetizing" powder or "a special case" of
something more explosive "exported abroad under the very nose
of the policeman on duty at the corner" (82). In *The Sacred
Fount,* literary self-consciousness is both undeniable and much
more thorough-going. Though the narrator is not described as
a writer, he nevertheless uses the language of James's Prefaces
and goes through processes now familiar from James's *Notebooks.* Like James, he has his "germ," and he constructs his
narrative with an eye for the kind of "ideal symmetry" that was
part of James's earliest thoughts about the novel.[27] The
"Preface" to *What Maisie Knew* begins by describing the "small
germ" from which the novel developed, and James then recalls
"promptly thinking that for a proper symmetry the second
parent should marry too – which in the case named to me indeed
would probably soon occur, and was in any case what the ideal
of the situation required."[28] In *The Sacred Fount,* the narrator
also makes fun of this tendency to construct his narrative in
terms of an "ideal symmetry" (*The Sacred Fount,* 169): he
produces the self-critical comic image of "opposed couples
balanced like bronze groups at the two ends of a chimney-piece,"
and notes that "Things in the real had a way of not balancing"
(182). Generally, however, his thoughts about the process of
constructing his narrative interpretation resemble Conrad's own
accounts of "the process by which stories...were produced"
(*WT,* 90). At one point, for example, he conceives that "there
was something quite other I possibly might do with Mrs Server"

(*The Sacred Fount,* 93); later, he feels pleasure because he had "got [his] point of view" (144); and then, later still he describes Mrs Server as "the real principle of composition" (167).[29] At the end, his pride in his theory produces a version of Jamesian organic form as he celebrates "that special beauty in my scheme through which the whole depended so on each part and each part so guaranteed the whole" (223). *The Sacred Fount,* then, not only lays out for inspection the narrator's working out of theories about "the sacred fount" (which involves the "mystery of mysteries," "the way other people could feel about each other" – 17), but also objectifies and explores James's ideas about curiosity, imagination, and narrative – foregrounding, in particular, the morality of curiosity, the exploitation involved in imagining and the coercion of narrative.

NOTES

1. "The Partner" was published in *Harper's Magazine* (November 1911) and collected in *Within the Tides* (1915). "The Informer" was published in *Harper's Magazine* in December 1906 and collected in *A Set of Six* (1908).
2. Cedric Watts, *Conrad's "Heart of Darkness:" A Critical and Contextual Discussion* (Milan: Mursia International, 1977), 22.
3. For example, "The Author of Beltraffio" (1884), "The Private Life" (1892), "The Middle Years" (1893), "The Death of the Lion" (1894), "The Next Time" (1895), "John Delavoy" (1898), "The Birthplace" (1903), "The Velvet Glove" (1909). *The Tragic Muse,* which was contemporary with "The Lesson of the Master" (James started it in 1887, and it was serialized from January 1889 to May 1890) also explores "the artist-life" and "the conflict between art and 'the world'" through the choice of life made by its central characters. See James's "Preface" to *The Tragic Muse* and Philip Horne, "Introduction" to *The Tragic Muse* (Harmondsworth: Penguin Books, 1995), VII, X.
4. The only references I have come across are both dismissive. Frederick Karl in *A Reader's Guide to Joseph Conrad* (London: Thames and Hudson, 1960) asserts that "The stories comprising this volume are among Conrad's weakest" (270). Lawrence Graver, in *Conrad's Short Fiction* (Berkeley: U. of California P., 1969) dismisses "The Partner" as adding "nothing new to our knowledge of Conrad's achievement as a short story writer" (158-9).
5. The writer's assumption of superiority is, of course, based on class, but his aesthetic response to the stevedore is also significant. Here, as elsewhere,

a consciously aesthetic response is used to suggest a disengagement from reality. Consider the writer's view of the rocks ("It was a delicate and wonderful picture, something expressive, suggestive, and desolate, a symphony in grey and black – a Whistler" – 91-2) and how it is challenged by the stevedore's.

6. "The Secret Sharer" had appeared in *Harper's Magazine* (August--September 1910).

7. The stevedore's concern for "hard truth" (94) contrasts with the storytelling of "patent-medicine chaps" who "think the world's bound to swallow any story they like to tell" (116). For an exploration of Conrad's interest in "the various inter-permeating aspects of the oral functions," see Tony Tanner, "'Gnawed Bones' and 'Artless Tales' – Eating and Narrative in Conrad," in *Joseph Conrad: A Commemoration,* ed. Norman Sherry (London: Macmillan, 1976), 17-36, 24.

8. Elsa Nettels, *James and Conrad* (Athens, GA: U. of Georgia P., 1977), 33.

9. *The Notebooks of Henry James,* eds. F. O. Mathiessen and Kenneth B. Murdock (New York: Galaxy Books, 1961), 87.

10. Edward Wagenknecht, *The Tales of Henry James* (New York: Frederick Ungar, 1984), 51. All references to "The Lesson of the Master" are to the New York Edition, *The Lesson of the Master* (New York: Charles Scribner's Sons, 1909).

11. Peter Barry draws attention to Overt's "professional opinion" of the study in "In Fairness to The Master's Wife: A Re-Interpretation of 'The Lesson of the Master'," *Studies in Short Fiction,* 15: 4 (Fall 1978), 385-9.

12. In *Searching for the Figure in the Carpet in the Tales of Henry James* (New York: Peter Lang, 1987), Benjamin Newman argues that Overt's positive view of Marian Fancourt is merely "the self-deception of romantic illusion" (42); that Overt fails to recognize her "indifference, shallowness, and insincerities" (42); and that she, far from contrasting with Mrs St George, actually mirrors her in being "quite indifferent to the ordeals of artistic creation" (44).

13. Henry James, *The Sacred Fount* (New York: Charles Scribner's Sons, 1901).

14. As Sara Chapman points out, "Paul's fear that St George will regain both youth and creativity as a result of his regained sexual power prefigures the narrator's theory in *The Sacred Fount*" (*Henry James's Portrait of the Writer as Hero* [Basingstoke: Macmillan, 1990], 42). For the vampiric theme, see Norma Phillips, "*The Sacred Fount*: The Narrator and the Vampires," *PMLA,* 76 (1961), 407-12.

15. John Berridge, the novelist-narrator of "The Velvet Glove," displays a similar tendency: "his inveterate habit of abysmal imputation, the snatching of the ell wherever the inch peeped out" (*The Finer Grain* [London: Methuen, 1910], 11-12). The attractive young couple with whom

he shares a train-compartment between Cremona and Mantua prompt a whole series of questions "all so inevitable and so impertinent:" "Who had they been, and what? Whence had they come, whither were they bound, what tie united them, what adventure engaged, what felicity, tempered by what peril, magnificently, dramatically attended?" (*The Finer Grain,* 12). Significantly, Berridge's habit of imputation does not save him from misinterpreting the situation, when he meets the young couple again later: he becomes, in effect, the victim of the story's joke.

16. Sara S. Chapman, *Henry James's Portrait of the Writer as Hero* (Basingstoke: Macmillan, 1990), 119.

17. Tzvetan Todorov, *The Poetics of Prose* (Oxford: Blackwell, 1977), 44, 46.

18. "The Partner," by comparison, seems to offer a *fable* without a *subject.*

19. R. P. Blackmur, *"The Sacred Fount," Kenyon Review,* 4 (Autumn 1942), 330-1.

20. We are told of his interest in new acquaintances: "He observes them, listens to them, penetrates them, measures them, and puts the memory away in the gallery of his mind" (*SS,* 73). The language is reminiscent of James's *Notebooks* and Prefaces.

21. Compare the dynamic of "Karain: A Memory:" while Karain is distanced from them as "other," the white men are able to contemplate with equanimity, the prospect "that some day he will run amuck amongst his faithful subjects and send *ad patres* ever so many of them;" subsequently, they form a bond with Karain by producing "woman" as other to both white men and Malay men; finally, once the strategy of "othering" Karain has been dropped, one of the Europeans, Jackson, is possessed by the sense that "Karain's story" has a greater reality than the urban life of London (*TU,* 45, 47, 55). For a more detailed account, see Robert Hampson, "Encountering the Other: Race, Gender and Sexuality in Conrad's Early Malay Fiction," *Tenggara: Journal of Southeast Asian Literature,* 32 (Kuala Lumpur, 1993), 108-18.

22. Carol Vanderveer Hamilton has commented on this strategy of "othering:" "A 'gulf of racial difference' would serve to naturalise their different attitudes towards politics and society; its absence makes the similarity in their cultural practices 'frightful'." See "Revolution from Within: Conrad's Natural Anarchists," *The Conradian,* 18: 2 (Autumn 1994), 31-48, 37.

23. The name "Sevrin" is perhaps chosen to point to Sacher-Masoch's Severin in *Venus in Furs.* Sevrin's apparent "stooping low as if to touch the hem" (97-8) of the Lady Amateur's garment would not be out of place in Severin's subservience to Wanda von Dunajew (which, indeed, includes kissing the hem of her robe). Bernard C. Meyer, in *Joseph Conrad: A Psychoanalytic Biography* (Princeton: Princeton U. P., 1967), suggested

that Conrad was familiar with Masoch's work, and that he drew on it for "The Planter of Malata" and *The Arrow of Gold* (308-16). Mr X might have chosen the name to suggest the masochism of "the well-fed bourgeois" (*SS,* 78) in general and of his auditor in particular.

24. For a detailed examination of the "joke" as part of Conradian narration, see Earl G. Ingersoll, "Tragic Jokes: Narration in *The Secret Agent*," *The Conradian*, 16: 1 (September 1991), 31-47. Ingersoll's approach to the "joke" has been very influential on the present essay.

25. Joseph Wiesenfarth, *Henry James and the Dramatic Analogy* (New York: Fordham U. P., 1963), 102.

26. Jean Frantz Blackall, *Jamesian Ambiguity in "The Sacred Fount"* (Ithaca, NY: Cornell U. P., 1965), 14.

27. The entry for 17 February 1894 concluded: "The two things – the two elements – beauty and 'mind,' might be correspondingly, concomitantly exhibited as in the history of two related couples – with the opposition, in each case, that would help the thing to be dramatic" – *Notebooks*, 151.

28. Henry James, *The Art of the Novel* (New York: Charles Scribner's Sons, 1934), 140-1.

29. Compare, for point of view, "Preface" to *The Princess Casamassima*: "my sense, sharp from far back, that clearness and concreteness constantly depend, for any pictorial whole, on some *concentrated* individual notation of them" (James, *The Art of the Novel*, 69); and "that provision for interest which consists in placing advantageously, placing right in the middle of the light, the most polished of possible mirrors of the subject" (70). Compare for "principle of composition" "Preface" to *The Spoils of Poynton*: "Fortunately in this case the principle of composition adopted is loyally observed" (139).

Josiane Paccaud-Huguet,
University Lumière-Lyon II,
Lyons, France

"Another Turn of the Racking Screw:"
The Poetics of Disavowal in The *Shadow-Line*

For the dead can live only with the exact intensity and quality of the
life imparted to them by the living. (*UWE*, 304)

Conrad's two "calm-pieces," "The Secret Sharer" (1910) and *The
Shadow-Line* (1916), share many secret bonds in structure and
theme. Quite strikingly, the concluding lines of the earlier tale
seem to contain the seeds of the later one: "Nothing! no one in the
world should stand now between us, throwing a *shadow* on the
way of silent knowledge and mute affection, the perfect communion of a seaman with his *first command*" ("The Secret
Sharer," *TLS*, 143).[1] The emphatic disavowals ("nothing," "no
one") actually fore shadow the obstacles lying between the
autodiegetic narrator of *The Shadow-Line* and his first command
– both as ship and speech-act, and ultimately in terms of the act of
writing itself. Conrad's novella was to be entitled "First Command" and became *The Shadow-Line* for reasons which he
explicitly related to the effect of the war.[2] Its discourse is
shadowed by a force of negativity which, I will argue here, is the
textual symptom of a struggle with the unspeakable horror. The
grapple with "that Thing" (115) – a fictional image of Lacan's
"*jouissance de la Chose*"[3] – makes of the captain-narrator and his
ship emblems of the tragic fate of mankind teetering over the edge
of the abyss whose most fitting metaphor is the *Gulf* of Siam.

Intertextual shadows

"A fairly complex piece of work" such are the words used by
Conrad to introduce his tale in "Author's Note" (*SL*, IX): this

complexity is reflected in the critics' bafflement about the significance of the tale,[4] even though the "technical problems of
narrative are much less conspicuous here than in *The Nigger of the
"Narcissus"* (Lothe, 132).[5] Daphna Erdinast-Vulcan speaks of "a
strong and inexplicable demonic element" (4) in this "puzzle-
-ridden novella" (36) while Jacques Berthoud wonders "what kind
of fact" Conrad sought to render. I would suggest that the
beginnings of an answer can be found in the complex intertextual
network in which this text is woven: more particularly in the
relation with Henry James's own fiction and literary criticism.

In his 1914 essay "The New Novel," James praises *Chance*
(1914) for its "extraordinary exhibition of method" (609) which
is the result of Conrad "multiplying his creators" so that "the
thing 'produced' shall, if the fancy takes it, once more glory in
a gap" (609). Conrad himself insisted in his "Author's Note"
that he wanted to interest people in a "vision of things which is
indissolubly allied to the style in which it is expressed." But
James seems also to imply that Marlow and his likes, by casting
"these dropping *shadow after shadow*" on the expanse of
narrative, have drained out the substance of the tale: no wonder
then if in 1916, at the time when he was working on *The
Shadow-Line,* Conrad wrote of James's remarks that it was "the
only time a criticism affected me painfully."

In his own earlier essay on James (1904), Conrad saw his
contemporary as one of those writers able to take their readers to
the

> threshold of the ultimate experience...courageous enough to interpret
> the last experience of mankind in terms of their tempera-
> ment...clustered on this threshold to watch the last flicker of light on
> a black sky, to hear the last word uttered in the stilled workshop of the
> earth. (Ingram, 64)

James's temperament, it seems, was keen on the fairy-tale – or
more precisely on its nineteenth century form, the ghost-story.
He offered a late flower of the genre in "The Turn of the Screw"
which he wanted to be "an excursion of chaos while remaining,
like 'Blue Beard' and 'Cinderella' but an anecdote" ("Preface,"

38). When he heard this "small and gruesome and spectral story"
from the Archbishop of Canterbury who himself had got it from
a friend, he felt that it was already the "shadow of a shadow"
(34) – as if story-telling were comparable with dealing with
ghosts. He then turned it into a fantastic tale whose characteristic is "epistemological uncertainty," hesitation between two
mutually exclusive worlds, the world of the living and the world
of unearthly shadows.[6]

Conrad's own modernist response – with a vengeance – to
James's poetics can I think be found in *The Shadow-Line* where
he dislodges the shadows from the dusty shelves of the fantastic
genre, projecting them on the very lines of his war novella. As
a modern writer convinced that humanity has "outgrown the
stage of fairy tales, realistic, romantic, or even epic,"[7] he also
aims at the excursion of chaos, at watching "the last flicker of
light on a black sky" but this time within the confines of this
world, including the world of words – which explains his
exasperation when a critic reviewed *The Shadow-Line* as a ghost-
-story (Baines, 486). The eerie effect of the tale stems from the
fact that the shadows no longer seem to loom from beyond – they
now lurk in the tragic folly of the kingdom of earth which
Conrad meant to be a chronicler of.

After days of dead stillness without a breath of wind, the
captain-narrator of *The Shadow-Line* finds himself in a situation
that certainly echoes James's story. He hears

> curious, irregular sounds of faint tapping on the deck. They could be
> heard single, in pairs, in groups. While I wondered at this mysterious
> devilry, I received a slight blow under the left eye and felt an enormous
> tear run down my cheek. Raindrops. Enormous. Forerunners of
> something...there was a renewed moment of intolerable suspense;
> something like an additional turn of the racking screw. (*SL,* 113-14)

Yet the fantastic dimension is immediately undercut by some
"naturalization effect:" the eerie sounds are nothing but the rain
– "Suddenly – how am I to convey it? Well, suddenly, the
darkness turned into water" (114). The reader now begins to see
the complexity of the intertextual bond with "The Turn of the

Screw:" whereas James's narrator exorcizes the ghost of Peter Quint by a naming process which grants a positivity to the verbal act, separating the living from the dead, Conrad manages to shift the dark kernel at the very heart of his tale – indeed at the core of the word "quinine" itself, possibly an ironic resonance of the name "Quint."

Which might well explain his insistence in the 1920 "Author's Note" that "this story was not intended to touch on the supernatural" or to reach "beyond the confines of the world of the living, suffering humanity." Conrad adds that if he had meant to put the strain on the supernatural, his imagination would have failed and exhibited "an unlovely gap" (*SL*, IX), as if in response to James's "glory in a gap." Displacing the gap then meant killing the fantastic tension according to the conviction that "whatever falls under the dominion of our senses must be in nature and...cannot differ in its essence from all the other effects of the visible and tangible world of which we are a self-conscious part" (IX). Therefore the concern of *The Shadow-Line* will be with the "intimate delicacies of our relation to the dead and to the living" (IX): more precisely with "the effect of a mental or moral shock on a common mind" (X).

The argument here will be that the shock in question bears on a loss of faith in the line of ancestry the young captain believed himself to be inscribed in by the magic of the word "command:" this loss casts shadows on the lines of generation, whether it be of the word or of the human subject, now confronted with the necessity of constructing subjectivity from the void which is the only inheritance. The episode of the bottles of quinine opens a gulf between the word and the thing "inside," the cursed inheritance being the effect of a symbolic father's fault/flaw – the late captain betrayed the tradition and sold the quinine which he replaced with salt. The shadow-line, then, is no longer a question of hesitation on the threshold of the marvelous: it comes to split up the whole spectrum of subjectivity by placing loss/the father's fault as the primordial experience before the constitution of the subject.[8]

Thus the death-urge lies at the core of the story, intra and metafictionally, not *supernaturally*. I think that the word "supernatural" bothered Conrad because of its transcendental resonances. It is surely not accidental if the novella's intertextual family is concerned precisely with the *lack* of transcendency, with a metaphysical gap that brings shadows into the very core of human experience. Three major references stand out here: the ghost of Hamlet's soliloquy on "The undiscovered country from whose bourn"//"no traveller returns" (*Hamlet*, III, I, 78-80) returns on the very first page of Conrad's text, embedded in a remarkable example of Freudian disavowal which I will further analyze in the light of Lacan's own study of *Hamlet*.[9] The "valley of the shadow of death" undertones are borrowed from David's Psalms in *The Old Testament*,[10] and "The Rime of the Ancient Mariner" resonates in the confessional undertones of *The Shadow-Line*. Coleridge gives the argument of his poem about "the nightmare LIFE-IN-DEATH" as "how as ship having passed the Line was driven by storms to the Cold Country towards the South Sea Pole."[11] The echoes in *The Shadow-Line* are strong, especially those concerning the passage into the Underworld:[12] under the glassy sheet of water, toward a stage where speech is nothing but maddening sound, pure signifiers devoid of significance – a theme rendered in Conrad's text by the violin of the old captain who has lost all *sound*ness of mind. It might also be useful to remember that the mariner murdered the albatross, the bird of life, and that the poem ends on the necessity of confession: "Since then, at an uncertain hour, // That agony returns: // And till my ghastly tale is told, // This heart within me burns" (582 and ff). The telling of the tale is then presented as a necessity providing relief from a sense of guilt obscurely related to the question of desire, itself evoked by the image of the burning heart – an image literalized in *The Shadow-Line* by a full-fledged character, Mr *Burns*. Last, but not least, a Baudelairean strain is overheard in the epigraph from "La Musique" which calls up the image of the glassy mirror of the sea. It is surely characteristic of Conrad's strategy of disavowal that he cut the poem's reference to the gulf, "*l'immense gouffre*" that tempts the desire of Baudelaire's *damné*.[13]

Of course, the polysemy and symbolism of the word "gulf" should not be overlooked; there are many analogies to be drawn between Decoud's last moments on the Golfo Placido,[14] his mortal plunge into the *jouissance de la Chose*,[15] and the experience of the captain-narrator on the Gulf of Siam after Captain Giles's parting words, "Don't let anything tempt you over" (*SL*, 45).

The valley of the shadow of death

The climactic moment in *The Shadow-Line* is precisely a moment of stillness, of literalization of desire, in the imaginary return to the primordial *jouissance* of being at one with the desired object, with "the thing that lies beyond the semblance of the thing" (Virginia Woolf).

The "undiscovered country" which is the unavowed object of the young captain's desire takes the shape of some pre-linguistic void, death being nothing but what man tries to imagine outside the realm of language, the area of the Thing itself.[16] In this place of undifferentiated matter – the Lacanian *Entre-Deux-Morts* – the creative function of the signifier hasn't operated yet. Such is the area of the madman's *jouissance* before and outside the advent of the symbolic order, an enjoyment which Lacan has pointed out in Hamlet's pretended madness and play on the limits of human speech: it is less biological death than death to the order of culture, a sort of zero degree of language figured in *The Shadow-Line* by the old captain's ex-centricity. It is in these footsteps that the successor follows, towards the realm of the unspeakable, in the silence of the primordial void where lies the maddening illusion of plenitude – or rather of *absence of lack*. One of the merits of Conrad's fiction is that it builds a meta-phorical network between the death-drive and a pseudo sea--story – or rather a "*see*-story" – which attempts to give a name and a shape to what a journalist returning from Sarajevo in 1995 called "the obscene *jouissance* of war."

Like many other modern narratives, *The Shadow-Line* comes

closer to imagining the "inconceivable terror and [...] inexpressible mystery" (108) that lies in the area of the Freudian Thing, at a moment of extreme tension comparable to the snapping of the cord of silence by the report of Decoud's gun in *Nostromo*: "In the tension of silence I was suffering from it seemed to me that the first crash must turn me into dust," the young captain notes. Such is the imagined moment of return to the mythical moment of being which impresses his senses beyond speech, in the presence of "the formidable work of the seven days, into which mankind seems to have blundered unbidden:" we are on *another scene* filled with spectral objects, giving "a foretaste of annihilation" and threatening the subject with literal dissolution: "To look around the ship was to look into a bottomless, black pit. The eye lost itself in inconceivable depths." Hence the sense of that "something going on in the sky like a decomposition, like a corruption in the air."

Here the pre-symbolic subject lies at one with un-differentiated matter, in "an immensity that receives no impress, preserves no memories, and keeps no reckoning of lives," an immensity recalling the "immense indifference of things" that engulfs Decoud into silent Oneness after the abolition of earthly limits which is the *negation of life* "poised on the edge of some violent issue" – to which *The Shadow-Line* gives a truly poetic shape: "I leaned on the rail and turned my ear to the shadows of the night. Not a sound. My command might have been a planet flying vertiginously on its appointed path in a space of infinite silence" (*SL*, 74). Thus the "infernal stimulant," the desire to encounter the Thing itself, leads the captain-narrator in Burns's wake – "Do you see it, sir?" (118) – and it seems that the ship has crossed the glassy surface, moving among the Baudelairean phosphorescent monsters: one of the men on deck looks like "a fish in an aquarium by the light of an electric bulb, an elusive, phosphorescent shape" (114) just before the narrator's nose, ears and eyes are filled by a heavy shower. And suddenly, "I could see It – that Thing! The darkness, of which so much had just turned into water, had thinned down a little. There It was! But I did not hit upon the notion of Mr Burns issuing out of the companion on

all fours till he attempted to stand up" (115). Here we can
measure the reference to – and the difference from – "The Turn
of the Screw:" at the moment of ultimate tension which in the
classic ghost story is founded on hesitation between the Uncanny
and the Marvelous, Conrad deflates the fantastic potentiality
and opts for the uncanny effect of *language* itself. Whereas the
very naming of the ghost in James's tale results in a narrative
event – young Miles's death – that puts an end to the story, in *The
Shadow-Line* the black unearthly substance operates on the
word itself, creates a story out of no-Thing: "*But I did not hit
upon* the notion of Mr Burns issuing out of the companion."
    Through the shadowy effect of the disavowal, the epistemo-
logical uncertainty becomes an effect of otherness in the
captain's very discourse, producing a moment of self-consciousness which is also a moment of separation from the
unspeakable horror.

The word arising from the primordial void

In this narrative, Burns and Ransome are two symbolic figures
on which the young captain's own unspeakable desires are
projected, their narrative function being to embody *subject
positions* in the face of constitutive otherness. It is a question of
the conflict between the magic view of speech – without a shadow
of otherness – and the other view acknowledging a share of
darkness at the very core of the human word.
    Burns figures the infantile belief in the magic of words,
whereby the subject finds himself as it were at the mercy of
a destructive wish like Isaac in the episode of Abraham's
sacrifice – hence the references to the burning bush. Burns's
"craziness" consists in seeing himself as the object of sacrifice
about to consume himself in the moment of fusion which is the
moment of stumbling into the gulf, of filling the Other's gaping
mouth. His superior sees him like a "predestined victim," prey to
"an invisible monster ambushed in the air" (*SL*, 67), burning
with "a passion of fear." But fear of what? Of a *literalization*

process that would be the terrifying accomplishment of Oneness if the mad captain's words were to become real, if he really *meant* every word of what he said (62): as if therefore this perverse father were about to engulf the "children of the sea." The other possibility that provides escape from the deadly fantasy, is to pay the ransom to the Other by accepting the share of otherness at the heart of human existence: the failing heart in Ransome's chest, the functional equivalent of the failure of the signifier "quinine" in the medicine chest, is the saving failure which undercuts the magic power of the destructive fathers' word. Here lies I think the gist of the metaphorical relation with the First World War, commonly viewed as a collective sacrifice to the Motherland at the request of the political fathers wishing death for humanity.

As a modernist writer, Conrad clearly opts for the second solution: rather than give up the ghosts of his protagonists according to the conventions of the fantastic story, he subjects them to a process of dispossession, making it clear that separation from the deadly *jouissance* out there, is the only possible origin from which the subject of speech might arise. The cathartic moment of liberation is characteristically a *splitting,* when the magic collapses, when the young captain becomes conscious of metaphoricity through a process of "*parolisation du manque*"[17] that simultaneously bars and protects Burns from the threat of the Other's infernal *jouissance*:

> Suddenly – *how am I to convey it?* Well, suddenly the darkness turned into water. This is the only suitable *figure*...and even without *the ghost of impact,* I became instantaneously soaked to the skin...the *idea of a bear* crossed my mind first.
> He growled *like one* when I seized him round the body. (114-15)

What happens here is that the captain-narrator experiences a lack in speech, he looks for words ("How am I to convey it?") *instead of* the Thing which is thus repressed and replaced by a figure, an idea, a metaphor ("*the ghost of impact*") turning the threatening ghost into a verbal effect, the very ghostly effect of metaphor founded on the recognition of lack.

The other ghostly effect occurs when the figure of the
destructive father – the fever devil in which Burns firmly believed
and which also tempted the young captain's desire – becomes
a mere shadow in the captain's mouth:

> "This is the sort of thing we've been having for seventeen days, Mr
> Burns," I said with intense bitterness. "A puff, then a calm, and in
> a moment, you'll see, she'll be swinging on her heel with her head away
> from her course *to the devil somewhere.*"
> He caught at the word. *"The old dodging Devil,"* he screemed
> piercingly, and burst into such a loud laugh as I had never heard
> before. (119)

What the text exposes here is the structural gap of *énonciation*
whereby the young captain is no longer in a position of
command, but uses unwittingly a figure of speech – "to the devil
somewhere" – which resonates in Burns's ear, recalling metaphorically the dead captain's ghost. Burns thus overhears the
possibility for his new master's discourse to be split by an
otherness that saves him from the terror of the literal effect, of
the one-to-one correspondence between word and thing that had
terrified him in the old master's word.

It is the recognition of this uncanny effect that liberates Burns
from the dead captain's threat. He overhears a resonance in
a phrase that escapes his interlocutor's control, making human
intercourse possible by unlocking desire from the master signifier – here "fever-devil." Thus Burns acknowledges a gap in the
line of his captain's discourse, a bar against the malevolent
Other[18] who has become a mere shadow in the spoken chain: the
devil has been named by a figure of speech that does not kill
anybody but simply splits the captain's utterance open. Thanks
to the shadowy effect of "to the devil somewhere," what had
been projected into the realm of the supernatural in James's
story has become with Conrad the very condition of language
and culture, made possible by the metaphoricity of speech:
which is not a curse but a gain, or at least a useful warning
against the word of the masters who lead mankind to slaughter
in war times.

What is also at stake is the position of the modern writer after the loss of certainty in meaning and inheritance, anticipated by the eerie effect of the doctor's letter that was supposed to guarantee the authenticity of the quinine – "a half-sheet of notepaper, which I unfolded with a queer sense of dealing with the uncanny" (80). The uncanny effect, equally conveyed by the diary – "a few detached lines, now looking very ghostly to my own eyes" (106) oozes from the letter once it has been cut from the unspeakable *jouissance*. The recognition of the ghostly essence of the human word is the ransom to be paid in exchange of existence which Lacan writes "ex-sistence" because it necessitates exclusion and expulsion from the realm of the unnameable Thing, a process achieved through the Name-of-the-Father structure:[19] for the modern writer this implies giving up the fantasy of authority and command, allowing shadowy effects to mar the sense of the tale – potentialities in which we might recognize a possible definition of Conrad's own *écriture*.

It is now time to come down to the text, to see if something has been captured in the shadows of its lines. Thus the forbidden *jouissance* might become a *jouissance inter-dite,* a remains in the letter of the text: a poetic resonance undermining the instrumental view of speech like a warning against its deadly consequences.

Disavowal: a ghost-effect

Compared to Conrad's other narratives, *The Shadow-Line* offers peculiarities that haven't escaped the critics' eyes: Hawthorn notes the absence of "narrative crutches," the concentration on "a sort of pure narrative voice" which I would analyze as Conrad's own response to James's bitter-sweet remarks about the shadowy presence of Marlow. Similarly, Berthoud notes in his edition of the text that "the authorial voice is not displaced by one or several narrators addressing a fictional audience, or enmeshed in irony-generating devices." Yet, as Lothe observes, "writing for Conrad was an activity that constituted negation – of itself, of what it dealt with...as an activity Conrad's writing negated and reconstituted itself, negated itself again, and so forth indefinitely, hence the extraordinary patterned quality of the writing" (108). Conrad himself spoke of the "shadowy impulses" that make the unearthly nature of fiction writing: in a letter to E. L. Sanderson he complains of its strangeness, as "One's will becomes the slave of hallucinations, responds only to shadowy impulses" (*CL*, II, 205).

The specific problem in *The Shadow-Line* was how to open gaps, how to dot with shadows the lines of first-person autodiegetic narrative, how to find new forms of distance and mediation after the sacrifice of Marlow's ghostly voice. My own view is that the pattern substituted for the narrator figure is something in the language itself, namely a use of negation and of Freudian disavowal which we find in disquieting quantity: a poetics that gives this text an amazing complexity beneath the glassy surface of words, a power to refract light in the darkness.

Disavowal is a figure of speech whereby one thing is affirmed and then immediately denied, so that the speaker simultaneously allows repressed material to be formulated and disowns responsibility/authority for the statement by means of expulsion out of the linguistic sphere of the ego ("You will think that this dream is about my mother, but this is not so" – was Freud's favorite example). Freud and Lacan recognized in this dis-torsion of sense – both in terms of meaning and direction – a manifestation of the Other's discourse and an affirmation of the death-drive in speech.[20] My argument is that the eeriness of the narrative in *The Shadow-Line* is the effect of the recurrence of various forms of negation producing the sense of "giving in before you start" which according to D. H. Lawrence "pervades Conrad and all such folks – the writers among the ruins" (Spittles, 174). I will concentrate first on the materials projected; secondly on the modernist effect of the device, and finally on the symptomatic character of a turn of speech where something of the lost *jouissance* remains as it were encapsulated.

The materials projected and then disowned are most of the time representations related to the motifs of loss and to the death-drive. The very rendering of the episode of the quinine produces that hole in the magic signifier – the missing original letter – on which the whole story is built: "You have guessed the truth already. There was the wrapper, the bottle, and the white powder inside, some sort of powder! But it wasn't quinine" (*SL*, 89). The truth, then, is no revelation about a transcendental object in the miraculous shrine – it is about a loss opening a gap in the predecessor's inheritance. It is thus not what the word "quinine" designates that gets the story started, but rather its failure to stand for anything. The very negation dramatizes the function of the semiotic bar which makes meaning impossible in the very act of calling it up, and thus delineates the area of culture.

Similarly the ghosts dormant in the repressed text will manifest themselves only to negate themselves: whereas "The Turn of the Screw" still relies on the positivity of speech to drive away the ghosts by naming them, in *The Shadow-Line* negativity contaminates the language of the text with ghostly effects. The ghost of the old captain who "being dead, had no authority, was not in anybody's way, and was much easier to deal with" (57) is marked by the very sign of negation. Its negative *quantity* becomes a *quality*: the negativity of speech, the line of resistance which threatens the captain-narrator's authority on the ship's/narrative's progress, but which also provides a glimpse at the unconscious forces motivating the telling of a story. The deleted passage of the captain's nightmare is worth recalling here:

> I upbraided myself for [? that] very existence of that unwholesome [sentiment] sensation...that [very] resistance [in] itself was a manifestation of a self-consciousness which was to me strange [to me?] experience, distasteful and disquieting....I dreamt of the Bull of Bashan...a fear woke up in me – that he would end by breaking through – not through the fence – through my purpose....Before my teeth began to rattle however the apparition spoke in a hoarse apologetic [?] but flesh [and blood] voice which no ghost would have [??] thought it necessary to adopt. Certainly not the ghost of that savage overbearing sinner....It was but the voice of a seaman on watch....

"Not through the fence – through my purpose" provides another
example of Freudian disavowal which lays bare the truth about
the captain's desire to break through the fence, to overstep the
limit between death and life, reason and madness, language and
the void. The next disavowal – "No ghost....Certainly not the
ghost of that savage overbearing sinner" both acknowledges and
denies the young captain's unconscious absorption in his
predecessor's figure. It is the very force of linguistic negation that
constitutes the resistance, the fence, the bar against the maddening temptation of such a reading which has yet been
formulated.[21] Likewise for the temptation of the underworld:
the captain catches sight of a seaman and beholds him "as one
sees a fish in an aquarium by the light of an electric bulb, an
elusive, phosphorescent shape. *Only he did not* glide away" (114).

In other cases it is the ghost of the Shakespearean intertext
which is called up: "'Oh, yes, I know what you mean, [the captain
says to Burns]' But you cannot expect me to believe that a dead
man has the power to put *out of joint the meteorology* of this part
of the world" (84). It is again as if the shadow of the other text
were barred in the very act of calling it up. But why, one might
ask? I would suggest that first it is because that half-confessed
kinship with a master text threatens narrative authority, and
secondly because that particular text also bears on man's
relation with the unavowable: *Hamlet* too is built on an empty
core, the death of the father whose sins leave the son gaping on
"the undiscovered coutry."[22] It is surely not accidental if the
very signifier of death in Shakespeare's play returns in *The
Shadow-Line* at a crucial moment of textual disavowal:

> One closes behind one the little gate of mere boyishness – and enters an
> enchanted garden. Its very shades glow with promise. Every turn of
> the path has its seduction. And it isn't because it is an undiscovered
> country. One knows well enough that all mankind had streamed that
> way. (3)

The reader begins to grasp here what devious paths indeed the
unavowable desire for the touch of death can take in order to
formulate itself: as the captain-narrator confesses rather per-

versely, "All roads are long that lead towards one's heart desire" (44).

Psychoanalysis has shown that the return of the Real is signalled by blinding moments of hallucination threatening the subject with dissolution: moments whose significance in *The Shadow-Line* is immediately neutralized by means of some disavowal which "naturalizes" the uncanny element. There are several such passages: the nightmare of the Bull of Bashan (a reference to the bulls threatening to devour David in Psalm 22) in which the spectral voice turns out to be "the voice of a seaman on watch;" the pseudo-scene of sacrifice in which Burns seems to be jabbing a pair of scissors at his own throat while "In reality he was simply overtaxing his returning strength in a shaky attempt to clip off the thick growth of his red beard" (90). Last, but not least, the confrontation with the Thing. The "naturalization effect" produced by the picture of Burns "issuing out of the companion on all fours" (115) builds up a fence at the moment when the subject is about to fade in the recognition of the desire to see what should not be looked at.

This leads us to wondering about the effect of disavowal in terms of narrative strategy – what kind of authority does the text thus own or disown? Jakob Lothe observes that "the narrative trick of making the narrator a firmly outspoken opponent to any sort of supernatural explanation" (128) results in allowing the supernatural to come off better. I would see more than a conscious narrative trick however in the pattern repeating itself insistently like a textual symptom, like the trace of a deep-rooted conflict between the temptation of negation – destructiveness aiming toward the ob-scene *jouissance* barred from the area of culture – and the writing impulse. I actually would tend to believe that Conrad is sincere when he writes in "Author's Note" that his story "was not intended to touch on the supernatural...there is nothing supernatural in it, nothing so to speak from beyond the confines of this world" (*SL,* IX-X). What is at stake rather is a poetics that, instead of situating death in the realm of fantastic story-telling includes it in the very speech act.

The autodiegetic narrator's discourse is also studded with

disavowals that cast shadows, often by means of modal verbs introducing epistemic doubt at the very heart of *énoncés*: "I might have smiled if I had not been busy with my own sensations, which were not those of Mr Burns." The various "might," "would," "ought to" seem to evoke a "possible other case" – Henry James's definition for irony – a possibility then denied. What is equally interesting here is that the possible other case is projected onto the sphere of the imaginary addressee – "You may think this, but it is not so" – so that the narrator's own authority remains unaltered. It is no accident that the denied materials are related to sensations and emotions that are thus safely displaced.[23] Elsewhere the narrator most deviously acknowledges the shadowy impulses at the base of his glossy narrative – "However, it's no use trying to put a gloss on what even at the time I myself half suspected to be a caprice" (4). The caprice, actually, was nothing but the dormant virtuality which it is the unavowable object of the tale to explore.

What conclusions can we draw from such changing positions? The first is certainly that Conrad's captain-narrator paradoxically assumes the role of the master-teller by giving himself up to "the licence of disconnexion and disavowal" which James also claimed for his narrator figures (Felman, 205). On the other hand, it is as if he also let go the helm that gives the narrative/ship a direction and a sense. The text's economy of contradiction affirms meaning as divided, introduces heterogeneity and raises the painful question of beginnings so characteristic of Conrad's fiction. Nowhere has the difficulty of asserting oneself through writing been more visible than here:

> It's the *only* period of my life in which I attempted to keep a diary. *No, not the only one.* Years later,...*I don't remember* how it came about or how the pocket-book and the pencil came into my hands. *It's inconceivable* that I should have looked for them on purpose.... *Neither* could I expect the record to outlast me. (*SL*, 105-6)

It might be useful to recall here that the problem of beginnings was precisely what poisoned the young seaman's existence on shore, where he felt a ghost to those men of pen and ink dealing with his name in offices (34). Before taking the magic command, he felt as if "[t]here was nothing original, nothing new, startling, informing to expect from the world" (23). It could be argued that the purpose of *The Shadow-Line* was initially to put a gloss on that negativity, to do as if there was something original to be done indeed, in order to deny the seaman's condition as a mere "subject for official writing," of a mere "ghost:" Conrad wanted to call the tale "First Command" and certainly had the idea of a simple story which the effect of the war – where soldiers are also mere ghosts in record books – then made impossible.

Thus the text moves back and forth, constantly denying its own sense/direction, delaying the moment of significance, offering glimpses at the void, playing with the negativity of the human word. The frustrated reader is placed in the position described by the young captain when he discovers the weight of the word "delay" (65). It is here that the poetics of disavowal distinguishes itself as a modernist gesture: mastery turns out to be dispossession, paralyzing self-consciousness. "Most of the details," Philippe Jaudel notes, "take on a new dimension when the text is read as a symbolic representation of the urge to create meaning and the risks it involves" (133). I would suggest here that the very movement of disavowal contributes to that dimension by producing *textual* loopings whose function is to bar the *sense* of meaning in the process of calling it up.

Loopings are turns comparable to the turn of a screw when one drives it in. In Conrad's tale, the "turn of the screw" effect is no longer a tightening of dramatic tension, it becomes a functional metaphor: the text, like a screw, turns in place, repeating the constitutive movement whereby "meaning indicates only the direction, points only at the sense toward which it fails" (Lacan, quoted in Felman, 113). For the reader such "racking" turns of the screw constitute the risk of reading, when repressed shades of meaning madden the ear and make us see not literally but rhetorically – a figure of speech is a *trope,* a word which comes from the Greek *tropein,* "to turn." It is only when we are blinded along the shadow-lines of meaning[24] that we can see in the dark:

the ghost story becomes a ghostly tale where the maddening threat of meaninglessness is overheard.

"This is not a marriage story," the captain-narrator insists at the beginning of his tale (*SL,* 4). Yet I would like to raise a last question: is there a relation to be drawn between the temptation of the mystical marriage with death, and this text's perverse determination to call up the original nonsense by foregrounding the negativity of language? Lacan has pointed out that speech is by definition *"l'appareil de la jouissance"* (*Séminaire,* XX, 52): it involves two modes, the phallic enjoyment of ordering and authorizing a world and another joy – *"la jouissance de l'Autre"* – which is the joy in sheer non-sense, of *"j'ouis-sens"* ("I can overhear other meanings") and *"jouis-sens"* ("I enjoy over-hearing them"). What is at stake here is the otherness overheard in the nonsense, in the music of language when meaningless signifiers resist significance, in the mere *composition* – Bloom's "other joy" that defeats the military word in *Ulysses.* It is likely that the very movement of disavowal which allows nonsense to blur sense, to jar the harmony, to thwart the speaker's command, constitutes a symptom on the textual body, pointing to the place where the lost fragments of the primordial senseless *jouissance* are encapsulated:[25] something in excess of narrative com-munication can be overheard in the opening of blank areas where discourse lets go the helm, where meaninglessness threatens, creating black holes that cast shadows on the mirror of sense.

It has often been argued that a writer's style is his symptom, an idiosyncratic way of erring on the limits of the language. Conrad's choice of the title "the shadow-line" instead of "first command" is surely symptomatic in that way. The shadows are the dark imprints on the letter of the text, splinters of the unnameable Real glimpsed through the ghostly effect of speech itself. Like the signifier "quinine" the letter of the text – its body – is imprinted with something that escapes narrative deter-mination, *"un petit-plus-de-jouir"* (Lacan), a trace of that other joy which can be sensed in the very movement whereby the text and its reader are dispossessed of meaning: the function of the word, then, will be no other than to circum*scribe* the void in

a process that re-enacts the narrative principle set up through
Marlow in "Heart of Darkness,"

> to him the meaning of an episode was not inside like a kernel but
> outside, enveloping the tale which brought it out only as a glow brings
> out a haze, in the likeness of one of those misty halos that sometimes
> are made visible by the spectral illumination of moonshine. (*YS*, 48)

The linguistic pattern of disavowal is that which makes the text
turn in place, constituting both the halo and the fence: an
experience of the limits of language where the Other *jouissance*
can bloom in something unheard which manifests itself in the
distorsions of articulate speech produced semantically, prag-
matically and textually by the process of disavowal. Thus the
text catches our ear on the unavowable desire for the gulf, on the
temptation of chucking one's berth/birth: "Nothing should ever
be taken for granted," is after all the first lesson learnt by the
captain on his phantom ship.

The Shadow-Line, therefore, can be read as a writer's symbolic
gesture of response to the nightmare of history: it explores chaos
without the excuse of the supernatural, erects itself as a barrier
against the deadly threat of taking the word for the thing itself,
thus anticipating the insights of psychoanalysis about the vital
necessity of the symbolic order which bars *homo loquens* from the
Jouissance de la Chose. It makes us see metaphorically into the
darkest impulses of humanity, into the danger of giving oneself
up to the desire for Oneness which is nothing but a denial of the
Otherness constitutive of human subjectivity. With the artist's
unconscious knowledge about non-knowledge, Conrad exposes
what Lacan later formulated thus: "When we wish to attain in
the subject what was before the serial articulations of the Word,
and what is promordial to the birth of symbols, we find it in
death, from which his existence takes on all the meaning it has"
(Wilden, 85). Last, but not least, through the power of its written
word *The Shadow-Line* offers its patient reader the "*petit-plus-
-de-jouir*" that gives it pride of place in the literature of this
century.

NOTES

1. Italics in quotations are my emphases, unless otherwise indicated.

2. Jeremy Hawthorn mentions in his "Introduction" that Conrad inscribed Richard Curle's copy in these terms: "This story had been in my mind for some years. Originally I used to think of it under the name of 'First Command.' When I managed in the second year of war to concentrate my mind sufficiently to begin working I turned to this subject as the easiest. But in consequence to my changed mental attitude to it, it became *The Shadow-Line*" (Hawthorn, 10). In a letter to S. Colvin of February 1917, Conrad observes that "to sit down and invent fairy tales was impossible then. It isn't very possible even now. I was writing that thing in Dec., 1914, and Jan. to March, 1915....Here I'll only say that experience is transposed into spiritual terms – in art a perfectly legitimate thing to do, as long as one preserves the exact truth enshrined therein. That's why I consented to this piece being published by itself. I did not like the idea of it being associated with fiction in a volume of stories. And this is also the reason I've inscribed it to Borys – and the Others" (Ingram, 84). The idea of transposition, i.e. of metaphor seems to me crucial for recovering the "enshrined truth" about "that thing."

3. Jacques Lacan's concept of *jouissance* "carries a wide range of meaning: enjoyment in the sense of legal or social possession, pleasure and the pleasure of sexual climax. Lacan uses the term emphasising the totality of enjoyment covered by it – simultaneously sexual, spiritual, conceptual" (Minow-Pinkney, 201) and, I would add, textual.

4. Jakob Lothe sees its thematic scope extending "beyond the specific test...during one particular voyage...to the challenge of how to write at all" (132). Philippe Jaudel argues in favor of "several levels of interpretation... – ethical, metaphysical, and metafictional...far from being mutually exclusive, these three levels coexist in a plural reading of the text" (130).

5. The mode of autodiegetic first-person narration is far simpler than the Marlow narratives; yet, as Conrad himself insisted, this does not mean that the piece is autobiographical in the common sense: "That the connection of my ships with my writing stands...recorded in your books is, of course, a fact. But that was biographical matter, not literary," he wrote to Richard Curle (Ingram, 106). Lawrence Graver notes that "For years readers have taken at face value Conrad's remark that the story is 'exact autobiography,' but the investigations of Norman Sherry and others have undermined the authority of the assertion" (179). Actually the subtitle "A Confession" with its implications of guilt, suggests that the autobiography might be oblique, metaphorical – to be found elsewhere than in *facts*. If Conrad was concerned with any fact here, as he insists in "Author's Note," it was in Mr Burns's *craziness*, the symptom of a temptation which the young captain narrator has to resist if the ship is to move on.

6. Brian MacHale, referring to T. Todorov's famous essay, defines the fantastic in these terms: "A text belongs to the fantastic proper only as long as it hesitates between natural and supernatural explanations, between the uncanny and the marvelous. Hesitation, or 'epistemological uncertainty,' is thus the underlying principle according to Todorov. Few texts manage to maintain this delicate balance to the end [like] James's 'The Turn of the Screw'" (74).

7. Essay on John Galsworthy, quoted in Ingram, 73.

8. In his "Introduction" to the Oxford edition, Jeremy Hawthorn underscores the intimate relation of *The Shadow-Line* with "The Secret Sharer" in words that invite a similar reading: "As in 'The Secret Sharer,' the young captain suddenly becomes conscious of his identity as something not given but (at least in part) to be constructed" (XI).

9. Here are some of the numerous references (the italicized terms indicate the textual echoes in Conrad's text): "I could be bounded in a nutshell, and count myself *a king of infinite space,* were it not that I have bad dreams....*A dream itself is but a shadow*" (II, II, 264, 273); "this most excellent canopy, the air, look you, this brave and o'erhanging firmament, this majestical roof fretted with golden fire, why, it appears to me *but a foul and pestilent congregation of vapours*" (II, II, 309, 311); "The spirit that I have seen // *May be the devil*" (II, II, 635); "There's a divinity that *shapes our ends,* // Rough hew them how we will" (V, II, 10-11).

10. In particular Psalms 22 and 23 whose chief motif is the lack of the father's response to the son's request – or in Nietzschean terms, the lack of a transcendental order.

11. The poem is a superb exploration of what Lacan in his essay on *Antigone* calls "*Entre-deux-Morts,*" a space between mental and biological death which the tragic protagonist seeks to imagine. But as Philippe Jaudel suggests, "in 'The Rhyme of the Ancient Mariner,' the supernatural signifies the existence of a transcendental universe, while in *The Shadow--Line* it exists, and most vividly indeed, only as the delusion of a diseased mind" (134). The loss of the transcendental order and the subsequent gap is precisely the inheritance of the modern imagination after the collapse of liberal humanism – what Lacan calls "*la fin de la veine humaniste*" (*L'Ethique de la psychoanalyse,* 319). One of the most poetic explorations of the theme in fiction is certainly Malcolm Lowry's *Under the Volcano* which itself overtly acknowledges its intertextual kinship with *Lord Jim* and "Heart of Darkness."

12. See for example verse 240 and following: "I looked upon the rotting sea, // And drew my eyes away; // I looked upon the rotting deck, // And there the dead men lay. // ... My lips were wet, my throat was cold, // My garments were all dank // Sure I had drunken in my dreams, // And still my body drank. // ... // We were a ghastly crew. // ... and now 'twas like all instruments, // Now like a lonely flute...."

13. The full reference is: *"Je sens vibrer en moi toutes les passions // D'un vaisseau qui souffre; // Le bon vent, la tempête et ses convulsions // Sur l'immense gouffre me bercent. D'autres fois calme plat, grand miroir de mon désespoir!"* The *damné* figure is more fully portrayed in *"L'irrémédiable:"* *"Un damné descendant sans lampe // Au bord d'un gouffre dont l'odeur // Trahit l'humide profondeur // D'éternels escaliers sans rampe // ou veillent des monstres visqueux // Dont les larges yeux de phosphore // Font une nuit plus noire encore // Et ne rendent visible qu'eux."* The *Shadow-Line* certainly means to explore that *"humide profondeur"* with its phosphorescent gleams.

14. Jakob Lothe rightly suggests that "the closest counterpart in Conrad...is probably the authorial description in *Nostromo* of Decoud's isolation and growing despair on the Grand Isabel in the hours preceding his suicide" (130).

15. *"L'aire de la Chose, de la jouissance innommée où domine le silence des pulsions...espaces vides...lieux d'attraction énigmatiques,"* Nestor Braunstein notes (98): the area of the Thing, of the unnamed *jouissance* dominated by the silence of drives, an area of enigmatic attraction (my translation).

16. Lacan defines it as the "primary exteriority of the subject" (Wilden, 297) – *"ce qui du Réel pâtit du signifiant"* (*L'Ethique de la Psychoanalyse*, 142), "that part of the Real which is excluded by the action of the signifier" (my translation). Nestor Braunstein defines it conceptually as *"la Chose, réelle et en même mythique, effet rétroactif de la symbolisation primordiale, objet absolu et perdu à jamais du désir"* (98): "the Thing, both real and mythical, the retroactive effect of primordial symbolization, the absolute object of desire, lost forever" (my translation).

17. *"La loi du langage déjouifie le corps. Le désir parolisant maintient la jouissance dans son horizon d'impossibilité"* (Braunstein, 103): the symbolic law of language deprives the body of *jouissance*. It is because of the interference of speech and desire that *jouissance* can remain out of reach, like an impossible object in the horizon (my translation).

18. Thus, Nestor Braunstein explains symbolic castration makes the subject immune against the Other's deadly *jouissance* and habilitates us for the other types of *jouissance* available in speech – *"une fonction d'habilitation pour la jouissance, celle qui porte l'immunité relative et précaire contre cette jouissance maligne qui rejette le sujet hors du symbolique"* (109).

19. The Name-of-the-Father being that first signifier (S1) which takes the place of the Thing and marks the possibility of the beginning of a spoken chain ("S1, S2, Sn"): *"Signifiant 1 qui prend la place de la Chose, de ce trognon du Réel...,signifiant zéro, inarticulable, et se place à la limite de la batterie signifiante, en dehors de l'Autre"* (Braunstein, 98).

20. "Lacan seeks to view affirmation or introjection as a 'primordial symbolisation' of reality and negation or expulsion as 'constituting the Real' as the domain which exists outside symbolisation" (Wilden, 280).

21. S. Felman makes a similar argument about "The Turn of the Screw:"

"The ghosts are themselves erased significations, barred signifiers -... marked by the very sign of negation and denial, prefixed by a 'no' which bars them in the very act of calling them up" (150).

22. Lacan's argument, inspired from Kierkegaard, is that Hamlet burns with the weight of his father's sins which are his inheritance: "*De quoi brûle Hamlet, si ce n'est du poids des péchés du père, que porte le fantôme dans le mythe d'Hamlet...l'héritage du père, c'est celui que nous désigne Kierkegaard, c'est son péché...c'est d'une profonde mise en doute de ce père idéal qu'il s'agit à tout instant*" (*Les Quatre Concepts...*, 35).

23. Like for example: "He would have amused me if I had wanted to be amused. But I did not want to be amused. I was like a lover looking forward to a meeting" (*SL*, 46); "I ought to have been moved to tears. But I did not even think of it" (34); "I don't suppose I would have screamed but I remember my conviction that there was nothing else for it but to scream" (114).

24. "Reading, then, begins with an awareness, with a perception of ambiguous signifiers: an enigmatic letter, an unfamiliar and uncanny ghost....The very act of reading implies at the same time the assumption that knowledge *is*, exists, but *located in the Other*" (Felman, 157).

25. The symptom appears when the return of the unknowable *jouissance* blurs the lines of organized discourse: "*Le parlant devient muet et, à sa place, apparaît le symptôme qui est la réversion du discours à la jouissance, une jouissance ignorée et déniée...non sentie, **non sense**, désarticulée. Le mot non-dit, maudit, il est symptôme et jouissance insensée, jouis-sens*" (Braunstein, 167).

WORKS CITED

Baines Jocelyn. *Joseph Conrad. A Critical Biography*. Harmondsworth: Pelican Books, 1971.

Braunstein Nestor. *La jouissance. Un concept lacanien*. Paris: Point Hors Ligne, 1992.

Brown Douglas. *Three Tales from Conrad*. London: Hutchinson Educational, 1960.

Erdinast-Vulcan Daphna. *Joseph Conrad and the Modern Temper*. Oxford: Clarendon P., 1991.

Felman Soshana. "Turning the Screw of Interpretation," in *Literature and Psychoanalysis: The Question of Reading Otherwise*, ed. Soshana Felman. Baltimore: Johns Hopkins U. P., 1982, 94-207.

Graver Lawrence. *Conrad's Short Fiction*. Berkeley: U. of California P., 1969.

James Henry. "The New Novel," in *James Henry, The Critical Muse: Selected Literary Criticism*. Harmondsworth: Penguin Classics, 1987.

James Henry. *"The Aspern Papers" and "The Turn of the Screw."* Harmondsworth: Penguin Classics, 1984.

Jaudel Philippe. "The Calm as Initiation: A Plural Reading of *The Shadow-Line*," *L'Epoque Conradienne,* 1988, 129-135.

Joseph Conrad. Selected Criticism and "The Shadow-Line," ed. Alan Ingram. London: Methuen, 1986.

Lacan Jacques. *Ecrits.* Paris: Seuil, 1966.

Lacan Jacques. *Les Quatre Concepts Fondamentaux de la Psychoanalyse.* Paris: Seuil, Le Champ Freudien, 1973.

Lacan Jacques. *L'Ethique de la Psychoanalyse.* Paris: Seuil, Le Champ Freudien, 1986.

Lacan Jacques. "Desire and the Interpretation of Desire in *Hamlet*," in *Literature and Psychoanalysis: The Question of Reading Otherwise,* ed. Soshana Felman. Baltimore: Johns Hopkins U. P., 1982.

Lothe Jakob. *Conrad's Narrative Method.* Oxford: Clarendon Paperbacks, 1989.

MacHale Brian. *Post-Modernist Fiction.* London: Methuen, 1987.

Minow-Pinkney Makiko. *Virginia Woolf and the Problem of the Subject.* Brighton: Harvester Press, 1987.

Paccaud-Huguet Josiane. "Conrad and Lowry: Two Voyages to Darkness," *L'Epoque Conradienne,* 1991, 1-21.

Spittles Brian. *Joseph Conrad.* London: Macmillan, 1992.

Wilden Anthony. *Speech and Language in Psychoanalysis: Jacques Lacan.* Baltimore: Johns Hopkins U. P., 1991.

Richard Hocks,
University of Missouri,
Columbia, USA

Teaching Henry James and Joseph Conrad

How I wish my title, "Teaching Henry James and Joseph Conrad," referred to a long successful career of teaching these two authors at the University of Missouri over many years, but I am afraid it does not. The truth is, I offered my course on Conrad and James for the first and only time during Winter semester, 1995, and I did so primarily because of the upcoming Canterbury conference in July of that year. I *have* taught Henry James for many years, to be sure, but not Joseph Conrad. In my specialized department, Conrad is considered to be outside my field, American Literature, and therefore is taught by my colleagues with appointments in early modern British Literature. On the other hand, I began to notice in recent years that, as certain colleagues in the Conradian slot have retired, or moved on, or became administrators, Conrad has been offered less frequently than in the past.

In any event, I finally proposed a James/Conrad graduate class with some hesitation, and I must now report, having completed it, that I never did feel as though my presentation of Conrad was as satisfactory as was my instruction of James. Moreover, I never felt as though what I myself learned along with the students, with our various assignments and reports, left me sufficiently informed of, and in command of the mystery and the magnitude of Conrad – at least not as much as with James. I felt instead, and still do, that it would probably take me the same number of years to become as truly knowledgeable of Conrad as it has of James, which only increases my admiration for colleagues like Elsa Nettels and Paul Armstrong, whose work on the two I shall cite throughout the course of this essay. So there came to be a sort of subtle imbalance to my class, not an imbalance of assignments or of attention but of deeper under-

171

standing and cumulative wisdom. Since this was one of my principal discoveries after the fact, that some imbalance, alas, may govern these remarks – much as a key signature governs even the simplest piece of music – despite my efforts to compensate.

The seminar pre-enrolled ten beginning graduate students and all except one quickly admitted to invincible ignorance of *both* Conrad and James, the one exception being a British student who participated in our exchange programme with the University of Manchester. Since they were starting from scratch and had no preferred titles except "Daisy Miller," "Heart of Darkness" and *The Turn of the Screw* – about the only texts they professed to know – I set about to cluster and configure the readings on my own without consulting their wishes further. It soon became obvious that representing the two writers equally would mean examining about five major fictions apiece together with appropriate scholarship – an American semester being slightly longer tnan an English term. My first decision, therefore, was to eliminate the early James corpus entirely on the grounds it would be better to read works by both authors composed approximately during the same time-period, while occasionally allowing some flexibility in order to combine works by each that invited comparison on other grounds. We began with *The Princess Casamassima* (1886) and followed it with *The Secret Agent* (1907) despite some disparity in chronology, because the two novels invited comparison thematically. With the help of older critics like Lionel Trilling and more recent ones like Mark Seltzer, John Carlos Rowe and Deborah Esch, the students developed a certain appreciation for *The Princess...* after initial puzzlement. F. R. Leavis and Paul Armstrong primarily guided us through *The Secret Agent,* along with Elsa Nettels' helpful comments about its grotesque elements.

These students seemed confused, however, about a novel that at times appeared to veer from cynicism to lugubriousness (although no-one in class ever used that particular word). They began to nod, however, when they encountered Eileen Sypher's Althusserian essay on "Anarchism and Gender in *The Princess*

Casamassima and *The Secret Agent*," where she asserts that both male authors domesticate political acts in an attempt to deal with the frightening "new Woman" and gender relations. Interestingly, *I* found that *The Secret Agent* held up magnificently just because of the issues they found confusing, especially the irony, which, as Paul Armstrong points out, presupposes a relation of mutuality with the reader, even a shared ironic awareness of the problems of irony. But my first major epiphany was the discovery that *these* students actually felt more secure in their understanding once Eileen Sypher told them that the real issues were feminist. Even the prospect of thematic parallelism in the two authors' social views of revolution and anarchy was, for them, less energizing than the feminist focus, especially if that focus swallowed up and redirected the political theme. As an older generation male critic, I began to resign myself, somewhat ruefully, to the idea that, for my students, whatever technical and social complexity might confuse, sexual politics might clarify.

The next cluster of readings were *The Spoils of Poynton*, "Heart of Darkness," and *In the Cage,* all written at about the same time, at the end of the 1890s. Although the class found James's "Preface" to *The Spoils...* somewhat daunting, much as they had "Preface" to *The Princess...*, they were generally pleased and impressed by his sensitive treatment of Fleda Vetch and the encaged telegraphist; and when a few began to notice that, although a man, Hyacinth Robinson shared a number of important features with both Fleda and the telegraphist – that is, all three were similarly sensitive, imaginative, "artistic," and came from the poorer classes – this allowed me to introduce the recent concept of James's narratology as perhaps double--gendered. On a different score, it was gratifying to see at least a few of them begin to respond to the special features of James's London topography – the Princess's purely "ideological" move to Paddington, for instance, over against the genuine pathos of the telegraphist standing alone at the edge of the Paddington canal, or else Fleda alone at the train station forced to return to the "Labyrinth of London." There was also a kind of implicit analogy between the trip to Greenwich Park by Hyacinth and

Paul Muniment near the end of *The Princess Casamassima* and
the momentous one by Verloc and Stevie in *The Secret Agent*.
    Meanwhile, I had originally hoped by grouping "Heart of
Darkness" with *The Spoils*... to suggest a parallelism between
James and Conrad's critical engagement with colonial ac-
quisitiveness; I also wanted to try out Paul Armstrong's point
– this time from *The Phenomenology of Henry James* – about the
unsuccessful rôle which the mystifying and alienated Poynton
objects play in mediating human relations, to see, that is, if
a similar point might be made regarding "Heart of Darkness."
My students were fairly receptive to ideas like these, but they
greatly surprised me by their very different interest in my own
long analysis of Fleda Vetch in *Henry James and the Pragmatistic Thought*..., I think because the very idea of her as a Romantic
pragmatist played havoc with their received notion of prag-
matism; one student thereafter even became immersed in the
pragmatic school of philosophy, although he gravitated more
toward Charles Sanders Peirce than William James. Another
idea that briefly emerged was the dubious moral status of
James's and Conrad's London in "Heart of Darkness" and *In
the Cage*.
    And yet, even though Conrad's great tale was the one work
most familiar to all of them previously, the spectacles of New
Historicism and post-Colonial critique found in Brook Thomas,
Chinua Achebe and others simply changed forever the look of
that text for them: what they had long assumed was Conrad's
indictment of Europe's colonial empire in Africa – "the horror"
– seemed now a case, at best, of ambivalence through complicity.
New-Historicist spectacles, moreover, to my own distress also
appeared to require the discarding of Jungian lenses. As
I listened to our class discussion, I began to sense, once more,
that perhaps the feminist insight carried a certain leverage: that
is, once we assert that Marlow's view of women, that they are
"out of it" and must remain out of it, is benighted, it is then more
natural to interpret Marlow's – and even Conrad's – stance
toward colonialism as similarly patriarchal. Meanwhile, however, James's *In the Cage* emerged as a "find" for these students

– a "find" in the sense that, although they had not read his other works, they all knew the ones they had been expected to read, and *In the Cage* was not among them. James's multidimensional tale seemed to have its levels of meaning lined up right: the tale is epistemological, hermeneutical, sexual and importantly sociological.

The next two works, *Lord Jim* and *The Ambassadors,* written at the same time, were two of the richest and, I think, pedagogically the most successful of the longer texts we read. *Lord Jim* seemed to engage my students right away, and the critical issues shaped themselves well. It also helped by now to have read just enough in James and Conrad to elicit some further retrospective points of comparison. For example, Jim's romanticism, both hubristic and vulnerable, seemed analogous to Fleda Vetch's; and of course the character of Marlow together with his narration – or intermediate narration, if you prefer – re-echoed "Heart of Darkness." Furthermore, Conrad's narrative virtuosity, which allows one to read the early third--person-voiced chapters as ironic, recalled *The Secret Agent,* while his complicated perspective on colonialism and revolution evoked both "Heart of Darkness" and *The Secret Agent,* yet did so in a way that now somehow appeared more impervious to reductive interpretation. As helpful as ever were our critical guides, particularly Elsa Nettes' keen analysis in *James and Conrad* of the parallels and differences between *Lord Jim* and *The Ambassadors* as symptomatic of the two authors as a whole, and Paul Armstrong's philosophically elegant chapter from *The Challenge of Bewilderment* on contingency, belief and interpretation in *Lord Jim.* There were some other critics too who helped shape the discussion, particularly Daniel Ross's essay on "The Saving Illusion" and Tracy Seeley on the novel as a "Modernist Romance." But we also heard from Padmini Mongia that in *Lord Jim* "Marlow becomes the artist of imperial myths," and that "Conrad's narrative innovations are ideologically complicit with European imperialism" – not, for instance, his critiquing "the romance" of the political scene as John Rowe had argued James does so brilliantly in *The Princess*

Casamassima. As an attempt to provide an antidote to a critic like Mongia, I insisted they look at Hans van Marle and Pierre Lefranc's meticulous essay identifying the real-life topography and geography in *Lord Jim,* but my students chafed at that essay and reacted with impatience. Feeling my age and generation once again, I told them sheepishly that I still remembered a time when the assumption that scholarship is the gradual elimination of error was not deemed naive.

The *Ambassadors* was another peak moment in our seminar, for it now became apparent that James's later fiction was both highly original and also the gateway into the post-romantic, post-realistic explorations found in Conrad, even though the issue of direct influence was at best a moot point. Once more, the critical literature greatly enhanced our discussion, although we could only survey a tiny portion of the vast *Ambassadors* scholarship. We looked at some older criticism like Laurence Holland's *The Expense of Vision;*... and tried to link it up with more recent work like David McWhirter's *Desire and Love.* We did the same thing with my *Henry James and the Pragmatistic Thought:*..., Armstrong's analysis of "The Composing Powers of Consciousness," and Susan Griffin's argument, "Strether's Principles of Psychology," from her book *The Historical Eye.* We also looked at chapters from a number of other books by critics like Ruth Yeazell, Nicola Bradbury and Dan Fogel, as well as Julie Rivkin's sinuous essay on Derridan supplementarity, "The Logic of Delegation."

The following unit, on *Nostromo* and *The Golden Bowl,* both published in 1904, was intended to be the high climax of the course, but it never attained the success of the preceding pair of novels, perhaps because these two books did not spark off one another as successfully as their two predecessors, or perhaps because of the disappearance of Marlow. I was somewhat consoled by the fact that my two or three strongest students did seem responsive to the challenge of *Nostromo,* but the others merely tolerated it – sort of like Henry James himself – which also made me wonder if I were turning these people into Jamesians but not Conradians, which was never my intent.

Whereas with *The Ambassadors* the scholarship we read had lit up a fire already glowing like coals within them from the novel itself, I found with *Nostromo* that the scholarship actually saved the day by making possible such discussion as we had. Keith Carabine's "Introduction" to the Oxford World's Classics edition, the one we used, was most helpful with its perspicacious focus on certain major thematic and technical elements; and Elsa Nettels' differentiation between the tragic novel in James and in Conrad also provided some help (although these students did not know *The Wings of the Dove,* her exemplary case from James). We also revisited briefly F. R. Leavis's *The Great Tradition.* The most satisfying of our readings, however, was Paul Armstrong's chapter on "The Ontology of Society" from *The Challenge of Bewilderment.* Other approaches included David Ward's essay on the "Problem of Identity," I. S. Talib's on the "Reader's Understanding of Anachronic Narratives," and particularly Nicholas Visser's fine discussion of "Crowds and Politics," Armstrong's chapter especially bridged the gap between our poor understanding and Conrad's genius: first, because he managed a comprehensive analysis of Conrad's breadth of canvas, his "wide, generous net;" and, second, because his exposition of the contradictory elements embedded in contingency, belief, semantics and historical horizons linked up with similar issues he already had treated in his criticism of *The Secret Agent* and *Lord Jim,* all providing a sort of "Armstrongian" motif not unfamiliar at this juncture in the course. Other than the powerful ironic enigmas and changing perspectives in the novel raised by the critical literature, the items of most interest to the class were: 1/ the symbolic, or sacramental, centrality of the silver mine; 2/ the character and suicide of Decoud; 3/ the corruption of Nostromo; and, for those who had finished the assignment, 4/ the questionable portrayal of the two sisters, Linda and Giselle. We also wondered briefly about the significance and relationship between the nomenclature of Nostromo as "our man" and Marlow's Jim as "one of us" – whether or not, that is, the two expressions evoked comparable resonances of meaning and irony.

The Golden Bowl was a wee bit more successful, although we never re-ascended to quite the heights of our discussion of *The Ambassadors*. The presence of a strong effective woman in Maggie Verver was most appealing, even though, just like the critics, there were some division in class as to whether she was all-for-love or else demonic, a question recalling Fleda Vetch, the so-called "free spirit," who, unlike Maggie, is unable to triumph in *The Spoils of Poynton*. As befits the nineties, however, no-one in this class condemned, or even considered condemning, Charlotte Stant, which led me to inform them that, had we read instead *The Wings of the Dove,* they probably would have ignored James and elevated aggressive, manipulative Kate Croy over saintly Milly Theale! Their benign view of Charlotte Stant did prejudice them, I thought, against the good features of Daniel Fogel's argument in *Henry James and the Structure of the Romantic Imagination*. As with Fogel's book, I had tended by now to assign a number of the same critics we had read for *The Ambassadors,* to see how their arguments applied to *The Golden Bowl*. This was especially crucial for Ruth Yeazell and for McWhirter's *Desire and Love,* whose theses really do build toward *The Golden Bowl* but the same procedure also helped fill out the arguments of Susan Griffith, Nicola Bradbury and Mark Seltzer – whom he had not revisited since *The Princess Casamassima*. We also considered Virginia Fowler's *Henry James's American Girl:...,* Dale Bauer's *Feminist Dialogics* and Christof Wegelin's *The Image of Europe....* Finally, we looked at a couple of essays, one by Daniel Brudney on the novel's "Moral Philosophy" and another by Arlene Young, an excellent one, on the novel's use of "Hypothetical Discourse." At the end of the day, I believe I convinced at least a few of them that *The Golden Bowl* really is James's equivalent to Joyce's *Ulysses,* a towering work, and one that elicits more discussion than any other James novel except whatever one just happens to be the present seat of controversy in his fiction – these days it is *The Bostonians*; it used to be *The Turn of the Screw*.

The final unit in the course, on Conrad's *Chance* followed by a sort of extended epilogue session on "The Secret Sharer," *The*

Turn of the Screw and "The Jolly Corner" was a case of utter failure followed by rather surprising success. I am sorry to report that the failure was with *Chance*. There was just no interest in or discussion of it, despite the return of Marlow – not even from my very best students. After some probing, I finally discerned that they were now all working on their longer term papers, due shortly at the end of the semester, and therefore had not time whatever to read the book itself. Faced with their silence and lack of preparation, I read to them several passages from James's tepid – if that is the right word – assessment of *Chance* from *The New Novel* or "The Younger Generation," as it was first called. Since *Chance* appeared to be an application of James's very own method of multiplied perspectives and self-reflexivity, his poor opinion of it, his damning with faint praise, struck us as rather peculiar. I tried to point out that James himself had "circled round and round" Milly Theale by a succession of narrative centers in *The Wings of the Dove,* so why not Conrad with the character of Flora? But then again, James also believed that that "circling" method created his structural problem, his "misplaced pivot," in *The Wings of the Dove.* And yet again, since these students did not know *The Wings of the Dove,* nor, in effect, *Chance,* their interest drooped. They could respond, however, to Conrad's profound personal disappointment and pain at James's adverse judgement of the work. On a different tack, I mentioned briefly, along with Herbert Klein's contention in "Charting the Unknown," that Marlow had so evolved in his understanding of women from "Heart of Darkness" through "Youth" and *Lord Jim* to *Chance* that his last viewpoint arguably reversed that of "Heart of Darkness." This idea did very much interest my students; it even allowed them to recall Marlow's encounter with Jewel in *Lord Jim* from a somewhat different perspective.

Our final class was an extended meeting during exam week, and their demeanor was very bright, probably because the course was ending, but presumably out of enthusiasm after reading "The Secret Sharer," which they did dutifully in reparation for recent sins with *Chance. The Turn of the Screw* they already

knew, and a number of them even discovered that they indeed
had read "The Jolly Corner" before and forgot to mention it at
the beginning of the course. I told them that, even though there
was truly superb scholarship on these three shorter works, they
did not have to read or report on any of it for this final class. It
was an upbeat session, in which we touched on the close ties
between *The Turn of the Screw* and "Heart of Darkness" the two
nested narratives with Conradian intermediate narrators, especially in view of Conrad's high opinion of James's tale which
he described much as *we* would describe "Heart of Darkness,"
that it "evades one, but leaves a kind of phosphorescent trail in
one's mind." Preliminary discussion of alter egos in these two
works led us into an energetic interchange regarding the authors'
terrific conceptions of alter egoism in the two later tales,
especially the psychoanalytic density achieved through their
different narrative choices. These students felt to a person that
"The Secret Sharer" and "The Jolly Corner" were vintage
masterpieces, and I felt the class running on its highest voltage
since the time of *Lord Jim* and *The Ambassadors*. They marvelled
not only at the social issues condensed in the two stories but at
certain resonant symbolic details, like the marker-hat in Conrad
or the image of the concave crystal bowl in James; I felt, almost
blissfully, that we were examining the equivalent of poetry or else
Beethoven's Quartets.

Fortunately the course ended on this high note, but it did have
its periodic "downs," as I have tried to convey. In what remains,
I wish to make some brief comments about this teaching
experience as a whole. One regret was that we spent too little time
on the biographical background of James's friendship with
Conrad as well as their common literary milieu. Partly this was
because the students by their own insistent admission were not
knowledgeable of the literature, much less any criticism, and
I felt they should place their effort in that area. Another reason,
perhaps a related one, is that I do not have the sense that these
two authors ever had the sort of symbiotic relationship found
most obviously, say, in Wordsworth and Coleridge, Hawthorne
and Melville, or Eliot and Pound. Even so, had the class been

better read in the authors' works and had I myself possessed a more subtle command of their personal and social milieu, something very worthwhile might have resulted. But neither the class nor I was sufficiently proficient. We did, however, read together Conrad's eloquent essay on "Henry James: An Appreciation," in his *Notes on Life and Letters,* and I tried to explicate some of its chief ideas in connection with James's later dramas of consciousness and renunciation alongside Conrad's probing of life's enigma found preeminently with Marlow. In that powerful essay, Conrad's provocative use of the term "temperament" in art especially interested me. It is a concept that rightly defines James's deep grasp of individual character and also, on his American side, one that goes back to Emerson's meditation in the essay "Experience," where "temperament" is designated one of the "Lords of Life." Although, as I say, we spent too little time on biographical background, I did ask one of the students with a particular prior interest to report on Jonathan Freedman's book *Professions of Taste,* dealing with British and American Aestheticism, in order to glean some literary ambience during the period of the works we read.

A real plus from this course, for me, certainly, was the occasion to read a number of essays in both *The Conradian* and *Conradiana.* I was familiar with the Don Holliday award--winning work published in *Henry James Review,* such as Barry Stampfl's essay "Mapping Conjecture in James and Conrad" (which we also noted in class), but this course gave me the opportunity to discover the excellent criticism found in those two Conrad journals.

I have already mentioned the student who eventually became interested in Charles Sanders Peirce by way of the two Jameses, William and Henry; but another vein that loomed more and more important as the semester progressed was that of the spiritual and moral kinship of both James and Conrad to Graham Greene. James and Greene have long been an interest of mine, I confess, but it seemed to me that Greene's critical analysis of James articulated elements that attached mutually to both James and Conrad, elements which they themselves never

articulated about each other's work – certainly James never did.
In any event, we took a bit of time in class for Greene's "Henry
James, The Private Universe," but we read it contextually with
respect not only to James but also to Conrad, and with an
awareness of the acknowledged power of *The Secret Agent*, for
instance, directly on Greene.

There were likewise some special interests of particular
students that became better refined in the course of the term. For
instance, one student entered the class with a great love of film
and a vague wish to work in that area. By the end of the semester,
she determined she would examine various film versions of
James's fiction later on in her Ph. D. programme; but the sort of
topic that augmented her interests and assisted this process was
the adaptation of *The Secret Agent* into Alfred Hitchcock's film
Sabotage – as distinct from his other film *Saboteur*.

On the whole, therefore, I believe this course to have been
worthwhile, although, as I said at the beginning, my grasp of
Conrad remains disproportionately low compared to James,
more so than I had reckoned with before I began the class. At the
same time, I was quite gratified by those students who said they
had now become fans of James or Conrad after this course: one
student in particular, who is an exceptional poet, wrote her
longer paper comparing *The Secret Agent* with the work of
Raymond Chandler, including some discussion of Agatha
Christie and Dorothy Sayers. I was pleased that someone with
those interests felt she had become a new fan of both James and
Conrad.

For me, however, the principal exciting and governing idea
between these two great writers remained perhaps the most
obvious one, the way the two of them configure or reconfigure
modernity. They convey the mindscapes of modernity, the
crossover in emphasis from the subject as interpreter to the
subject and perceiver's mind in its own reflexive activity and
agency; to the observer as subject as much as, or more than, what
he or she observes. In *The Turn of the Screw,* for instance,
Douglas reads in a drawing-room, re-enacting the attempt of
Apollonian civilization to control Dionysiac primitive energy

– a situation analogous to Marlow's in the *Nellie* in Conrad's tale published the next year. And both Marlow and the Governess subsequently become imprisoned by the nightmare of their choice. The mindscapes of modernity and even post-modernity created by the re-situating art of James and Conrad work in much the same way as does modern and expressionist painting, wherein the viewer's gaze weaves a pattern to complete, or as Paul Armstrong prefers to write, "construe" the meaning. I suspect that any time I try to teach James and Conrad together, this type of issue will remain for me the quintessential one, even though the precise articulation of it frequently seems elusive to our kernels of formulation and instead envelops the consonance and parallelism between the two writers much as – and I quote from "Heart of Darkness" – "a glow brings out a haze, in the likeness of one of these misty halos that sometimes are made visible by the spectral illumination of moonshine" (*YS*, 48). In regard to their shared content, that "spectral moonshine" so emblematic of the Jamesian "imagination of disaster" and the Conradian "destructive element" also links these two backward to their respective countrymen Hawthorne and Coleridge – but that would be another course.

WORKS CITED

Achebe Chinua. "An Image of Africa," *Massachusetts Review*, 18 (1977), 782-94.

Armstrong Paul B. *The Challenge of Bewilderment*. Ithaca: Cornell U. P., 1987.

Armstrong Paul B. *The Phenomenology of Henry James*. Chapel Hill: U. of North Carolina P., 1983.

Armstrong Paul B. "The Politics of Irony in Reading Conrad," *Conradiana*, 26: 2-3 (1994), 85-101.

Bauer Dale M. *Feminist Dialogics*. Albany: State U. of New York P., 1988.

Bradbury Nicola. *Henry James: The Later Novels*. Oxford: Clarendon P., 1979.

Brudney Daniel. "Knowledge and Silence: *The Golden Bowl* and Moral Philosophy," *Critical Inquiry*, 16 (1990), 397-437.

Conrad Joseph. "Heart of Darkness," (1899), Norton Critical Edition, ed. Richard Kimbrough. New York: W. W. Norton, 1971.

Conrad Joseph. *Nostromo* (1904), ed. Keith Carabine. Oxford: Oxford World Classics, 1984.

Esch Deborah. "Promissory Notes: The Prescription of the Future in *The Princess Casamassima*," *American Literary History*, 1: 2 (1989), 317-38.

Fogel Daniel Mark. *Henry James and the Structure of the Romantic Imagination.* Baton Rouge: Louisiana State U. P., 1981.

Fowler Virginia C. *Henry James's American Girl: The Embroidery on the Canvas.* Madison, WI: U. of Wisconsin P., 1984.

Freedman Jonathan. *Professions of Taste: Henry James. British Aestheticism and Commodity Culture.* Stanford, CA: Stanford U. P., 1990.

Greene Graham. "The Private Universe," in Graham Greene *The Lost Childhood and Other Essays.* New York: Viking P., 1951, 21-30.

Griffin Susan. *The Historical Eye: The Texture of the Visual in Late James.* Boston: Northeastern U. P., 1991.

Habegger Alfred. *Henry James and the "Woman Business."* New York: Cambridge U. P., 1989.

Hocks Richard A. *Henry James and the Pragmatistic Thought: A Study in the Relationship Between the Philosopher William James and the Literary Art of Henry James.* Chapel Hill: U. of North Carolina P., 1974.

Hocks Richard A. *Henry James: A Study of the Short Fiction.* Boston: Twayne Publishers, 1990.

Holland Lawrence. *The Expanse of Vision; Essays on the Craft of Henry James.* Princeton, NJ: Princeton U. P., 1964.

James Henry. "The New Novel," in *Henry James Literary Criticism: Essays on Literature, American Writers, English Writers.* New York: Library of America, 1984, 124-59.

Klein Herbert G. "Charting the Unknown: Conrad, Marlow, and the World of Women," *Conradiana*, 20: 2 (1988), 147-57.

Leavis F. R. *The Great Tradition.* London: Chatto and Windus, 1954.

Marle Hans van and Lefranc Pierre. "Ashore and Afloat: New Perspectives on Topography and Geography in *Lord Jim*," *Conradiana*, 20: 2 (1988), 109-35.

McWhirter David. *Desire and Love in Henry James.* New York: Cambridge U. P., 1989.

Mongia Padmini. "Narrative Strategy and Imperialism in Conrad's *Lord Jim*," *Studies in the Novel*, 24: 2 (1992), 173-86.

Nettels Elsa. *James and Conrad.* Athens: U. of Georgia P., 1977.

Rivkin Julie. "The Logic of Delegation in *The Ambassadors*," *PMLA*, 101 (1986), 819-31.

Rowe John Carlos. *The Theoretical Dimensions in Henry James.* Madison, WI: U. of Wisconsin P., 1984.

Seltzer Mark. *Henry James and the Art of Power.* Ithaca: Cornell U. P., 1984.

Stampfl Barry. "Marlow's Rhetoric of (Self-)Deception in 'Heart of Darkness'," *Modern Fiction Studies*, 37: 2 (1991), 183-96.

Stampfl Barry. "Mapping Conjecture in Henry James and Joseph Conrad: A Stylistics Approach," *Henry James Review*, 14: 1 (1993), 99-114.

Sypher Eileen. "Anarchism and Gender: James's *The Princess Casamassima* and Conrad's *The Secret Agent*," *Henry James Review*, 9: 1 (1988), 1-16.

Talib I. S. "Conrad's *Nostromo* and the Reader's Understanding of Anachronic Narratives," *Journal of Narrative Technique*, 20: 1 (1990), 1-21.

Trilling Lionel. *The Liberal Imagination: Essays on Literature and Society.* Garden City, NY: Doubleday, 1953.

Visser Nicholas. "Crowds and Politics in *Nostromo*," *Mosaic*, 23: 2 (1990), 1-15.

Ward David Allen. "'An Ideal Conception:' Conrad's *Nostromo* and the Problem of Identity," *English Literature in Transition (1880-1920)*, 35: 3 (1992), 288-98.

Wegelin Christof. *The Image of Europe in Henry James.* Dallas: Southern Methodist U. P., 1958.

Yeazell Ruth B. *Language and Knowledge in the Late Novels of Henry James.* Chicago: U. of Chicago P., 1976.

Young Arlene. "Hypothetical Discourse as Fichelle in *The Golden Bowl*," *American Literature*, 61 (1989), 382-97.

Part II

Conrad, James and Other Relations

Hugh Epstein,
London, England

Victory's Marionettes: Conrad's Revisitation of Stevenson

I

Robert Louis Stevenson seems to have acted upon Conrad like some sort of irritant. Whilst Stevenson's apparent facility in writing earned Conrad's grudging admiration, it also provoked an envious rancor of the sort which recently led Jeanette Winterson to dub him, with some justice, "the Salieri of letters."[1] The first mention of Stevenson in Conrad's letters is in connection with W. E. Henley's consideration of *The Nigger of the "Narcissus"* for publication in *New Review* in 1896. Conrad writes to Ted Sanderson: "Next week I shall hear from Henley and let you know what the patron of Kipling and Stevenson thinks" (*CL,* I, 320). The faintly ironic edge here announces a distance that Conrad will maintain even as he seeks acceptance; and when, writing to Henley himself two years later, he says, "RLS – Dumas – these are big names" (II, 107), one cannot be sure that there is not some ironic deprecation playing below the apparent homage. However, Conrad can also use his irony to acknowledge Stevenson's achievements. When Ford proposed to print the dates of the beginning and the end of the composition of *Romance,* Conrad felt this would scarcely redound to their joint credit and used the example of Stevenson to say so. He speaks of "sneers at those two men who took 6 yrs to write 'this very ordinary tale' whereas RLS single handed produced his masterpieces" (III, 59). Conrad may not have thought them masterpieces, but he knew they had the popularity he craved and that they were written with an apparently effortless speed he could never command. And four years later, in 1907, Conrad, as so often, apologizes defensively to Pinker for his slowness by saying, "I wish I had that careless sunny nature

189

people talk of in connection with Stevenson. But then Stevenson perhaps – but never mind" (428). This half-declared mixture of envy, condescension and contempt hints at a lasting entanglement with Stevenson: and by examining one particular, undeclared, engagement with the earlier writer's work, I hope to illuminate an aspect of the art of *Victory* to indicate just how persistent a figure in Conrad's literary landscape Stevenson was, and what he made of him.

Conrad's other references to Stevenson in his letters are far more openly disparaging. When he wishes to insist upon the difficulty of serious composition, Conrad finds Stevenson a convenient butt for his sense of injury and neglect. So he complains to Pinker in 1902, "I am no sort of airy R. L. Stevenson who considered his art a prostitute and the artist as no better than one" (II, 371). And it is clearly Stevenson of whom Conrad is thinking when he writes to Pinker in January 1908, "I have no charm, no flow of wit or of facetiousness or mere patter to fill in chinks with. I have only a mind a quite different gift from the gift of the gab. I have no literary tradition even which will help me to spin phrases – the chewed up silly phrases." One can hear Conrad bolstering hurt pride by fashioning an image of lonely heroism to the point at which he can turn the implicit comparison explicit: "I am not a 'Sedulous Ape.' I wish sometimes I were" (IV, 21). Laurence Davies reminds us that "Stevenson confessed to his sedulous aping of dead writers in *Memories and Portraits,* Chapter 4." This one-sided battle with Stevenson (who had, after all, been dead for fifteen years by this time) seems to have exercised Conrad particularly in the early months of 1908 when he was writing "Razumov," the work of Conrad's most concerned with personal identity. In February he writes to Ford praising *The Heart of the Country,* and his antagonism to Stevenson breaks out memorably in the exclamation, "That anybody could mention, in connection with you, that Virtuoso Cymballist Stevenson passed my comprehension" (47). That image of Stevenson as a talented performer – but a performer only, and thus bearing the implication that Conrad by comparison was the true laborer in the field of composition – surfaces in a letter to Knopf in 1913, when he asserts, "When it comes to popularity, I stand much nearer the public mind than Stevenson who was superliterary, a conscious virtuoso of style."[2] Stevenson seems to have cast a long shadow for Conrad which he somewhat disingenuously turns to his own uses. When Conrad wishes to deny his fears (of being unpopular, or of being an over-literary stylist), an image of Stevenson can supply what he wishes to deride or to dismiss.

The Stevenson that Conrad represents in his letters is the early writer of romances who wanted to be popular and considered that his duty was his pleasure, which was simply to entertain. Whilst it is clear that it was important for Conrad's ideal construction of himself as a serious artist to distance himself from this popular conception of Stevenson, covertly he must have perceived how closely some of Stevenson's preoccupations resembled his own. They are both persistent writers about fathers and sons. In their own lives they both had to struggle against crushing paternal legacies, though very different ones. "The Story of a Lie," "The Misadventures of John Nicholson" and, of course, *Weir of Hermiston* represent Stevenson's progressive attempts to deal with his relationship with his father through fiction. And Conrad returns again and again to the damage inflicted upon the son by the absent, distant or surrogate father: Mr Gould and Charles Gould, Mr Verloc and Stevie, Prince K– and Razumov, Carleon and Captain Anthony, the elder Heyst and the younger. The brutal manner in which the necessities of survival sometimes enjoin us to struggle with a second or related self, had been depicted by Stevenson through three penetrating literary doubles – Dr Jekyll and Mr Hyde, James and Henry Durie, Archie Weir and his father Adam, Lord Hermiston. These are paired figures who need, or who are possessed by one another to the point of destruction: Mr Hyde and the Master of Ballantrae prey upon their milder counterparts; their fierce energy, like that of the hanging judge Lord Hermiston, will not be denied. In "The Lagoon," "Karain," "The Duel," Conrad explores the same terrain through the motif of pursuit; Marlow's struggle is to understand his loyalty to the dark heart represented by Kurtz and to the fair promise gone rotten represented by Jim: both remain haunting presences whose stories are his story and mere repudiation would be self-betrayal; the captain must both save and release the outlaw Leggatt; Razumov is brought to confess his betrayal of Haldin and, in so doing, to find his loyalty to this lonely brother-spirit who has, it seems, so unfairly claimed him; the scepticism of Heyst must confront the scepticism of Mr Jones in mutual destructiveness. It is not difficult to see how Stevenson's fictional exploration of the unacknowledged connections between men sounds a strong resonance in so much of Conrad's work.

To be working in the same area of experience, however, is not necessarily to owe a debt to a predecessor. Stevenson's achievements with narrative supply a more certain pointer to artistic influence, for all Conrad's denials. In *The Master of Ballantrae,* for instance, the sense that what we are reading is a product of its telling is inscribed in the use of the three narrators, Ephraim Mackellar, Francis Burke and John Mountain. But more particularly, the device of having a fussy, cautious, rational man to be the prime participant narrator in a tale of violent deeds, high passion and supernatural mysteriousness must surely have been interesting to the creator of Captain Mitchell, the teacher of languages, the Marlow of *Chance,* and of Davidson. Although Conrad chose to maintain an image of Stevenson as careless and flippant about art, it was Stevenson who wrote tellingly of the art of narration in his "Humble Remonstrance" to Henry James (*Longman's,* December 1884): "Literature....So far as it imitates at all, it imitates not life but speech: not the facts of human destiny, but the emphasis and the suppressions with which the human actor tells of them."

As far back as his collaboration with Fanny on *The Dynamiter* (1885), Stevenson's interest in multiple narrators, or multiple focalizers of the narrative, begins to lend unsettling perspectives to adventure tales. The nature of that disturbance to a genre which generally offered confirmation to a readership of English gentlemen or army officers is the critical issue that demands consideration in connection with Conrad. *The Beach at Falesa* has long earned critical currency as "Conradian" because its subject matter, a ruthless struggle to monopolize trade, so conspicuously prefigures *Almayer's Folly, An Outcast of the Islands,* "An Outpost of Progress" and "Heart of Darkness;" and its cast of opportunistic and criminal adventurer-traders so clearly belongs to the same world as that which Conrad depicts. However, the narrative achievement is equally pregnant for Conrad's art, if not more so. Andrea White, in her discussion of *Almayer's Folly,* raises the issue of "monologic telling, shaped by the popular travel writing and adventure fiction of the day and by such influential periodicals as *The Illustrated London News, The Graphic* and *Blackwood's Magazine.*" She claims that Conrad's "insistence upon multiple story tellers disrupt(s) the authorial centre, and interrupt(s) the monologic repetitions of the white man's story, marking the demise of the dream those tellings shaped."[3] Whilst *The Beach at Falesa* offers a conspicuously monologic telling in the mouth of the white trader Wiltshire, the monologic vision and judgement upon people and events is radically modified by the voice in the text sounding against the received rhetoric of the genre: the full force of Stevenson's tale relies upon this irony to produce two voices out of one, and a corresponding uncertainty of final judgement on the part of the reader. It would be a paradigm text in which to study what Bakhtin calls "the internal dialogism of the word (which occurs in a monologic utterance as well as in a rejoinder)." Bakhtin's assertion that "The prose artist...creates artistically calculated nuances on all the fundamental voices and tones of this (social) heteroglossia"[4] offers the perfect introduction to the aspects of both Stevenson's and Conrad's art that I wish to highlight; the interesting point is how differently, as artists, they locate this heteroglossia and calculate their nuances. In a voice subtly touched with class inflections quite beyond Conrad's scope, Stevenson maintains Wiltshire's coarsened imperialist sensibility to the end, yet wins the reader's assent to his brutal actions in revenging himself on his fellow trader Case for the latter's earlier destruction of two white traders and wounding of Wiltshire's island wife Uma. However, if Wiltshire

learns commitment to a people and a place, he is not a reconstructed figure at the end as he looks forward with relief to being
able to move to a different island and abandon his pledge that he
will "deal fairly with the natives:" "I was half glad when the firm
moved me on to another station, where I was under no kind of
a pledge and could look my balances in the face" (169).[5] As
exemplified in the wit of the last phrase, Stevenson's positioning
of the reader in many places between admiration and contempt
for Wiltshire is masterly; the story reveals him as the great realist
depictor of the colonial situation and far from the Virtuoso
Cymballist of Conrad's dismissal. It is a story, of course, of the
greatest interest to readers of *Victory,* where the gentlemanly and
refined sensibility of Heyst prevents the decisive action of which
the reader might have approved.

II

Conrad, however, owes a much more specific debt to Stevenson
than the inheritance of a subtly altered terrain of psychological
and adventure fiction from which so many later writers could
profit. *The Ebb Tide,* written in collaboration with Lloyd
Osbourne and published in the year of Stevenson's death, 1894,
against the advice of his (and later Conrad's) friend, Sidney
Colvin, is the work of Stevenson's that recurred to his memory
and imagination most often.[6] As Stevenson's most pitiless
exposure of the illusions men construct in the pursuit of the ideal
construction of the self, this constant yet concealed revisitation is
scarcely surprising. That Conrad *did* use the prompting of
Stevenson's work has been established by Robert Hampson in
his essay "*Chance* and the Secret Life" in which he points out the
features of plot shared between *Chance* and Stevenson's story
"The Pavilion on the Links" from *New Arabian Nights* (1882).[7]
If we were to subject *The Ebb Tide* to proper comparative
analysis we would not have to excavate very far before we found
vestigial representations of its features in *The Nigger of the
"Narcissus," Lord Jim* and "The End of the Tether." Stevenson's

London clerk Huish, "who called himself sometimes Hay and
sometimes Tomkins, and laughed at the discrepancy" (*The Ebb
Tide*, 177), is a clear literary forerunner to Donkin, as has been
pointed out by Andrea White, Jenni Calder and, indeed, by
Harold Frederic, who reviewed *The Nigger of the "Narcissus"*
for the *Saturday Review* in 1898.[8] The central drama of *The Ebb
Tide* lies in Robert Herrick's loss of honor and the possibility of
his redemption, a drama which parallels that of *Lord Jim* too
closely for Conrad to have been unaware of it in all the groaning
labors of his composition. In both novels, Jim and Herrick seek
a rescue from dishonor on their respective islands: Herrick's
appeal to Attwater, "Can you do anything with me?," sounding
very much like Marlow's appeal on Jim's behalf to Stein. Both
men are found out by "gentlemen," that is Gentleman Brown
and Attwater himself; and the play with the notion of the
gentleman extends to "The End of the Tether" in which Captain
Whalley deceives himself that he has not fallen below the
standard of gentlemanly conduct until finally he is forced to
reflect that "The light had ebbed forever from the world."[9] In
practice, for all his high-mindedness, Whalley's sin is that of
Robert Herrick of *The Ebb Tide* who "had complied with the ebb
tide in man's affairs and the tide had carried him away" (257).
Conrad's tones are darker: "the world" is a grander image than
"man's affairs;" and we might propose a reversal of the usual
account, in that, rather than Conrad finding in Stevenson the
romantic adventure tale which he appropriates in the service of
a more searching examination of human motives, it is Conrad
who is the more romantic in his reworking of certain shared
motifs, whilst Stevenson serves up, as had his fictional Captain
Davis in order to chasten Huish, "a plain man's masterpiece of
the sardonic" (283).

But it is in *Victory,* Conrad's examination of the evolutionary
blind alley represented by the refined sensibilities of the gentleman, that *The Ebb Tide* resurfaces to provide a fundamental
structure for at least one part of the novel. There are three sorts
of literary influence at work in *Victory*. First are those that create
it as an intertextual novel – most significantly *The Tempest,*

Hamlet, Villiers de L'Isle Adam's *Axel,* and, in a different
manner, Schopenhauer's *The World as Will and Idea.* The
reader's pleasure is heightened when he recognizes these strains
in the measure that the novel gains scope and resonance by these
interactions with other enquiries in the same field of experience.
Second are the specific aids to composition – borrowings of
phrases and ideas from Maupassant and Anatole France (as
Paul Kirschner and Owen Knowles have shown).[10] These are of
interest to scholars who wish to understand Conrad's working
methods in the construction of his novel, but surely they are not
features he would have hoped to see recognized. Third are works
perhaps only flickeringly present to Conrad's consciousness,
whose scenarios he glances at again in writing his own novel,
works whose terrain he uses as a literary anchorage, as if in the
security provided by their literary precedent he can allow the
memories of his own experience to evolve into something more
rich and strange. And perhaps one should say that behind these
lies again the pervasive shaping example of Dickens, whose zest
for grotesque comic deformity animates Conrad's writing too.
    The Ebb Tide is of this third kind, not a source like
Maupassant's *Fort Comme La Mort* from which Conrad directly
borrowed phrases and ideas, but one that cleared some ground
for new sorts of artistic expression. Stevenson's story is a masterly depiction of class antagonisms as played out in the colonial
Pacific misadventure. Its technical achievement, quite different
from Conrad's whether in *Victory* or elsewhere, arises from his
mobile, acebric yet always receptive observation of motivation
and interaction. To use Andrea White's term, there is no
monologic telling from a position of moral rectitude – whether
that of gentleman (or woman) or honest artisan, the two fixed
points to be inherited from the nineteenth-century novel – and
a reader's judgement on the proceedings arises almost entirely
from an encounter with the presented drama with only rare
promptings from an authorial center. Whilst in one sense this is
no more than Wayne Booth's old distinction between telling and
showing, its subversive quality within the genre of colonial
adventure fiction needs emphasizing in order to make clear the
very different sort of artistic destabilization at work in *Victory.*

The Ebb Tide takes three types, Herrick, the disgraced gentleman, Davis, the disgraced and criminal captain, and Huish, the cocky clerk who won't reveal his past, and observes them in a common fight for survival that strips each one of his pretensions. While the text primarily invites us to share the perspective of the gentleman Herrick, the moral authority of his vision ebbs as the story proceeds, and Stevenson's powers of verisimilitude compel the reader to share the viewpoint of each participant even as the moral degradation of the whole "adventure" invites a pitiless detachment. Whilst Herrick offers the perspective of individual honor, and Davis that of pragmatic energy, into Huish is written, Thersites-like, an ironic commentary debased to cynicism. For instance, after Davis has earned the threesome a meal by playing the concertina to a ship's crew of Kanakas, and then been ejected by the Scopts captain, Herrick flings himself on the ground:

> "Don't speak to me, don't speak to me. I can't stand it," broke from him.
> The other two stood over him perplexed.
> "Wot can't stand now?" said the clerk. "Asn't he 'ad a meal? *I'm* lickin' my lips."
> Herrick reared up his wild eyes and burning face. "I can't beg!" he screamed, and again threw himself prone.
> "This thing's got to come to an end," said the captain, with an intake of breath.
> "Looks like signs of an end, don't it?" sneered the clerk. (188)

The nature of that "end" is the ground of enquiry that both links and separates Stevenson and Conrad. The fiction of a gentleman's adventure cannot recover from this sort of assault; in *The Ebb Tide* Stevenson so thoroughly evacuates a fictional territory which we may have thought he pretty well owned, that in *Victory* Conrad can comically, ironically reinhabit it with an exhausted cast of make-believe desperadoes and a weary recluse without destroying a genre, but indebted to a great work of realism which had already altered it irreparably for serious artists. There was something already achieved to stylize.

In *The Ebb Tide* Stevenson's obsession with the nature of the gentleman receives its final expression and perhaps its death--blow. The tale shows us not the romance of travel, the sea or even of illusions, but an inheritance embracing clerk, captain and gentleman (including the so-gentlemanly Attwater when we meet him) of rootless knavery. Uneasily united on a schooner they propose to steal, they discover that half the cargo of champagne is in fact water. Davis pieces out the plot of which they have become an unwitting part: the American merchant has paid the previous captain to lose the ship so he can collect the insurance money for a full cargo of champagne. The enormity of the crime is conveyed in Davis's calm reflection, "If you're going to lose a ship, I would ask no better myself than a Kanaka crew" (228). As in *Lord Jim*, but even more cynically so, non-whites are simply an invisible expenditure. Stevenson is uncompromising in his depiction of the colonial trading inheritance and allows no moral agency to Herrick beyond hollow protest. Davis' drunken lavishness has run the stores of the schooner so low that it will be impossible for them to make a landfall. Faced again with a struggle for survival the trio's association is exposed as being purely vicious. Huish mocks Davis tellingly, concluding with a broad threat which prefigures one of the watchwords of the amiable faithful retainer, Martin Ricardo: "You droor it mild, John Dyvis; don't 'andle me: I'm dyngerous" (233). Herrick's new-found allegiance to Captain Davis entails this gentlemanly admonition to Huish:

> "I hope I shall die very soon; but I have not the least objection to killing you before I go. I should prefer it so; I should do it with no more remorse than winking. Take care – take care, you little cad!"
> The animosity with which these words were uttered was so marked in itself, and so remarkable in the man who uttered them, that Huish stared.... (233)

The animosity arises from the gentleman discovering his own impotence once he has been named, as Huish has just done by calling him a "stuck-up sneering snob." The trio are at the point of complete fracture. Davis humiliated and Herrick and Huish declared as class enemies, when land is sighted, Attwater's improbable island.

The subtitle of *The Ebb Tide* is "A Trio and a Quartette," which hints at what the writer of the allegorical *Victory* found to inspire him in the earlier realist text. Conrad's trio of thirst--crazed desperadoes arrive at an island – retreat to encounter a gentleman as disconcerting in his distant civility as is Attwater in his prescient power. Having dropped his frame narrator and Davidson in Part 2 Chapter 2, Conrad seems in need of some artistic invention to shape Heyst's forced encounter with the world. He takes the geometric configuration provided by Stevenson's tale and exactly reverses the focalization: instead of encountering Attwater from the point of view of those landing, the reader is invited to share Heyst's uncomprehending gaze as it rests upon the three grotesque voyagers; Attwater is armed both as a Christian militant and as a crack shot with a rifle, whilst Heyst is disarmed by a scepticism which robs him of all "force and conviction," and also literally by Wang when he robs Heyst of his revolver; the self-composure of Attwater's command of the situation casually delivered in his "I have some information which you think I might impart, and I think not" (245), is replaced in Conrad's redrawing of the confrontation by Heyst's bewilderment at this fantastic invasion as he is quite unable to perceive what its motive could be. The ambiguity of Herrick's status as the fallen gentleman of the trio is replaced by the more fundamental ambiguity of the nature of "plain Mr Jones," the gentleman-adventurer of *his* trio; Attwater's hatred of women is displaced onto Mr Jones rather than transferred intact to Heyst; Huish's cockney may have had a part to play in the formation of Ricardo as already hinted, though a clearer connection is provided by the function of each in his respective trio as the wielder of underworld, as opposed to gentlemanly, violence; *The Ebb Tide* offers no prototype for Pedro as he is not a creature of Stevenson's social class depiction but rather of the evolutionary chain which Conrad makes of it. In addition to these reversals and variations a single more verbal echo suggests the kind of compositional impetus Conrad might have been given by a recollection of *The Ebb Tide*: the three still on board their schooner *The Fallarone* await "in a perfect vacancy of mind, the coming of the stranger who might mean so much to them. They had no plan, no story prepared; there was no time to make one" (240). So when Conrad's trio have refreshed themselves with water at Heyst's jetty, Ricardo is similarly unprepared for the strange encounter: "At that precise moment he had no explanation ready for the man on the wharf, who, as he guessed, must be wondering much more at the presence of his visitors than at their plight" (*V, 232*).

Whilst the reminiscence may be more conceptual than verbal, the similarities are too pronounced to be overlooked as coincidental. Perhaps Conrad thought so too. The majority of "Author's Note" to *Victory* is taken up with an account of the real life models of Mr Jones, Ricardo and Pedro, concluding with the assertion, "It seems to me but natural that those three buried in a corner of my memory should suddenly get out into the light of the world – so natural that I offer no excuse for their existence" (XV). Surely the combination in which these dark creatures are exposed to the light of readership is as much literary in its prompting as "natural." The feeling that Conrad is here engaged in obscuring the traces of literary antecedents is strengthened by reading Frederick Karl's account of the origins and development of the novel, in which he says, "(a) key image...later cut, is that of deliquescence, of two figures caught in liquid, of pieces of straw floating aimlessly, of the ebbing tide washing away traces of human habitation." Karl talks of Heyst the father's "'ebbing' philosophy" and quotes from Part 1 Chapter 3 of the manuscript:

> And it is also possible that Mr Berg the father would have explained and commented and qualified his laconic advice (that is, "Look on – make no sound") later on if the later on had not slipped away from him in the shade of the night, gently like a receding tide that will have no flood. Like the veriest fools and indeed like every one of us Mr Berg the elder had been taken unawares by the finality of that ebb leaving some worlds unexplained and taking with him some words unspoken – for no one yet has ever said his last word on earth.[11]

This gives an idea of the un-Stevensonian territory into which the resonances of Stevenson's haunting title took Conrad many years later; but we should now look more closely at how they each work the common ground, the encounters of the respective trios with their respective gentlemen.

III

Stevenson's treatment of the encounter puts Attwater in command of the situation immediately, and with a confidence born of physical prowess, proprietorship, class and religious conviction, he sets about turning the unwelcome intrusion to his own advantage with well-bred ease. He has little to do as, after his opening gambit of "'Ope we don't intrude!'" (241), Huish's vanity and lack of affectation or restraint reveals the enterprise in a moment: "We're all equal, all got a lay in the adventure; when it comes to business, I'm as good as 'e (Davis); and what I say is, let's go into the 'ouse and have a lush, and talk it over among pals. We've some prime fizz" (*The Ebb Tide,* 242).

Stevenson perfectly observes the manoeuverings and embarrassments that arise from class recognition and divided allegiances: "The presence of the gentlemen lighted up like a candle the vulgarity of the clerk; and Herrick instinctively, as one shields himself (sic) from pain, made haste to interrupt." Stevenson might be making his own declaration of allegiance in that "one" but, as perhaps the grammar suggests, this authorial center is ill-defended against attack. Herrick having introduced himself under his alias of Hay, Attwater continues:

> "Well! this is a queer place and company for us to meet in, Mr Hay," he pursued, with easy incivility to the others. "But do you bear out....I beg this gentleman's pardon, I really did not catch his name."
> "My name is 'Uish, sir" returned the clerk, and blushed in turn.
> "Ah!" said Attwater. And then turning again to Herrick. "Do you bear out Mr Whish description of your vintage? Or was it only the unaffected poetry of his own nature bubbling up?" (242)

To point out the subtle inflections and sneers of this would be to rob it of its point, which is to be understood perfectly and instantaneously by Robert Herrick and a readership of gentlemen. Yet within the single discourse that operates, engaged as it is dialogically with the centers of power and learning located thousands of miles away from where thé men are standing on a deserted beach, Herrick's ambivalence and Huish's pert persistence keep open the possibilities of discomfiture. "Herrick was embarassed; the silken brutality of their visitor made him blush; that he should be accepted as an equal, and the others pointedly ignored, pleased him in spite of himself, and then ran through his veins in a recoil of anger" (242).

The alignment of the reader is slightly re-adjusted with each addition to the conversation and narrative comment. Attwater invites the trio to dinner, and with sentiments entirely opposed to Heyst's, but which suggest the self-dramatizing, self-allegorizing tones of Mr Jones, he turns to verse:

> "For my voice has been tuned to the note of the gun. That startles the deep when the combat's begun" quoted Attwater, with a smile, which instantly gave way to an air of funereal solemnity. "I shall particularly expect Mr Whish," he continued. "Mr Whish, I trust you understand the invitation?" "I believe you, my boy!" replied the genial Huish. (243)

This, in my reading, is Huish gaining a verbal revenge, but the placing of "genial" allows the line to hang suggestively between naivete and irony.

After Attwater's departure, the hidden agenda is exposed by Davis: "*We've* got no use for that fellow, whatever you may have. He's your kind, he's not ours; he's took to you and he's wiped his boots on me and Huish. Save him if you can!" (247). Ironically, Herrick goes ashore only to experience how lost he is and to find a man already saved by his own conviction, an "Angel of God's wrath," a catcher of souls himself. Conrad, of course, makes this powerful but simple irony more interesting: Heyst imagines himself a saved man in his fastidious withdrawal, only to discover his vulnerability to attack and his inability to defend either himself or Lena. The invading trio treat Heyst with unnecessary caution, comically regarding him as dangerous; the savior, repaying Heyst's earlier rescue of her from the odious Schomberg and the Zangiacomos, is Lena.

Both Robert Kiely (1964) and Jenni Calder (1979) concur in regarding *The Ebb Tide* as an account of Herrick's dilemma of choice;[12] but if this is so, the novella offers no affirming framework to endorse his choice to be saved from crime by a fellow gentleman (who is himself a slave runner) rather than stand in solidarity with his criminal fellow-adventurers. Davis is saved, yet he becomes, as Herrick mocks, "Attwater's spoiled darling and pet penitent" (301), a mockery earned by the final reduction of the pragmatic, maudlin, vicious and resourceful figure he had been to mere mouthing hollowness: "O, why not be one of us? Why not come to Jesus right away, and let's meet in yon beautiful land?" (301) finds no supporting rhetoric in this hard-bitten text. Herrick, equally, is left a morally empty figure: his drifting indifference brings the novella to its inconclusive ending as, after all his agonies, he lights the conflagration that scuppers *The Fallarone* and erases the record of their crime. Heyst's earnest last words and the purifying or apocalyptic flames that light the final dark pages of *Victory* show Conrad reworking the material in the other direction. In *The Ebb Tide* the tyrant Attwater, it would seem, is accorded the victory, though it is not one the reader can enjoy. In fact, the pleasure is likely to have come a little earlier in the way in which the despised and degenerate Huish is allowed further to destabilize and to discomfort in this gentleman's story, I cannot agree with Jenni Calder that he is "so totally repellent" that he makes Herrick's choice to side with Attwater all too easy. Robert Kiely's "even Huish has his charms" is better, but does not go far enough in acknowledging the force of Huish in the story.

When Davis cannot come up with a strategy to kill Attwater, Huish, at first coolly and then with "venemous triumph," instructs him how "Mr J. L. 'Uish will proceed to business" (285). He will kill Attwater by throwing a four-ounce jar of vitriol in his face, from which Davis recoils in horror. What

judgement are we to make? Here is the narrative focalized
through Davis:

> Huish sat there preening his sinister vanity, glorying in his
> precedency in evil; and the villainous courage and readiness of the
> creature shone out of him like a candle from a lantern. Dismay and
> a kind of respect seized hold on Davis in his own despite. (287)

While some readers will find Huish comically diminished in
the implicit comparison with Milton's Satan, certainty of
judgement ebbs away, or shifts uncomfortably, the more we
read. Here is Huish himself:

> Look as long as you like....You don't see any green in my eye! I ain't
> afryde of Attwater, I ain't afryde of you, and I ain't afryde of words.
> You want to kill people, that's wot *you* want; but you want to do it in
> kid gloves and it can't be done that w'y. Murder ain't genteel, it ain't
> easy, it ain't safe, and it tykes a man to do it. 'Ere's the man. (288)

The debased voice utters some home truths that are not
opposed by any equivalently convincing voice from within the
tale. Huish, does not, of course, provide the tale's moral, but like
a true grotesque he takes his revenge on those who would.

IV

To understand the creative transformation that Conrad applies
to his memory of Stevenson's sour comedy, we need to have
some sympathy for those tendencies in Conrad's imagination
which led him to find one of his abiding masters in Dickens. The
extent of Dickens's penetration into Conrad's habits of composition is vividly revealed in this letter to Marguerite Poradowska written in 1891. Conrad projects a feeling of hurt isolation
onto the comically alarming gestural permanency of his dolls in
a way that combines Esther Summerson's maudlin recollections
of her doll with the verve of the grotesque depiction of the
Smallweeds:

> The Punch of my childhood, you know – his spine broken in two, his nose on the floor between his feet; his legs and arms flung out stiffly in that attitude of profound despair, so pathetically droll, of dolls tossed in a corner....He was a faithful friend....He was a gentleman....This evening I seem to be in a corner, spine cracked, nose in the dust. Would you kindly scrape together the poor devil, put him tenderly in your apron, introduce him to your dolls, make him join the dinner party with the others. I can see myself at that banquet from here, nose besmeared with jam, the others watching me with that air of cold astonishment natural to well-made dolls. (*CL*, I, 98)

Six years later, the self-pitying appeal to Poradowska has hardened into an aesthetic that he asserts to another recipient of his most searchingly intimate letters, Cunninghame Graham. Conrad had been reading the Stevenson and Henley play "Admiral Guinea," and whilst he admits that it is his "dark and secret ambition" to write a play himself, he works himself into a stage of "anger and loathing" at the "transparent pretences" of actors. The attempt to create the illusion of real-life through the representation of character by actors disgusts him with its "false light." Then, with a sudden swerve, he writes:

> But I love a marionette show. Marionettes are beautiful – especially those of the old kind with wires, thick as my little finger, coming out of the top of the head. Their impassibility in love, in crime, in mirth, in sorrow, is heroic, superhuman, fascinating. Their rigid violence when they fall upon one another to embrace or to fight is simply a joy to behold. I never listen to the text mouthed somewhere out of sight by invisible men who are here today and rotten tomorrow. I love the marionettes that are without life, that come so near to being immortal! (*CL*, I, 419)[13]

The wonderful word "impassibility" may help to explain Conrad's dedication in *Victory* to the representation of just recognizably human figures who perform the same routine over and over again without giving any of themselves away. So when Davidson encounters Mrs Schomberg he tells us that "she jumped exactly like a figure made of wood, without losing her rigid immobility" (*V*, 39); and the frame-narrator claims, with a relish that recalls the letter just cited, and an ironic latitude never allowed to the fastidious old man: "Nobody had ever suspected her of having a mind....One was inclined to think of her as an It – an automaton, a very plain dummy, with an arrangement for bowing the head at times and smiling stupidly now and then" (40). The marionette motif is irrepressible, disrupting Lena's pathetic tale of her childhood with a gratuitously comic note in her father's demise: "After he had a paralytic stroke, falling over with a crash in the well of a music-hall orchestra during the performance, she had joined the Zangiacomo company. He was now in a home for incurables" (78). The marionette image declares itself explicitly at the moment Jones realizes Ricardo's apostasy and reinterprets the words "on the track" and "on the scent" to mean – of a woman. "Heyst looked on, fascinated by this skeleton in a gay dressing gown, jerkily agitated like a grotesque toy on the end of an invisible string" (389). The coolly self-possessed Mr Jones is revealed as a puppet of his own humor, entirely without self-volition as soon as the spring of his fear and hatred is touched. No enquiry or explanation is possible of a doll that dances to reflex action, and the reader is left to reconcile his laughter and his repugnance as he will.

In contrast to the cloudy shifts of human consciousness (here today and rotten tomorrow) the puppetry of human folly and rapacity is permanent and complete. As opposed to Conrad's delight in this absolute spectacle, Stevenson's account in *An Inland Voyage* tells us "The marionettes made a very dismal entertainment," whilst he feels of all strollers it is actors who embody the romantic impulse of life: "But if a man is only so much of an actor that he can stumble through a farce he is made free of a new order of thoughts....He has gone upon a pilgrimage that will last him his life long, because there is no end to it short of perfection."[14] *The Ebb Tide* gives us a much darker picture, but Herrick, Davis and Huish are at least not derided by the narrative they inhabit as they stumble through their farce.

One of Conrad's hallmarks, however, at least in *The Secret Agent* and *Victory,* is a seemingly gratuitous licence given to the narration to be vindictive at the expense of the characters. It is a means of displaying a most un-Stevensonian feeling for the "ghastly, jocular futility of life" as Conrad expressed it to Cunnighame Graham, an artistic development of the cold astonishment of dolls and the rigid violence of marionettes into a grotesque excess of gesture over interiorization. This gloomy and ferocious sense of humor found its way into art through the example of Dickens's ghastly comic mode with its violent delight in the depiction of the "maimed and distorted." For instance, in an apt moment from *Little Dorrit,* Arthur Clennam, shown his room at the top of the house by Flintwinch, encounters "a washing stand that looked as if it had stood for ages in a hail of dirty soapsuds," a phrase quite wonderful for the brutal swiftness with which silent immobility opens upon furious activity that turns out incongruously to be a permanent punishment by cleansing in grime. The violence of the fantasy is then projected towards a sort of forbidden laughter as Arthur proceeds to "a bedstead with four bare atomies of posts, each terminating in a spike, as if for the dismal accomodation of lodgers who might prefer to impale themselves."[15] The comic play on "accomodation" instantly displays the correspondence between the desired bed and a hidden world of torment and unhappiness: we are in the same mode of apprehension as the Conradian grotesque which enters *Victory*, even before the trio, with the famous description of the Zangiacomo Ladies' Orchestra:

> The uproar in that small, barn-like structure, built of imported pine boards, and raised clear of the ground, was simply stunning. An instrumental uproar, screaming, grunting, whining, sobbing, scraping, squeaking some kind of lively air; while a grand piano, operated upon by a bony, red-faced woman with bad-tempered nostrils, rained hard notes like hail through the tempest of fiddles. (*V,* 68)

This has local brilliance enough to provide its own justification and also to provide a perfect illustration of Ford's observation of Conrad's writing that "each sentence is a mosaic of little crepitations of surprise and (that) practically every paragraph contains its little jolt."[16] However, the collision here between

Heyst's "desperate mood" and the vulgar violence of the world's
traffic, felt as a dismaying affront to the senses, is also the figure
which is at the heart of the novel as we will see when we look at
Conrad's version of the encounter between the trio and the
gentleman; and when we read that "The Zangiacomo band was
not making music: it was simply murdering silence with a vulgar,
ferocious energy" (68), the Dickensian delight in comic deformity also sounds a note in a larger disharmony felt as the spacious
silence of Samburan is subject to a ghastly intrusion.

Whilst Stevenson's comedy is governed by his ear for realistic
dialogue, Conrad's comedy is both far less responsible to the
observable world and far more anarchic. Another way of putting
it is to say that Stevenson is a brilliant mimic, whilst Conrad is an
irrepressible parodist who, in *Victory,* is driven by this urge to
oppose the realist mode of his central story, of Heyst and Lena.
Whatever Conrad's protestations in his "Author's Note," his
trio are not drawn from life (while Conrad makes a sustained
attempt with Ricardo, Huish, in all his economy, is far the more
substantial *character*); but they take their place in this novel as
a surreal visitation accorded the power to take fantasized
retribution on the world of sham civilization represented by
Schomberg's *table d'hote*:

> The new guest [Mr Jones] made answer that he liked a hotel where one
> could find some local people in the evening. It was infernally dull
> otherwise. The secretary, in sign of approval, emitted a grunt of
> astonishing ferocity, as if proposing to himself to eat the local people.
> All this sounded like a longish stay, thought Schomberg. (101)

What we enjoy here is the witty mobility of the narrative voice in
comparison with Schomberg's obtuseness, an effect that reaches
its comic climax in the projected leap of "as if proposing to
himself to eat the local people," which exceeds what Schomberg
is thinking but which might figure forth his desperate fantasy.

This sort of comic-ironic internal dialogue is almost exposed
to the reader in Schomberg's desperate interruption of Ricardo's
narrative of the killing of Antonio:

"Look here," exclaimed Schomberg violently, as if trying to burst some invisible bonds, "do you mean to say all this happened?" [and Ricardo's retort], "No," said Ricardo coolly. "I am making it all up as I go along, just to help you through the hottest part of the afternoon" (140)

Here it is as if Ricardo has taken on the sardonically unmoved quality of the narrative commentary, and at least one of the invisible bonds entrapping Schomberg is that he is the object of a joke whose terms always elude him. This is true even when the writing apparently offers to represent Schomberg's own thoughts about the trio. Mr Jones proposes Pedro as a waiter to assist the gambling venture. The "unlucky" Schomberg thinks:

But Pedro, at any rate, was just a simple straightforward brute, if a murderous one. There was no mystery about him, nothing uncanny, no suggestion of a stealthy, deliberate wild-cat turned into a man, or of an insolent spectre on leave from Hades, endowed with skin and bones and a subtle power of terror. (115)

A stricter technique would require the free indirect speech to inform the interior narrative more rigorously. But here, by the time we come to the incomparable phrasing of "on leave from Hades," we are offered a wit too swift for Schomberg and this excess delivers a more unstable, hybrid mode of narration than Stevenson's. On all these occasions the discomposing of mono-logic telling is not merely a matter of setting Schomberg's point of view at odds with the narrator's, but of thrusting upon the reader with comic violence the conditions of a heteroglossia highlighted by Schomberg's complete unawareness of the sort of dialogues in which the novelist has engaged him. Whilst the target is Schomberg, we are comfortably entertained by our complicity; when, later, the target becomes Heyst, the effect is more disturbingly tragic.

V

In keeping with his guarded statement about the aim of creation
– "I would fondly believe that its object is purely spectacular"
(*PR,* 92) – Conrad typically focuses upon the sensational
aspects of the encounter between Heyst and his unexpected
visitors. Stevenson's trio suffer "a sense of being watched and
played with, and of a blow impending, that was hardly bearable"
(*V,* 239) but the battle to be fought is indubitably a verbal one,
each participant picking his way through the nuances of social
speech. A verbal coincidence enables us to gauge exactly the
difference of Conrad's treatment, in which the impression of the
image upon the retina is paramount and interpretation struggles
afterwards in the locked world of Heyst's solitude. Wang's
sighting of the boat in the strait is so incongruous in his
experience that it is "as if his vision had received a blow" (226).
As Heyst looks, the emptiness of Diamond Bay leads him to
entertain the idea of "some strange hallucination" (226) or "a
phantom boat;" and, in a manner which is one of the great
artistic achievements of the novel, the comprehension of the
scene, although from this point perceived entirely through
Heyst's eyes, ebbs away from his authority. The irony will be that
he will indeed see as phantoms and a hallucination what his eyes
rightly presented as fearful.

     The endemic violence of this encounter has begun with Wang
receiving a blow and continues with the vertiginous sensation of
Heyst's first view of the boat: "His sight plunged straight into the
stern sheets of the big boat....His eyes fell on the thin back of
a man doubled up over the tiller in a queer, uncomfortable
attitude of drooping sorrow" (227). Of course, we don't see
exactly what Heyst sees. We know who these people are and
what they have come for, and to see Mr Jones as a collapsed
marionette discomforted by sorrow suspends his threat in an
incongruous melancholy that is funny. A "second man glared
wildly upward, and struggled to raise himself but to all
appearance was much too drunk to succeed." Despite Heyst's
assurance to Lena earlier, "Appearances – what more, what

better can you ask for? In fact you can't have better. You can't
have anything else" (204), now that he is faced with nothing but
appearances he is left to flounder in suppositions diametrically
opposed to the truth. The desperate plight of these arrivals, so
alarming to Heyst, is comic to the reader, who had viewed their
activities with apprehension but is now almost gratified to find it
is they rather than Heyst who have become the odious Schomberg's immediate victims ("by some extraordinary mistake one
of the two jars put into the boat by Schomberg's man contained
salt water").

We are positioned painfully between apprehension for Heyst
and progressive detachment from him as he is unable to
interpret what is evident to us as readers. The pain is also
touched with a cruel laughter that none of the characters
in the scene can share, though Ricardo typically, is the first
to recover sufficiently to do so. "Heyst had never been so
much astonished in his life...these men were not sailors...but
their apparition in a boat Heyst could not connect with
anything plausible" (227). The fun with "apparition" is swiftly
superceded by the particular resonance of "plausible," as
in "a plausible story," which breaks away from Heyst's consciousness to acknowledge that there are two stories here,
one meditative-philosophical, the other a melodramatic pot-
-boiler, and there is a problem about which one Heyst is
in. So, later, Jones will play with the same figure in a parody
of Heyst's astonishment: "As to finding assistance, a wharf,
a white man – nobody would have dreamed of it. Simply
preposterous!" (240). Meanwhile, Jones and Ricardo remain
problematic for the reader as they seem to be harbingers
of tragedy yet they act as agents of comedy. Ricardo "uttered
faintly a hoarse, dreamy 'Hallo!'" and, questioned whether
he is wounded as he has blood on him, "glanced down,
reeled – one of his feet was inside a large pith hat – and,
recovering himself, let out a dismal grating sound in the
manner of a grim laugh" (228). When Wang brings a crowbar
to loosen the water tap, Ricardo dimly apprehends an attack:
"'Crowbar? What's that for?' he mumbled, and his head

dropped on his chest mournfully" (229), that last word wonderfully chosen to allow a delicious fantasy momentarily to flicker
of Ricardo acquiescing in his own death.

We are pleased that we know from prior experience how to
take Ricardo's performances, whilst Heyst doesn't. But he *does*
mean the blow that "resounded all over the quiet sweep of Black
Diamond Bay" and the abandon of the psychopath is horrifying.
Response is surely destabilized to an extreme degree here, and
eventually to the point that it is no longer Heyst's sense of the
incongruity of the strangers that we share, but rather the other
way round, as he is unable to respond appropriately to the three
who have come to rob and, if necessary, murder him. Heyst
apologizes "'I am prevented from offering you a share of my own
quarters.' The distant courtliness of this beginning arrested the
other two suddenly, as if amazed by some manifest incongruity"
(242). It is as if these unreal cardboard cut-out figures have not
only invaded Heyst's island but also the novel itself, in the sense
that they threaten to wrest the genre of the novel into their own
possession. Whilst in *The Ebb Tide* the reader is presented with
competing points of view, in *Victory* he is confronted by
competing forms of artistic representation, a feature highlighted
by Heyst's inability to conceive of the intrusion upon his solitude
as real. He muses, "now that I don't see them, I can hardly
believe these fellows exist" (247). With much greater exasperation, when Wang has rejected his proposals, he cries
roughly, "All this is too unreal altogether" (347), and finally
addresses Ricardo with "You people...are divorced from all
reality in my eyes" (364).

Daphna Erdinast-Vulcan cleverly relates this aspect of Heyst's
characterization to the consciously literary and intertextual
quality of the novel's procedures:

> The blatant textuality of this novel, the fact that it parades itself as
> a literary text by numerous allusions to other texts, is a significant
> correlative of the protagonist's frame of mind. For Heyst the reader,
> a man who views reality as a spectacle or a mesh of appearances, is so
> afflicted with this textual or literary view of life, that he can never
> suspend his disbelief and respond to the drama of reality as if it were
> real indeed.[17]

On this reading, the novel becomes Conrad's critique of the affliction of his own dominant aesthetic; and Robert Hampson uses R. D. Laing to good effect when he writes: "Laing suggests that one development for 'the person who does not act in reality' is the increasing impoverishment of reality and a corresponding impoverishment of the self until 'the world is in ruins and the self is (apparently) dead',"[18] which connects Heyst to Decoud, Conrad's other examination of his own sceptical tendencies.

These suggestions almost convince me that it is the Heyst philosophy which produces the gaudy, two-dimensional flatness of much of the third and fourth part of *Victory*. We can only save the idea of the organic unity of the novel by a reinstatement of Heyst as the generating consciousness of the whole fiction. I would contend, however, that the trio, and indeed the whole configuration, that Conrad inherited from Stevenson has a more independent life than this, disrupting more fundamentally the realistic-mimetic mode of representation applied to Heyst and Lena; and anyway, their flaunted unreality cannot logically be seen to be a product of Heyst's view of the world because, as we have seen, this mode of representation accompanies them from their entrance into the novel and their dealings with Schomberg, long before they encounter Heyst in Part 3 Chapter 6. Rather than trying to reclaim the grotesque elements of *Victory* for a single and singularly realized conception of the novel, I would propose that *Victory* offers a particularly exposed example of an intentional hybrid within what Bakhtin calls the "parodic--travestying" tradition in European literature. Of medieval Latin literature he says:

> This reciprocal orientation of each word to the other occurs across the entire spectrum of tones – from reverent acceptance to parodic ridicule...exactly like the modern novel, where one often does not know where the direct authorial word ends and where a parodic or stylised playing with the characters' language begins.[19]

At one end of the spectrum this describes Jane Austen's brilliant use of free indirect speech in that most seamless of all novels,

Emma; and at the other end this points to Conrad's trio operating in conscious travesty of the conduct of the realistic novel. Most obviously this occurs in Jones's self-allegorizing "I am the world itself, come to pay you a visit....I am a sort of fate – the retribution that waits its time" (*V*, 379), where the relish in imposing this mode of speaking upon the more realistic dialogue is Conrad's as much as it is Jones's. More subtly, towards the very end of the novel, we have this:

> Mr Jones, after firing his shot over Heyst's shoulder, had thought it proper to dodge away. Like the spectre he was, he had noiselessly vanished from the verandah. Heyst stumbled into the room and looked round. All the objects in there – the books, the gleam of old silver familiar to him from boyhood, the very portrait on the wall – seemed shadowy, unsubstantial, the dumb accomplices of an amazing dream-plot ending in an illusory effect of waking.... (403)

So many phrases here, like small ambushes, ask us to re-examine the discourse in which the story is being told. The gentleman's "had thought it proper" is placed unsettlingly next to "dodge away;" "like the spectre he was" (not "like a spectre") is a manner of speaking but here offers itself as confirmation of a fact; and the transfer to Heyst's stumbles raises irreconcilable readings of the unreality he confronts – have the objects in the room played the part of impotent by-standers unable to prevent Jones and company writing the script of Heyst's nightmare? or is it that Heyst's reading is still purblind? These collisions remain unresolved and help to construct *Victory* into the hybrid of adventure tale, meditation and masque which for many Conrad critics counts as artistic failure. *The Ebb Tide* is about the failure of adventure and the failure of fictions to return to health the man who has escaped the mendacity of society; *Victory's* stylization of Stevenson's portrayal of the underside of imperialism is less sardonic, more apocalyptic, riven and agonized in its exposure of a sense of civilization to "the tragic brutality of the light" (216) that decomposes it. Readers are no less anguished and divided over whose is the "victory" at the end of the tale. To Heyst himself, his father, Lena and Wang – all candidates for the award of final victor – I would bleakly add one more who bears intimations of the coming European conflagration and the end of the gentleman indeed: Schomberg, certainly the most parodic of the candidates, travestying the gravity of the novel's close. As Conrad pondered the title of his novel ("the last word I had written in peace time" – VII) did a memory of Stevenson's *The Dynamiter* cross his mind? Dr Grierson holds up a flask "three parts full of a bright amber liquid....As he saw me he raised the flask at arm's length. 'Victory!' he cried, 'Victory, Asenath!' And then – whether the flask escaped his trembling fingers, or whether the explosion was spontaneous, I cannot tell."[20]

NOTES

1. Jeanette Winterson, *Art Objects: Essays on Ecstasy and Effrontery* (London: Cape, 1995).

2. Quoted in Frederick Karl, *Joseph Conrad: The Three Lives* (New York: Farrar, Straus and Giroux, 1979), 733.

3. Andrea White, *Joseph Conrad and the Adventure Tradition* (Cambridge: Cambridge U. P., 1993), 128.

4. M. M. Bakhtin, "Discourse in the Novel," in M. M. Bakhtin, *The Dialogic Imagination,* ed. Michael Holquist (Austin: U. of Texas P., 1981), 279.

5. Robert Louis Stevenson, *The Strange Case of Dr Jekyll and Mr Hyde and Other Stories,* ed. Jenni Calder (Harmondsworth: Penguin, 1979). All references to *The Ebb Tide* are to this edition.

6. Cedric Watts has already written on the connection between the two novels: see his essay "*The Ebb Tide* and *Victory*," *Conradiana* (forthcoming). We both saw the connection quite independently of each other and our essays are very different in tenor.

7. Robert Hampson, "*Chance* and The Secret Life," in "Conrad and Gender," *The Conradian,* 17: 2 (1993).

8. Reprinted in *Conrad: The Critical Heritage,* ed. Norman Sherry (London: Routledge and Kegan Paul, 1973), 98-100.

9. As readers will swiftly recognize, this essay is little more than an illustrative footnote to Tony Tanner, "Joseph Conrad and the Last Gentleman," *The Critical Quarterly,* 28: 1/2 (1986), 109-42.

10. Paul Kirschner, *Conrad: The Psychologist as Artist* (Edinburgh: Oliver and Boyd, 1968), 181-287. Owen Knowles, "Conrad, Anatole

France and the Early French Romantic Tradition," *Conradiana,* 11: 1 (1979), 41-61.

11. Frederick Karl, "*Victory,* Its Origin and Development," *Conradiana,* 15: 1 (1983), 38.

12. Robert Kiely, *Robert Louis Stevenson and the Fiction of Adventure* (Cambridge MA: Harvard U. P., 1964). Jenni Calder, "Introduction" to *The Strange Case of Dr Jekyll and Mr Hyde and Other Stories,* 22.

13. I have long thought that this passage about his tastes constitutes one of Conrad's most revealing statements about his own art. Soo Young Chon makes excellent use of this extract in her article "Conrad's *Victory*: An Elusive Allegory," *English Language and Literature,* 35: 1 (1989), 88-101.

14. Robert Louis Stevenson, *An Inland Voyage* (London: Thomas Nelson), 242, 231.

15. Charles Dickens, *Little Dorrit* (Harmondsworth: Penguin, 1967), 77.

16. Ford Madox Ford, "Introduction" to *Joseph Conrad, The Sisters* (New York: Crosby Gaige, 1928).

17. Daphna Erdinast-Vulcan, *Joseph Conrad and the Modern Temper* (New York: Clarendon, 1991), 180.

18. Robert Hampson, *Joseph Conrad: Betrayal and Identity* (London: Macmillan, 1992), 247.

19. M. M. Bakhtin, "From the Prehistory of Novelistic Discourse," in *The Dialogic Imagination,* 77.

20. Robert Louis Stevenson with Fanny Van de Grift Stevenson, *The Dynamiter* (Stroud: Alan Sutton, 1984), 44.

Garry Watson,
University of Alberta,
Edmonton, Canada

Fundamental Information: *The Secret Agent, Billy Budd, Sailor* and the Sacrificial Crisis

I will be arguing in this essay that we will be better able to appreciate some of the more significant things that Joseph Conrad's *The Secret Agent* and Herman Melville's *Billy Budd, Sailor* have to offer us if we read them alongside one another, and in the light of Rene Girard's theory of the sacrificial crisis. Since Melville died (in 1891) well before the publication of *The Secret Agent* (in 1907), and since *Billy Budd, Sailor* (which Melville was still revising at the end of his life) was not published until 1924 (the year of Conrad's death), there can obviously be absolutely no question of any direct influence here, either way. But, as I understand it, both the similarities and dissimilarities between these two works are broadly explicable in terms of the fact that Melville and Conrad shared a common interest. Like many others, they were both interested in the research into, and speculation about, the world's mythologies that flourished throughout the second half of the nineteenth century and into the beginning of the twentieth.[1] More specifically, I would say that, on the evidence of these two works, they were both interested in the *kind* of research that appeared to be motivated by the hope of discovering what George Eliot once, famously and ironically, referred to as the key to all mythologies; and that took the form of a search for a real origin.

Of course, this particular project into origins was abandoned a long time ago. But this is where Girard comes in. In the work he has been producing since 1972 (when his *Violence and the Sacred* was first published), Girard has almost single-handedly revived this form of what – in his *Things Hidden Since the Foundation of the World* – he aptly calls Fundamental Anthropology. He has been operating on the assumption that it is, in his words,

217

"foolhardy to condemn the search for a real origin simply because the search has not been successful so far" and that the "relative failure of Frazer, Freud, or Robertson Smith is no reason to regard their insistence on getting to the bottom of things as foolish or outdated."[2] And he leaves us in no doubt but that he believes he himself has actually got to the bottom of things and discovered there the key to all mythologies.[3]

In short, Girard is every bit as interested as Conrad and Melville in the kind of "information" which, because it is both basic and also concerned with origins and foundations, Conrad appropriately calls "fundamental" (while suggesting that there is a sense in which we may be better off without it). And while it is true that Girard is the only one of the three to talk explicitly about a sacrificial crisis, it seems to me clear enough that Melville and Conrad have a major contribution to make to our understanding of the concept. Even, that is to say, though they don't use the *term, Billy Budd, Sailor* and *The Secret Agent* nevertheless constitute not only dramatizations of, but also major theoretical reflections on, the thing itself.

Girard's theory: In the beginning

The concept of the sacrificial crisis is an integral part of Girard's argument concerning the origin of human society. Girard argues that "[h]uman society does not begin with the fear of the 'slave' for the 'master,' as Hegel claims, but – as Durkheim maintains – with religion" (Girard, *Violence*..., 306-7). We need to know, however, that Girard uses the term "religion" (or "religious") very broadly to define "[a]ny phenomenon associated with the acts of remembering, commemorating, and perpetuating a unanimity that springs from the murder of a surrogate victim" (315). And from this, two things follow: first, that something happens *before* the beginning of human society or culture and "the original event must have been a murder" (92). And secondly that we need to distinguish between "the original *event*"[4] – in the sense of a decisive occurrence that marks the transition from nature to culture – and "a real origin." If we press our search for the latter as far back as the *cause* of the murder, we *then* find it is the kind of violence that is principally characterized by its essentially imitative or mimetic nature. And if, as Andrew McKenna notes in his recent attempt to reconcile the thought of Girard and Derrida, this is "the mimetic violence of all against all, having its origin solely in another's violence, which it imitates," then the consequence may seem somewhat disconcerting, at least to those of us who would have preferred something more concrete:

> In the beginning is imitation, not an origin....When the violence of all against all becomes the violence of all against one a victim is produced, which is likely to happen when a difference, a weakness, marks out a single member of the melee for destruction. So in a sense we can say with Derrida that in the beginning was the mark, the trace of a violence that has no origin except in another's violence, a trace of nonorigin or an arche-trace....[T]he victim is the trace of a violence that has no origin except in "itself," that is, in another's violence.[5]

The search for a real origin ends up by producing not so much an origin as the "trace" of an origin. Or, to be more exact, since we obviously don't have direct access to the surrogate victim, this search produces a trace of a trace.

Girard's account of our origins isolates three main stages, the first of which, *violent mimesis,* spreads throughout a group in an intensifying crisis until it culminates in a *murder.* This – the murder of a more or less arbitrarily chosen victim, together with the peace and calm this murder restores – forms the second stage. And it in turn makes possible the third stage, *religion,* which is the attempt to understand and come to terms with this murder.

Over a period of time, and with the help of the misinterpretations fostered by religion, the group's perception of its victim changes. Whereas to begin with the victim was held responsible for all that was troubling the group, after a suitable passage of time he (or she) is credited with the social unity and peace his (or her) death has ushered in. Hence as interpreted by religion, the two faces of the sacred – the Latin for which (*sacer*)

is, as Girard points out, "sometimes translated 'sacred,' sometimes 'accursed,' for it encompasses the maleficent as well as the
beneficent" (Girard, *Violence*..., 257) – as the victim is transformed into a god.[6]

As Girard understands it, the *sacred* is an essentially violent
phenomenon – indeed, for him, "violence and the sacred are one
and the same thing" (262) – and the function of religion is to
protect us from it. The trouble is that the "only barrier against
human violence [has been] raised on misconception" (135); that
"religion protects man [only] as long as its ultimate foundations
are not revealed." And our problem today is that these
foundations are now becoming increasingly visible.

This is perhaps nowhere more apparent than in the fact that
our judicial system, which has taken over the role played by
religion in earlier societies, "no longer enjoys the obscurity it
needs to operate effectively" (23).[7] For it to operate effectively
we need to be able to believe that its primary function is not so
much to guarantee security as to ensure the possibility of justice.
And we are now living at a time when it doesn't seem
outrageously cynical to assert, as Girard does, that "the judicial
process is more concerned with the general security of the
community than with any abstract notion of justice" (22). How
has this come about? What has made it seem increasingly
plausible to believe that the judicial process is more concerned
with security than justice? Girard's answer, in the work he has
produced after *Violence and the Sacred,* is that it is the influence
of a non-sacrificial version of Christianity that has very gradually, over a period of many centuries, made the decisive difference.

But this is not the answer that I myself wish to give. Without
assuming that Girard would necessarily disagree with me,
I simply want to suggest that, among the many other things that
have no doubt contributed to this new awareness, such texts as
The Secret Agent and *Billy Budd, Sailor* have also made
a significant difference. I'm thinking, on the one hand, of the
obvious enough fact that Melville's Captain Vere is *much* more
concerned with security than with justice when he decides that
Billy Budd must be executed. And, on the other, of the various

ways in which Conrad's novel forces us to reflect on the nature and function of our judicial system. Of course, the fact that Karl Yundt thinks of the law as "the pretty branding instrument invented by the overfed to protect themselves against the hungry" (*The Secret Agent*) may not, in itself, seem surprising. After all, he is an anarchist and isn't this the sort of thing we expect anarchists to believe? But Winnie Verloc is no anarchist. So what are we to make of the fact that, even though she detests Yundt, her view on this matter – "They [the police] are there [she tells her brother] so that them as have nothing shouldn't take anything away from them who have" (*SA,* 173) – is substantially the same as his? I am *not* suggesting that Conrad is pursuing the same project as the Professor, another of his anarchist characters, who wants "[t]o *destroy* public faith in legality" (my italics). But I *do* think that the overall effect of such details – as the resemblance between the views of Yundt and Winnie and as the fact that the principal act of violence at the center of *The Secret Agent* is, as the Assistant Commissioner rightly says, "not the work of anarchism at all" but of "some species of *authorized* scoundrelism" (my italics) – is inevitably to *weaken* our faith in legality. At least in so far as our "faith" has been, up until this point, unquestioning.

According to Girard, it is, at any rate, precisely at the moment when we begin to lose our faith in legality, when the distinction between law and lawlessness begins to blur, that we find ourselves in the kind of legitimation crisis he calls sacrificial; a term I too prefer because it seems to me that its ability to encompass the crisis in legitimation while reaching to a deeper level gives it a greater power of explanation.[8] In brief, then, Girard defines a sacrificial crisis as "a crisis of distinctions." And since, in his view, the "cultural order is nothing more than a regulated system of distinctions in which the differences among individuals are used to establish their 'identity' and their mutual relationships," this means that a sacrificial crisis is one "affecting the [entire] cultural order" (Girard, *Violence...,* 49).

From Girard's point of view, it is no accident if sacrificial crises coincide "with the disappearance of the difference between impure violence [for example, vengeance] and purifying violence [pure and purifying because enacted in the name of justice]." Because, as he sees it, this particular distinction is absolutely crucial:

> When this difference has been effaced, purification is no longer possible and impure, contagious, reciprocal violence spreads throughout the community.
>   The sacrificial distinction, the distinction between the pure and the impure, cannot be obliterated without obliterating all other differences as well. One and the same process of violent reciprocity engulfs the whole. (49)

What, Girard argues, tended to happen in the past was that after violent reciprocity had engulfed the whole it would "trigger the mechanism of generative unanimity," thus enabling the violence to focus on a surrogate victim whose murder – so long, at least, as the victim was not seen (accurately) as a merely arbitrary scapegoat – would restore "a social system based on multiple and sharply pronounced differences" (188). But even if we wanted this to happen, we could no longer count on its doing so. And if, as Girard says, "[c]enturies can pass before men realize there is no real difference between their principle of justice and the concept of revenge" (24), how – when we finally *do* realize this – can we possibly pretend that we don't? How, in other words, are we to get out of *our* sacrificial crisis?

For our purposes here it suffices merely to have raised this question. In any case, I don't propose to try to answer it, any more than I propose to answer equally legitimate and important questions concerning the evidence for Girard's assertions and some of the possible implications of his argument. All I have been trying to do up to this point is provide a clear enough explanation of what Girard means by a sacrificial crisis. We are now ready to consider the ways in which Melville and Conrad understand it.

Melville and Conrad

The Secret Agent and *Billy Budd, Sailor* are similarly organized in terms of a conflict between those who would prefer to remain on the surface and those who are determined to get to what Conrad, like Girard, calls "the bottom of things." In "Author's Note" that Conrad wrote for his novel in 1920, he explains that it focuses on "the absurd cruelty of the Greenwich Park explosion" and that its characters relate "directly or indirectly to [Winnie Verloc's] tragic suspicion that 'life doesn't stand much looking into'" (*SA*, XII-XIII). But, when we turn to the novel itself, we discover that not all of its characters share the lack of curiosity in which – in Winnie's own case, at least – this "tragic suspicion" manifests itself. It's true that Winnie's husband does. We are told, for example, that Winnie's "disdainful incuriosity" is "the foundation of their accord in domestic life" and that what this accord means is that they "refrained from going to the bottom of facts and motives." But Winnie's mother doesn't seem to share this incuriosity.[9] And neither does Stevie, as Conrad makes quite explicit in the eighth chapter, in which we see Stevie's pained but thoughtful reaction to the sorry condition of the cab-driver and his horse, who are conveying Winnie's mother to the charitable institution she has decided to settle in.

After making a considerable effort, Stevie has managed to articulate the thought "Bad world for poor people" (171). And then – in response to his protest ("Beastly!") – his sister has told him that "Nobody can help that." This thought plunges Stevie into gloom until it occurs to him that she has forgotten the police. "'Police,' he suggested, confidently." But no, Winnie won't have it. She informs him that the "police aren't for that." At which point, we are told that "it was with an aspect of hopeless vacancy that he gave up his intellectual enterprise" (172). But he only gives it up temporarily – and I take it, incidentally, that it *is* a genuinely "*intellectual* enterprise" – because "[u]*nlike his sister, who put her trust in face-values, he wished to go to the bottom of the matter*" (173; my italics). Stevie therefore "carried on his inquiry by means of an angry

challenge" (173). And in response to his reiterated question
– "What are they for then, Winn?" – his sister produces the
answer which, as we have already noted, is very similar in its view
of the law to the one expressed much earlier in the novel by the
anarchist Karl Yundt: "Don't you know what the police are for,
Stevie? They are there so that them as have nothing shouldn't
take anything away from them who have" (173). Not surprisingly, this provokes Stevie – "He was impressed and startled now,
and his intelligence was very alert" – to ask for further
clarification: "'What?' he asked at once, anxiously. 'Not even if
they were hungry? Musn't they'?" And his sister, whose
intelligence is obviously *not* very alert, who clearly doesn't
realize the implications of what she is saying, responds as
follows: "'Not if they were ever so,' said Mrs Verloc, with the
equanimity of a person untroubled by the problem of the
distribution of wealth" (173). This, one might add, is the
equanimity of someone who – "put[ting] her trust in face values"
– doesn't even realize when (for once) she has actually (if
unintentionally) *got* "to the bottom of the matter." As a result
she also fails to realize how disturbing "the matter" she has got
"to the bottom *of*" *is*. In fact, it isn't until near the end of the
novel, after she has murdered her husband, that Winnie, "who
always refrained from looking deep into things," is "*compelled*
to look into the very bottom of this thing" (my italics). And what
she sees there is something that "terrifie[s]" her: an object, "the
gallows," "that last argument of men's justice."

So we have Winnie and her husband preferring to stay on the
surface while Stevie, his mother and Conrad himself are
interested in going beneath it. What is immediately striking
about "Author's Note" is the way in which Conrad explicitly
offers to talk about what he refers to, in its opening sentence, as
the "origin" of his novel. Finding himself "reproved for having
produced it" (VII), he tells us that he feels the need "to explain
that there was no perverse intention, no secret scorn for the
natural sensibilities of mankind at the bottom of [his] impulses"
(VIII). But to say this, he then notes (somewhat ruefully, it seems
to me), is to risk "becoming a bore; for the world generally is not

interested in the motives of any overt act but in its consequences. Man may smile and smile but he is not an investigating animal. He loves the obvious. He shrinks from explanations" (VIII). Unlike Man-in-general or Winnie Verloc (who "did not investigate her brother's psychology") in particular, Conrad *is* precisely "an investigating animal," someone like Stevie and his mother who won't rest until he gets to the bottom of things.

In *Billy Budd, Sailor* there is an obvious enough conflict between the surface view of things that Captain Vere insists his officers adopt during Billy's trial – "War looks but to the *frontage,* the *appearance*" (my italics) – and the inner view implicit in the work's subtitle – "*An inside narrative.*" But if *The Secret Agent* is preoccupied with the question of either avoiding or trying to get to the bottom of things, in *Billy Budd, Sailor* this preoccupation gets expressed in terms of a concern with directness or indirectness. For example, we are told that the view of Captain Vere held by some of his officers (men "[w]ith minds less stored than his and less earnest") is that "there is a queer streak of the pedantic running through him." As the narrator explains, this criticism is based on the fact that "not only did the captain's discourse never fall into the jocosely familiar, but in illustrating of any point touching the stirring personages and events of the time he would be as apt to cite some historic character or incident of antiquity as he would be to cite from the moderns." But, as the narrator continues, this criticism is made to rebound on the men who make it:

> He seemed unmindful of the circumstance that to his bluff company such remote allusions, however pertinent they might really be, were altogether alien to men whose reading was mainly confined to the journal. But considerateness in such matters is not easy to natures constituted like Captain Vere's. Their honesty prescribes to them directness, sometimes far-reaching like that of a migratory fowl that in its flight never heeds when it crosses a frontier. (Melville, *Billy Budd,...,* 341)[10]

This firmly establishes that in this novel we are to expect *directness* in the form of what may well, at first glance, look like *in*directness – in the form, that is, of remote citations and

allusions. And it is Melville, of course, rather than his character
Captain Vere, who makes easily the greatest use of allusions.

As for *Vere's* directness, however, I would say that we are
encouraged to see it as manifesting itself in his willingness to
pierce through surface conventions to a Nature that is presumably to be found at the heart or bottom of things.[11] We are told,
for example, that he admires "unconventional writers like
Montaigne, who, free from cant and convention, honestly and in
the spirit of common sense philosophize upon realities" (340).[12]
And the surgeon's reaction to Vere's decision to call a drumhead
court to try Billy – the "way dictated by usage" would be "to
place Billy Budd in confinement...and postpone further action in
so extraordinary a case to such time as they should rejoin the
squardon, and then refer it to the admiral" (379) – makes it clear
that he, at least, believes this to be a definite breach of
convention. If Vere goes on to instruct his officers to obey
"martial law" (387) (which he claims means that their allegiance
is not to Nature but to the King), this is not necessarily the
contradiction it could at first appear to be. What he is actually
appealing to here is something *in between* nature and culture, the
sacred: in the form of "the God of War – Mars" (398).

Even before we learn about Vere's impatience with the
conventional, the narrator's use of allusions in the three opening
paragraphs of the novel – to refer to the phenomenon of the
Handsome Sailor – has already taken us beyond the "frontage"
or "appearance" of things. This opening and thrice-made
identification between the Handsome Sailor and Taurus is of
course an obvious enough allusion both to the sacrificial practice
of making an offering to the gods and also to the frequent
transformation of the proferred victim into a god in his own
right. And the allusion functions as the first of a number of
strikingly direct anticipations – "the priestly motive," for
example, that we are told led Nelson at Trafalgar to adorn
"himself for the altar and the sacrifice" (336); or the possibility
that, in his private interview with Billy near the end, Vere may
have caught Billy to his heart, "even as Abraham may have
caught young Isaac on the brink of resolutely offering him up"

(392) – of the moment later on the novel when Billy will be sacrificed by Captain Vere.

Recalling what (in Shakespeare's *Julius Caesar*) Brutus says to Caius on the eve of the assassination – "Let's be sacrificers, but not butchers, Caius....O, that we then could...not dismember Caesar!...Let's carve him as a dish fit for the gods, // Not hew him as a carcass fit for hounds" (*Julius Caesar*, II, I, 166-74) – it seems appropriate (especially in view of the eating imagery that pervades *Billy Budd, Sailor*) to say that in Melville's novel Billy is offered up by Vere precisely as "a dish fit for the gods."[13] And yet this particular allusion is to be found not in Melville's novel but in Conrad's. As I understand it, Conrad alludes to this passage in three distinct but related ways. First, in some of the words Mr Vladimir speaks to Mr Verloc while instructing him to provoke an outrage against science – "the sacrosanct fetish of today" – by setting off a bomb at the Greenwich observatory. "I am," says Mr Vladimir, "a civilized man. I would never dream of directing you to organize a mere butchery, even if I expected the best results from it" (*SA*, 33). Second, in the various references to butchers throughout the novel, especially the one that turns up in the description of Stevie's remains, as they have been gathered up and placed on a table, after the explosion.[14] Thus, moments after we are told that the remains "might have been an accumulation of raw material for a cannibal feast" (86), we read that "Chief Inspector [Heat] went on peering at the table with a calm face and the slightly anxious attention of an indigent customer bending over what may be called the by-products of a butcher's shop with a view to an inexpensive Sunday dinner" (88). And third, in the various references to a carving knife, two in particular, starting with the one Winnie makes while telling her husband that Stevie has been reading in one of the F. P. (Future of the Proletariat) tracts the story "of a German soldier officer tearing half-off the ear of a recruit, and nothing was done to him for it." "I had," she then explains, "to take the carving knife from the boy....He would have stuck that officer like a pig if he had seen him then" (60). This subsequently turns out to be the same carving knife that Winnie – while haunted by the "vision" of "a rainfall of [Stevie's] mangled limbs" and "decapitated head" – later sticks into her husband, who has of course more than once in the novel been himself likened to a pig, a "fat-pig," ready presumably for the sacrifice.

But what are we to make of the fact that, unlike Billy Budd, Stevie Verloc is definitely *not* carved "as a dish fit for the gods?" Or, indeed, of the obviously related fact that in Conrad's novel Mr Verloc is the one who gets carved while Stevie gets butchered and dismembered. After all, Stevie and Billy do resemble one another in a number of ways, three of which seem to me especially worth noting. First, their apparent child-like innocence; second, Billy's "occasional liability to a vocal defect" (*Billy Budd*,..., 331) and Stevie's "stammer;" and third, their shared duality. I'm thinking here of the way in which Melville's Billy is characterized as one of the "fighting peacemakers" (*Billy Budd*,..., 326) and of the passage in which Conrad tells us that Winnie fails to "fathom" the "twofold character" of Stevie's excitement. As it happens, this is the passage in which we are told that Winnie is not interested in acquiring "fundamental information" and it is strongly suggested, I think, that this is what Conrad is offering *us* in his description of Stevie's excited state. To begin with, as Stevie watches the cabman and his horse disappearing into the night (the cabman "limping"), our attention is drawn to Stevie's hands, which are in his pockets and which are "clinched hard into a pair of angry fists." We then get the following:

> In the face of anything which affected directly or indirectly his morbid dread of pain, Stevie ended by turning vicious. A magnanimous indignation swelled his frail chest to bursting, and caused his candid eyes to squint. Supremely wise in knowing his own powerlessness, Stevie was not wise enough to restrain his passions. The tenderness of his universal charity had two phases as indissolubly joined and connected as the reverse and obverse sides of a medal. The anguish of immoderate compassion was succeeded by the pain of an innocent but pitiless rage. (*SA*, 169)

In what sense, then, is the information this offers us "fundamental?" In the sense that it is about the sacred, the two faces of which it strikingly illustrates. If, as Girard can help us to see, the first two of the resemblances between Billy and Stevie are characteristic signs of the victim both *before* (when victims are often identified by some physical infirmity, such as precisely a vocal effect, or a limp) and *after* a scapegoating (when victims are transformed into innocent gods), the third resemblance reminds us of the fact that these newly-created representations of the sacred never remain wholly innocent.[15] On the contrary, like Billy and Stevie, they have two sides, the one indeed innocent and compassionate but the other enraged and with angry fists at the ready (think, for example, of the fist that strikes Claggart dead).

Still, despite these similarities, the deaths of Billy and Stevie are undeniably very different. Why? Partly, no doubt, because of the very different crises – or what may possibly be seen as the very different moments or stages in the same ongoing crisis – to which Melville and Conrad are responding. Let's look first at the earlier crisis (or moment) and of the three metaphors Melville uses to characterize it. The first metaphor conveniently comes in the midst of a sketch of the historical context that Melville provides in his third chapter:

> It was the summer of 1797. In the April of that year had occurred the commotion at Spithead followed in May by a second and yet more serious outbreak in the fleet at the Nore. The latter is known, and without exaggeration in the epithet, as "the Great Mutiny"....To the British Empire the Nore Mutiny was what a strike in the fire brigade would be to London threatened by general arson....[T]he bluejackets, to be numbered by thousands, ran up with huzzas the British colors with the union and cross wiped out; by that cancellation transmuting the flag of founded law and freedom defined, into the enemy's red meteor of unbridled and unbounded revolt. Reasonable discontent growing out of practical grievances in the fleet had been ignited into irrational combustion as by live cinders blown across the Channel from France in flames. (*Billy Budd,...*, 332-3)

Here, also from Chapter three, is the second metaphor: "To some extent the Nore Mutiny may be regarded as analogous to the distempering irruption of contagious fever in a frame

constitutionally sound, and which anon throws it off" (334).
And here, from Chapter seven, is the third one: Captain Vere's
"settled convictions were as a dike against those invading waters
of novel opinion social, political, and otherwise, which carried
away as in a torrent no few minds in those days, minds by nature
not inferior to his own" (340). According to Girard, each one of
these three metaphors – fire, infectious or contagious disease and
flood – has been widely used (together with tempests and
plagues, among others) to describe sacrificial crises.[16] And this
seems appropriate enough, of course, since each of them so
powerfully evokes the irresistibly mimetic and distinction-eras-
ing nature of violence.

Now in between his employment of the second and third of
these metaphors Melville's narrator announces that he is "going
to err into...a bypath" (334), which I suggest is analogous to
those allusions that seem self-indulgently pedantic to Captain
Vere's "bluff company" but that actually take us where we want
to go in the quickest possible time. What we actually want is the
solution to the crisis, and it is implicitly provided by the brief
account of Nelson's death that we are given in this chapter. If
Nelson's name is now "a trumpet to the blood," this is because of
the way in which he has theatrically staged his own death as
a sacrifice on the altar (336). So by implication this, or something
like it, is what Vere needs to do if he is to defeat *his* enemy. And it
is of course precisely what he does do: he effectively stages Billy's
death as one of those "measured forms" that is intended to
provide at least some protection against "the disruption of forms
going on across the Channel and the consequences thereof"
(404).

Except that it *could* be said that it is not so much Vere as
Melville himself who stages Billy's death. This aside, however,
there can be no question but that the death is indeed elaborately
staged. As we see, for example, in the perfect timing with which,
just at the very moment when the last signal is given, "it chanced
that the vapory fleece hanging low in the East was shot through
with a soft glory as of the fleece of the Lamb of God seen in
mystical vision, and simultaneously therewith, watched by the

wedged mass of upturned faces, Billy ascended; and, ascending, took the full rose of the dawn" (400-1). The theatrical quality of the event can also be seen in the perfect way it achieves the effect it is so clearly designed to produce: the turning of potentially "bad" (in the sense of revolutionary) mimesis – the possibility that "the deed of the foretopman" might have awakened some "slumbering embers of the Nore among the crew" (381) – into "good" (in the sense of obedient) mimesis – the kind exemplified by the way in which "with one voice" the ship's crew involuntarily finds itself producing a "sympathetic echo" of Billy's last words, "God bless Captain Vere" (400). The entire event concentrates for us the unmistakable aura of the sacred.[17]

I now want to return to *The Secret Agent* and to the question as to why Stevie's death is so different. I have already suggested that part of the answer is to be found in the very different crises (or moments in an ongoing crisis) to which Melville and Conrad are responding. The world of *The Secret Agent* is one in which an all-engulfing Flood has broken through the "dike" that Captain Vere had managed to erect, and for a while successfully maintain, against it ("against those invading waters of novel opinion social, political, and otherwise, which carried away as in a torrent no few minds" – 340). While there are moments in Conrad's novel when it seems as if a flood is on the way (as, for example, when Winnie reacts to the trickle of blood from her husband's dead body as if it "had been the first sign of a destroying flood"), we mostly get the impression that it has already come and gone. If at one point a street can seem to the Assistant Commissioner "as if swept clear suddenly by a great flood," the London of this novel mostly seems to be covered by the kind of mud one might expect to find after a flood has receded. A more characteristic moment, therefore, is when we are told that the Assistant Commissioner's "descent into the street was like the descent into a slimy aquarium from which the water had been run off. A murky, gloomy dampness enveloped him. The walls of the houses were wet, the mud of the roadway glistened with an effect of phosphorescence" (*SA*, 147).

Girard says that the sacrificial crisis coincides "with the

disappearance of the difference between impure violence and purifying violence. When this difference has been effaced, purification is no longer possible and impure, contagious, reciprocal violence spreads throughout the community" (Girard, *Violence*,..., 49). Unlike the world of *Billy Budd, Sailor* – in which Captain Vere has had at least some success in enforcing "the difference between the pure and the impure" and also, therefore, various other differences as well – the world of *The Secret Agent* is one in which this crucial distinction has been effaced, with the result that "purification is no longer possible" in it and "violent reciprocity engulfs the whole" (59).[18] As a result, the world of *Billy Budd, Sailor* is quite simply clean (and fresh and relatively innocent) – with Billy likened at one point to Adam before "man's Fall," his virtues having been "transmitted from a period prior to Cain's city" (*Billy Budd*,..., 331) – while that of *The Secret Agent* is dirty (and soiled and muddy and jaded). In the first we see the world *before* the Flood, in the second, the world *after* the Flood.

We still need an explanation that will be less obviously mythological than this one. Recall Girard's insistence that the distinction between purity and impurity "cannot be obliterated without obliterating all other differences as well" (Girard, *Violence*,..., 49). If Girard is right, then we would expect *The Secret Agent* to be full of supporting evidence. Let's quickly note three examples. First, that of the Italian restaurant that causes the Assistant Commissioner "to lose some more of his identity" when he visits it and that causes its patrons to lose "all their national and private characteristics" and to become "as denationalized as the dishes set before them" (*SA*, 149). It is as if the main function of this restaurant, which specializes in "fraudulent cookery," is to dissolve the identities (which is to say, the differences) of its customers. It operates in much the same way as the dirt that can be found everywhere in the London of this novel but especially in the gutters. Thus, for our second example, consider the "dismal row of newspaper sellers standing clear of the pavement [who] dealt out their wares from the gutter. It was a raw, gloomy day of the early spring; and the grimy sky, the mud of the streets, the rags of the dirty men, harmonized excellently with the eruption of the damp, rubbishly sheets of paper soiled with printers' ink" (79). This shows what is simultaneously happening in this novel both to humans and to the Logos: both are relegated to the gutter, which is where we also find the "Apollo-like" Comrade Ossipon in the penultimate paragraph of the novel ("marching in the gutter," his broad shoulders bowed "as if ready to receive the leather yoke of the sandwich board" – 311).[19] And finally, for our third example, note how the distinction between savage and civilized is put into question when Chief Inspector Heat reminds the Assistant Commissioner of "a certain old fat and wealthy native chief" he once knew. "It was bizarre. But does not Alfred Wallace relate in his famous book on the Malay Archipelago how, among the Aru Islanders, he discovered in an old and naked savage with a sooty skin a peculiar resemblance to a dear friend at home?"

It is true, however, that there does appear to be *one* important difference left. I am referring to the difference that bothers the Chief Inspector when he encounters the Professor in an alley. We are told that he can understand "the mind of a burglar, because, as a matter of fact, the mind and the instincts of a burglar are of the same kind as the mind and the instincts of a police officer" (92). From his point of view, thievery is "not a sheer absurdity." *Absurdity* is what bothers Chief Inspector Heat, and he associates it with the likes of the Professor, anarchists or terrorists. To Heat, the Professor embodies a real difference (Heat doesn't recognize him "as a fellow-creature" but as someone "impossible – a mad dog to be left alone"). And there is no doubt but that – except for the fact that her sees it in a more positive light – the Professor is in essential agreement with this. "Like to like," he says, when comparing Heat to Karl Yundt. "The terrorist and the policeman both come from the same basket" (69). But though *he* obviously believes that he comes from a *different* basket, there is no need for us to agree. After all, in at least one respect, the Professor is just like both the Chief Inspector – in his private dealings with Verloc ("It's a private affair of my own") – and also Verloc himself. In fact, it could even be said that, in this one respect, the Professor is like just about everyone else in the novel, including Mr Vladimir. He too is a secret agent.

The clue we need to pursue is found not so much in the character of the Professor as in "the general idea of the absurdity of things human," an idea that the novel associates less with the Professor than with Mr Vladimir. Of course, in terms of politics, these two would seem to be at opposite poles: Mr Vladimir, the arch-conservative, who wants Mr Verloc to influence "the public opinion here in favour of a universal repressive legislation;" the Professor, the perfect anarchist, who wants to "break up the superstition and the worship of legality." Yet *these* differences may be less significant than what Mr Vladimir and the Professor have in common – not just the fact that they are both secret agents but that they are also both terrorists. Somewhat para-doxically, then, if Mr Vladimir *is* significantly different, what makes him so – in addition, that is, to the key structural position he occupies in the novel's plot – is the way in which he manages to summarize and express sentiments that he *shares* not only with the Professor and other anarchist characters in the novel but also with many historical figures *outside* of the novel, most of whom we don't think of as anarchists at all. In the course of the exchange with Verloc in the novel's second chapter, Conrad manages to articulate through Mr Vladimir an astonishing distillation of some of the key preoccupations of avant-garde thinkers from the beginning of the nineteenth century through to the 1960s and 70s.

I'm thinking first of his observation that the "sensibilities" of the middle classes are "blunted" and "jaded," an observation that was perhaps originally made by Wordsworth in his famous "Preface." Then of his frequently reiterated insistence that "the middle classes are stupid" and "idiotic," which might remind us of Flaubert, whose obsession with stupidity is well-known, and – in the generally "scorn[ful]" and "contemptuous" manner in which he expresses his detestation of the "imbecile bourgeoisie" – of any number of thinkers from Flaubert down to Sartre.[20] And, finally, I'm thinking of his idea that what is needed is a "series of outrages," of the kind that will constitute an attack *on meaning* itself:

> But what is one to say to an act of destructive ferocity so absurd as to be incomprehensible, inexplicable, almost unthinkable; in fact, mad? Madness alone is truly terrifying, inasmuch as you cannot placate it either by threats, persuasion, or bribes....The attack must have all the shocking senselessness of gratuitous blasphemy. (*SA*, 33)

Once again, this is an idea or, perhaps, more accurately, a cluster of ideas, one or another of which can be found, again in Flaubert and then later on, in successive generations, in André Gide, Albert Camus and eventually Roland Barthes and others in the 1960s.

So what are we to make of all this? I think that it means two things. First, Mr Vladimir strikingly *embodies* the crisis he has taken it upon himself to *solve*. Secondly, what makes this crisis (or this stage of the crisis) so much more advanced than the one dramatized in *Billy Budd, Sailor* is the fact that whereas the earlier one threatened differences, this one threatens *difference--as-such*, which is to say that it directly threatens *meaning,* or the *logos,* as such. We can be reasonably sure, in other words, that we understand Mr Vladimir's intention: he wants to break the law in order to strengthen it and to destroy meaning in order to recreate it. The irony is that, whereas the means he has chosen to solve the crisis only aggravate it, the novel makes us aware of the sense in which, in different circumstances, his intervention *might* have helped to produce a solution to the crisis. Conrad encourages us to reflect what *might* have happened if Chief Inspector Heat had done what he wanted to do, which was to arrest Michaelis, the anarchist, and make him into a scapegoat. What if "the public" had "roar[ed] with...indignation" and he had "thrown [Michaelis] down [to them]?" Then, I take it, Michaelis might have been dismembered as Stevie is dismembered and, like Stevie's, Michaelis's bodily parts might have also resembled "raw material for a cannibal feast." In different circumstances, a community might then have formed in the unanimity generated in the public by this killing of an anarchist. And in the course of time Michaelis, like Stevie, might even have come to seem like a kind of savior.

But of course if any of this had happened it would have been unintentional. Mr Vladimir may be occupying a place in *The Secret Agent* analogous to the one occupied by Captain Vere in *Billy Budd, Sailor* but, unlike Vere, he clearly lacks the fundamental information, concerning the creation and function of the sacred, he needs. Which is why the accidental, pointless, meaningless and absurd death of Stevie, whom Mr Vladimir doesn't even know, is so different from the death of Billy Budd.

As Conrad explains in his "Author's Note," the challenge he faced was to find a way of dealing with the sheer absurdity of it all. In fact, at first the "story of the attempt to blow up the Greenwich Observatory [seemed] a blood-stained inanity of so fatuous a kind that it was *impossible to fathom its origin* by any reasonable or unreasonable process of thought" (X; my italics). He started to feel differently when a friend casually remarked that "that fellow was half an idiot. His sister committed suicide afterwards." But why? Why did *this* piece of information suddenly seem so "illuminating?" It may in itself have suggested to him that the way to write the story was as a sacrificial crisis that fails to resolve itself. My reason for thinking this is that Conrad writes about Winnie and Stevie exactly as if they are the kinds of twins that turn up so often in myth and that, according to Girard, frequently get transformed, during the course of a sacrificial crisis, into the kind of monstrous double that gives us another version of the two faces of the sacred. Thus, a second or two before Mr Verloc's death, we read the following: "As if the homeless soul of Stevie had flown for shelter straight to the breast of his sister, guardian and protector, the resemblance of her face with that of her brother grew at every step, even to the droop of the lower lip, even to the slight divergence of the eyes" (262). And this occurs, incidentally, even though Mr Verloc (who clearly feels himself safely ensconced in "familiar sacredness – the sacredness of domestic peace") "did not see [it]." It occurs for *our* eyes.

Whether or not it was the idea of this brother and sister that suggested a failed sacrificial crisis to Conrad, there can, it seems to me, be no doubt about its appropriateness. After all, what could be more effective than the decision to view this apparently meaningless and absurd event as an *attack* on meaning that unintentionally produces the kind of victim or victims – Stevie *and* Winnie – out of which meaning was originally generated?[21] Nor can there be any doubt but that this *is* the framework he chose for his story. Hence, of course, the various explicit references to sacrifice and scapegoating: the Professor suggesting on one of their meetings that Chief Inspector Heat has "a fine opportunity of self-sacrifice;" Chief Inspector Heat thinking it "an excellent thing to have [Michaelis] in hand to be thrown down to the public should it think fit to roar with any special indignation in this case" (90); Winnie's mother "sacrificing Winnie" and herself to try to protect Stevie; Winnie's own "self-sacrifice." And so on.

In such a crisis almost everyone has either already been a victim or has the potential to become one. Including, for example, the father of Stevie and Winnie who was, we are told, "wounded in his paternal pride, declaring *himself* obviously *accursed* since one of his kids was a 'slobbering idjut and the other a wicked she-devil'" (my italics).[22] Indeed, the list of victims even includes Mr Vladimir who is "[d]escended from generations victimized by the instruments of an arbitrary power." Which means that almost everyone could potentially find that he or she is no longer being recognized as "a fellow-creature" but as something monstrous, like "a mad dog," instead. Or like the "Hyperborean swine" or "dog-fish," which are two of the ways in which Mr Vladimir gets recognized, by Mr Verloc and the Assistant Commissioner. In this sort of crisis the truth – that, like Mr Verloc, Mr Vladimir too is "a human being – and not a monster" – becomes increasingly difficult to hold onto. Furthermore, if, in such a crisis, everyone is potentially interchangeable as a victim, by the same token, it can also be said that virtually everyone is a kind of revolutionary (like Sir Ethelred) or radical ("All the damned professors are radicals at heart").

Finally, there is the question as how to get out of this kind of crisis, how to bring it to an end. And to this there would seem to be no easy answer. Conrad's description of the effect of being driven in the horse-driven cab hints at the nature of the problem: "the effect was of being shaken in a stationary apparatus like a mediaeval device for the punishment of crime, or some very new-fangled invention for the cure of a sluggish liver" (163). Mr Vladimir's insistence that "[w]e don't want prevention – we want cure," and his advising Mr Verloc that "[w]hat we want is to administer a tonic to the Conference in Milan," ignore the problem, which is precisely the difficulty in distinguishing something that might provide a "cure" from something that might only deepen the crisis. We might think, in this connection, of the sequence that ends up with Stevie swallowing a "terrifying statement [made by Karl Yundt] with an audible gulp, and at once, as though it had been swift poison, [sinking] limply in a sitting posture." In other words, the problem is the one Derrida examines in his now famous discussion of the dual nature of the Greek *pharmakon,* as remedy and as poison.[23] It is that the same thing – or what looks, at any rate, like the same thing – can either save or kill us.

In his "Author's Note," Conrad defends himself against criticism by saying that he hasn't "intended to commit a gratuitous outrage on the feelings of mankind" (XV). Which inevitably reminds us – as does the frequent use of such terms as "contempt" and "scorn" throughout the novel – of the language used by Mr Vladimir. And since, only two paragraphs earlier, Conrad has admitted that there were of course "moments during the writing of the book when I was an extreme revolutionist" (XIV)("I was," he explains, "simply attending to my business"), how can we not conclude that at moments he inevitably occupies the position of Mr Vladimir? But, if so, he is surely being forgetful when he claims that "the thought to elaborate mere ugliness, to shock...has never entered [his] head" (VIII). It *must* have entered his head, at the same time as Mr Vladimir did. In a similar way, though it seems obvious enough at times that he is being ironical at the expense of Comrade Ossipon's belief in science-in-general (as if it were something sacred), and Lombroso-in-particular (Lombroso being the one who identifies criminals by their teeth and ears), Conrad himself tends to make a point of noticing the teeth of many of his characters (and it is clear that, in various ways, he attaches the greatest of importance to hearing).[24]

As far as irony is concerned, Conrad tells us (again, in "Author's Note") that he deliberately applied "an ironic method" to the subject in the belief that it alone would enable him to say all he had "to say in scorn as well as in pity." Nearer the end of the Note, we find the following:

> Lately, circumstances,...have compelled me to strip this tale of that literary robe of indignant scorn it has cost me so much to fit on it decently, years ago. I have been forced, so to speak, to look upon its bare bones. I confess that it makes a grisly skeleton. (XIV-XV)

What this seems to suggest is that Conrad's irony functions as a kind of "robe" that effectively covers up the grim and even indecent truth. And I find this misleading, at least as far as Conrad is concerned. Yet it seems to me a useful way of thinking about *Billy Budd, Sailor*. In that work Melville does indeed – some of the time, at least – use his art to conceal. On the other hand, in the discussion which the surgeon has with the purser after Billy's execution Melville opens up the kind of gap in which later writers and readers could clearly perceive (what William Burroughs has called) Billy's "cheating profile."[25] Melville's art both conceals *and* reveals. But I see no concealment in *The Secret Agent* at all.

I want to end up by commenting very briefly on the argument that Paul B. Armstrong has recently made about Conrad's irony. Writing as a "liberal ironist" in Richard Rorty's sense of the term (as explained in Rorty's book *Contingency, Irony, and Solidarity*), Armstrong argues that Conrad provides liberalism with the kind of challenge it needs to confront if it is not to fall "into political complacency and epistemological naivete."[26] The challenge derives from the fact that Conrad has "a tonic, illuminating anguish about a contradiction Rorty would have us embrace – the contradiction, namely, between an ironic awareness of the contingency of all norms, beliefs, and values and the necessity nonetheless to affirm a commitment to community,

compassion, and self-invention." This seems to me well said
and, like Armstrong, I too find Conrad's way of dealing with
"the unresolvability of the contradiction between contingency
and commitment more revealing, defensible, and intellectually
honest than Rorty's commonsensical advice that we should stop
worrying about a problem we cannot solve." But I have a slight
reservation when Armstrong characterizes this in terms of what
he calls "Conrad's rigorous bitterness and unrelenting anguish
about the unresolvability." While I agree about the presence of
an "illuminating" and "tonic" bitterness and anguish in Conrad's work as a whole (and in *The Secret Agent* in particular),
I think that the use of the word "unrelenting" may be a bit
misleading. At least insofar as it might encourage us to overlook
the fact that Conrad's irony is often extremely funny.

I will cite just two instances, the first of which uncannily
anticipates the example Louis Althusser was to choose years
later as an ilustration of how ideology transforms individuals
into subjects. It does so, Althusser explains, "by that very precise
operation which I have called *interpellation* or hailing, and which
can be imagined along the lines of the most commonplace
everyday police (or other) hailing: 'Hey, you there'!"[27] But in
The Secret Agent it is Mr Verloc who does the hailing and
a policeman is the one who gets interpellated: "'Constable!' said
Mr Verloc, with no more effort than if he were whispering; and
Mr Vladimir burst into a laugh on seeing the policeman spin
round as if prodded by a sharp instrument" (24).

The second example of the kind of humor I have in mind is
made up of the various references to unreadability and writing in
the great eleventh chapter of the novel. They occur in the
sequence that culminates in Winnie's murder of her husband.
First we see Mr Verloc contemplating his wife's "unreadable
stillness." Next we are told that he "saw no writing on the wall."
We then see Winnie gazing at a wall and we learn that it is
a "blank wall – perfectly blank." And finally, after Verloc has
tried again to get through to Winnie and been defeated by her
"still unreadable face," in the split second before his death, he
does actually see something on "the wall." But it isn't writing. It

is "the moving shadow of an arm with a clenched hand holding a carving knife" (262). Making use of Conrad's biblical allusion, we might, I suggest, call this sequence in which Mr Verloc fails to read the writing on the wall.

I would suggest that one way to understand the presence of such irony, at once anguished, hilarious and exuberant, might be to ponder Georges Bataille's claim that the solution to the enigma of sacrifice is to be found "in laughter."[28] According to Bataille, "*when anguish arises, then laughter begins*" (70). Yet, as he sees it, sacrifice is "*the communication of anguish*" and "laughter is the communication of its dispersion." He speaks, therefore, of "the borderline between laughter and the deep gravity of anguish" and maintains that "to laugh and to be serious at the same time is impossible" (73). But it seems to me that *The Secret Agent* forces us to question this. It may be that what is *most* disturbing about this novel is the way it even dissolves the distinction between laughter and anguish. But, if so, this doesn't make it any the less serious: it simply makes it even more challenging.

NOTES

1. Where Melville is concerned, see, for example, H. Bruce Franklin's *The Wake of the Gods: Melville's Mythology* (Stanford: Stanford U. P., 1963). And though I can think of no one book of comparable stature to Franklin's that is exclusively devoted to Conrad's interest in the subject, it is probably true to say that many of the important works on Conrad take it for granted and deal with various aspects of it in passing.

2. René Girard, *Violence and the Sacred,* trans. Patrick Gregory (Baltimore: Johns Hopkins U. P., 1977), 91.

3. Thus, with reference to the question concerning "a real origin" (91), Girard maintains that "[t]he sacrificial crisis and the surrogate-victim mechanism fulfill all the conditions required of a satisfactory hypothesis" (92). And he makes it clear that, in his view, the surrogate victim is "the key that opens any religious text" (316).

4. Or events. Girard explains that he is *not* arguing either "that the murder was a single historical event or that it belongs exclusively to prehistory" (92).

5. Andrew J. McKenna, *Violence and Difference: Girard, Derrida, and Deconstruction* (Urbana: U. of Illinois P., 1992), 69. My other quotation from this book is from the same page.

6. This is not to say that all victims are transformed into gods. As Girard points out, in the course of distinguishing between mythological texts and what he calls texts of persecution, "[m]edieval and modern persecutors do not worship their victims, they only hate them." See *The Scapegoat,* trans. Yvonne Freccero (Baltimore: Johns Hopkins U. P., 1986), 38.

7. If the judicial system can best operate when "the aura of misunderstanding" has formed "a protective veil around [it]" (*Violence*..., 22), this, according to Girard, is because, in the last analysis, it shares the same function as the institution of sacrifice.

8. See Jurgen Habermas's *Legitimation Crisis* (Boston: Beacon Press, 1975).

9. Not, at any rate, if we judge by the early exchange in which we find her "trying to get to the bottom" of her daughter's response to the question as to whether or not Mr Verloc isn't "getting tired of seeing Stevie about."

10. Herman Melville, *Billy Budd, Sailor (An inside narrative)*, in Herman Melville, *Billy Budd, Sailor and Other Stories,* ed. Harold Beaver (Harmondsworth: Penguin, 1970), 341. All references are to this edition.

11. For a different view of this character, see "Melville's Fist: The Execution of Billy Budd" – in *The Critical Difference* (Baltimore: Johns Hopkins U. P., 1980) – where we find Barbara Johnson referring to his "allegiance to martial law and conventional authority" (100) and claiming that, "[f]or Vere, the functions and meanings of signs are neither transparent nor reversible but fixed by socially determined *convention*" (100).

12. It seems to me that this association of convention with cant and unreality is reinforced by such things as the narrator's telling us that we should consider Billy's "occasional liability to a vocal defect," his "stutter" (*Billy Budd*,..., 331), as evidence that Billy "is not presented as a conventional hero" (332).

13. I recommend Richard Chase's *Herman Melville* (New York: MacMillan, 1949) in this connection. Chase argues that the "real theme of *Billy Budd* is castration and cannibalism, the ritual murder and eating of the Host" (269).

14. Given the various allusions to the Greek gods in the novel, it is worth recalling that – as Lucien Scubla points out in a very different context – "in Ancient Greece...the butcher's shop was a sort of annex to the temple." See "The Christianity of René Girard and the Nature of Religion," in *Violence and Truth: On the Work of René Girard,* ed. Paul Dumouchel (Stanford, CA: Stanford U. P., 1988), 274 (n. 24). See too, in this connection, Marcel Detienne's "Culinary Practices and the Spirit of Sacrifice," in *The Cuisine of Sacrifice among the Greeks,* trans. Paula Wissing, ed. Marcel Detienne

and Jean-Pierre Vernant (Chicago: U. of Chicago P., 1989), 1-20. Detienne explains that "[i]n the city the cook, whom the Greeks call *mageiros*, is indissociably both butcher and sacrificer" (8). He tells us that this "butcher-cook-sacrificer" was "attached to a temple" and refers to "the butcher's art" as that of "carving" (11, 13). He has some interesting reflections on the carving knife, or "sacrificial weapon" (12), and on the need to maintain a distinction between cooking and hunting (8); a point that seems to me relevant to our understanding of the hunting scenes on the walls of the Silenus Restaurant (as described at the opening of the fourth chapter of *The Secret Agent*).

Marlow's well-known references to the butcher in "Heart of Darkness" are also worth reflecting on here. "Here you all are...a butcher round one corner, a policeman round another....You can't understand. How could you? – with solid pavement under your feet...,stepping delicately between the butcher and the policeman, in the holy terror of scandal and gallows and lunatic asylum" (*YS*, 114, 116).

15. See Girard's *Things Hidden Since the Foundation of the World*, trans. Stephen Bann and Michael Metteer (Stanford, CA: Stanford U. P., 1987), 120-5.

16. Girard discusses this in a number of places but see, for example, *Violence...*, 29-31.

17. R. W. B. Lewis's essay on *Billy Budd, Sailor* in *The American Adam* (Chicago: U. of Chicago P., 1955) is probably the best known example of a reading that accepts this on its own terms. It could be said, incidentally, that Billy's execution is meant to guarantee the victory of the *Bellipotent* (Vere's ship) over the *Athee* or *Atheist* (the ship it in fact meets and predictably defeats shortly afterwards) and for the significance of this see Bruce Franklin's *The Wake of the Gods*, 198.

18. I should note at this point the useful distinction Barbara Johnson makes between differences *within* and differences *between*. She argues that the "political content in *Billy Budd* is such that on all levels the differences *within* (mutiny on the warship, the French revolution as a threat to 'lasting institutions,' Billy's unconscious hostility) are subordinated to differences *between* (the *Bellipotent* vs. the *Athee*, England vs. France, murderer vs. victim)." And she concludes by maintaining that "[w]ar, indeed, is the absolute transformation of all differences into binary differences" ("Melville's Fist," 106). In other words, the differences Vere enforces are the ones Johnson calls binary (differences *between* entities).

19. This might remind us of the fate of Don José Avellanos's "Fifty Years of Misrule," the pages of which ended up "floating in the gutters" and "trampled in the mud." *Nostromo* is also preoccupied with the obliteration of differences. A particularly striking example is to be found in the way in which, after insisting in Part One that "we Goulds are no adventurers," Charles Gould is eventually forced, in Part Three, to admit that he and the

adventurer Hernandez are "equals before the lawlessness of the land" and
even that he is "an adventurer in Costaguana, the descendant of adventurers," with "something of an adventurer's easy morality." Similarly, in
Part Two, we learn that Nostromo and Decoud are "merely two
adventurers."

20. Here, for example, is Nietzsche on the subject: "The psychologists of
France...still have not exhausted their bitter and manifold delight in the
betise bourgeoise....Flaubert, for example,...in the end no longer saw, heard,
or tasted anything else any more" (*Beyond Good and Evil*, trans. Walter
Kaufmann «1886; New York: Vintage, 1966», sec. 218, 146-7). As Jean
Paul Sartre explained it, Flaubert's idea was "to combat the stupidity of
other people without ever attacking it, but quite the contrary, *by
experiencing it,* by becoming its medium and its martyr – until he manifests
itself in his own person. In a word, Flaubert dreams of taking upon himself
all the Stupidity in the world, of becoming its scapegoat" ("Class
Consciousness in Flaubert," in *Madame Bovary,* trans. Lowell Blair, ed.
Leo Bersani «New York: Bantam, 1972», 408). For Flaubert's influence on
this novel see also William Bysshe Stein's "*The Secret Agent*: The Agon(ies)
of the Word," *Boundary,* 2, 6: 2 (Winter 1978), 521-40.

21. To say, as Girard does, that "the mechanism of the surrogate victim
gives birth to language and imposes itself as the first object of language"
(*Violence...*, 235), is to say that it gives birth to meaning.

22. Considering, in the light of this, the central role played by Captain
Vere in Melville's novel, we can say that another way of registering the
difference between the worlds of *Billy Budd, Sailor* and *The Secret Agent* is
in terms of the failure, in the latter, of its various father-figures.

23. See "Plato's Pharmacy," in Derrida's *Dissemination,* ed. and trans.
Barbara Johnson (Chicago: U. of Chicago P., 1981), 61-171. See too
Girard's brief discussion of this in *Violence...*, 296-7.

24. Both in this novel, incidentally, and often elsewhere. See, for
example, the reference to Ricardo's teeth in *Victory.* And if, in the same
novel, it is Mr Jones who summarizes "the way of the world" in the
expression "gorge and disgorge," the sentiment describes an attitude that
can be found in many of Conrad's other works.

25. William Burroughs, *The Soft Machine* (New York: Grove Press,
1967; Evergreen Black Cat Edition), 169-70.

26. Paul B. Armstrong, "The Politics of Irony in Reading Conrad,"
Conradiana, 26: 2 (1994), 85. My other quotations are also from this page.

27. Louis Althusser, "Ideology and Ideological State Apparatuses
(Notes towards an Investigation)," in *Lenin and Philosophy and Other
Essays,* trans. Ben Brewster (New York: Monthly Review P., 1971), 174.

28. Georges Bataille, "Sacrifice" (1939-40), *October,* 36 (Spring 1986),
68. This is a special issue of *October* entitled "Georges Bataille: Writings on
Laughter, Sacrifice, Nietzsche, Un-Knowing."

Wiesław Krajka,
Maria Curie-Skłodowska University / University of Wrocław,
Lublin / Wrocław, Poland

Making Magic as Cross-cultural Encounter:
The Case of Conrad's "Karain: A Memory"

Joseph Conrad was a writer of many cultures. His twenty years of service in the British Merchant Navy and journeys in the Mediterranean, to the West Indies, the Congo, Australia, and especially the Far East, exposed him to non-white cultures and races. In Conrad's time, crews on English ships formed multinational communities (as exemplified in *The Nigger of the "Narcissus"*). Ethnic differences and identities were not pronounced in them, as seamen conformed to unwritten laws of the ethos of the British Merchant Navy.[1] Neither are they articulated in the records of young Conrad's travels in the Mediterranean nor to the West Indies. In "Heart of Darkness," which depicts Marlow's (Conrad's) journey up the Congo river, the racial/cultural differences between the whites and the blacks are articulated, but real interracial communication does not take place, as the culture of the black people is not explored in any depth. It is indeed in Conrad's novels and short stories of the Malay Archipelago that the cross-cultural and cross-racial encounter is presented in a more pronounced and detailed way. In Conrad criticism, this encounter is usually treated by reference to imperialist and feminist perspectives.[2] "Karain: A Memory" belongs to these works: it was written in 1897 and included in his first published collection of short stories, *Tales of Unrest* (1898). Somewhat disregarded by critics, "Karain" is a significant text in Conrad's literary career: it initiated the writer's fortunate connection with *Blackwood's Edinburgh Magazine,* and it also introduced techniques and effects typical of Conrad's entire literary output.[3]

"Karain" marks a turning-point in Conrad's delineation of native characters. In *Almayer's Folly* and *An Outcast of the*

Islands they are presented from a white narrator's distanced point of view; they are stereotypical and vaguely drawn – even those who play significant roles in the action of these novels (Mrs. Almayer, Lakamba, Babalatchi, Dain). Only the portrayal of Aïssa reveals an attempt at penetration of a native psyche, but she also conforms to racial stereotype, as she opens her mind neither to Willems nor to Lingard nor to the white narrator. In the first part of "Karain" the distanced mode of presentation continues and is magnified by the use of theatrical imagery with Karain as an actor who plays the main part of an omnipotent ruler on the stage of his "kingdom." His exaggerated power, magnificence and majestic bearing, as well as the splendor of his royal retinue, strengthen the barrier separating him from his white friends. His behavior is unauthentic, his movements and speeches are carefully studied:

> he presented himself essentially as an actor, as a human being aggressively disguised. His smallest acts were prepared and unexpected, his speeches grave, his sentences ominous like hints and complicated like arabesques. ("Karain: A Memory," *TU,* 6)

The real change in Conrad's presentation of Malays comes in the course of "Karain" when the protagonist, haunted by Matara's ghost, escapes in panic on board his white friends' schooner to seek spiritual consolation. This event is followed by his dropping his former pose and his authentic auto-presentation. Under the circumstances created by his white friends, he opens his heart, externalizes his culture, feelings, mind and inner conflicts in his highly subjective and expressive narration.[4] Karain's confessional narration, triggered off by extraordinary external circumstances, is Conrad's first successful attempt at penetration of a native psyche, the first instance of a breaking of the inter-racial/intercultural barrier in his fiction. This results from sincere friendship between the white gun-runners and Karain, expressed here by the authorial narrator for the first time in Conrad's canon:

> There are those who say that a native will not speak to a white man. Error. No man will speak to his master; but to a wanderer and

a friend, to him who does not come to teach or to rule, to him who asks for nothing and accepts all things, words are spoken by the camp-fires, in the shared solitude of the sea, in riverside villages, in resting-places surrounded by forests – words are spoken that take no account of race or colour. One heart speaks – another one listens; and the earth, the sea, the sky, the passing wind and the stirring leaf, hear also the futile tale of the burden of life. (26)

However artificial, unauthentic and idealized this situation may seem, when applied to Karain's confession it definitely increases its verisimilitude.

Conrad's bold venture at psychologically convincing presentation of interracial communication is continued in "The Lagoon" and *Lord Jim*. Arsat's confession in "The Lagoon" is the only other (apart from "Karain: A Memory") instance of a Malay opening his heart and mind to a white man and being understood by him. The motif of a genuine friendship between a white man and a Malay is developed in the relationship between Jim and Dain Waris in *Lord Jim*. However, their fraternity is merely stated, taken for granted; real psychological union of these two characters is not depicted in the novel. All other cases of interracial/intercultural contact between whites and Malays occurring in Conrad's fiction lack such profound intercommunication as that presented in "Karain" and "The Lagoon" and hinted at in *Lord Jim*. They mostly assume the form of protection and philanthropy for natives, as exemplified by Lingard in the Malay trilogy, Jim in the Patusan part of *Lord Jim*, Van Wyk in "The End of the Tether," and such episodic characters as Jasper Allen in "Freya of the Seven Isles," Morrison in *Victory* and Jörgenson in *The Rescue*.[5]

Karain experiences a conflict of loyalties, is isolated by his former transgression, tormented by a sense of guilt (caused by his killing his friend Pata Matara) and feels anguish and remorse.[6] He is Conrad's first attempt at this kind of character creation. "Karain," as well as "The Lagoon" (featuring the same kind of hero), paved Conrad's way for the writing of *Lord Jim*, the protagonist of which embodies this kind of guilt-tormented character in its utmost complexity and ambiguity. The creation

of Karain meant breaking new ground, as this kind of individual
became quintessentially Conradian, impersonated in such cru-
cial figures as Nostromo, Razumov, Leggatt and the captain-
-narrator in "The Secret Sharer," the protagonist of *The
Shadow-Line,* as well as in such lesser guilt-ridden characters as
Big Brierly in *Lord Jim,* the commander-owner of the tug-boat in
"Falk," Captain Whalley in "The End of the Tether," Doctor
Monygham in *Nostromo,* Davidson in "Because of the Dollars,"
Bunter in "The Black Mate," the commanding officer in "The
Tale."[7]

Karain's account of his past experiences reveals his extreme
superstitiousness. Irrational belief in supernatural beings and
phenomena shapes his imagination and perception of reality.
Figures of women, especially powerful ones, fix themselves
deeply in his mind. Karain's tale reveals reverence for his mother
who had authority over "a small semi-independent state on the
sea-coast at the head of the Gulf of Boni" (14). Later, his white
friends' tales stimulate his extreme respect and wonder for the
English Empress:

> He...inquired about the Queen. Every visit began with that inquiry; he
> was insatiable of details; he was fascinated by the holder of a sceptre
> the shadow of which, stretching from the westward over the earth and
> over the seas, passed far beyond his own hand's-breadth of conquered
> land. He multiplied questions; he could never know enough of the
> Monarch of whom he spoke with wonder and chivalrous respect
> – with a kind of affectionate awe! Afterwards...we came to suspect
> that the memory of his mother (of whom he spoke with enthusiasm)
> mingled somehow in his mind with the image he tried to form for
> himself of the far-off Queen whom he called Great, Invincible, Pious,
> and Fortunate. (12-13)

During the search for Matara's sister, Karain's psyche
becomes more and more dependent upon her image, and he even
comes to regard her as his inseparable companion (33-5). Her
figure fills his imagination, helps to preserve his peace of mind,
and supports him in the quest: "She gave me [confesses Karain]
courage to bear weariness and hardships...she soothed me...she

soothed the pain of my mind" (35-6). This dependence develops into a real psychic symbiosis:

> The consoler of sleepless nights, of weary days; the companion of troubled years!...I had seen her for years – a faithful wanderer by my side....Her touch caressed me, and her voice murmured, whispered above me, around me,... (37)

Karain's fear of getting separated from this illusion triggers off the fatal shot (37-8). His fusion of real and illusory phenomena is manifest in his perception of both this woman (39) and of Matara's ghost – viewed as a real person tormenting him (41-2). Karain's psychic wound is later healed by his old Malay servant, who is inseparable from the ruler as his sword-bearer; his words murmured into Karain's ear, or his mere assistance, had the power of pacifying Karain's fears and anguish. The Malay ruler views his confidante as the wizard who "warded from [him] the shade of the dead [Matara]," who "could command a spirit stronger than the unrest of [his] dead friend" (42).

After the sword-bearer's death, Karain becomes enslaved by the ghost haunting him, as "The power of his [the sword-bearer's] charm has died with him" (43): his plight becomes desperate as the safe zone around him is annihilated. Karain hopes that his white friends' unbelief will create a substitute area of comfort for him: he escapes on board their schooner, the only safe enclave (25-6), and entreats them either to take him to their land or provide him with an adequate phylactery. Hollis yields to the Malay ruler's entreaties and, assisted by the other gun-runners, fakes a charm.[8] They use a syncretic code of magic: words, gestures and atmosphere. At the outset of this performance, their grave, powerful and compelling looks contribute to creating the necessary atmosphere, conducive to effective magic actions.[9] Hollis speaks in terms adjusted to Karain's mentality and makes magical gestures: his hands hover above his box, he takes a coin and a ribbon out of it, sews the coin in leather and sews the leather to the ribbon, ties its ends together, lifts his arms and throws the ribbon over Karain's head (47, 50). He desires to transform this object into an amulet, "a thing like those Italian

peasants wear" (50).[10] It is meant to shield Karain from both the
ghost of his former friend and his own compunction. According
to the white narrator, Hollis achieves the desired result: Karain
views the contents of the box as "Amulets of white men! Charms
and talismans!" (48). And just before he obtains the created
amulet he "was the incarnation of the very essence of still
excitement" (50). Hollis manages to impress him with the
English Queen's supernatural power.

Hollis's attempts aim at making their Malay friend believe in
the magic properties of the newly-created amulet, at making his
attraction to this object extreme. He entreats his fellow-gun-
-runners to help "make him [Karain] believe – everything's in
that" (50). His speech and gesticulation play an analogous role
to that used in prayers and rituals: mainly to increase the
addressee's belief in the power of the magic object. The white
narrator enforces Hollis's endeavors by complementing them on
the verbal level. He increases Karain's trust in Hollis ("He is
young, but he is wise. Believe him!" – 50) and eventually utters
the magic formula ("Forget, and be at peace!" – 50). Its language
is that of an incantation: it lends magical properties to the coin,
expresses belief in the supernatural power of the pronounced
words and aims at imparting this faith to the Malay ruler.

In consequence of all these actions, he regains his former
self-confidence: "Karain seemed to wake up from a dream...
shook himself as if throwing off a burden. He looked round with
assurance" (51). Having pronounced the magic formula, the
white narrator suggests the magical impact of the amulet: "'He
[Matara's spirit] is not there,' I said, emphatically, to Karain. 'He
waits no more. He has departed forever'" (51). The repetition of
his words by the Malay – "'No! He is not there waiting,'...'I do
not hear him,'...'No!'...'He has departed again – forever!'" (51)
– indicates his belief in the message imparted to him. Like
incantations, these utterances have supernatural power, they
lead to the fulfilment of the expressed wish – annihilation of the
phantom tormenting Karain. His belief is strengthened by the
white gun-runners: "We assented vigorously, repeatedly, and
without compunction," in the hope that "we affirmed our faith

in the power of Hollis's charm efficiently enough to put the matter beyond the shadow of a doubt" (51). The transformation in Karain is reflected in the reality surrounding him – its descriptions evoke the romantic conception of nature, functioning as a parallel image of a character's frame of mind: Karain's restored self-confidence coincides with a change in the aspect of nature, which seems to express its concern for him and to share in his cheerful mood and happiness: "above his head the sky, pellucid, pure, stainless, arched its tender blue from shore to shore and over the bay, as if to envelop the water, the earth, and the man in the caress of its light" (51). The effectiveness of the charm is finally confirmed by the self-assurance with which Karain returns to his domain: "He left us, and seemed straightway to step into the glorious splendour of his stage, to wrap himself in the illusion of unavoidable success" (52). He reassumes his former role of omnipotent ruler, worshipped by his subjects.

The performance by Hollis and his fellow gun-runners may be viewed as a ritual, a shamanic mystery. The charm created in it is effective symbolically and instrumentally (it determines Karain's later actions and mentality). It is sympathetic (that is, operates on the principle that like produces like), "white" and protective, as it produces beneficial effects for Karain: it shields him from Pata Matara's ghost, brings about his catharsis and restores his self-confidence, allowing him to continue normal activities. The successful wizard manages to turn "mana" into a force which influences Karain's mind and conduct favorably.

The jubilee sixpence, presented by Hollis to Karain, is a typical amulet which protects its owner against evil forces. It functions as a medium: it enables Karain to restore his former status (he returns to his "kingdom" as if reborn, free from anxiety and unpleasant hallucinations). This amulet has a round shape, which is a symbol of perfection, divinity, internal harmony, spiritual rebirth, the sun. It is like a magic ring which ensures safety and wards off evil spirits. The engraved image of the English Empress is its most essential element (in folk symbolism women were generally understood to be associated with supernatural powers). Karain comes to believe in this impersonation. He trusts that the magic power of the amulet has been transferred to him, its owner. He manifests an animistic sense of reality (according to which all the surrounding world is alive, pervaded by invisible forces or spirits which have the power to determine human existence), which gives birth to magical thinking, to the creation of magic. In this performance Hollis plays the role of a shaman: a magician, a medium and a healer. As such, he is an altogether different kind of person: he has access to external mystical forces beyond the ordinary human sphere. He functions as a mediator between the realm of supernatural power and the protagonist – it is through him that this power is channelled and directed at Karain to alter his predicament. Hollis the shaman is a liminal figure – both mortal and immortal, human and supernatural, tame and wild. Karain credits him with the power of establishing communication with the other world. Karain believes that Hollis comes into contact with spirits on his behalf, the white man's soul enters their realm to nullify the influence of Matara's ghost. Hollis succeeds in rendering its destructive power harmless, inactive and inoffensive, in shielding his Malay friend by means of appropriate magic, enveloping him in a kind of protective armor. Hollis uses standard shamanic techniques: manual, verbal, symbolic, purifying, sympathetic, cathartic and sacrificial. At the outset of his ritualistic performance, he applies the typically shamanic devices of ecstasy and hypnosis: he achieves mystical communion with the spirit world during a hypnotic/auto-hypnotic trance. His mysterious gestures transfer the coin from the realm of the profane to the realm of the sacred, transform it into a magic object, make safe and sacred the space around Karain. Hollis hypnotizes his Malay friend, impresses him with his seeming supernatural power (as well as partly his fellow-gun-runners and himself). The shaman's power prevents Matara's spirit from doing its will. Hollis's gestures and words are directed towards the coin, which constitutes the focal point of this ritual performance: the attention of all its participants is centred on it. His movements and utterances function like a prayer which is to exorcize an evil spirit. They make the spell effective and heal Karain's psychic wound. Hollis's technical actions acquire the status of expressive actions, they create magic, symbolic communication. Hollis's success largely results from producing a highly dramatized atmosphere, from the quasi-theatrical nature of his performance. The magical communication between the white sailors and Karain is mysterious, secret and private: they are his only confidantes, their knowledge of his secret isolates all of them from other people, makes intimate Karain's confession and their interactions with him. Hollis's shamanic performance is enacted in a time and place appropriate for such rituals: in isolation (away from Karain's people) and at daybreak (see the symbolic contrast between the dark of the night of Karain's enslavement and the light of the day of his liberation from his anguish). The narration of this scene skilfully depicts three basic components of this ritual performance: the experiences of the shaman, the audience and the person impressed with the magic.[11]

However, the narration of "Karain" applies typically Conradian strategies of ambiguity and re-interpretation.[12] The Malay ruler's superstitiousness and dependence on illusions and phantoms turns him into an object of both Hollis's pity and irony.[13] Hollis's magic-making is an act of sincere compassion and help: his desperate endeavors result in a real service rendered to his Malay friend, in termination of his anguish, in a "white lie" (a prefiguration of the "white lie" in "Heart of Darkness"); they constitute a humane extension of the "white man's burden." But simultaneously, his attitude is permeated with a sense of racial superiority and irony: upon his arrival on board the schooner he is called by Hollis a "[c]eremonious beggar" (22). Later Hollis is reprimanded by his companions for cynicism (47); he also seems to question the possibility of a white man's friendship with a Malay (47). In the course of the shamanic mystery, Hollis treats the object of his endeavors with irony and scorn. He communicates a double message: an impressive-magic utterance in Malay directed to the protagonist and a commentary upon it in casual English, addressed to his white friends: "he talked to us ironically, but his face became as grave as though he were pronouncing a powerful incantation" (47).

The communication among gun-traders (constituting an essential element of the narrative structure of this short story)[14] frames the relation of the shamanic mystery discussed above by making its privacy and secret public, with the whites acting parts, like in a play. However, their attitude undergoes significant evolution in the course of this scene. At its outset they are at a loss not knowing how to help Karain (45-6), and they disapprove of Hollis's sense of superiority, irony and sarcasm toward Karain ("Don't be so beastly cynical" – 47). After a while, they yield to the persuasion of Hollis's magic and to the ghosts, charms and amulets of white men which seemed to be shut in Hollis's box to be later released (48-9); they look bewildered by Hollis's actions ("We did not know whether to be scandalized, amused, or relieved" – 49). Yet in the final, decisive phase of this process (50-1), they express whole-hearted approval and support of Hollis's actions ("We did our best; and I hope we affirmed our faith in the power of Hollis's charm efficiently enough to put the matter beyond the shadow of a doubt" – 51).

The strategy of ambiguity and re-interpretation is also manifest in Conrad's use of the concept of illusion, essential to this story. Karain's request for help is grounded in his profound conviction about a fundamental difference between irrationality and superstitiousness in Malays (like himself) and unbelief and rationality in white representatives of the Western civilization (like the gun-runners):

> With you I will go [Karain says]. To your land – to your people. To your people, who live in unbelief; to whom day is day, and night is night – nothing more, because you understand all things seen, and despise all else! To your land of unbelief, where the dead do not speak, where every man is wise, and alone – and at peace! (44; see also 24)

This sense of duality seems to be shared by the white narrator who, in the course of Karain's narration, feels the invisible presence in their cabin "of noiseless phantoms, of things sorrowful, shadowy, and mute," from which protection and relief is given by "the firm, pulsating beat of the two ship's chronometers ticking off steadily the seconds of Greenwich Time" (40). But this distinction is soon undermined by his claim that Western people's rationality is a façade, a pretence. In reality they are strongly irrational and persecuted by their own illusions, ghosts and memories – not unlike Karain. The white narrator gets an impression that in the course of charm-making

All the ghosts driven out of the unbelieving West by men who pretend to be wise and alone and at peace – all the homeless ghosts of an unbelieving world – appeared suddenly round the figure of Hollis bending over the box; all the exiled and charming shades of loved women; all the beautiful and tender ghosts of ideals, remembered, forgotten, cherished, execrated; all the cast-out and reproachful ghosts of friends admired, trusted, traduced, betrayed, left dead... (48-9)

The power of the newly-created charm is undermined, too: a sixpence may be associated with a fake, and Karain's unbounded admiration for Queen Victoria may be viewed as mimicking Disraeli's elevation of her as the Empress of India and the late Victorian worship of the British Empire.

Illusion is the central element in the conception of *teatrum mundi* (the playhouse of the world) which constitutes a crucial organizing principle of this short story.[15] Karain is constantly placed in a world in which illusory phenomena acquire the status of reality and real phenomena acquire the status of illusion, in which reality and illusion blend into a homogeneous mode of existence. This real/illusory world is at first created both by Karain's playing-living on the stage of his "kingdom" and by his psychic symbiosis with the phantoms treated by him as real human beings (Matara's sister – in the course of pursuit, and Matara – after the fatal shot). Later, Karain's experiences, as confessed on board the schooner, are compared by the white narrator to a dream (26), and he is called one of "the men that wander amongst illusions" (40). The scene of charm-making, too, is presented as having a real/illusory status: having got the

new amulet from Hollis, "Karain seemed to wake up from
a dream [of his confession and of the shamanic performance]"
(51) to return to the stage of his kingdom to play-live his rôle
there as the ruler protected by the amulet: "He left us, and
seemed straightway to step into the glorious splendour of his
stage, to wrap himself in the illusion of unavoidable success"
(52). Thus, Karain's belief in spirits and amulets erases the
border between fiction and reality. His acting on the stage of his
"kingdom" and communication with ghosts form two kinds of
illusoriness mixed with actuality – essential for his mode of
existence.

The final narrative situation, reporting the white narrator's
meeting with Jackson in a London street, further emphasizes the
real/illusory status of Karain's experiences and prevents the act
of magic-making from being concluded on a triumphant note of
racial superiority. Here again Western rationalism turns out to
be a mere pretence, as the white narrator's conversation with
Jackson reveals that whites cherish illusions, like Karain. The
two gun-runners ponder the real/illusory status of Karain's
realm and their successful charm-making, as well as of the
London reality surrounding them. This ambiguity is enhanced
by the description of London, which combines the tendencies of
realistic and impressionistic presentation (54-5). Some critics
stress that Karain's world is more real and morally superior to
the London reality enveloping the white narrator and Jackson.[16]
Thus, the final episode of this story re-interprets Hollis's act of
charm-making and makes it more ambiguous.

"Karain" is an interesting and remarkable text in many ways.
It terminated Conrad's creative impasse. It constitutes a successful attempt at penetration of a native psyche, one of very few
instances in Conrad's fiction of psychologically convincing
presentation of cross-racial and cross-cultural communication,
of an authentic friendship between a white and a Malay.
"Karain" makes an interesting and complex use of the conception of *teatrum mundi*, manifest in all the cases of merging of
reality and illusion, in Karain's acting on the stage of his
"kingdom," in his communication with various ghosts, in

Hollis's charm-making. All these elements turn "Karain" into both an outstanding artistic achievement and an important prefiguration of themes and ideas developed in *Lord Jim*.[17] This short story also uses other quintessentially Conradian themes and motifs which integrate it into the writer's canon and pave the way for such masterpieces as *Lord Jim*, "Heart of Darkness," *Nostromo* and *Under Western Eyes*. It presents the typically Conradian guilt-ridden hero, isolated by his former transgression and tormented by a sense of guilt. It also uses essentially Conradian strategies of ambiguity and re-interpretation (manifest in Hollis's attitude of compassion and irony, in various treatments of the concept of illusion, in undermining the whites' rationality and unbelief and the power of Hollis's charm--making, in mimicking the unbounded admiration for Queen Victoria and the British Empire). And this short story is a unique instance of literary presentation of a ritual, a shamanic performance.

NOTES

1. See W. Krajka, *Isolation and Ethos. A Study of Joseph Conrad* (Boulder, CO: East European Monographs, 1992), 111-271.

2. See e.g. A. Fleishman, "Colonists and Conquerors," in A. Fleishman, *Conrad's Politics: Community and Anarchy in the Fiction of Joseph Conrad* (Baltimore: Johns Hopkins, 1967); R.F. Lee, *Conrad's Colonialism* (The Hague: Mouton, 1969); and the articles by H. Krenn ("The 'Beautiful' World of Women: Women as Reflections of Colonial Issues in Conrad's Malay Novels"), G. Fraser ("Empire of the Senses: Miscegenation in *An Outcast of the Islands*"), P. Mongia ("Empire, Narrative and the Feminine in *Lord Jim* and 'Heart of Darkness'") and P. Armstrong ("Misogyny and the Ethics of Reading: The Problem of Conrad's *Chance*") in the section "Gender" of *Contexts for Conrad*, eds. K. Carabine, O. Knowles and W. Krajka (Boulder, CO: East European Monographs, 1993).

3. See W. Krajka, "Betrayal, Self-Exile and Language Registers. The Case of 'Karain: A Memory'," *L'Epoque Conradienne*, 19 (1993), 47-69.

4. See *ibid.*, 53-9.

5. See W. Krajka, *Isolation and Ethos....*, 202-9.

6. See A. Gillon, *The Eternal Solitary: A Study of Joseph Conrad* (New York: Bookman Associates, 1960), 122; A. J. Guerard, *Conrad: the Novelist*

258 Wiesław Krajka

(Cambridge, MA: Harvard U. P., 1958), 91; B. M. Johnson, "Conrad's 'Karain' and *Lord Jim*," *Modern Language Quarterly*, 24:1 (1963), 13-20; W. Krajka, *Isolation and Ethos*...., 85-8; O. Andreas, *Joseph Conrad. A Study in Non-conformity* (London: Vision Press, 1962 «1959»), 31-4.

7. See W. Krajka, *Isolation and Ethos*...., 73-90, 180-201.

8. On the psychological portrait of Karain, the function of his sword-bearer and Hollis's act of magic, see T. E. Boyle, *Symbol and Meaning in the Fiction of Joseph Conrad* (London: Mouton, 1965), 63-5; B. M. Johnson, "Conrad's 'Karain' and *Lord Jim*;" W. Krajka, *Isolation and Ethos*...., 85-8, 95. R. F. Lee interprets Hollis's charm as a laudable realization of "the white man's burden" (*Conrad's Colonialism*, 23-33). R. Humphries's "'Karain: A Memory:' How to Spin a Yarn," *L'Epoque Conradienne*, 1983, 9-21 presents an opposite view.

9. This atmosphere is prepared earlier: Karain's subjective-expressive narration brings about his presentation as a man in a trance (22-4, 35, 40).

10. Ethnographic sources testify to the appearance of this kind of amulet in various cultural areas. For example Polish peasants wore it, trusting it would protect them from dangers and evil forces: see H. Biegeleisen, *Lecznictwo ludu polskiego* (Kraków: Państwowa Akademia Umiejętności, 1929), 347.

11. The understanding of "magic" and "shamanic rite" applied here is based on the following sources: *The New Illustrated Columbia Encyclopedia* (New York: Columbia U. P., 1978-9), vol. 14, 4120 ("magic"), vol. 20, 6164 ("shaman"); *The Encyclopedia Americana* (New York: Americana Corporation, 1957), 655 ("shamanism"); *The New Encyclopedia Brittanica*, ed. P. W. Goetz (Chicago: U. of Chicago P., 1991), vol. 7, 671-2 ("magic"), 692-3 ("shaman"), vol. 25, 89-91 ("occultism"); H. Biegeleisen, 347-55; E. Leach, *Culture and Communication: The Logic by which Symbols are Connected* (Cambridge: Cambridge U. P., 1976), 29-32, 71-2, 82; C. Lévi-Strauss, *Antropologia symboliczna*, trans. K. Pomian (Warszawa: Państwowy Instytut Wydawniczy, 1970), 253-5; M. Mauss, *Socjologia i antropologia*, trans. M. Król, K. Pomian, J. Szacki (Warszawa: Państwowe Wydawnictwo Naukowe, 1973); M. Popko, *Magia i wróżbiarstwo u Hetytów* (Warszawa: Państwowy Instytut Wydawniczy, 1982); H. Swienko, *Magia w życiu czowieka* (Warszawa: 1964), 69-79; S. A. Tokariew, Pierwotne formy religii, trans. M. Nowaczyk (Warszawa: Książka i Wiedza, 1969).

12. On functions of various types of narration applied in this short story see W. Krajka, "Betrayal, Self-Exile and Language Registers...."

13. On the use of irony, see B.M. Johnson, "Conrad's 'Karain' and *Lord Jim*," 18-19; C. R. La Bossière, "'A Marvellous Thing of Darkness and Glimmers:' The Conradian Playhouse of the World," *Kwartalnik Neofilologiczny*, 25:2 (1978), 173-4.

14. On various functions of narrative framing in "Karain" see W. Krajka, "Betrayal, Self-Exile and Language Registers....," 60, 65-7.
15. See C. R. La Bossière, "'A Marvellous Thing of Darkness and Glimmers:'...," 169-74.
16. C. Watts, "Conrad and the Myth of the Monstrous Town," in *Conrad's Cities: Essays for Hans van Marle*, ed. G. M. Moore (Amsterdam: Rodopi, 1992), 21-2; J. McLauchlan, "Conrad's 'Decivilized' Cities," in *ibid.*, 61-2; R. Hampson, "'Topographical Mysteries:' Conrad and London," in *ibid.*, 161-3. It is significant that their third companion, Hollis, representing the attitude of irony and condescension to Karain, is absent in the final scene, depriving it of these overtones.
17. According to J. Batchelor, *teatrum mundi* functions as a principal mode of presentation of the protagonist in *Lord Jim*: see J. Batchelor, "'Honour,' 'Dream' and 'Tragedy:' *Hamlet*, *La Vida es Sueño* and *Lord Jim*," in J. Batchelor, *Lord Jim* (London: Unwin Hyman, 1988).

Tim Middleton,
University College of Ripon and York, St John,
York, England

Re-reading Conrad's "Complete Man:" Constructions of Masculine Subjectivity in "Heart of Darkness" and *Lord Jim*

Masculinities are lived out in the flesh, but fashioned in the imagination. (Graham Dawson, *Soldier Heroes*)[1]
Egoism is good, and altruism is good, and fidelity to nature would be best of all, and systems could be built, and rules could be made – if only we could get rid of consciousness. (To R. B. Cunninghame Graham, 31 January 1898, *CL*, II, 30)

In this paper I offer an account of some of the ways in which Conrad draws upon extant modes of representation (the imperial gothic[2]/the boy's own story) and their associated construction of masculinity in order to suggest their failure to account for the complexities of lived experience in the modern world. It is something of a commonplace amongst the more general commentators on the early twentieth-century novel that Conrad's fictions offer what might be called "boy's own" adventure stories reworked into a modernist aesthetic, but I want to suggest that in these novels Conrad offers new ways of seeing which seem to me close to a Lyotardian desire to represent what is unrepresentable.[3] In this desire the stories of Kurtz and Jim may be read as tales of abjection in Julia Kristeva's sense that the abject is "that which disobeys classification rules peculiar to...[a] given symbolic system."[4]

In what follows I will attempt to ground these introductory remarks in a reading of the texts which draws upon the cultural politics from which they emerge. I will examine the textualized construction of masculine subjectivity and suggest some of the ways in which it relates to debates in the period and, in particular, to versions of national identity (broadly) contemporaneous with the texts' production. Secondly, I suggest some

ways in which the representation of masculine subjectivity in
these works allows for a reassessment of Conrad's modernism;
a reassessment which begins to move towards developing
Frederic Jameson's suggestion that Conrad be read "not as an
early modernist, but rather as an anticipation of...post-mod-
ernism, or schizophrenic writing."[5]

Imagining Masculinities in the 1890s

Masculinities cannot be analyzed in the abstract: as Peter
Middleton argues, they are "fluid, unstable, constantly reconstructed and embedded in the symbolic realm."[6] Masculine
subjectivity is an effect of discursive interaction, and masculinities are "produced in and by different discourses of
representation."[7] Approaching masculinity as a discursive construct allows the critic to focus upon textual representations as
sites in which competing accounts of masculinity from the wider
culture are put into dialogue, and from this perspective literary
representations of gender may be claimed as part and parcel of
an era's construction of gender.[8] In order to unpack the
discourses which contributed to the construction of masculinity
in Conrad's early fiction it is necessary to establish (briefly) the
wider cultural politics in which his representations signify.

Many critics have explored the interrelation between the new
imperialism of the late nineteenth century, and "the crisis of
identity for men" of that *fin de siècle*.[9] What happens in the later
1890s is, of course, an intensification of trends evident much
earlier; as Graham Dawson notes:

> during the mid-to-late nineteenth century, heroic masculinity became
> fused in an especially potent configuration with representations of
> British imperial identity...[a] dominant conception of masculinity
> – the "true Englishman" – was both required and underpinned by the
> dominant versions of British national identity. (Dawson, *Soldier
> Heroes,* Chapter 1, 1-3)

Empire was projected as a mythic or imaginary space in which
the era's dominant cenceptions of masculinity could be enacted.

Central to the projection of masculinity in imperialist discourse is the notion of the English gentleman:

> He was an amateur furnished with ability – the apotheosis of the amateur. But the essence was a code of conduct – good form: the not doing of the things which are not done: reserve: a habit of understatement....It was in many ways a curious code...it was a mixture of stoicism with medieval lay chivalry, and of both with unconscious national ideals half Puritan and half secular....It is impossible to think of the character of England without thinking also of the character of the gentleman. But it is also impossible to think of the character of the gentleman clearly. It has an English haze. The gentleman is shy, yet also self-confident. He is the refinement of manliness; but the manliness is sometimes more obvious than the refinement.... (Ernest Barker, "An Attempt at Perspective," *The Character of England* «1947»)[10]

> the Englishman feels very deeply and reasons very little. It might be argued, superficially, that because he has done little to remedy the state of things on the Congo, that he is lacking in feeling. But, as a matter of fact, it is really because he is aware – subconsciously if you will – of the depth of his capacity to feel, that the Englishman takes refuge in his particular official optimism. He hides from himself the fact that there are in the world greed, poverty, hunger, lust or evil passions, simply because he knows that if he comes to think of them at all they will move him beyond bearing. He prefers, therefore, to say – and to hypnotise into believing – that the world is a very good – an all-good – place. He would prefer to believe that such people as the officials of the Congo Free State do not really exist in the modern world. People, he will say, do not do such things...the especial province of the English nation is the evolution of a standard of manners. For that is what it comes to when one says that the province of the English is to solve the problem of how men may live together....It is true that in repressing its emotions this people, so adventurous and so restless, has discovered the secret of living...this people which has so high a mission in the world has invented a saving phrase which, upon all occasions, unuttered and perhaps unthought dominates the situation. For, if in England we seldom think it and still more seldom say it, we nevertheless feel very intimately as a set rule of conduct, whenever we meet a man, whenever we talk with a woman: "You will play the game." (Ford Madox Ford, *The Spirit of the People* «1907»)[11]

Crudely summarized, these passages provide a check-list of English masculinity in the early twentieth century which can

serve as a context for understanding Conrad's representation of
masculinity in "Heart of Darkeness" and *Lord Jim*. The
Englishman is an amateur – this idea is tinged with a social
Darwinist sense of racial fitness for survival in-as-much-as the
Englishman doesn't need to specialize in order to be successful;
the Englishman has a code of conduct tied closely to what Barker
calls stoicism and lay chivalry; the Englishman is shy but
self-confident, manly rather than refined, and whilst capable of
feeling deeply is unreflective about his emotions; indeed rather
than face contradictions he will take refuge in what Ford calls
"official optimism;" this capacity for self-delusion means that
the English have solved the problem of how to live together.
These notions are central to accounts of the role of the gentleman
in Britain's imperial mission: empire was both a place where one
could be "a real man" and a place in which the Englishman was
supposed to offer a shining example of "how to be" to the
empire's subject-races. The reality frequently fell rather short of
these ideals as the work of historians like Ronald Hyam makes
clear.[12] Between the "official optimism" of imperialist ideology
and the pessimistic accounts of degeneracy theorists there exists
a range of positions concerning masculine subjectivity which
relate in productive ways to the representations on offer in the
Conrad texts I plan to address. Before turning to the texts I want
to briefly consider how Conrad's notion of the "complete man"
draws upon his own socialization.

Conrad's "complete man"

Writing in the *Daily News* in 1915 Conrad lamented the impact
of "progress" upon seamanship; characteristically the world of
the ship does service for a wider world:

> More and more is mankind reducing its physical activities to pulling
> levers and twirling little wheels. Progress! Yet the older methods of
> meeting natural forces demanded intelligence too; an equally fine
> readiness of wits. And readiness of wits working in combination with
> the strength of muscles made a more complete man.[13]

This tension between readiness of wits and the strength of muscles finds a counterpart in the split subjectivity which arises from Conrad's (peculiar) socialization. The kind of qualities which Conrad is identifying here in sailors – "Seeing things through to their conclusion, tenacity, loyalty, persistence, good workmanship, judgement – these were all Uncle Tadeusz qualities" and in the early fictions under consideration in this essay we will see that "Conrad dramatizes the contrast between these virtues and the flamboyant virtues of his father – idealism, risk-taking and self-sacrifice" (Batchelor, 20).[14] In "Heart of Darkness" and *Lord Jim* Conrad draws upon his own experience of masculinities – the impact of figures as diverse as Uncle Tadeusz, Roger Casement and Dominic Cervoni has been well documented by his biographers – and of the "realities" of Africa and the East in order to cut across the period's dominant constructions of both place and identity.[15] In both texts he is concerned with subjectivities which are beyond the comprehension of the "haggard utilitarian lies" (*LJ*, 282) of extant discursive formations. In these works Conrad explores the dominant notions of masculine subjectivity and reworks them in ways which are profoundly critical not just of the opposition between men of action and men of intellect but, more radically, of the bourgeois fiction of the subject-as-essence.

"Heart of Darkness" and the crisis of subjectivity

"Heart of Darkness" works within a (largely) nineteenth--century episteme in which identity is an essence – a "lonely region of stress and strife" ("Preface," *NN*, VIII): Kurtz's withdrawal into his alienated self – "he had kicked the very earth to pieces...alone in the wilderness...[his soul] had looked within itself and [...] had gone mad" (*YS*, 144-5) – draws upon late nineteenth-century notions of the opposition between madness and civilization, but in my reading "Heart of Darkeness" goes beyond the *fin de siècle* concerns it draws upon. Through the "gap" between Marlow's experiences in Africa and his later meditations upon them the novella is able to counter the period's "haggard and utilitarian" fictions about the continent. The novella doesn't simply suggest Africa as a place in which civilization's writ does not run (the imperial gothic version) nor is it offered as a proving ground for Marlow's masculinity (the Haggardian boy's own version): rather it uses the story of Marlow's journey and of Kurtz's "degeneration" as a vehicle for a critique which encompasses not only the dominant ideologies of imperialism but also the dominant accounts of subjectivity. In "Heart of Darkness" Conrad undermines the whole edifice of the Victorian rational subject by suggesting that consciousness is an effect of language *qua* discourse.

The novella's ability to do this rests upon its bifurcated narrative; it is the gap between the narrating and experiencing Marlow which Conrad exploits in order to offer his critique of the period's notions of subjectivity. Marlow's narrative literally presents individual subjects to the reader as an effect of language; in the gap between the experienced narrating Marlow and the story of his younger experiencing self, we can find a representation of masculine subjectivity not as something which is fixed or essential but, rather contingent on its inter-relation with place. Here the figure of Kurtz is crucial for it is in his troubling capacity as multiple subject – skilled trader, emissary of "enlightenment;" white man gone native; populist politician, visionary, artist, to name but a few of his incarnations – that Conrad furnishes his tale with a register of a very different kind of subjectivity to that adhered to by either the young Marlow or the men who make up the mature Marlow's audience on board the *Nellie*.

The story of Kurtz offers a characteristically *fin de siècle* world-view in which "ideals are mere specious rationalizations of material interests" and language becomes "the reflex of power and desire."[16] Marlow's narrative offers not the sustaining illusion of meaning – but rather a tri-partite meditation upon the impossibility of meaning; on the impossibility of narrating that which lies beyond the "threshold of the visible." It records a narrativization of experience and points up the gaps between the experience and its telling to the extent that some have argued that the Marlow of Part 1 and that of Part 3 have a radically different perspective.[17]

At the center of "Heart of Darkness" is the young Marlow's failure to place Kurtz within extant categories of discourse.[18] The reason he cannot make sense of Kurtz rests with his socialization: Marlow is an Englishman, apt – as Ford suggests – to take refuge in established codes of behavior, bewildered by those who – like Jim and Kurtz – do not adhere to them. In *Lord Jim* he notes that "one *must*" take refuge in "the sheltering conceptions of light and order" which civilization offers. The younger Marlow's sturdy Englishness equips him with a world--view that is utterly at a loss to make sense of Kurtz's eloquent, depraved and multi-faceted self.

For much of the journey (as opposed to his later narration of it) Marlow is a good example of Conrad's "complete man" with little time for introspection or passivity. Marlow's code of conduct – his "deliberate belief" – seems to be associated with the kind of "singleness of intention" he identifies in Towson's *Inquiry into Some Points of Seamanship*.[19] Indeed, it is the lack of these qualities which leads him to suggest that Kurtz is an incomplete man – with no "true stuff." Kurtz's lack of any "singleness of intention" is part and parcel of his multi-faceted subjectivity; the end of the novella reveals that he has been a myriad of things to a wide range of people. In part this is tied into the novella's concern to reveal subjectivity as contingent upon a specific social order but, arising out of Marlow's perplexed yet probing re-telling of his experiences is – as Michael Levenson has cogently argued – a profoundly modern (some might even say postmodern) notion of the subject:

> "Heart of Darkness" does not simply record the unfolding of an action; it unfolds its own mode of understanding action, and by the time it reaches its conclusion it has redrawn its portrait of society, redefined a notion of subjectivity.... (Levenson, 38)

By the end of "Heart of Darkness" Conrad appears to be offering an almost Nietzschean account of the self as "a

multiplicity of subjects, whose interaction and struggle is the
basis of our thought and our consciousness in general."[20]
Marlow's naration foregrounds what Butler terms "the subject
as multiplicity" (Butler, 92): it restages the splitting of the subject
(contingent upon the entry into the symbolic order of language)
by reproducing in Marlow's narration of his earlier experiences
the disjunction between lived experience and the discourses
through which one attempts to communicate that experience.
The novella explores the interconnections between social contexts and subjectivity whilst insisting upon the difficulty of so
doing because language cannot access the Real: the text
foregrounds the ways in which "language...[is]...[a]lways seeking
to 'rationalise,' to 'repress' the lived experience, [and thus
ensures] reflection will eventually become profoundly divergent
from that lived experience."[21] As Marlow puts it: "it is
impossible to convey the life-sensation of any given epoch of
one's existence – that which makes its truth, its meaning – its
subtle and penetrating essence. It is impossible" (*Lord Jim*).
"Heart of Darkness" explores a world "beyond the end of
telegraph cables and mail-boat lines" (*LJ*, 282) in order to offer
"a glimpse of truth" which those readers of *Blackwood's
Magazine* expecting an imperial gothic fiction undoubtedly had
not asked for. The horror revealed in "Heart of Darkness" is not
the marginal experience of a madman but rather serves as the
occasion for "an unveiling of the abject, an elaboration,
a discharge, a hollowing out of [the] abjection" (*Powers of
Horror,* 208) which characterizes the other side of the ideals of
imperialism.[22] More broadly, the "horror" which Marlow's
narrative rests upon is the late nineteenth-century anxiety about
the dissolution of the subject in a world without God; the
"sheltering conception" of rational subjectivity is replaced by
the abject self. We do Conrad a disservice if we read the novella
simply in terms of the established discourses of the era of its
production – seeing it "merely" as a text concerned with
individual regression or the failure of civilization to withstand
the shock of the primitive because, as Marlow's interview with
the Intended and his asides to his audience suggest, the truth

which Kurtz glimpses cannot be transposed into the period's categories. As Levenson argues: "it was when Conrad thought past the former possibility, the degradation of a virtuous man...that 'Heart of Darkness'...disclosed another region of subjectivity" (Levenson, 49). It is this other region of subjectivity which is to the fore in *Lord Jim*.

Lord Jim – towards a (post)modern subjectivity

In many ways the reading offered of "Heart of Darkness" can be applied to *Lord Jim*: again we have an individual who seems to represent the idealized virtues of his community (Jim's Englishness/Kurtz's idealistic imperialism). Jim is "outwardly so typical of that good, stupid kind we like to feel marching right and left of us in life" (*LJ*, 44); more than this, he appears to be "one of us" and so, as was the case with Kurtz, the simplest way of accounting for his actions is to suggest a fatal flaw: as in Marlow's suggestion that there is some "infernal alloy" (45) in Jim. Yet the text works to undermine this reading through its insistence upon Jim's fidelity to a code of conduct which is shown to be increasingly out of step with his lived experience. Jim's whole life is a sequence of roles which – until he gets to Patusan – he has botched; but it isn't this which troubles Marlow: as with Kurtz, Jim's story is disturbing because it cuts across the "official optimism" of Marlow's own deeply in-grained Englishness: "I was aggrieved against him, as though he had cheated me – me! – of a splendid opportunity to keep up the illusion of my beginnings" (131). Marlow is the reader's main source of material on Jim but by his own admission he cannot understand him – "[u]pon the whole he was misleading" (76). Marlow continually returns to the incomprehensibility of Jim's actions and he is uncertain even when he attempts to summarize:

> The truth *seems to be* that it is impossible to lay the ghost of a fact. You can face it or shirk it – and I have come across a man or two who could wink at their familiar shades. Obviously Jim was not of the winking sort; but *what I could never make up my mind about* was whether his line of conduct amounted to shirking his ghost or to facing him out. (197; emphasis added)

As readers of *Lord Jim*, we are presented with a text which appears to be full of anomalies and, in my reading, central to these is the fact that, for Marlow, Jim appears to be the epitome of those codes of English good conduct which his audience hold dear (43-6) and yet this appearance is mere illusion. Conrad uses Marlow's meditations upon the enigma of Jim to move his readers beyond the novel's *Maga* friendly opening chapters. Through Jim's illusory Englishness Marlow's narrative works to disclose a vision "of remote unattainable truth" (323) about the ways in which the beliefs and values of Englishness fail to equip someone as "imaginative" (224) as Jim to deal with Otherness.[23] As Marlow suggests, there is "something abject" (121) about Jim's case and his abjection rests upon the ways in which his life has become blighted by his failure to live up to rules peculiar to the symbolic systems of Englishness. At the start of the novel Jim is shown to be let down by his imaginative egocentrism; paralyzed before his sense that the "brutal tumult of earth and sky...seemed directed at him" (7) he fails to live in accordance to the heroic codes of English masculinity projected in the "light--literature" (6) which impels him to become a merchant seaman. The same imaginative facility leads him to abandon the *Patna* and also, after his trial, to imagine slights from all and sundry. It is "pitiless wedding with a shadowy ideal of conduct" (416) that drives him to Patusan; a place in which he hopes he can realize "his hope of a stirring life in the world of adventure" (6) or, as he puts it, a place which could give him "the certitude of rehabilitation" (248). The close of the novel sees him consciously acting in accordance with his "ideal of conduct" and that this leads to his death seems to me to be a part of Conrad's critique – not so much of Jim's adherence to the codes of English masculinity but rather to the ways in which those codes fail once the specific cultural conditions that generated them are far away.

Conrad's foregrounding of the tensions which arise when one adheres to any single set of principles regardless of circumstances is part of the novel's *fin de siècle* pessimism. The fragmentation of Marlow's re-telling of Jim's story is a device that seeks to ensure that the reader shoulders the burden of interpretation or, as Marlow puts it, "the onlookers see most of the game" (224). In this remark of Marlow's, Conrad offers a hint to the reader: to adapt a comment of Barbara Johnson's about the act of reading, Marlow's narrative offers Jim's attempts to be a stereotypical English gentleman as: "an already-read text;...the already read is that aspect of a text which it must have in common with its reader in order for it to be readable at all" (Johnson, "The Critical Difference...," 165).[24] Jim himself is "already-read," both by Marlow and, more importantly, by the discourses of Englishness which constitute his subjectivity. For Marlow, the tragedy of Jim is that his actions point up the hollowness and idealism of the discourses which are the bedrock of his sense of self. Out of this schizophrenogenic double-bind arises a text which, as Jameson suggests "has discovered the symbolic" (Jameson, 224) with the associated discovery of subjectivity as an effect of language (qua discourse).

Discovering the symbolic: split subjects

From this perspective Conrad's constructions of masculine subjectivity can be read in terms of the Lacanian account of the construction of the subject. Lacanian enquiry focuses on the question of how society and law – the symbolic – enter the individual, with particular emphasis being placed on the role of language as a means of conferring a social meaning.[25] Whilst the psychological and social are inseparable the relationship between the two categories is founded upon misunderstanding: the constructed self is always based upon misrecognition: the entry into the symbolic distorts and deforms the individual.[26] The idea that one's sense of self is a limiting, socially derived constraint placed upon the subject is central to Jim's predicament and in his final act Conrad seems to offer a glimpse of a more radical account of subjectivity; one which might be termed postmodern.

Jean Baudrillard argues that indifference is a characteristic of the postmodern subject: "[t]he subject has...become quietly indifferent to his own subjectivity, to his own alienation."[27] This indifference turns around the disappearance of otherness, a disappearance of norms for behavior arising out of the end of grand narratives (Marlow's "sheltering conceptions") which leads to the increasing dehumanization of the subject that, for me, is revealed in the closure of *Lord Jim*. Gentleman Brown and Jim are – in their own ways – paradigms of the indifferent subject of postmodernity. Brown's case is straightforward: a man of "aggressive disdain" who is "tired of his life, and not afraid of death" and would "stake his existence on a whim" (*LJ*, 354). At the end of the novel Jim's actions can also be read as an act of abject indifference: "Everything was gone, and he who had been once unfaithful to his trust had lost again all men's confidence....loneliness was closing in on him....'I have no life,' he said....There was nothing to fight for....'Nothing can touch me'" (409-13). Whilst Kurtz cries out at the "horror," Jim casts his life away in silence – "with his hand over his lips he fell forward, dead" (416): whilst both are ultimately beyond any understanding which Marlow can put into language Jim's death – for "a shadowy ideal of conduct" – seems to suggest a subjectivity which cannot operate outside of the discursive categories which construct it; Jim lets his body be killed because its actions only have meaning within codes of conduct by whose terms he has failed. Jim's horror is the realization that "what we articulate in our most authentic acts is absolutely not ourselves" (Eagleton, 17): from this perspective it is not Jim who dies on Patusan but the clichés of English heroic masculinity.

Conclusion: re-defining the subject

A central claim in this paper has been that fictional constructions of subjectivity reveal the contradictions of the cultural conditions from which they emerge. In both texts, beliefs and values associated with the maintenance of a particular symbolic order – the myths of enlightened imperialism in "Heart of Darkness," the ideals of Englishness in *Lord Jim* – are shown to be "haggard and utilitarian lies" (*LJ*, 282): unable to withstand the contradictions of lived experience. In my reading, Conrad's account of the dissolution of the rational subject isn't simply an expression of a *fin de siècle* pessimism but a plea for the development of new ways of seeing consciousness not as fixed and stable but as "fluid, unstable, constantly reconstructed and embedded in the symbolic realm" (Middleton, 145). As such, it may be argued that Conrad engages with what Michael Foucault has identified as *the* "political, ethical, social, philosophical problem" of the late twentieth-century, namely:

> not to try to liberate the individual from the state and from the state's institutions but to liberate us both from the state and the type of individualisation which is linked to the state. We have to promote new forms of subjectivity through the refusal of this kind of individuality which has been imposed on us for several centuries. ("The Subject and Power")[28]

Conrad's critique of what he might have termed consciousness makes him not just "a modernist at war with modernity"[29] but also a postmodernist, sceptical of the meta-narratives of the age. As an individual whose own life provided first-hand experience of being a multiplicity of subjects – son of a revolutionary; British Merchant Marine seaman and Captain; man of letters – Conrad's concern with the construction of the subject reveals a Lyotardian desire to seek out "new presentations not in order to enjoy them but in order to impart a stronger sense of the unrepresentable" (Lyotard, "What Is Postmodernism"). As he comments in "Preface" to *The Nigger of the "Narcissus,"* simply to tell the story of a "passing phase of life" (*NN*, XIII), however innovatively, is not enough – is "only the beginning of the task" (XIII). The narrative techniques Conrad deployed in "Heart of Darkness" and *Lord Jim* in order to reveal the constructed nature of consciousness are not simply the product of a (modernist) poetics but are a part of a (postmodernist) politics of the subject which highlights the limitations of extant models of subjectivity and confirms the need for resistance to imposed models of selfhood.

NOTES

1. Graham Dawson, "Introduction: Soldier Heroes, Masculinity and British National Identity," in Graham Dawson, *Soldier Heroes; British Adventure, Empire and the Imagining of Masculinities* (London: Routledge, 1994).

2. Patrick Brantlinger coined this term: the key features are "individual regression...; an invasion of civilisation by the forces of barbarism...and the diminution of opportunities for adventure and heroism in the modern world." See *Rule of Darkness: British Literature and Imperialism 1830-1914* (Ithaca: Cornell U. P., 1988), 230.

3. J. Lyotard, "What is Postmodernism," reprinted in *Art in Theory,* eds. Harrison and Wood (Oxford: Blackwell, 1992), 1014.

4. Julia Kristeva, *Powers of Horror* (Ithaca: Cornell U. P., 1982), 92.

5. Frederick Jameson, *The Political Unconscious: Narrative as a Socially Symbolic Act* (London: Methuen, 1981), 219.

6. P. Middleton, *The Inward Gaze: Masculinity and Subjectivity in Modern Culture* (London: Routledge, 1992), 145.

7. Carolyn Born, Ann Cullis and John Mumford, *Laws of Gender: Concerning Some Problems Encountered in Studying Representations of Masculinity* (Birmingham: Birmingham U. P., 1985; CCCS), 1 – cited in Middleton, *The Inward Gaze:...,* 142.

8. Teresa de Laurentis, *Technologies of Gender* (London: Macmillan, 1987), 3.

9. Elaine Showalter, *Sexual Anarchy* (London: Bloomsbury, 1991), 8.

10. Reprinted in *Writing Englishness 1900-1950,* eds. Giles and Middleton (London: Routledge, 1995), 59.

11. *Ibid.,* 46-52.

12. R. Hyam, *Empire and Sexuality: the British Experience* (Manchester: Manchester U. P., 1990).

13. Cited in Spittles, *Joseph Conrad* (London: Macmillan, 1992), 13. The article is reprinted in *Notes on Life and Letters.*

14. J. Batchelor, *The Life of Joseph Conrad: A Critical Biography* (Oxford: Blackwell, 1994), 1-20.

15. See for example, Batchelor's discussion, *ibid.,* 21-46.

16. Terry Eagleton, "The Flight to the Real," in *Cultural Politics at the Fin de Siècle,* eds. Ledger and McCracken (Cambridge: Cambridge U. P., 1995), 18.

17. On this see Michael Levenson's reading in *Modernism and the Fate of Individuality: Character and Novelistic Form from Conrad to Woolf* (Cambridge: Cambridge U. P., 1991), 1-77.

18. John Batchelor makes a similar point in his account of the novella, see *The Life of Joseph Conrad:...,* Chapter 4, 91.

19. I take this point from Batchelor, *ibid.*

20. Christopher Butler, *Early Modernism: Literature, Music and Painting in Europe 1900-1916* (Oxford: Clarendon P., 1994), 92.

21. Jacques Lacan (London: Routledge and Kegan Paul, 1977) trans. David Macey, 53.

22. This was more forcibly the case with the serial text as that version was less circumspect about Kurtz's aberrations: in Kimbrough's Norton edition (*"Heart of Darkness:" An Authoritative Text: Background and Sources: Criticism*, ed. R. Kimbrough «New York: Norton, 1988») a short sequence of dialogue from the serial is reprinted in which Kurtz declares that he wants more "blood, more heads on stakes, more adoration, rapine, and murder" (72).

23. Marlow, it will be recalled, somewhat disingenuously declares that he has "no imagination" (*LJ*, 223).

24. Reprinted in *Untying the Text: A Post-Structuralist Reader,* ed. Young (London: Routledge and Kegan Paul, 1981), 162-73.

25. I take this gloss from David Fisher's, *Cultural Theory and the Psychoanalytic Tradition* (New Brunswick: Transaction Publishers, 1991), 5.

26. I use the term "constructed self" rather than "ego" as I am working with a (broadly) phenomenological frame of reference in which the subject is constructed by a culture through discourse and its associated iconography. The ego is only part of the subject but is that which has been modified by the direct influence of the external world. (See Freud's "The Ego and the Id" «1923», in *Standard Edition: Volume 19* or *The Essentials of Psychoanalysis* «London: Pelican, 1986», 439-83).

27. Baudrillard, "The Melodrama of Difference," in *The Transparency of Evil* (London: Verso, 1993), 125.

28. M. Foucault, "The Subject and Power" appears in *Art after Modernism: Rethinking, Representation,* ed. Brian Wallis (New York: New York Museum of Contemporary Art, 1984), 417-32. I quote from Robert Siegle's *Suburban Ambush: Downtown Writing and the Fiction of Insurgency* (Baltimore: Johns Hopkins, 1989), 396.

29. D. Erdinast-Vulcan, "Introduction," in D. Erdinast-Vulcan, *Joseph Conrad and the Modern Temper* (Oxford: Clarendon P., 1991), 5.

Paul Hollywood,
London, England

The Artist as Anarchist: Henry James's *The Princess Casamassima* and the Prospect of Revolution

The Dictator, the Despot, is always cowardly. He suspects treason everywhere. And the more terrified he becomes the wider ranges his frightened imagination, incapable of telling real danger from the fancied.... (Alexander Berkman, *The Anti-Climax*)[1]

Get thee glass eyes,
And like a scurvy politician seem
To see the things thou dost not. (Shakespeare, *King Lear*)[2]

"A spectre is haunting Europe...[declared Marx and Engels in 1848] – the spectre of communism. All the powers of Old Europe have entered into a holy alliance to exorcise the spectre: Pope and Czar, Metternich and Guizot, French Radical and German police spies."[3] Their words, poetically capturing the very spirit of this age of revolution, strike the keynote of the theme which was to obsess the minds of writers, journalists, politicians of all persuasions, and everyone concerned with the social and political issues of this time. Indeed, in putting it quite like this, they clearly had in mind to evoke the type of "spectral" worries from which Prince Metternich, the Austrian Chancellor, had famously suffered in his letter to Tsar Alexander of December 1820:

Kings have to calculate the chances of their very existence in the immediate future; passions are let loose, and league together to overthrow everything which society represents as the basis of its existence; religion, public morality, laws, customs, rights and duties, all are attacked, confounded, overthrown, or called into question. The great mass of the people are tranquil spectators of these attacks and revolutions, and of the absolute want of any means of defence. A few are carried off by the torrent, but the wishes of an immense majority are to maintain a repose which exists no longer, and of which even the first elements seem to be lost....

Metternich, the scourge of revolutionaries throughout Europe, was an extreme and apocalyptic conservative. "All revolutions are lies," he wrote and, in an impossible fiction of political stability, wanted European history brought to a "full stop."[4] Ironically, however, his dramatic vision of Europe verging on revolution, born of a sense of vulnerability and fear of "passions...let loose" and in "league" against him, are the perfect realization of the sense of dread and disintegration that Marx and Engels later wished to capture and provoke with their "spectre of communism." With very different feelings, it seemed, the extreme conservative and the extreme revolutionary could at least be united in the conviction that nineteenth-century Europe was on the brink of revolution.

I begin with these contending observations for two reasons. Firstly because it is only in that curious coincidence between the political expectations they express, that we can begin to understand the difficult position of those novelists who undertook to write artistic fiction about politics and revolution at this time, and who wished not to merely propagandize. Secondly because, despite their greatly differing ideological purposes, Marx and Metternich provide us with equally good examples of the language of politics and propaganda against which genuine artists would need to define their work: a discourse typically consisting of visionary statements which, despite their essentially fictional or notional status, nevertheless claim to have a real reference and power in the world. Characteristically politicians attempt to agitate their audience by constructing gaps between their own ideologically engaged and authorized vision and the unengaged vision available to the individual "spectator" of the political scene. Thus, to revolutionary and conservative alike, "the revolution" is a powerful imaginative and linguistic construct by which they mean to direct the vision and control the minds of men for their own political ends. Indeed, in raising this promise or threat of revolution, both Marx's "haunted" Europe and Metternich's "immense majority" in "repose" are turned into the audience for the politician's attempt to transform his implicitly ideological fictions of revolution, his new and energizing descriptions of a crisis-ridden Europe, into the realities of the political world. The novelist who enters this political theatre, and who wishes to construct a representation of the world which is not politically committed, is thus faced with a unique difficulty and a unique temptation: the difficulty of not merely re-producing and adding to the propagandistic myths, fictions and half-truths with which he must inevitably deal; and the temp-tation to exploit the power of expression and representation which acquiesence in those myths would bring.

Thus when, in the mid-1880s, Henry James came to write *The Princess Casamassima* (1886), a novel dealing with the revolu-tionary world of London, he did so against the problematic political background of a world which seemed threatened and dominated by the promise of impending social turmoil: a prom-ise which issued, with equal urgency, from the most reactionary quarters of the political establishments of Europe and from the most revolutionary of their socialist and anarchist opponents. I say "seemed" because, as so many of the critics of his novel have pointed out and as James himself acknowledged, he had no precise information on European political matters and was therefore dependent for his notion on what revolution was upon the pronunciations of prominent statesmen and revolutionaries, and the journalists and writers who interpreted them. His novel was most directly a response to the myths and political fictions of his age, as they emerged from the twin authorities of the revolution and the state. His problem therefore, as an artist whose instinctive tendency was to withdraw from the political world, was to construct an imaginative realization of those myths which remained ideologically and formally distinct from their original political meanings and expressed James's own point of view. *The Princess Casamassima,* as an artist's political fiction, is James's attempt to find an individual language in which to represent the revolutionary "spectres" of the public world; and, in the event, a construction of them which reveals the contradictions and difficulties at the heart of the literary engagement with the fictions of political thought.

I

The extent of the influence that such pronunciations and forecasts of revolution had over James can be gauged by those letters he wrote to his friends and family in the 1880s, in which he describes his impressions of England and takes the prospect of social conflict very seriously indeed. Consider these well-known and rather pessimistic reflections, in a letter to Grace Norton of January 1885:

> there is very little "going on" – the country is gloomy, anxious, and London reflects the general gloom. Westminster Hall and the Tower were half-blown up two days ago by Irish dynamiters, there is a catastrophe to the little British Force in the Sahara in the air...and a general sense of rocking ahead in the foreign relations of the country – combined with an exceeding want of confidence – indeed a deep disgust – with the present ministry in regard to such relations. I find such a situation as this extremely interesting and it makes me feel how much I am attached to this absurd country....The possible *malheurs*...the "decline," in a word, of old England, go to my heart, and I can imagine no spectacle more touching, more thrilling and even dramatic, than to see this great precarious, artificial empire, on behalf of which, nevertheless, so much of the finest stuff of the greatest race (for such they are) has been expended, struggling with forces which perhaps, in the long run, will prove too much for it. If only she will struggle, and not collapse and surrender and give up a part which, looking at Europe as it is today, such may be great, the drama will be well worth watching from (such) a good, near standpoint as I have here.[5]

James's imagination of conflict and "collapse" often tends to be greater than his grasp of the "forces" which will bring it about, and here his sense of little "going on" is overcome by his visualization of a forthcoming struggle. Here in fact one has the basic dramatic ingredient of *The Princess Casamassima* in the vision of England "struggling with forces," the nature of which James does not specify or identify beyond feelings of "gloom" and visions of imagined and dramatic "spectacles." Like Marx's "Europe," James's "old England" is a world threatened by "forces," or haunted by "spectres," which it does not really understand; or, maybe to be more precise, which it does not have the language to describe and so figures in terms of those feelings and visions. Consider another of his letters, this time describing the British ruling class to Charles Eliot Norton in 1886:

> The condition of that body seems to me to be the same rotten and collapsible one as that of the French aristocracy before the revolution – minus cleverness and conversation; or perhaps it is more like the heavy, congested, and depraved Roman world upon which the barbarians came down. In England the Huns and Vandals will have to come up – from the black depths of the (in the people) enormous misery, though I don't think the Attila is quite found....At all events, much of English life is grossly materialistic and wants bloodletting.[6]

Now, in his search for a language to describe those "forces" which threaten the "old" world, James reaches back into historical precedents and myths of other revolutions: into narratives which impose their own ideological structure on events and seem to give them coherence, but which ultimately get him no nearer to his subject. Indeed, what is "going on" in the present is almost totally dissolved and so James can indulge in his image of "bloodletting" without appearing cynical.

The relevance of these letters to *The Princess Casamassima* is not so much that they confirm James's expectation of a forth-coming social conflict, an expectation which he, after all, shared with a great number of his contemporaries, but that they provide an example of the way in which he represents that conflict and are another phase of his search for a way to describe the political world which became the novel. Indeed it becomes clear in these letters, in James's constant straining and reaching out for the right words, that his personal difficulty was in many ways a version or mirror of that most central political tension of the nineteenth century: that somewhat helpless sense, felt keenly by Metternich and attested to everywhere in the literature of the day, that the known world was collapsing and dissolving under the pressure of forces beyond the senses, beyond the ken, and beyond even the naming power, the existing linguistic range, of the ordinary individual. Of course it is this sense of lacking an effective language and vision that Marx and Engels parody with their talk of "exorcisms" and "specters," and to which they also explicitly offer a solution: a way out of political fantasy, of James-like speculation on "barbarians" and "Attilas," in the form of the new language of power and history that James so obviously lacked. Implicit within the Marxist ideological construct is the assumption that there is always a gap or a time-lag between material reality and our consciousness of it, between the world and the worlds we use to represent it, so that in times of rapid material or technological development we are inevitably subject to the seeing of "spectres:" to apprehending our material experiences and instinctive feelings only in terms of haunting presentiments of future understanding, shadowed forth in an imagistic or narrative form, and without ever directly or consciously engaging with them. However, what Marx and Engels were offering in the "manifesto," in response to that problem, is nothing less than a new way of looking at, and describing the world which claims to cut through those "spectral" narratives and visions and bring about the destruction not only of "old Europe's" social and economic systems but, as Metternich and seemingly James feared, also of its entire cosmology, art, ideologies and language.[7] "Communism" is a new narrative of history and a fresh, more direct and "scientific" way of using words to bridge the gap between the past and future, the world and consciousness, material reality and ideology.

This formulation of the Marxist understanding of ideological language places the process of representation which James undertook at the very forefront of political struggle and has, therefore, a direct bearing on any discussion of the connections between ideology and artistic political fiction. As Gramsci was later to argue, "The founding of a ruling class is equivalent to the creation of a *Weltanschauung*;"[8] and any such world-view must control, of course, not only the content but the very forms and terms of expression permitted within it. Political fiction is itself a major determinant of the political reality it claims to represent.

For Marx and Engels, then, it is within that gap or time-lag between reality and its representation, that the "holy alliance" and fictional "nursery tale of the spectre of communism"[9] arise and impose a rigid, conservative and authoritarian representation on the internal dynamic of society towards change. These representations, based on an outmoded religious narrative of history, cut across our direct observation of the world and force our attention out towards a larger supernatural reality of good and evil, saints and devils, "specters" and "exorcisms:" a *Weltanschauung* which derives its power and authority from the fact that it is irrefutable by the individual, because based on realities assumed to exist beyond the evidence of the senses and only to be encountered as mediated through the established institutions of church and state. Operating within the context of power and taking their meaning from, it rather than from anything they actually say about the world, these authorized fictional representations render "communism" as a threatening and secret "power" lurking beneath the visible surface of life: as the evil which must be "exorcized" from the soul of mankind in a gigantic struggle between the forces of order and anarchy.

It is, then, in opposition to such large metaphysical notions of history that Marx and Engels hold out their "manifestation" of communism their revelation of a "history of class struggle," based upon a different type of language use: a language which derives its meaning, not from its social power context, but from its objective and verifiable reference in the world and which can therefore bring "before the face of the whole world"[10] those facts which are overlooked by the discourse of traditional power. "Communism" is the promise of a future controlled by knowledge as opposed to myth; in which there is the guarantee of a "scientific" bonding between the words one uses and the reality one wishes to represent; and which gave rise to new notions of realism in language and in art which inspired theoretists like Zola and eventually Maxim Gorky and the socialist realists.

James, on the other hand, was explicitly concerned to deny the determining power of his fiction and the ideological implications of his choice of language. As an American and as an artist, he characteristically imagines himself to be outside of the political world he observes: to be a fascinated, but detached and private spectator of a conflict in which he is not involved and cannot describe, except in the most self-conscious and unscientific of ways. James's consistent strategy for representigng that conflict is therefore to build himself into it as its audience: with his fascination for its drama justified or politically neutralized by his own disengaged, powerless and self-conscious position as spectator. Consider this reaction to the aftermath of a violent political riot outside of his new Piccadilly home in February 1886, as described in a letter to his brother William:

> I was at Bournemouth (seeing R. L. St.) the day of the *émiente,* and lost the spectacle, to my infinite chagrin. I should have seen it well from my balcony, as I should have been at home when it passeed, and it smashed the windows in the houses (3 doors from me) on the corner of Bolton Street and Piccadilly....The wreck and ruin in Piccadilly and some other places (I mean of windows) was, on my return from Bournemouth, sufficiently startling, as also was the manner in which the carriages of a number of ladies were stopped, and the occupants hustled, ruffled, or slapped and kissed, as the case may be, and turned out. The real unemployed, I believe, had very little share in all this: it was the work of the great army of roughs and thieves, who seized, owing to the formidable nature of their opportunity, a day of licence. It is difficult to know whether the real want of work is now, or not, so very much greater than usual – in the face of positive affirmations and negations; there is, at any rate, immense destitution. Every one here is growing poorer – from causes which, I fear, will continue.[11]

Whilst James displays a quite natural curiosity to see such a dramatic "spectacle," his attitude towards it does at first sight seem strange. He makes it sound as if the events he had missed were not so much a serious public disturbance as the latest instalment of some ongoing popular drama which he could watch, with the air of the fascinated but detached observer, from the safe formal distance of his "balcony." Thus the imaginary scenario he constructs is a situation in which he, James, is looking at "it," the riot, unable to forget his own alien social and literary identity. Even the journalistic mythology, the postulation of an innocent "real unemployed" and of a "great army of roughs and thieves" behind the trouble, falls neatly into James's evocation of a thoroughly melodramatic social and political world of which he, as an outsider, is the bemused and powerless witness.

In his novel, of course, James turned this private act of witness into his literary perspective on the "forces" which threaten England. Whilst he was obviously free to express his imaginative visions and vague political fears in his private correspondence, it is clear that once those imaginings became part of an artistic expression in a public context, then James felt the need to defend his position and to deny the political import of his work. In his "Preface" to the novel, for example, James makes an explicit point of this:

> My Scheme called for the suggested nearness (to all our apparently ordered life) of some sinister underworld, heaving in its pain, its power and its hate; a presentation not of sharp particulars, but of loose appearances, vague motions and sounds and symptoms, just perceptible presences and general looming possibilities.[12]

Whilst in the central tradition of the then burgeoning popular fiction of revolution,[13] this is a highly melodramatic "scheme," it is also a loosely-veiled apology for the lack of "sharp particulars" in his novel. James, of course, was aware of the literary background against which his novel would be received: a dominant tradition of social realist novels which included European realists like Zola, with their claims to "scientific objectivity" and "sharp particulars," and the English social protest novels, with their apparently close knowledge of working-class life and conditions. He was, therefore, concerned to distinguish his work from both aspects of this tradition and to establish it as belonging to another genre altogether: to the melodramatic literature of the city, shot through with feelings of isolation, alienation and unknown "possibility" that James himself evidently felt as he tried to "guess" at the truth behind those threats and promises of revolution. Indeed James's "scheme" clearly emerges from his own conception of artistic experience and practice as a privileged mode of vision which involves, as he put it in "The Art of Fiction" (1884), "the power to guess the unseen from the seen, to trace the implications of things, to judge the whole piece by the pattern."[14] Accordingly, far from offering any kind of objective, "scientific" or omniscient perspective in the world it depicts, *The Princess Casamassima* takes an excited imagination working on a lack of knowledge as the very starting-point of all its observations, and James implicitly foregrounds this fact at crucial points throughout the book.

This is clear, for example, in the description of Hyacinth taking the air outside of the *Sun and Moon* anarchist club, shortly before he take his revolutionary "vow:"

> The puddles glittered round about and the silent vista of the street, bordered with low black houses, stretched away in the wintry drizzle to right and left, losing itself in the huge tragic city where unmeasured misery lurked beneath the dirty night, ominously, monstrously still, only howling for its pain in the hated human cockpit behind him. Ah what could he do? What opportunity would rise?...If he had a definite wish while he stood there it was that that exulted deluded company should pour itself forth with Muniment at its head and surge through the sleeping world and gather the myriad miserable out of their slums and burrows, should roll into the selfish squares and lift a tremendous hungry voice and awaken the gorged indifferent to a terror which would bring them down.[15]

Here it is the city in its psychological dimensions which interests James most closely. Such is the geography of the city, that whatever social realities it can be said to contain must remain, for the most part, hidden and unspoken in the "lost" "silent vistas" of its physical perspectives. Thus Hyacinth is able to see the "unseen from the seen" and to project his agitated anxieties onto the outward aspect of his city world: his sense of its stillness becomes "monstrous" and "ominous;" the silence of the street gives way to a "howl" of "pain;" and his own misery, his own sense of paralyzed alienation and need of an "opportunity," is transposed into the form of an almost embodied figure of lurking "misery." This itself gives way to the more overt fantasy of Hyacinth's friend Paul Muniment leading an exciting revolutionary "surge:" an act of visualization which reproduces James's own invention of this novel which, as he assures us in "Preface," "proceeded quite directly, during the first year of a long residence in London, from the habit and exercise of walking the streets." Indeed he descriebes how "The history of little Hyacinth Robinson...sprang up for me out of the London pavement."[16] For James, on his lonely night-time walks, the city was a theater of fantasy, and Hyacinth is the correlative of his author here as he imaginatively projects his internal hopes and fears onto an external fictional narrative (Hyacinth's subsequent "vow" to be an instrument of the revolution is, of course, the equivalent of James's commitment to verbal constructions of his own).[17]

The prospect of the revolution, then, becomes itself the product and subject of melodramatic fiction to James: in terms of his character's understanding of it, of his own highly self-conscious engagement with its dramatic appeal and power, and, by implication, in his denial of the capacity of a realist technique to describe it. The realist novel is based, of course, on the ideal of the precise documentation of phenomena in language which is an objective and scientific representation of the world. As Zola famously argued, "the goal of the experimental method...is to study phenomena in order to control them;"[18] by which he meant that the language of realist fiction is a language of power authorized by the claim to objective "truth" and the assumption of a direct connection between the word and the world: between the writer's description and the thing described. James's imaginative constructions of "loose appearances," however, consciously dissipate the claim of reference and clearly belong to a dimension of political reality and a language-use in which there is no necessary or desired connection between the word and the world and where referentiality is self-consciously abdicated or denied. James's "possibilities" are no more than an individual and overtly self--referential construction of, and submission to, the authority of those myths of revolution which seemed to dominate the public world he observed. James is the recipient and "reverberator," but not the author, of the set of myths and fictions which are the political world of his revolutionary London.

Thus *The Princess Casamassima*, again as so many critics have pointed out and as he himself admitted in "Preface," represents a new departure for James in his attempt to represent the world: an abandonment of omniscient narration for the new technique of the central recording consciousness, which displaces narrative authority and excuses the author from the responsibility to provide a direct and final interpretation. James's use of this new technique of spectatorship to embody his vision of the forth-coming social crises becomes an implicit formulation of the inadequacy or unavailability of the realist novel, and of the linguistic theories of "scientific" representation which underlie it, to the type of political phenomena he wishes to describe. Indeed his "sense" of the rising revolutionary forces in society becomes even more unknowing, detached and thoroughly unscientific as put into the mind of his confused and divided hero, his central recording consciousness "little Hyacinth Robinson:"

> – the sense, vividly kindled and never quenched, that the forces secretly arrayed against the present social order were pervasive and universal, in the air one breathed, in the ground one trod, in the hand of an acquaintance that one might touch or in the eye of a stranger that might rest for a moment on one's own. They were above, below, within, without, in every contact and combination of life; and it was no disproof of them to say it was too odd they should lurk in a particular form. To lurk in improbable forms was precisely their strength and they would doubtless have still clearer features to show.... (*The Princess Casamassima*, 415)

Hyacinth's almost schizophrenic vision discloses the contradictions at the heart of James's engagement with the "forces" of the revolution which, like the "spectre" of revolution, he renders as simultaneously absent and omnipresent. Once again those "forces" are imaginatively conceived as a ghostly presence "lurking" beneath the visible surface of society and, as such, the perfect material for the melodramatist's novels and the ideologue's myths, but not for the realistic documentation of "things as they are." These "forces" emerge here as both a fantasy and a potentially unlimited power, and James, in a sense, wants it both ways: he wants to evoke, or express, his own "sense" of social crises at the same time as he wishes to disclaim responsibility for adding to the crises in doing so. These reflections, for example, are presented to us through the heavily ironic veil which James uses to distance himself from Hyacinth: the point registered is that such things as "secret" revolutionary "forces" can exist only in the mind of the perceiver and that the belief in them, like any other political or cultural phenomenon, is what constitutes their only reality. "[A]mong the disinherited there's a mystic language which dispenses with proofs," promises Eustace Poupin, Hyacinth's revolutionary friend and one of his mentors, "a freemasonry, a reciprocal divination; they understand each other at half a word" (233). James uses Hyacinth's solipsistic tendency and submission to such ecstatic forms of language to shift the responsibility for the authorship of those "forces" to the imagined authors of the revolution by whom Hyacinth is influenced: for example, to the shadowy revolutionary Hoffendahl, the great "composer" of the revolutionary "symphonic massacre" (280) from whom Hyacinth receives his direction, and in life to the socialists and anarchists whom James could have read about in any newspaper or journal.

James's difficulty, projected into his "little" hero, is that he did not have any knowledge of revolutionary activities, nor even a grasp of scientific or "realistic" language, to abate his fear of what the revolution was; and so he could not attain to, or provide any kind of a positive vision of what was happening in the world outside of his own social circles to counterbalance his sense of impending turmoil. His novel becomes a fiction which is only a fiction, a personal Jamesian language, with no external concrete reference in the world; and his vision of the "forces secretly arrayed against the present social order" turns into a form of cultural despair, with no boundaries other than those of his own frightened imagination. *The Princess Casamassima*, and the tradition of criticism to which it has given rise, thus becomes the search for some kind of certainty and substance for what James suspects "goes on" (his own self-consciously vague phrase used continually in "Preface") beneath the surface of society: the search for a plot or narrative to give formal shape, expression, and hence a "sense" of reality to that general public ignorance and fear of the "looming possibilities" that are the revolution. It becomes, in fact, James's search for his own personal political and social boundaries constructed in narrative form.

It is this which makes *The Princess Casamassima* an interesting and essentially political novel in the sense that, despite its obviously derivative content, it does nevertheless struggle to realize an authentic, if loosely defined, position which is at once political and individual. However, the precise nature and value of that position is a difficult question and one which has proved to be a contentious issue. Until recently critics have tended to locate the politics of the novel in James's presentation of the London anarchist scene and have therefore largely dismissed its political significance by pointing to James's patent ignorance and reliance on others for his material.[19] Indeed many have argued that James's absorption in technical matters of narration means that the novel is not really political at all.[20] Irving Howe, for example, criticized James's "view of politics" as the clichéd politics of the popular press:

> James, despite many fine touches, was relying far too comfortably on his celebrated lack of knowledge and justifying far too easily his acceptance of second-hand impressions. The result was a novel in which the most brilliant insights into political character jostle with a view of politics that reminds one, a little uncomfortably, of the catch-words of melodramatic journalism.[21]

For Howe, the value of the novel derives from the fact that James was "superbly conscious of his handicap,"[22] and its significance must be sought more in its artistic techniques, in what James makes of that "handicap," than in its overt political subject. He is right, of course, in the sense that the novel does sometimes have an uncomfortable effect upon the reader and that James has nothing particularly interesting or new to tell us of the world of London anarchism. However, it is not quite correct to then propose, as Howe implicitly does, so sharp a distinction between an interesting artistic technique and an uninteresting political subject, or to limit our attention to the formally "artistic" elements of the novel. On the contrary, it is more accurate to say that subject begets technique with James, particularly so here, and that his reflections on his limitation to "second-hand" subject matter become more and more the bearer of the politics of the novel. Indeed James's narrative techniques, the deliberate impressionism and the constant disavowing of his authority, are what allow him to articulate the political position which is the true subject of the novel: the position of those consciously outside of, or alienated from the political scene, of those made aware of the limitations of their own perspective as they curiously read the newspapers and walked the streets of London, as James did. In this case, of course, the paradigm of that position is the artist, but also more generally it is the position of the mass of people who do not possess an adequate vision or an authentic voice within the organized political world, however incoherent or confused by the "catch-words of melodramatic journalism" that voice may be.

In one sense, of course, this is merely another way of saying what Howe said: that the politics of the novel are those of the politically ignorant and alienated. What Howe does not add, however, is that such conditions as ignorance and alienation are themselves at least potentially symptomatic of a more conscious disaffection with the world of politics and that, by giving voice to them in a public context, James effectively politicizes them. More recent critics have recognized the political dimension of James's technique more readily and have restated the political position and intention at the heart of the novel in various ways. Mark Seltzer, for instance, has argued that James's central theme is the continuity, in a modern technological culture, between seeing and power and between the "techniques of the novel and the social technologies of power that inhere in these techniques."[23] James both constructs and deconstructs his authorial power in order to "police" the fictional world without incurring the blame that the possession of power, of an authorized vision and voice, involves in the real political world.

His techniques are a cover for his own formally distinct exercise of power: his "non-political," "artistic" supervision of the world:

> The recession of narrative supervision in *The Princess Casamassima* appears as one further "shifting of the shame," a displacing of responsibility, culpability,.... The shifting of narrative authority makes reference to an uneasiness concerning the shame of power. If James's novel is systematically the story of a criminal continuity between seeing and power, this continuity is finally disowned. If James works towards a demystifying of the realist policing of the real, this police work is finally remystified, recuperated as the "innocent" work of the imagination.[24]

For Seltzer, James's foregrounding of the realist continuity between language, vision and power becomes a method of establishing or defining his own artistic, literary identity. It is what allows him to look at the political scene without taking responsibility for what he sees in the way that a political thinker must. Wendy Graham, in another and more radical interpretation, draws attention to the implicit homo-eroticism of the novel and offers a reading which seeks to emphasize its subversive elements:

> The novel undeniably expresses a desire to subvert a repressive power of the highest order; in depicting this underlying aim, the novelist participates in the subversion of that authority even as he shores up its appearance of invulnerability....Recasting the terms in which *The Princess Casamassima* may be read as social commentary, it is possible to see the novel's anarchist melodrama as a screen for the underlying theme of sexual subversion.[25]

Graham believes that the energy of James's writing directs attention to the inadequacy of the highly conventional social and political references of the novel and thereby reveals how repressive such references are to the individual imagination and to the values and desires which actually drive James's art. Thus he shows, whether consciously or not, how repressive social values, and the literary/narrative structures which sustain them, are produced and employed.

Clearly, then, it is possible to see the position that James attempts to describe in a number of ways, and this is undoubtedly because James himself did not know exactly what it was. However, what is common to nearly all interpretations is the idea that James, the conservative, did something other than write a simple conservative novel: that in looking for the revolution, he found not it but something equally subversive.

II

Of course James need not have actually looked too far into what he calls the "depths" of London life to get the "impression" that the revolution was a hidden force in preparation and only waiting for the right moment before it "awoke."[26] As I said, he could hardly have failed to gather that much from any of the newspapers and periodicals of the time. He could have read of it, for instance, in the pages of the *Contemporary Review* of May 1884 in which Elisée Reclus, the infamous anarchist geographer, threatened and thrilled his audience with revelations of the London "horrors" which lie beyond their presumed middle-class purview:

> A sincere man owes it to himself to expose the frightful barbarity which still prevails in the hidden depths of a society so outwardly well-ordererd. Below the London of fashion is a London accursed, a London whose only food are dust stained fragments, whose only garments are filthy rags, and whose only dwellings are fetid dens....Others may turn their eyes away from these horrors, we socialists look them full in the face and seek out their causes.[27]

As Conrad once sardonically reflected, "the demagogue carries the amateurs of emotion with him" ("The Informer," *SS*, 76), and throughout this article Reclus carries his unknowing and impressionable readers on an imaginative journey into the hidden secrets of life in the city. The ideological journey is, of course, towards the proposition that "socialism" is something akin to James's conception of his art: a mode of vision that

begins with the willingness to distrust the "outwardly well-
-ordered" aspect of society, and ends with the ability to see the
"unseen" that lies below it, in a realm of melodramatic
"possibilities" and "horrors" just waiting to be discovered.

The excerpts quoted from James's novel are, of course,
a sophisticated joke and parody of the type of "revelatory"
ideological language at which Reclus excels and yet at the same
time an almost paranoid construction of it. Reclus is making the
factual assertion that there exists an unseen or wilfully ignored
misery and horror beneath the surface of London life. James was
simply expressing what was, for the uninformed but curious
reader of the *Contemporary Review,* the *imagined* consequences
of the existence of that misery and horror: that the "apparently
ordered life" of the middle-class gentleman was, as the phrase
suggests, a sham based on fantasy, called ignorance, and the
careful control of information by a repressive state: "the value
I wished most to render and the effect I wished most to produce,"
James writes in his "Preface," "were precisely those of our not
knowing, of society's not knowing, but only guessing and
suspecting and trying to ignore, what 'goes on' irreconcilably,
subversively, beneath the vast, smug surface."[28] So, again in
"Preface," James poses the question which lies at the heart of his
novel:

> what would be the effect of...having so many precious things
> perpetually in one's eyes, yet of missing them all for any closer
> knowledge, and of the confinement of closer knowledge entirely to
> matters possibly pass for a privilege? Truly, of course, there are
> London mysteries (dense categories of dark arcana) for every
> spectator, and it's in a degree an exclusion and a state of weakness to
> be without experience of the meaner conditions, the lower manners
> and types, the general sordid struggle, the weight of the burden of
> labour, the ignorance, the misery and the vice. With such matters as
> those my tormented young man would have contact – they would have
> formed, fundamentally, from the first, his natural and immediate
> London. But the reward of a romantic curiosity would be the question
> of what the total assault, that of the world of his work-a-day life and
> the world of his divination and his envy together, would have made of
> him, and what in especial he would have made of them. As tormented,
> I say, I thought of him,...[29]

The point is that James's vision of the world and of "the ignorance, the misery and the vice" is as much a fantasy, as much a product of the things he has read and imagined, as his "little bookbinder's" romantic vision of the "precious things" which he supposes makes up the "mysterious" aristocratic world which fascinates him. James is, in fact, engaging in an elaborate form of imaginative transference here: change some of the terms and one has the difficulty and the "weakness" which James confronted in trying to "make" something of the revolution; and his protagonist is endowed with all the doubt, the ignorance and the curiosity from which James himself suffered, only from the reverse social angle. Thus his Hyacinth Robinson, his child of the slums and "*ab ovo* a revolutionist" (*The Princess Casamassima*, 232), becomes an interloper between two worlds and gains a footing in the world that James himself really did not know: the "outwardly well-ordered" circles of London society. This allows James the ironic perspective to debunk his illusions, expose his vanity and reveal his political ideas as solipsistic fantasy, without having to confront or invent the concealed "horrors" of the social conditions his ideas "represent."[30] Hyacinth's construction of imaginary narratives concerning what "goes on" in aristocratic salons is a reversed correlative of James's story of what "goes on" in the revolutionary world. Both are effectively debunked as total fiction.

The effect and purpose of this debunking can most clearly be seen in James's use of Hyacinth's aestheticism, the essentially artistic nature of his experience and perception, which becomes the means by which James saves himself from having to lie in his representation of the revolution. A heavily ironic treatment of his hero becomes the means by which James examines and criticizes his own fears and anxieties. Consider in a little more detail Hyacinth's conception of the "revolution," as revealed to the Princess, in a moment of intimacy at her country house at Medley:

> Nothing of it appears above the surface: but there is an immense underworld peopled with a thousand forms of revolutionary passion and devotion....And on top of it all society lives. People come and go,

and buy and sell, and drink and dance, and make money and make
love, and seem to know nothing and suspect nothing and think of
nothing; and inequities flourish, and the misery of half the world is
prated about as a "necessary evil," and generations rot away and
starve in the midst of it, and day follows day, and everything is for the
best in the best of possible worlds. All that is one half of it; the other
half is that everything's doomed! In silence, in darkness, but under the
feet of each one of us, the revolution lives and works. It's a wonderful,
immesurable trap, on the lid of which society performs its antics....The
invisible, impalpable wires are everywhere, passing through everything, attaching themselves to objects in which one would never think
of looking for them. What could be more strange and incredible for
instance that they should exist just here. (276)

Some critics, most famously Lionel Trilling, have praised the
very vagueness of James's portrait of the revolutionary movement, arguing that it effectively suggests the moderation and
lethargy of the British political scheme compared to the intense
activity of continental Europe. Indeed Trilling contends that the
novel offers us a "brilliantly precise representation of social
actuality."[31] This argument is unconvincing because it leads to
a misunderstanding of James's purposes in the novel. If these
hallucinatory visions of "A thousands forms of revolutionary
passion and devotion" can be said accurately to evoke the
self-delusion of the British revolutionary movement, then that
must be largely the result of accident or at least be incidental to
the novel's scheme. Hyacinth remains a most unbelievable
historical representation of a revolutionary because his suitabili-
ty as a central character is premised, not upon James's wish to
represent what was really happening at this time, but upon his
psychological similarity to James in his possession of an artistic
consciousness. It is this which allows him to see the "invisible"
and touch the "impalpable" and which therefore necessarily
condemns him, like James himself, to misunderstanding social
and political realities. Hyacinth is James's figure of the artist in
the modern world in which the aesthetic is political and there, as
Reclus would have us believe, the ideologue has usurped his
function as bearer of a higher and more comprehensive truth.

III

Ultimately then, James's irony, his sophisticated and somewhat corrosive jokiness at Hyacinth's expense, becomes in his novel a double-edged sword which, paradoxically, takes him closer to a vision of the darker, more subversive truth which he assumes to lie below the surface of things. Thus both the novel and "Preface," like Marx's evocation of a "specter"-haunted Europe, are dominated by the imagery of strained vision and barely adequate senses, of "just perceptible presences," of "vague motions, sounds and symptoms," and of having "things perpetually in one's eyes, yet of missing them:" as if the consciousness of a changing world, and the rise of revolutionary forces within it, would be experienced firstly and poetically as personal crises of confidence in the evidence of one's own senses. Consider where these extending perspectives and visions left James as he walked the streets of London and, attempting to "guess the unseen from the seen," worked in isolation on his novel: imaginatively confronting a world where all order, including the "vast, smug surface" of the social order, is always at least potentially a sham designed to hide the unpleasant, even horrific truth; in a world of a perpetually immanent anarchy overlain with delusions and narratives of order. On a purely abstract or theoretical level, and with no concrete knowledge to contain it, James's ironic distance has its logical conclusion in an almost anarchistic detachment from the political world.

Unable to construct an omniscient perspective, James had no way to free himself from his fears. Unable to adopt a political stance, he had to negate everything in the political world. And he was not, at times, averse to expressing this potentially anarchistic strain in his thought more directly:

> Well that's one way of living – treating life as not "all" solitude and syntax – that has much to be said for it. But I have the imagination of disaster – and see life as ferocious and sinister.[32]

Here, in a letter written some years after *The Princess Casamassima*, James is prepared to make explicit the avoided and unspoken implications of a novel which presents us with a world of isolated individuals, each controlled by a web of verbal inventions which finally subject and victimize them. Hyacinth, for example, dies uselessly and becomes the victim of the vast terrorist conspiracy of which he imagines he is a part. The "imagination of disaster," that "ferocious and sinister" vision of life, is thus generated by the failure of verbal invention to protect the individual and is driven by the recognition that all our nobler ideals and passions are only "syntax." It is a particular temptation of the isolated and verbally-orientated individual like Hyacinth or of the professional artist in words like James: the artist conscious of the nature of the material of his work and of his own separation from the world. But it is also a symptom of a cynical and potentially anarchistic, even if not exactly revolutionary, cultural despair: a despair leading James to deny or at least to suspect all order and culture as mere rationalization over, and disguise of the miseries and injustices that the social system generates. For James, in his role as artist, words and "syntax," the values of art and fiction, are the only thing which give life meaning and save the individual from "solitude." Yet words, from the politically alienated perspective forced upon the conscious artist, are also ultimately only "syntax:" an artificial medium serving to shape our direct sensual experiences into a coherent, formal and falsifying narrative or plot. Paradoxically, James's practice as an artist brought him uncomfortably close to the anarchistic despair and isolation he feared.

It is also clear, however, that James was not prepared to accept or acknowledge easily such an isolation. The anguish at the center of *The Princess Casamassima* is born of the desire to "connect" in more than a purely linguistic sense and the fear that, in the modern political world, it may not be possible to do so. This anguish is the source of the opposition between art and politics which, as so many critics have pointed out, runs throughout James's novel. Politics and art are equally and similarly a linguistic response or answer to the chaos of our direct experience; with the difference that political language serves to connect the events of the public world into the plots and stories of conspiracies which give them coherence and form, whereas art does the same for our private world. James himself, in the form of Hyacinth's suicide at the end of the novel, seems to come down on the side of art as a way of life and thought, advising withdrawal from the political arena. That is hardly surprising, not simply because James was himself an artist who did not understand the public world of politics and revolution, but because the outcome of his ignorance was a suspicion that all public commitments and relationships were inescapably problematic and always potentially "sinister." The artist, by contrast to the political actor, is ideally independent of public commitments and free to connect with his fellow man on a different basis. However, by the end of the novel it is clear that this too is a delusion: Hyacinth's drastic withdrawal from the political world is finally a commitment only to words and fiction, art and culture divorced from the conditions in which they actually exist and can have value.

Ultimately, then, Hyacinth's death can affirm no such choice in James's part and achieves nothing but negation. Indeed it almost seems as if the politics/art opposition through which James presents his story of Hyacinth's revolutionary adventures (culled from a European tradition of fiction, but principally from Turgenev's *Virgin Soil* – 1871),[33] is employed mainly to obfuscate and avoid the difficult political issue of commitment and, quite simply, to give him the illusion of a choice to make. The honest writer like James, caught in the conflict between the values of art and those of political life, between detachment and commitment, tends to evade the issue and to withdraw to an ivory tower of art; an ultimately self-defeating movement which simply implies a despair with the social and political process. As the anarchist literary critic George Woodcock reflected: "The conscious avoidance of being implicated shows that in...a writer's mind politics holds a place, even if an unpleasant one. The Ivory Tower is as much a symbol of inescapable social problems as the air-raid shelter is of the inescapable evils of war."[34]

It is here, of course, that one encounters the whole range of conceptual complexities and contradictions which face the writer of political fiction. Correspondingly it is also here that the appeal of anarchism comes most into play, since it is the political theory which most closely addresses the tensions inherent in the literary artist's position and it also apparently resolves his dilemma by reducing the world of politics itself to a purely imaginary but socially authorized series of tyrannizing fictions, against which the true artist's and true anarchist's task is defined. Anarchist theory tends to place great stress upon the criticism of the negative role and power of unacknowledged fictions in our social organization and yet, in an apparent contradiction, offers a committed vision of individual power and freedom in a future society which is itself an imaginative and fictional construction: one which is distinguished from what it negates only by the fact that it is a formally powerless discourse which acknowledges its own fictionality and individual source. In Emma Goldman's terms:

> The state has no more existence than gods and devils have. They are equally the reflex and creation of man; for man, the individual, is the only reality. The state is but the shadow of man, the shadow of his opaqueness, of his ignorance and fear.[35]

In a world of "shadows," present power and order are simply invented and thought into existence and can just as easily be unthought, if an alternative form of expression can be found for the needs they represent. Indeed the anarchist propagandistic ideal of a language of action, mixing violent iconoclasm with a positive assertion of imaginative visions, grows directly out of this perception and is a use of words which aims to create the thing it apparently describes and to remould the "plastic" human soul. It is also, of course, a model of communication which would appeal in obvious ways to the writer of imaginative literature, since it seems to confer his imagination with power in the political arena *and* absolves him from the responsibility to directly engage with social and political realities.

Perhaps when James wrote *The Princess Casamassima* he was temporarily under the influence of anarchism or rather, like

Conrad when he came to write *The Secret Agent* (1907) some twenty years later, the isolation and imaginative effort of writing brought him to think and feel like an anarchist.[36] Or perhaps, and what is more likely, James's attraction to anarchistic ideas and analyses was the unconscious outcome of his years of practice as a writer: that the ideas and understanding of the world that he developed in his work as a literary artist were also essentially anarchistic ideas. "The really independent writer," writes George Woodcock, "by the very exercise of his function, represents a revolutionary force....The novelist who shows the hollowness of middle class life, the poet who displays without comment the spiritual agonies of war, as well as the painter who shows on his canvas a symbol of the schizoid futility of a modern city, are all playing a part in subverting a corrupt society....In this way any honest writer is an agitator, an anarchist, an incendiary."[37] Woodcock articulates the assumption behind the readings of critics like Wendy Graham: that James's individual creative energy was implicitly yet necessarily opposed to the repressive social codes and conventions in which he was forced to realize it.

Whatever the truth of James's attraction to anarchism, it is in any case certain that he could have met with anarchist ideas and analyses, posed in specifically linguistic terms, in the works of Stirner, Proudhon, or Bakunin;[38] the most likely sources to which he would have turned if he had tried to research anarchism at all. Or perhaps, as has been suggested by Taylor Stoehr,[39] he was influenced by his longstanding friend Henry B. Brewster, an anarchist theorist of language who published *The Theories of Anarchy and of Law: A Midnight Debate* (1887) very shortly after James's novel. Brewster is a particularly interesting potential influence on James because he addressed his whole philosophy, what he called "syntacticism," to the problem that lies at the very center of James's concerns: the isolation, the sense of "disconnection," engendered by the apparently reductive idea that our mental life is "all" and only "solitude and syntax." Brewster, however, quite readily embraced solipsism and accepted verbal isolation as a universal human condition, and so this was not such an unwelcome idea for him as it was for James.[40] Indeed, for Brewster, it is only our unwillingness to acknowledge and accept this idea that creates our problems.

In *The Theories of Anarchy and of Law:...*, Brewster argues that the fundamental origin of our social and political conflicts, in fact of all our suffering as social beings, resides in the mistaken belief that the language of social and political thought has a truth content: that the words we use to express our beliefs and ideals act in reference to an objective reality and can be said to "represent" the world. It is only what Brewster calls "disconnected utterances," the most simple of verbal units with a direct reference to an object of sense, that can be said to work in this way and truly to reflect the "disconnected" and chaotic structure of experience. Any more complex statement, any structure of words which seeks to connect one thought or verbal unit to another, ceases to "represent" the world and begins instead to create and form it. Thus, declaring the power of speech to be "one of the primary ingredients of the universe,"[41] Brewster sees the creative and poetic capacities of language as far more important than "truth" and far more integral to our constitutions than we understand: words themselves, in their syntactic "connective" function, are the creative force which invents our world and makes us human. Structures of words, what he calls "connected utterances,"[42] are not a medium for reflecting reality, but are the only reality we can partake of:

> They express nothing, they are something. They form part of the stock and riches of the world, even as the organic forms. Far from being products of our mind, that is to say, secondary or manufactured wares like our knowledge, they exist not by us but we by them. Behold in the connective power they display, one of the threads which man spins not but of which he is woven.[43]

Brewster, remember, was an anarchist and as such was concerned to break the hold of all authoritative and transcendent ideas, and especially to free the individual from the shackles of those political ideologies which impose fixed interpretations and total resolutions on the chaotic conditions of our existence. "[N]o expression can be that of the total," he wrote "any great doctrinal unity is a misuse of language."[44] Like James in his novel, Brewster's discussion of all social and political issues tends to draw attention to its own inadequacy and fictionality and to transfer one's attention from the referential to the formal aspects of the words: from the content of ideas, what they translate, to the mode of their grouping and orchestration, what they create.

Yet, despite this negative view of language as an interpreter of reality, Brewster turns this "connecting" and falsifying quality of language into an affirmation of its very power and importance:

> I would neither get the world out of man's mind nor our mind out of the progressive integration of matter. I would get them both out of speech and say to those who discuss their priority: you are expressing no reality, you are creating one: you are singing after a fashion – go on![45]

Brewster is content to see everything reduced to speech. Everything, all possible ideas and feelings, exists in the structure of language as "one of the possible cases of the concatenation of thoughts,"[46] and our thought is merely the fulfilment of its pre-existent possibilities and relations; to be judged, if at all, only by the aesthetic and formal criteria we employ to judge a phenomenon like a poem or novel. Indeed, for Brewster "all" that makes us human, or that makes human life valuable, is our capacity to engage in such poetic exercise of language without having to believe in the ultimate truth and authority of what we say:

> There is no complete life without some great lie of romance, some dream of love or grandeur, whose value is in its falseness. There is no idealess reality. There is no true world of here below unless there is, under some guise or other, a kingdom of heaven.[47]

Thus whilst "dreams," "lies" and fictions are necessary to our existence, as the formal work of the imagination which make a coherent mental life possible, their real value is in their "falseness:" in the fact that they express, not truth or reality, but simply the unrealizable desire to "connect" and therefore do away with the "isolation of the individual"[48] within a purely fictional element. Like the novelist in his verbally created world, the social and political "philosopher" seeks value and connection in a form which he knows is "all poetry and teaches us nothing."[49]

This, of course, is a familiar enough idea but what makes Brewster's formulation of it unusual, and reminiscent of James's and Hyacinth's commitment to fiction as fiction, is the readiness with which he embraces the "value" of "falseness," the power of deliberate and self-conscious illusion, and accepts the fictionality of all thought and understanding. It is like another, more politically and philosophically justified version of the writer's isolation in the ivory tower of art.

In a sense, then, the linguistically aware anarchist like Brewster approaches the world from a position identical to that of the conscious artist like James, and his adoption of a simplified language of "poetry" as a means of understanding and moving it, forms a model of communication which both challenges and reflects the very basis of the writer's undertaking. It challenges the writer's ideal of a uniquely individual and non-political commitment to the world in fiction; since, in the anarchist world-view all "representation" of the world is the covert expression of the political power and order in which it occurs, and inevitably involves the writer in the subjection of individual vision to the systematized falsehoods of the public world. Art, particularly literary art, must simply take its place amongst the other products of speech: the other fictions which construct our world, and with nothing to distinguish it formally from the fictions of the politician. However, since anarchism conceives of our social life in terms of a conflict between the truth of individual experience and the innate falsehood of its social and political representation, Brewster's model of communication also offers a reflection and sanction for the writer's claim to be able to offer individual imaginative truth and to connect with the world through fiction. If we understand the language of fiction aright, if the writer like James constantly negates his own authority and the illusion of reference behind the words he uses, then literary art can become the perfect model of speech: that purely formal medium which builds connection, not between us and an objective world, but between isolated and "disconnected" consciousnesses.

We cannot know, at this stage, whether James ever read Brewster's work or took any conscious interest in his ideas, and perhaps it is not important if he did or not. What is certain, however, is that the type of questions and difficulties that Brewster raises, and the model of communication he describes, are ones that would have both frightened and appealed to James; and that he would have had to confront in the composition of his "political" novel. Indeed, along with many other of the most politically conservative writers of this time, James's fictional handling of the "myths" of revolution can be seen as a kind of implicit engagement with the language of anarchistic isolation.

I have dwelt upon James because his dilemma in confronting his own ignorance and fear of the revolution is a complex but clear version of that faced by many other novelists of this time. James mediates his glimpses of "the misery and the vice" of London life by regarding them within the narrative context of a vast terrorist conspiracy against the "present order:" a narrative which thrills and terrifies by its threat of revolution, yet which nevertheless defuses the more ferocious and formless fear engendered in those glimpses by making them seem comprehensible and so controllable. A threat which is part of a conspiracy, a social and conventional intention, is understandable and so less terrifying than a pure unmotivated threat; a truth clearly registered by Elisée Reclus:

> It is said that when the magicians of the middle ages wanted to raise the devil, they began their incantation by painting his image on a wall. For a long time past modern exorcists have adopted a similar method for conjuring anarchists.[50]

Like Reclus, James understood that representation and plot themselves are a means of controlling the fear of anarchy. It is as if the very act of telling the story of the revolution was an expression of authority over it; as if words themselves were, as Brewster and the anarchists insisted, a means of power.

This, then, is the purpose of *The Princess Casamassima*. That purpose can be seen as an attempt to find a boundary to the potentially anarchistic cultural despair engendered by talk of "specters" and the suspicion, re-inforced by casual and disconnected glimpses, that "below the London of fashion is a London accursed." The final point is, of course, that all this is an anarchistic analysis or at least the beginning of one: that the perception James reaches through the practice of his art, a kind of disillusioned conservatism and commitment to art as art, is in many respects the outcome of an anarchistic rejection of politics as itself no more than fiction.

NOTES

1. Cited by Paul Berman in *Quotations from the Anarchists* (London: Praeger, 1972), 43 (hereafter: Berman).

2. Shakespeare, *King Lear*, IV, VI, 170-2.

3. Karl Marx and Frederich Engels, *The Communist Manifesto*, ed. A. J. P. Taylor (Harmondsworth: Penguin, 1964), 51 (hereafter: *Manifesto*).

4. Cited by Stuart Millar in *Modern European History* (London: Macmillan, 1980), 53.

5. *The Letters of Henry James*, 2 vols., ed. Percy Lubbock (London: Macmillan, 1920), vol. 1, 114 (hereafter: Lubbock).

6. *Ibid*, 125.

7. It was this fear that the whole of European culture would collapse that made James a conservative. He was, however, a conservative of a very open-eyed and at least potentially subversive kind, who was ultimately prepared to question the value of his own attachments and prejudices. James's doubt about the rectitude of his overt political position has been vividly described by Irving Howe in his classic 1957 study of the novel, which I quote at length in order to give a flavor of the force of Howe's appreciation of James:

> there is something admirable in James's creative bravado, his boldness in summoning the unknown and his economy in exploiting his ignorance; there is something even more admirable in his readiness to face the possibility – he seems to have thought it a likelihood – that the society to which he was committed by taste and habit was on the edge

of disaster. For if it was James's conscious intention in writing *The Princess Casamassima* to discover how far he could extend the powers of his art into an unfamiliar subject, he was also moved by more intimate needs. The book registered his fear that everything he valued was crumbling, and it would be gratuitous to question the depth or sincerity of this fear; but it also betrayed his doubt whether in some ultimate moral reckoning that was beyond his grasp, everything did not deserve to crumble. This could hardly affect his conservative temper, which by now had become thoroughly ingrained, but it did permit him an openness and breadth of feeling greater than is usually available to those in whom conservatism is merely an opinion. (*Politics and the Novel* «New York: Horizon, 1957», 141; hereafter: Howe).

8. Cited by Giuseppe Fiori in *Antonio Gramsci: Life of a Revolutionary* (London: New Left Books, 1970), 235.

9. *Manifesto*, 53.

10. *Ibid.*, 53.

11. Lubbock, vol. 1, 121.

12. "The Preface to *The Princess Casamassima*" in *The Critical Muse: Selected Literary Criticism,* ed. R. Gard (Harmondsworth: Penguin, 1987), 502; hereafter: Preface.

13. I mean the novels of writers like Flaubert, Turgenev, Dostoyevsky and Conrad, all of whom directed their attention to the prospects of revolution; but more especially I mean the works of these great novelists as they were filtered through and imitated by the popular fiction of this period. In Britain, the years 1880 to 1920 saw the growth of a huge tradition of highly melodramatic popular novels which took revolution as their subject or setting and sought to exploit its obvious exciting dramatic appeal. Even a brief survey of these popular novels reveals that their writers' understanding of revolution is largely imported from European and more particularly Russian sources, and that the melodramatic treatment that it receives was an effective way of obfuscating the British public's understanding of the revolutionary forces in their own society.

14 "The Art of Fiction," in *Henry James: Selected Literary Criticism,* ed. Morris Shapira (Cambridge: Cambridge U. P., 1981), 57.

15. *The Princess Casamassima* (New York: Harper and Row, 1959), 243-4. All further page references in the text are to this edition.

16. *Preface*, 498.

17. Conrad could well have had James's paranoid artistic imaginations in mind in his "Author's Note" to *The Secret Agent* (1907). He recalls how, in the composition of the novel, he "had to fight hard to keep at arm's length the memories of my solitary and nocturnal walks all over London in my early days, lest these should rush in and overwhelm each page of the story as these emerged one after another from a mood as serious in feeling and thought as any in which I ever wrote a line" (*SA,* XIII).

18. "The Experimental Novel," in *Documents of Modern Literary Realism*, ed. George J. Becker (Princeton: Princeton U. P., 1963), 168.

19. It is a curious anomaly in the criticism of the novel that, whilst it is almost universally recognized that James constructed his plot from the most commonplace elements of journalism and popular fiction, many critics still devote a great deal of attention to historícal sources, as if he had some special understanding or information. Barbara Melchiori, for example, speculates on his sources at length in *Terrorism and the Late Victorian Novel* (London: Croom Helm, 1985), as does Hermia Oliver in *The International Anarchist Movement in Late Victorian London* (London: Croom Helm, 1983).

20. See, for example, J. M. Luecke in *"The Princess Casamassima*: Hyacinth's Fallible Consciousness," in *Henry James: Modern Judgements*, ed. Tony Tanner (London: Macmillan, 1969); or Manfred Mackenzie, *Communities of Love and Honour in Henry James* (Cambridge, MA: Harvard U. P., 1976).

21. Howe, 146.

22. *Ibid.*, 153.

23. Mark Seltzer, *"The Princess Casamassima*: Realisation and the Fantasy of Surveillance," in *Henry James: Critical Assessments*, ed. Graham Clarke (Mountfield: Helm Information, 1991), vol. 4, 549.

24. *Ibid.*, 548.

25. Wendy Graham, "Henry James's Subterranean Blues: A Rereading of *The Princess of Casamassima*," *Modern Fiction Studies*, 40: 1 (1994), 52-3.

26. It is, of course, with this sort of imaginative and poetic language, replete with the imagery of awakenings and heroic violence, that Hyacinth attempts to transform the world into an image of his own desire, as he does the clientele of the *Sun and Moon*:

> When gathering at the "Sun and Moon" was at its best, its temper really seemed an earnest of what was the basis of all its calculations – that the people was only a sleeping lion, already breathing shorter and beginning to stretch its limbs and stiffen its claws – at these hours, some of them thrilling enough, Hyacinth waited for the voice that should allot him the particular part he was to play. (246)

Hyacinth, himself the novelist *manqué*, is a character apparently in search of an author.

27. *The Contemporary Review* (London), May 1884, 629-35.

28. *Preface*, 501.

29. *Ibid.*, 507.

30. The interloper between classes is a familiar type of hero in the tradition of fiction to which *The Princess of Casamassima* belongs. Heroes who belong to two classes, or more commonly who originate in the privileged classes but become politically committed to the proletariat, allow

the author a double perspective and the power to criticize the existing social structure whilst simultaneously exposing what is limited or absurd in the alternative. To name but two examples from this tradition: G. B. Shaw used it in *An Unsocial Socialist* (1884) and "Isabel Meredith" (the pseudonym of the Rossetti sisters) in *A Girl Among the Anarchists* (1903).

31. Lionel Trilling, *The Liberal Imagination* (New York: Viking Press, 1950), 42.

32. From a letter to A. C. Benson, in *Henry James: Letters to A. C. Benson and Auguste Monod,* ed. H. F. Benson (New York: Charles Sembrer's Sons, 1930), 35.

33. Turgenev's *Virgin Soil* was perhaps the most important single source for James: particularly Turgenev's treatment of Nejdanov, his hero, as caught in an antagonism between his sympathy for the people, associated with his proletarian mother, and his personal aestheticism, associated with his aristocratic father. At a bitter moment of crisis, Nejdanov reflects:

How I loathe this irritability, sensitiveness, impressionableness, fastidiousness, inherited from my aristocratic father! What right had he to bring me into this world, endowed with qualities quite unsuited to the sphere in which I live? To create a bird and throw it in the water? An aesthetic amidst filth! A democrat, a lover of the people, yet the very smell of their filthy vodka makes me feel sick! (trans. Rochelle S. Townsend «London: Dent, 1963», 240).

This is also the central predicament of Hyacinth Robinson and James imported it, along with Hyacinth's somewhat crude biological determination, from Turgenev.

34. George Woodcock, *The Writer and Politics* (London: Porcupine Press, 1948), 10 (hereafter: Woodcock).

35. Berman, 93.

36. Interestingly Conrad described, in his "Author's Note" to *The Secret Agent,* how "there had been times during the writing of the book when I was an extreme revolutionist" (*SA,* XIV). Under the pressure of imaginative commitment, there is little to divide the writer plotting revolutionary destruction in a fictional world and the anarchist doing so in the "real" world.

37. Woodcock, 17-18.

38. Mikhail Bakunin, one of the most notorious anarchists of all, was possibly an important source for James's idea of anarchists. Not only did he write at length on the subject of language but his ideas on revolutionary organization and his habit of inventing imaginary brotherhoods of which he was the master, suggest that he could have been the model for the mysterious and "invisible" Hoffendahl. Indeed, some of Bakunin's more far-flung statements on the revolution describe Hoffendahl's role very closely. Consider his letter to Albert Richard, a fellow Paris Communard, in 1881:

There must be anarchy, there must be – if the revolution is to become and remain alive, real and powerful – the greatest possible awakening of all the local passions and aspirations, a tremendous awakening of spontaneous life everywhere....We must bring forth anarchy, and in the midst of the popular tempest, we must be the invisible pilots guiding the revolution, not by any kind of overt power but by collective dictatorship of all our allies, a dictatorship without tricks, without official titles, without official rights, and therefore all the more powerful, as it does not carry the trappings of power. (Cited by Eugene Schulkind in *The Paris Commune of 1871: The View from the Left* «London: Cape, 1972», 38.)

39. See Taylor Stoehr, *Words and Deeds* (New York: A. M. S. Press, 1986).

40. Brewster (1850-1908) was a wealthy French-born American with extensive connections amongst the literary and artistic circles of London and Paris society. A thoroughly eccentric and reclusive man, he spent much of his life guarded from the world by a devoted and jealous wife, the daughter of a German statesman, who thought him a great philosopher and universal genius. Much of his life was taken up with quiet contemplation and abstract speculation on metaphysical matters, and the alacrity with which he accepted solipsism as a universal human condition is perhaps most reflective of his own life habits, since he had neither the need nor the desire to "connect" with the world outside of his own philosophical seclusion. James's case is clearly different in all respects except the central one: the isolation and loneliness of his writing life.

Brewster's somewhat eccentric ideas are now mainly of interest for the influence he may have had on his acquaintances, and his proper place in the history of thought is probably no more than a footnote. His ideas *are* interesting, however, because Brewster can be seen as grasping at some very modern ideas whilst lacking the modern language in which to formulate them. His principled abstention from theories and from any "all-embracing point of view," his insistence that all ideological thought is "misunderstanding the nature and overstepping the boundaries of truth, which is forever fragmentary" (*The Theories of Anarchy and of Law: A Midnight Debate* «London: Northgate and Williams, 1887», 34; hereafter: Theories), is not simply a product of a modernist scepticism but, given the specifically linguistic emphasis, also looks forward in many ways to more recent developments like structuralism.

William James, whose ideas are in many ways pre-dated by Brewster's, is known to have possessed and carefully annotated a copy of *The Theories of Anarchy and of Law*:... Henry James regarded Brewster with great fondness and, after his death, wrote that Brewster "remains for me, with his accomplishments, his distinction, his extraordinary play of mind, and his too tragic death, the clearest case of cosmopolitan culture I was to have known" (*Notes of a Son and Brother* «London: Macmillan, 1914», 409). They are known to have corresponded frequently but, unfortunately, it seems that James destroyed the letters.

41. *Theories*, 20.

42. It is in relation to Brewster's use of this concept of "connected utterances," that his modernity can most easily be appreciated. His ideas are fundamentally based on the distinction between the types of meaning generated by the types of sentence structure we use and on the recognition that the meaning of all but the most simple acts of speech and thought is never final:

> disconnected utterances conveying information owe their strength to a previous work of some of our sense simple or combined, which they translate into words. Connected utterances bearing strength with them owe that strength to the fact that they embody, instead of translating a primary reality....Truth, however much you may get of it, is but a factor in a larger work, and its greatest value is not in that which it declares, but in what the declaration is ignorant of but tends to fashion and form. Whatever you may express, you are at the same time co-operating in the growth of a reality of a different kind, you are making something different from what you express. Truth is but a parcel of some becoming reality. (*Theories*, 19-21)

43. *Ibid.*, 20.
44. *Ibid.*, 34.
45. *Ibid.*, 20.
46. *Ibid.*, 18.
47. *Ibid.*, 39.

48. This phrase is derived from an unpublished note found amongst Brewster's papers many years after his death. In a very interesting point, Brewster reflects on the nature of "myth:" "Myths are neither images of exterior realities nor symbols of interior ones. Their value lies in the collective desire they embody. A collective desire is neither an exterior fact nor an interior one; it effaces the distinction between the two by doing away with the isolation of the individual." (Cited by Martin Halperin, *The Life and Writings of Henry B. Brewster* «Harvard University: *Doctoral Thesis, 1957*», 309.) As elsewhere, Brewster clearly pre-dates the modern use and understanding of the term "myth."

49. *Theories*, 19.
50. *The Contemporary Review*, May 1884, 637.

Philip Horne,
University College London,
London, England

The Lessons of Flaubert:
James and *L'Éducation Sentimentale*

For Henry James, Flaubert presented an unsettling case, one on which his writings repeatedly touch, with disapproval and admiration, from various angles. He saw Flaubert in a fluctuating, partly in an increasingly warm light, without ever quite overcoming his reservations. I start by quickly sketching the curve of James's relation to Flaubert as it manifests itself through his career.

Flaubert's first mention in Jamesian print comes in the *Nation* of 14 September 1865, where a review of Elizabeth Rundle Charles's *Chronicles of the Schönberg-Cotta Family* finger--waggingly recommends to the foreign "realist" some salutary but improbable reading: "For an exhibition of the true realistic *chique* [sic] we would accordingly refer that body of artists who are represented in France by MM. Flaubert and Gérome [sic] to that class of works which in our own literature are represented by the 'Daisy Chain' and 'The Wide, Wide, World,' and to which the 'Chronicles;' before us essentially belong."[1] In April 1868, reviewing a book on French art, he again links Flaubert to Gérôme in connection with *"heartlessness"* (James, *Literary Criticism: Essays on Literature,...,* I, 1038). On 5 February 1874 a review of Jules Sandeau starts by remarking that "M. Gustave Flaubert seems to have told the one good story he had to tell."[2] In April 1874, in the *North American Review,* James wrote of Turgenev as having "an apprehension of man's religious impulses...never dreamed of in the philosophy of Balzac and Flaubert, Octave Feuillet and Gustave Droz" (James, *Literary Criticism: French Writers,...,* 974). Having thus warmed himself up with glancing blows, James came right out on 4 June 1874 with a severe review of *La Tentation de Saint Antoine* where Flaubert was seen as "a writer outliving his genius," typically French insofar as neglecting the "spiritual" for the "pictorial" and thus "morally stranded and helpless" (290, 294).

Yet after actually meeting Flaubert in 1875 James recorded in a letter his surprisingly charmed state – "He is not at all what his books led me to expect."[3] Personal acquaintance gave James friendly feelings about the "great, stout, handsome, simple, kindly, elderly fellow" (*Henry James Letters*:..., II, 14) which partly qualified his general revulsion at French amorality. This good impression was soon afterwards reflected in a changed vision of the works: "Since knowing him I see his books in a different light" (24).[4] Not that James's Gallophobia was dispelled – he notoriously described himself in 1876 reading Daniel Deronda in "this beastly Paris, and realizing the superiority of English culture and the English mind to the French" (30).

The ambivalence about Flaubert signalled in these divergent responses issued thereafter in a succession of critical meditations: despite his new light, James produced in 1876 a restrictive essay on "Charles de Bernard and Gustave Flaubert." In 1893 the posthumous violation of Flaubert's cherished privacy by his niece's publication of his letters enlisted James's sympathy as well as exposing the uncle to further limiting judgements in a survey based on the *Correspondence de Gustave Flaubert*. In 1899 the French critic Emile Faguet published a critical study emphasizing the analogy between Flaubert himself and his character Emma Bovary as each, in slightly differing degrees, "an embodiment of helpless romanticism" (James, *Literary Criticism: French Writers*,..., 322). This seems to have affected James by tracing a vein of feeling he had previously missed, a warmth like that of the inspiring "love of each seized identity" which partly constituted for him "The Lesson of Balzac" in the 1905 lecture on that French master (131). In 1902, then, in a general introduction to Flaubert for a translation of *Madame Bovary,* this novel has *its* lesson, the lesson af Art: "The work is classic because the thing, such as it is, is ideally *done,* and because it shows that in such doing eternal beauty may dwell" (325). "The value of Flaubert for us," further on, "is that he admirably

points the moral," of "what composition, distribution, arrangement can do, of how they intensify the life of a work of art"
(333). Then the last pages of James's final New York Edition
"Preface," that to *The Golden Bowl* in 1909, bring in Flaubert for
a valedictory appearance, privileged as the arch-representative
of the artist in prose (and by implication closely aligned with
James himself).

But the classic *Madame Bovary* is only one of Flaubert's major
works, and the others – except the *Trois Contes* – suffer by
comparison in James's esteem. To one in particular
– *L'Éducation Sentimentale* – he keeps returning with scarcely
diminished wonder and dismay as "the most unfathomable of
anomalies" (176). In the 1870s it is one of the Flaubert novels he
calls "unmistakeably still-born" in their uninteresting subjects,
their "fatal charmlessness" (290); it is "mechanical and inanimate," and reading it is like "masticating ashes and sawdust"
(171, 176). In 1893 it is "cold as death" because it makes us
"breathe the air of pure aesthetics" (306) – being undiluted, we
can infer, by moral or emotional interest in the story. And even
in 1902, where James's reservations are most temperately stated,
he joins Faguet in judging this "strange,...indescribable work"
to be, "by the measure of its quantity of intention, a failure"
(327). His prime doubt, as expressed in 1902, concerns Frédéric
Moreau, the novel's hero, lover and loser, "man of every
weakness" ("*homme de toutes les faiblesses*").[5] "'Why, why
him?'" asks James (326).

In the 1893 essay James spoke of Flaubert's enemies as
mocking (in general) his "immense ado about nothing" (307)
– thus anticipating the 1907 "Preface" to *The Portrait of a Lady*,
where, conscious of the unconventionality of his own choice of
subject, he portrays himself organizing "an ado about something,...an ado about Isabel Archer" (1077). Why *her*? – James is
conscious of the same question. Well, Isabel is a "mere young
thing," he knows, a "frail vessel" in George Eliot's phrase; but
the novel has been careful to "Place the centre of the subject in
the young woman's consciousness," and "It was naturally of the
essence that the young woman should be herself complex" (1078,

1079, 1080). James's own choice of central figure here has been controversial, as with F. R. Leavis, who felt "invited to share a valuation of Isabel that is incompatible with a really critical irony."[6] About Frédéric Moreau, for James, Flaubert's irony *is* "really critical," but excessively so; lowering our valuation of him to such an extent that the book is impoverished. Flaubert's "ado" in *L'Éducation Sentimentale,* which is as great as five years of agonized planning, research and composition could make it, James declares to be *about* too little: "Why did Flaubert choose," he wonders, "as special conduits of the life he proposed to depict, such inferior and in the case of Frédéric such abject human specimens?" (326).

The objection to the hero affects James's evaluation of Flaubert's whole book. Because Frédéric Moreau is not only the subject but also the "reflector" or "register" or "conduit" of the action, present in, and main perceiver of nearly every scene, his alleged abjectness, "the poverty of Frédéric's own inward or for that matter outward life" (328), hobbles the novel. James finds missing the breath of moral life with which its central character *should* have inspired this "epic of the unusual," and supplies a metaphorically inflated image for Flaubert's deficiency. James's swellingly punitive image expands on his earlier judgement of "mechanical and inanimate:"

> it affects us as an epic without air, without wings to lift it; reminds us in fact more than anything else of a huge balloon, all of silk pieces strongly sewn together and patiently blown up, but that absolutely refuses to leave the ground. (328)

Here too James anticipates one of his Prefaces, that for *The American,* where his own balloon has seemingly left the ground without trouble, and where the differently applied image conveys the distinction between realism and romance:

> The balloon of experience is in fact of course tied to the earth, and under that necessity we swing, thanks to a rope of remarkable length, in the more or less commodious car of the imagination; but it is by the rope we know where we are, and from the moment that cable is cut we are at large and unrelated. (1064)

Successful realism takes off, but stays attached to the earth by rope; romance floats off and cuts the rope; successful romance cuts the rope without our noticing. *L'Éducation Sentimentale,* says James, "absolutely refuses to leave the ground." Few would claim that Flaubert was planning in a romantic way to cut the cable that tied his action to the earth, and certainly his agonizing researches into funeral arrangements, the stock market, socialist theory and so forth – quite apart from the reductively earthward lines of the story – suggest the opposite; but the very scale and ferocious accuracy of his social panorama, of the depiction of Frédéric's life in Paris, might be thought to have raised *L'Éducation Sentimentale* at least a short way above the ground. James shows excessive animus, that is, in his allegation of an absolute want of animation in it, animus of a revealing kind.

An explanation of his reaction has been tendered. Edmund Wilson in "The Ambiguity of Henry James" calls James "especially invidious on the subject," and offers a brilliant reading which sees James as too full of sympathy with "the sensitive young man" not to be stung at the sight of Flaubert "flaying remorselessly the squemish young man of this type."[7] The reading is magnificently unfair, and we start to object that the same "type" can't quite be in question both in France and the United States; but Wilson then – with a generous and ex-hilarating turn – points out, and makes capital of, this very national difference. James's strong reaction correlates, that is, with the refusal in America's new society of the class-system which gives the word *bourgeois* its damning power for the intemperate Flaubert, to whom "hatred of the Bourgeois is the beginning of virtue."[8] In the United States, Wilson says, abstaining lovers like Frédéric and Madame Arnoux would have a supporting context that would give meaning to their non--consumption (like that in James's early tale *Madame de Mauves*): Americanized, "Their scruples and renunciations have a real moral value."[9]

We can connect James's exaggeration, and the touchiness it may indicate, with anxieties about his own creative activity at the time of writing this final essay on Flaubert (for which he seems to

have at least partially reread *L'Éducation Sentimentale*). It was
sent off to Edmund Gosse in September 1901, and so must have
been written while he was at work on *The Wings of the Dove*
– a work, we might want to say, with an intense moral purpose,
albeit indirect, of the kind Flaubert seems to eschew, but which
nonetheless opened James himself to accusations like those he
levels at Flaubert – the charge by one critic, for example, of
failing to "breathe the breath of life into the dust of romance."[10]
In his weak young man, Merton Densher, James could be said to
come as close as he ever does to Flaubert's Frédéric Moreau, in
the sense that Densher adores, quasi-religiously, one woman,
Milly Theale, who is thus an equivalent of Mme Arnoux, and
finds sexual consummation (rendered in a manner as sensual as
anywhere in James) with another, Kate Croy, who might offer
a parallel to Frédéric's mistress Rosanette. James takes pains to
make Densher engaging despite his passivity, and to convey the
pressures of the situation which edges him into conspiracy; but
attracting the reader's sympathy for such a figure is a risky
occupation and one critic bluntly referred to Densher as "the
villain,"[11] while another harshly put it that "for Merton
Densher's fascination we have only the author's rather anxiously
reiterated word."[12]

The parallel becomes even more striking when we examine
James's account of the woman Frédéric Moreau worships
throughout, Madame Arnoux. Here it is that James reveals what
he has meant earlier by "a defect of [Flaubert's] mind" (326); for
it is in connection with Madame Arnoux that he finds Flaubert
guilty of a compromising blunder "the unconsciousness of error
in respect to the opportunity that would have counted as his
finest" (330). He praises Flaubert's "conception" of her and of
the never-consummated relation between her and Frédéric in
terms which might be applied to Milly Theale, especially in the
last stages of *The Wings of the Dove*:

> Almost nothing that she says is repeated, almost nothing that she does
> is shown. She is an image none the less[,] beautiful and vague, an image
> of passion cherished and abjured, renouncing all sustenance and yet
> persisting in life. (330)[13]

Milly, dying, *doesn't* persist in life; and is more a protagonist than Madame Arnoux (she is the "center" in Books Four, Five and Seven). Yet as a source of value in the book she is given a status at least equal to that of Madame Arnoux; and her value is in the end chiefly registered by a wavering young man. Something close to James's praise of Flaubert's conception here has been levelled, as blame, at James's treatment of Milly – by Leavis, scourge of James's heroines: "A vivid, particularised Milly might for him stand in the midst of his indirections, but what for his reader these skirt around is too much like emptiness."[14] Leavis seems in this to ignore Milly's centrality in three out of ten Books, and to be unduly prescriptive in his demand for "vivid particularisation" as the mode in which all heroines are to be represented. James himself – Leavis-like – goes on to contrast Flaubert's "conception" of Madame Arnoux with the execution in the novel: he criticizes Flaubert's kind of indirectness in her presentation, the point of view from which she is seen:

> She has for real distinction the extreme drawback that she is offered us quite preponderantly through *Frédéric's* vision of her, that we see her practically in no other light. Now Flaubert unfortunately has not been able not so to discredit *Frédéric's* vision in general, his vision of everyone and everything, and in particular of his own life, that it makes a medium good enough to convey adequately a noble impression.

And James declares that "to propose to register in so mean a consciousness as that of such a hero so large and mixed a quantity of life as *L'Éducation*... clearly intends" is a mistake "somehow moral" (330). Urbane as his treatment of Flaubert has become over the years, that is, he retains in 1902 a moral objection to the tenor of French fiction, and in this case his edge of disappointment seems particularly sharp because Flaubert, with his "conception" of the figure of Madame Arnoux, has come so apparently close to James's own ethic and aesthetic. Yet we may not wish immediately to accept James's understanding, either of Frédéric's vision as so discredited or of Flaubert's aim with regard to Madame Arnoux as quite being "a noble impression."[15]

The novel's hero fails for James as an adequate "conduit," it seems, through his many delusions (drily noted by Flaubert's narration) and egotistical self-deceptions (James does not appear, it may be noted, to bring forward as damning Frédéric's involved sexual infidelities). It seems that, like Edmund Wilson, James thinks that Flaubert "considers Frédéric a worm"[16] – though relishing the supposed persecution less than the more politically motivated 1930s critic. Yet this summary-view (approving or not) neglects a good deal in the novel, overlooking the tonal ambiguity of Flaubert's characteristic ironies – for a description like "ironic tone" only takes us so far – overlooking, that is, the inscrutability of ultimate attitude which is one of the resources and liabilities, one of the conditions, of the *style indirect libre*.

There is no mistaking the profusion of bathetic effect to which Frédéric's vision is at times subjected. Sometimes the fallibility of his Romantic taste, as a creature of his age, is exposed by explicit narratorial judgement: "What he valued above all was passion: Werther, René, Franck, Lara, Lélia and others more mediocre than these filled him with enthusiasm almost equally;"[17] or, more damagingly, his self-estimate is thrown comically into question by the impassive notation of his poetic sense of superiority to those around him: "On the other hand, the consciousness of being more valuable than these men diminished the fatigue he felt in looking at them."[18] At times the effect is epigrammatic, a curt deflating phrase setting off a carefully charged set-piece in Frédéric's face. When he looks at the smudged, confusing sketches of the copiously bragging painter Pellerin, "*Frédéric les admira*" (37) is the last sentence of a paragraph.

But whether this exposure, bitter as it is, amounts to "flaying remorselessly," in Wilson's Swiftian phrase, is another question. In the first of these cases, "*almost* equally" ("*presque également*") qualifies the damage done by the narrator's "mediocres" in a description of what is anyway adolescent taste; in the second, we may smile in a superior way at the character whose unexamined sense of superiority has been laid bare, but too smug a scorn for him on our part will lay us open to the same criticism; and in the third, the excusably ignorant, because young, Frédéric is admiring works "whose originals he wasn't acquainted with."[19] We should not forget, either, the generosity of Frédéric to his friends, especially Deslauriers and Arnoux and the worker Dussardier, which, although qualified in every case by some degree of selfish compromise, is beyond the strict call of duty; nor "the sweetness of the young man,"[20] which endears him to Arnoux.

More important is the question of the overall architecture into which the attenuations of Frédéric's estimability fit. Flaubert's stated purpose in the work – in a letter written as he began work on it – has a bearing here: "I want to do the moral history of the men of my generation; 'sentimental' would be truer. It is a book of love, of passion; but of passion in the only form in which it can exist nowadays, that is to say, inactive."[21] Frédéric's passion, from the beginning of the book to the end, attaches him to Madame Arnoux, despite all the occasions on which "his grand passion for Mme Arnoux began to be extinguished,"[22] or "this affection had become tranquil and resigned;"[23] and despite his despairing, complicated involvements with Louise Roque, Rosanette and Madame Dambreuse – despite, also, his repeated unsuccessful attempts at politics and public affairs, and his participant-observer contacts with the upheavals surrounding the Revolution of 1848 (which James barely mentions). She becomes poetically associated for him with all sorts of scenes and objects and ideas, and is often evoked in the "beautiful passages" (James, *Literary Criticism: French Writers*,..., 329) James admits the book to contain. Thus a magnificent enumeration of the squalid rainy outskirts of Paris culminates in an image of her: "but two eyes which to him were equal in value to the sun itself shone behind the mists."[24] Even making up to Madame Dambreuse late on, he is reminded of evenings with his deepest love: "similar evenings, with the same kinds of silence, came confusedly back to him."[25]

James seems, then in the 1902 essay to be making an inappropriate demand on *L'Éducation Sentimentale,* based perhaps on his immersion in *The Wings of the Dove,* where, according at least to the title and to the "Preface" a few years afterwards, Milly Theale is the focus of interest and Densher and Kate Croy are primarily being used as reflectors of her value. He takes for granted first that it is Flaubert's intention to establish the beauty and value of Madame Arnoux through the medium of Frédéric's life, treating him in effect as a device; and, second, that it is a failure on Flaubert's part that "she seems scarcely to affect, improve or determine it" (330). I'll take these in reverse order. The second judgement is unconvincing, in the sense that the great set-piece scenes of exotic and erotic yearning undeniably show Madame Arnoux profoundly affecting Frédéric; though whether she improves his life is debatable; and because their love is unfulfilled it is determining for him mainly in a negative way, preventing the whole-hearted pursuit of any other interests (when he says to her: "you are my sole occupation,"[26] it is truer than he means).

James's first apparent assumption, that Frédéric is a medium, a reflector for Madame Arnoux's value, seems equally insecure. The novel's devastating double ending (in Chapters VI and VII of the *Troisième Partie*) gives us first, certainly, the final encounter with the white-haired Madame Arnoux, after a separation of sixteen years and all the previous anguish of their protracted non-consummation, when she comes to see Frédéric, who "suspected Mme Arnoux of having come to offer herself to him."[27] James does not mention this scene, but it distinctly smudges the "image of passion cherished and abjured" for which he has idealizingly praised Madame Arnoux. Like many James characters, Frédéric is drawn by inner necessity not to take advantage of the opportunity, but he refrains out of a mixture of impulses in which Flaubert painfully details the base alongside the noble:

> *Frédéric* suspected *Mme Arnoux* had come to offer herself; and he was seized again by a lust now stronger than ever, furious, enraged. At the

same time, he felt something inexpressible, a repulsion, and a fear, as of incest. Another fear held him back, that of being disgusted afterwards. And then, what a fuss it would all be! – so, at once from prudence and not to degrade his ideal, he turned away and started to roll a cigarette.[28]

The state of inward conflict, of protective paralysis, rendered here has Madame Arnoux for its object; but by the last chapter of all, she has left the novel – "And that was all" – sees her out.[29] Frédéric and his old friend Deslauriers end *L'Éducation Sentimentale* by reminiscing about their visit in adolescence, thirty years before, to the brothel *"chez la Turque"* in Nogent, an abortive episode to which allusion has been glancingly made over four hundred pages before, and Frédéric says, somewhat puzzling Deslauriers: "It's there that we had the best thing of all!"[30] That the book's focus lies on Frédéric himself (as the subtitle of the whole work announces) is strongly intimated by a further scene of paralysis, of inactivity, placed at the very conclusion. What he remembers as their best moment is not the sexual intercourse one might expect in a brothel:

The heat, the apprehension of the unknown, a sort of remorse, and the very pleasure of seeing in a single sweep of the eye so many women available to him, these moved him so that he became very pale and stayed where he was, without a word.[31]

Anticipation rather than consummation controls Frédéric's imagination, it seems, and a fetishistic implication emerges from his tremulous remark to Madame Arnoux at their last meeting: "The sight of your foot disturbs me."[32] The terrifying sense of waste and painfully partial self-deception of these final pages, coming as the climax of the grim build-up of complications, bafflements and small humiliations that *L'Éducation Sentimentale* has massively documented, denies Flaubert's characters the compensations achieved by James's defeated heroes and heroines, whose imaginative life and moral sensitivity frequently give them inner satisfaction of some kind, even if sometimes only the satisfaction of a completed development.

James's 1902 essay at one point describes *L'Éducation Sen-timentale,* with a restrictive intention, as "large, laboured, immensely 'written,' with beautiful passages and a general emptiness, with a kind of leak in its stored sadness...by which its moral dignity escapes" (329). The "leak" in question for James is Frédéric, the imperfect "conduit;" but as I have tried to suggest it is possible to see Frédéric's imperfection and the correspond-ing escape of "moral dignity" as part of Flaubert's "conception" – he wrote declaredly *à contre-coeur*[33] – and part of his achievement. The imaginative triumph of the work in this view would lie, paradoxically, in its refusal to give the imagination the easy ride it mostly gets in works of the imagination, a refusal anticipating the rigors of Beckett. The reticent intensity of the narration over such a span establishes a potent and moving relation with the awed reader that gives a surprising weight to these final poised chapters. Flaubert's unflinching confron-tation, to the last, of a sensuously thronged world and a corre-spondingly flawed self that together offer almost nothing but circumstantial obstacles to the realization of an ideal – this is what he offers us as the overwhelming climax of his painful work.

The lesson of James's discussion of Flaubert's novel for us is also painful, in part. It is indeed in a sense tragic that great writers, even when great critics also, should be often unable to appreciate the achievements of others, as if the concentrated singularity of perspective which holds together their imaginative world entailed in this respect a tight economy of speculative experience. That he was closed off to Flaubert's vision of things is perhaps a sign of the sacrifices James had had to make in order to be able to write *The Wings of the Dove,* itself a great and powerful, though formally flawed, novel – one which, unlike *L'Éducation Sentimentale,* finds a value in consciousness and its evolution through experience that may amount to a not particularly Christian version of the *felix culpa.* I have not meant to say that one cannot share James's misgivings about *L'Éducation Sentimentale* – more that it does very powerfully something James could never do. Just as James in his novels does things Flaubert never could.[34]

NOTES

1. Henry James, *Literary Criticism: Essays on Literature, American Writers, English Writers* (I), eds. Leon Edel and Mark Wilson (New York: Library of America, 1984), 827.

2. Henry James, *Literary Criticism: French Writers, Other European Writers, The Prefaces to the New York Edition*, eds. Leon Edel and Mark Wilson (New York: Library of America, 1984), 799.

3. *Henry James Letters: Volume II. 1875-1883*, ed. Leon Edel (Cambridge, MA: Belknap Press, 1975), 14.

4. *"Depuis que je le connais j'envisage ses livres autrement que je n'ai fait jusqu'ici."*

5. Gustave Flaubert, *L'Éducation Sentimentale: Histoire d'un jeune homme*, ed. and Introduction Édouard Maynial (Paris: Garnier, 1964), 300. All subsequent quotations in French followed by bracketed page numbers are from this edition.

6. F. R. Leavis, *The Great Tradition: George Eliot, Henry James, Joseph Conrad* (1948) (Harmondsworth: Penguin, 1972), 132.

7. Edmund Wilson, "The Ambiguity of Henry James," in Edmund Wilson, *The Triple Thinkers: Twelve Essays on Literary Subjects* (Harmondsworth: Penguin, 1962), 117-18.

8. *The Letters of Gustave Flaubert, 1857-1880*, ed. and trans. Francis Steegmuller (Cambridge, MA: Belknap Press, 1982), 105 (Letter to George Sand of 17 May 1867).

9. "The Ambiguity of Henry James," 119.

10. By J. P. Mowbray in "The Apotheosis of Henry James" (November 1902), reprinted in *Henry James: The Critical Henry James: A Study of the Late Novels*, ed. Roger Gard (Cambridge: Cambridge U. P., 1989), 137.

11. H. R. Hays in *Hound and Horn*, quoted in F. R. Leavis, *The Great Tradition:...*, 181.

12. Harriet Waters Preston in the *Atlantic Monthly* (1903), reprinted in *Henry James: The Critical Heritage*, 334. The contrast seems to be between saying and doing on the one hand, and *being*, being an image, on the other. James's "none the less" confusingly doesn't work with "vague" (since the lack of speeches and acts makes her all the vulgar).

14. *The Great Tradition:...*, 183.

15. David Gervais comments persuasively that "the phrase 'a noble impression' is too cold and words like 'beautiful and vague' make her too evanescent to evoke the woman who is made real to us in her frustrated love for Frédéric and her humiliating marriage" (*Flaubert and Henry James: A Study in Contrasts* «London: Macmillan, 1978», 209). James's phrases here, though, refer respectively to Flaubert's intention (unfulfilled according to him) and his actual achievement in the novel. Gervais's discussion of *L'Éducation Sentimentale* is extremely stimulating; and there is a helpful section on it in Philip Grover, *Henry James and the French Novel: A Study in Inspiration* (London: Paul Elek, 1973).

16. "The Ambiguity of Henry James," 117.

17. "*Il estimait par-dessus tout la passion: Werther, René, Franck, Lara, Lélia et d'autres plus médiocres l'enthousiasmaient presque également*" (15).

18. "*Cependant, la conscience de mieux valoir que ces hommes atténuait la fatigue de les regarder*" (66).

19. "*dont il ne connaissait pas les modèles*" (37-8).

20. "*la douceur du jeune homme*" (315).

21. Quoted in "Introduction," *L'Éducation Sentimentale*, I. It comes from a letter to Mlle. Leroyer de Chantepie of 6 October 1864. "*Je veux faire l'histoire morale des hommes de ma génération; 'sentimentale' serait plus vrai. C'est un livre d'amour, de passion; mais de passion tel qu'elle peut exister maintenant, c'est-à-dire inactive.*"

22. "*sa grande passion pour Madame Arnoux commençait à s'éteindre*" (26).

23. "*cette affection était devenue tranquille et résignée*" (97).

24. "*mais deux yeux qui valaient pour lui le soleil resplendissaient derrière la brume*" (103).

25. "*des soirs semblables, avec des silences pareils, revinrent dans son esprit, confusément*" (367).

26. "*vous êtes mon occupation exclusive*" (271).

27. "*soupçonna Mme Arnoux d'être venue pour s'offrir*" (422-3).

28. "*il était repris par une convoitise plus forte que jamais, furieuse, enragée. Cependant, il sentait quelque chose d'inexprimable, une répulsion, et comme l'effroi d'un inceste. Une autre crainte l'arrêta, celle d'en avoir dégoût plus tard. D'ailleurs, quel embarras ce serait! – et tout à la fois par prudence et pour ne pas dégrader son idéal, il tourna sur ses talons et se mit à faire une cigarette*" (423).

29. "*Et ce fut tout*" (423).

30. "*C'est là ce que nous avons eu de meilleur!*"

31. "*la chaleur qu'il faisait, l'appréhension de l'inconnu, une espèce de remords, et jusqu'au plaisir de voir, d'un seul coupo d'oeil, tant de femmes à sa disposition, l'émurent tellement qu'il; devint très pâle et restait sans avancer, sans rien dire*" (427).

32. "*La vue de votre pied me trouble*" (422).

33. He complained: "What I find desolating is the conviction that I am doing something useless, I mean something opposed to the aim of Art, which is vague exaltation." ("*Ce qui me désole, c'est la conviction de faire une chose inutile, je veux dire opposée au but de l'Art, qui est l'exaltation vague* «quoted in "Introduction»," *L'Éducation Sentimentale*, II; it comes from a letter to Mme. Roger des Genettes of December 1864).

34. Acknowledgement is gratefully made to *The Yearbook of English Studies*, 1997 for permission to reprint this essay in revised form.

George Smith,
Maine College of Art, USA

Manet, James and Postmodern Narrative

Thanks to cultural studies, interartistic criticism is booming, especially when it comes to modernist fiction and painting, and perhaps most especially when it comes to Henry James studies. More often than not, though, the ever-burgeoning interest in the relationship between modernist fiction and painting has been preoccupied with comparative analysis. This is not what Raymond Williams had in mind when he talked about relationships. Insofar as modernism is about pure form, the trouble lies partly in the object of study. While modern forms appropriate from one another, they do not blend, and thereby remain pure and essentially autonomous, in keeping with the principles of modernist aesthetics. Which is to say that modernist interartistics has really been a case of appropriation without formal hybridization. The analogical approach to this problem has proven what we already know: a style of fiction can be like a style of painting, and vice versa. In making this gross oversimplification, I do not mean to suggest that all interartistic criticism begs the question, so what? The serious discussion of modernist interartistics goes at least as far back as Joseph Frank's 1945 essay on "Spatial Form in Modern Literature." True, in this proto-cultural critique Frank did not go so far as to problematize the ideology of modernist appropriation. Philip Rahv and Frank Kermode did, however, and they denounced spatial fiction as a fascist aesthetic.

Be that as it may, modernist painters have made any number of raids across the literary borders, and again, this is usually a matter of hostile if subtle appropriation. As Greenberg put it, "Modernist painting asks that a literary theme be translated into strictly optical, two-dimensional terms before becoming the subject of pictorial art – which means its being translated in such a way that it loses its literary character" (17). What Greenberg is

327

describing here and what Frank is talking about in his essay on spatial form in modernist literature is the monological structure of formalism. The description of formalism as a monological or one-voiced aesthetic is perfectly correct. In interartistic terms this means that when literature is put to use in modernist painting it is stripped of its autonomy and serves painterly aspirations. Often as not these aspirations have to do with painting's struggle against literature for hegemony within what Bourdieu calls the cultural field. The same holds true when the spatial form of visual art is subjected to appropriation by modern literature.

This kind of appropriation obeys the categorical imperative of Kant's modernist aesthetic and abides as well by Lessing's proscriptions against mixing temporal and spatial form, and as I suggested, these matters do give rise to serious critical debate. But while such polemics tend to be more sophisticated than the analogical analysis I complained about earlier, all too often the effect is more deleterious. Rarely in these discussions do we hear anything but the possibility of monological formalism in the so-called modernist epoch, and this powerful underwriting of a presumptive aesthetic monolith has pulled the wool for a long time. But if feminists have begun to see that dominant patriarchal modernism was not the only game in town, it is also true that modernist interartistics was not the only kind of interartistics going on in the period in question. In fact there can be discerned in the nineteenth century a dialogical relationship between painting and fiction. This postmodern development includes authors and painters long held critical hostage to modernist history – Manet and James perhaps foremost among them.

In what follows I want to discuss the way Manet contradicts the critical and discursive history by which his painting is still defined. I then want to look at the way Manet's postmodern aesthetic turns up in James. Is this to say that Manet and James were absolute postmodernists? No. But I *will* suggest that their interartistic aesthetic comes very close to what Suleiman has in mind when she says that the "appropriation, misappropriation, montage, collage, hybridization, and general mixing-up of visual and verbal texts and discourses, from all periods of the past as well as from the multiple social and linguistic fields of the present is the most characteristic feature of what can be called the 'postmodern style'" (191). As such, I will argue that Manet and James advance a dialogical interartistic form against the monological aesthetics of modernist ideology.

Insofar as the advent of modern painting marks a refusal to represent anything but painting itself, the premodernist pictorial narrative, whether history or myth, gives way to an arrangement of paint on a flat surface. In a word, form erases content, leaving itself as the sole arbiter of the judgement of taste. So at any rate runs the history of modernism. I have already quoted Greenberg's remark about the way "Modernist painting asks that a literary theme be translated into strictly optical, two--dimensional terms." According to Greenberg, modern painting begins with Manet, precisely because he was the first to liberate painting from its literary dependence. With Manet, Greenberg argues, painting became a "purely optical experience" (15). Greenberg is hardly alone in his opinion. And yet while it may be true that formalism was established as a modernist school of practice by the Impressionists, who supposedly followed Manet in this regard, the same does not apply to Manet at all. Far from doing away with literary content, Manet inverts the social literariness of French painting to a private psychoanalytical frame of literary representation. This inversion of what can be called the style of Poussin marks a Copernican revolution in Western aesthetics.

Here I am speaking most particularly of *Olympia*. With this painting more than any other, Manet situates himself *against* the dominant modernism that Greenberg and others see emerging in *Les fleurs du mal, Madame Bovary* and *Olympia* at roughly the same time.[1] This is not only to say that postmodernism begins much earlier than previously thought and that it runs coeval with modernism; it is also to say that although postmodernism is described as a lately formulated feminist aesthetic, its resistance to the patriarchal/dominant modernism constituted in Baudelaire and Flaubert was there from the start, when Manet exhibited the work in 1863. Along these lines T. J. Clark and Charles Bernheimer have already shown that *Olympia* represents a primary challenge to the male look, which in its discursive construction of nineteenth-century bourgeois patriarchal hegemony had become nothing less than a full-blown ocular centrism. But this kind of analysis has yet to be squared with its own designation of *Olympia* as the first modernist painting. Through the recognition of Manet's development of a center of consciousness point of view in *Olympia,* we can see how this mode of narrative address allows Manet to represent consciousness and the unconscious, and this in turn will open an approach to the painting's feminist postmodern aesthetic.

In the center of consciousness point of view, the traditional narrator is done away with, and the job of narration is given to one of the characters. This character does not tell the story; rather, the story is dramatized through his/her eyes. If the point of view is rendered in absolute terms, we see nothing that this character does not see, and, as far as that goes, the character who plays the role of center of consciousness is never seen, just as we never see ourselves, unless looking in a mirror. Famously and erroneously attributing the invention of the center of consciousness point of view to his friend Henry James, Percy Lubbock remarks of *The Ambassadors*: "Throughout...Strether's point of view still reigns; the only eyes in the matter are his. There is no sight of the man himself as his companion sees him. Miss Gostrey is clearly visible, and Madame de Vionnet and Little Bilham, or whoever it may be; the face of Strether is never turned to the reader" (James, *The Ambassadors,* 165). And just as we alone are privy to our own thoughts and to no one else's, in this narrative point of view we have access to the thoughts of the center of consciousness and to no-one else's in the text. In developing the center of consciousness narrative point of view, Manet takes example from Velazquez's *Las Meninas*.[2]

In the Velazquez a mirror reflects the image of the royal couple who occupy the space just outside the visual confines of the frame, whence they, along with us, look back into the painting. The mirror is located behind Velazquez, who addresses his canvas with an eye toward his sitters. Meanwhile various members of the court, including Fantata and her dog, occupy themselves in the foreground of the picture. As Foucault suggests, we are inclined to take in the scene from the psychological viewpoint of the king and queen. We see the drama as they would see it, not as a painting, but as a moment in their lives, complicated by the imperious demeanor of the artist, who for the present is dominating the action and seems an all but threatening, if not usurping royal power. If we consider *Olympia* within the context of this mirror play, with which Manet was familiar, we can begin to see that Olympia is looking at someone outside the painting's visual field much as Velazquez is looking at Philip and Mariana. While the royal presence is established in the mirror behind Velazquez, Manet, I want to suggest, has similarly established an unseen presence, by way of a "mirror effect" in Olympia's glossy black, impenetrable eyes. In order that we catch this intertextual play with the mirror diagesis in *Las Meninas*, Manet has laid down several markers.

For one thing, Olympia's scandal immediately associates her with two other prostitutes notorious to the Parisian art world: Baudelaire's whore, Phryne, who "freeze[s] the world in a perfect mirror: // the timeless light of [her] wide eyes" (Baudelaire, 24), and also Emma Bovary, whose black eyes reflect back at Charles the image of himself: "mirrored in miniature" (23-4).[3] Here we should note the suggestion of castration in Baudelaire's allusion to Medusa and in Charles's shrinkage to tiny inconsequence. Along these lines Bernheimer observes that Manet has set up "a mirror effect whereby Olympia reflects back to the male viewer the desire motivating his gaze" (Bernheimer, 15). As he goes on to say,

> the painting initiates this discursive reflection by constructing its beholder as male. It is evidently to a male viewer that Olympia offers her availability as a "token triumph over the threat of castration and a protection against it" (Freud). She appears to be displayed as an erotic spectacle signifying passive submission to male desire. She seduces her viewer by seeming to confirm his mastery, reinforcing his illusion of narcissistic wholeness by presenting herself iconically as

a magnifying mirror of his phallic power. But this tricky mirror is
a trap. Instead of hiding its operation, the mirror reveals its distortions
disseminated throughout the representational field. (15-16)

Indeed when he subsequently refers to the "beholder" of
Olympia as "Olympia's client," Bernheimer implies his sense of
a center of consciousness narrative point of view, and this adds
weight to T. J. Clark's earlier and identical sense of the matter,
remarked in his attempt to "specify where Olympia came from
and *whom she was looking at*" (Clark 86; my italics). (Clark picks
this up, by the way, from one of the painting's first critics, who
insisted that "Arthur is certainly in the ante-chamber waiting"
– quoted in Clark, 87).

If everybody agrees that the maid has brought the flowers on
behalf of a client, this client has yet to be recognized as the object
of Olympia's gaze. And yet the bouquet bears no card, indicating
that the giver's identity is not represented in writing precisely
because he is there in person. Manet has given other hints to the
same effect, such as the startled look in the maid's eyes, the
scared cat and the fact that Olympia is actually in the act of
sitting up and lifting her head off the pillow, indicating her own
sudden surprise. All of this points to something like the
following scenario. A client arrives bearing flowers. While he
waits in the anteroom, the maidservant brings Olympia the
bouquet, along with the client's request for an audience. As the
maidservant is presenting the flowers, the client barges in
unannounced. It is this moment that Manet dramatizes, with
Olympia staring her intruder down at the threshold. This
explains why the cat's back is up and its tail is stiff, and why it is
glaring wide-eyed at the same point in space toward which
Olympia directs her gaze. It also explains why the startled maid is
not so much presenting the flowers as actually flinching away
from Olympia, as if the intrusion might be blamed on her.

So, do we have here a young man, romantically inclined, fallen
in love with a professional lover, bursting in to proclaim his
affections only to be met with a castrating cut by the object of his
desire? Whatever the case, we do in fact have an unseen third
party, through which Manet has constructed a center of

consciousness narrative point of view. Which is to say that we do not look at Olympia directly, as long supposed. Just as we are positioned directly behind Strether's eyes in *The Ambassadors,* in *Olympia* we are positioned directly behind the eyes met by Olympia's gaze. Looking through those eyes, we witness the image of Olympia, glaring back at her intruder as he stands at the threshold of her suddenly violated private space. As Paul B. Armstrong has pointed out,[4] the viewer of the painting is not "dismissed by" Olympia's gaze, as Foucault says of Velazquez's gaze in *Las Meninas* (Foucault, 4). Rather, the viewer is implicated by, and involved in the diagetic tableau, so that Olympia's effect on the center of consciousness has a similar effect on whomever is looking at the painting (which no doubt goes a long way to explain the outrage the painting ignited when it was first exhibited, at the *Salon des Refuses*).

This narrative construct reflects the male look as it is virtually arrested in the appropriation of the Other. Here we have a story of self-apprehension as well as arrest. In the mirror image of Olympia's gaze, Manet's center of consciousness witnesses himself stopped dead in his tracks, exposed in the act of scopophilac appropriation. This anti-climax marks a startling shift, culturally and art-historically. As Heidegger points out, "being" is dependent on "dwelling," the latter itself depending on clearly-bounded borders. In this sense, woman is represented in the history of the nude as non "being," insofar as she is contained within the borders of patriarchal space. Titian's *Venus of Urbino* is a good case in point, as is the Ingres *Odalisque*. Everything about the marriage *boudoir* and the *seraglio,* from the architecture to the furnishing and rich fabrics, is a representation of phallic space, within which the Other is secured and displayed as patriarchy's most prized possession. Intertextually engaged with both of these paintings, *Olympia* represents woman as "being" – precisely insofar as Olympia controls her own space, as her gaze cuts off the male look at the borders of her domain.

More specifically, of course, we are dealing with the look as a matter of psychoanalytical aesthetics. In this regard Mulvey reminds us that Freud "associated scopophilia with taking other people as objects and subjecting them to a controlling and curious gaze" (Mulvey, 363). As she goes on to say, "this [look] begins in childhood, most notably as it concerns the child's curiosity about other people's genital and bodily functions, about the presence or absence of the penis and retrospectively about the primal scene" (363). Inasmuch as we are headed directly for the primal scene in the present analysis, Mulvey can take us a little further along the way. Bringing her discussion to the matter of cinemagraphic gaze/body dynamics, she says that the "mode of representation of woman and the conventions of diagesis" are both "associated with a look: that of the spectator in direct scopophilic contact with the female form displayed for his enjoyment (connoting male fantasy)" (368). But this has to do with the idea that woman

> also connotes something that the look continually circles around but disavows: her lack of a penis, implying a threat of castration and hence unpleasure. Ultimately, the meaning of woman is sexual difference, the absence of the penis is visually ascertainable, the material evidence on which is based the castration complex essential for the organization of entrance to the symbolic order and the Law of the Father. Thus the woman as icon, displayed for the gaze and enjoyment of men, active controllers of the look, always threatens to evoke the anxiety it originally signified. The male unconscious has two avenues of escape from castration anxiety: [the first is voyeurism and the second is the]...complete disavowal of castration by the substitution of a fetish object or turning the represented figure itself into a fetish so that it becomes reassuring rather than dangerous.... (368)[5]

The remarks on the second, fetishistic avenue lay out for us precisely what Manet's nude refuses the center of consciousness: flight from castration anxiety through the fetishistic register. I want to elaborate on this process, after which we can examine the way James imposes the same refusal on *his* center of conscious through the voyeuristic register.

The analytical approach to Manet's representation of thwarted fetishistic gaze would seem to be through Lacan's mirror stage, if only because of Olympia's mirror reflection thereof. Because of its closer proximity to the origins of castration anxiety and the Oedipal complex, however, *Nachträglichkeit,* or deferred action is in this case the more productive approach to the problem at hand. This is the memory dynamic by which the thwarted scopophilic/fetishistic impulse we are describing is re-routed back to the primal scene. According to Lacan, *Nachträglichkeit* lies at the center of Freud's theory of subjectivity, and indeed, according to Malcolm Bowie, it lies at the center of Lacan's as well. Rather than the mirror stage in and of itself, it is this mnemonic mechanism that is represented through Manet's center of consciousness narrative point of view.

We can illustrate how *Nachträglichkeit* works by way of the Wolfman case. In this case voyeurism instead of fetish is the scopophilic defence put into place in the effort to avert the primal scene, but as Mulvey suggests, it is always a matter of either voyeurism or fetish when it comes to preventing the return of the repressed primal scene during moments of castration anxiety brought on by scopophilia. According to Freud, at the age of one and a half, the child Wolfman "witnessed a coitus *a tergo* [from behind] three times repeated; he was able to see his mother's genitals as well as his father's organ, and he understood the process as well as its significance" (37). Two years later, the young Wolfman comes upon the housemaid Grusha on her knees, scrubbing the floor. He sees her from the same angle he occupied during the primal scene, and as with the primal scene, his viewpoint is voyeuristic. Because of the mnemonic relation between the image the Wolfman sees from behind (the housemaid Grusha on her knees scrubbing) and the repressed event (his mother in the same *a tergo* position and making the same motion during the primal scene), the Wolfman's initial scopophilic encounter with the maid Grusha causes castration anxiety of such force that it overloads the sadistic function of voyeurism, and the short-circuited repressive mechanism triggers *Nachträglichkeit.* Organizing the fundamental structure of the Wolfman's psychological development around the original effect of the primal scene – linked always to the trauma of castration – the Wolfman's future is punctuated by a long series of *a tergo* visual crises like the one with Grusha, all of them voyeuristic and all of them referring back, through *Nachträglichkeit* or deferred action, to the primal scene and the origins of the castration complex. Each time the Wolfman is caught up by *Nachträglichkeit* he understands the primal scene in a new light, shaded by all the previous returns, and as a result of this experience, he undergoes re-subjectification.

As Bernheimer says of the male spectator we have identified as Manet's center of consciousness, Olympia "reflects back to him the fetishizing desire in his gaze, forcing him to respond to the scandalous lack she represents in his unconscious" (24). In other words, in the confrontation with Olympia's castrating look, there is no way to fetishize what he perceives in her nudity as a "castrated body," no way to "build up the physical beauty of the object," so as to transform it "into something satisfying in itself" (Mulvey, 368). Moreover, the fetish *per se* – where it shows up specifically in the black bootlace around Olympia's neck and in the black cat's erect tail – works against its own function. From the bootlace hangs an oval pearl pendant (signifying the female genitalia, i.e., castration); and likewise, the cat's fear-driven hostility reverses its own fetishistic function, invoking the very thing it is meant to alleviate: castration anxiety. Which is to say that Olympia's deconstruction of the male look takes place here, at the point where the unchecked castration anxiety is channeled back, retroactively, to the one traumatic visual event that fetish is supposed to provide *a detour* around: namely, the castration trauma that resides in the primal scene.

To sum up, *Nachträglichkeit* takes place in the unconscious of the center of consciousness as he attempts to disavow the castration assigned to Olympia's body. Here we see the construction of decentered, poststructural subjectivity as Lacan describes it. Its resistance to the ideology of dominant modernism cannot be over-stressed. As for the process of the construction, according to Silverman, "Masculinity is perhaps never so fully troubled as it is within the primal scene. It is not merely that knowledge fails there to provide power, or to shore up sexual difference, but that vision, which is culturally coded as a phallic function, and which indeed helps constitute masculinity, turns back against the [subject, causing] a sense of inadequacy and exclusion" (Silverman, "Too Early/Too Late:...," 158). As for poststructural subjectivity per se, it has long been established as a feminist stronghold and needn't be reestablished here. Suffice it to say that in its nullification of humanist essentialism, poststructural subjectivity upsets the bourgeois patriarchal order of things. I would only add that the artistic representation of poststructural subjectivity can be described as the postmodern aesthetic *par excellence*.

In the space remaining I want to suggest how James represents Manet's narrative aesthetic through the center of consciousness narrative point of view in *The Ambassadors*. When Strether arrives at the river's edge, in the famous recognition scene, his look focuses on the two lovers in the boat, and the visual (spatial/pictorial) dynamics shift from scopophilia to that of voyeurism. This scene is so notoriously interartistic that I will not bother to situate it within the particulars of the oblong g[u]ilt frame. I will only remark that the passage unfolds with Strether's view of the French countryside. What he sees replicates a Lambinet he had lost the chance of acquiring twenty years earlier, and the memory of this loss is now returned from the repressed. This return of a long repressed loss is a classic screen memory that veils, and at the same time signifies, the more deeply repressed image of primal castration. As Silverman argues, Strether's subsequent voyeuristic discovery of the sexual relationship between Chad and Madame de Vionnet does indeed reproduce the primal image and the castration trauma that goes with it (*The Ambassadors*, 165). And it does so in the same way that *Olympia* reproduces the primal image for Manet's center of consciousness/fetishist and the maid Grusha reproduces the primal image for the Wolfman/voyeur. Indeed the primal scene that James represents through Strether's voyeuristic discovery of the sexual relationship between Chad and Madame de Vionnet bears out the precise details of the primal scene as Freud describes it in the Wolfman case.

In this case – and according to Freud this happens frequently

– the primal scene is interrupted by the child-voyeur's scream, resulting from his passing a stool in reaction to the sexual drama. At this point, the little Wolfman's parents freeze and turn and look at the cause of the interruption. In Strether's case, James has positioned Chad and Madame de Vionnet face-to-face in the small boat, about the size of a bed, Chad rowing, his back going to and fro, making a motion similar to what the Wolfman saw when he came upon Grusha scrubbing the floor. When she discovers the voyeur staring at them from the river bank, Madame de Vionnet gives Chad a look that "bid[s] him keep still" (*The Ambassadors,* 307-8), whereupon Chad stops in mid-stroke. For Strether this analogical mnemonic image triggers *Nachträglichkeit,* which James calls the "suddenly-determined *absolute* of perception." For James, this is the moment wherein "an old latent and dormant impression, a buried germ, implanted by experience and then forgotten,...flashes to the surface...and there meets the vivifying ray" ("Preface" to *What Maisie New,* Blackmur, 151). Which is to say that Strether has reached what Lacan would describe as another "turning point where the subject restructures himself" (48). Re(self)structured through the process of *Nachträglichkeit,* Strether becomes, in other words, a renewed – poststructural – subject. In relation to Manet, James's narrative/pictorial representation of *Nachträglichkeit* is intertextual and historical. As I have suggested elsewhere, James first dramatized *Nachträglichkeit* through a tentative center of consciousness point of view in the recognition scene in *The Portrait of a Lady,* and *Nachträglichkeit* formulates the Jamesian aesthetic all the way through the major phase (Smith, 1992).

Always represented through variations on the center of consciousness narrative point of view, *Nachträglichkeit* determines the postmodern aesthetic in painters and writers such as Degas, Cezanne, Proust, Joyce, Woolf and Djuna Barnes. The idea that these supposed modernists ought to be reconsidered in terms of postmodernism is hardly new. I cite for example Silverman's recent discussions of James and Proust (1992), and even ten years ago, in her essay on "The Body Politic,"

Smith-Rosenberg insisted that "Feminist modernists spoke the political language of post-modernism," insofar as "they constructed a female subjectivity that was decentered" (117). And while Smith-Rosenberg is speaking here of content, we should not forget that the postmodernist construct we have been describing is also a matter of dialogical form in discursive opposition to monological formalism. Anyhow, contemporary feminist postmodernists such as Sherrie Levine, Barbara Kruger, Cindy Sherman, Richard Prince, Jenny Holzer and Sue Coe further develop the anti-modernist aesthetic we have brought forward. They hybridize word and image, time and space, picture and narrative in the same dialogical form that we see in Manet and James, and they do so in order to represent *Nachträglichkeit* against the dominant modernism that begins in Baudelaire and Flaubert.

NOTES

1. While it might be objected that Manet was a close follower of Baudelaire, critics have begun to challenge this long-standing oversimplification (see Lethbridge). As for Flaubert, I would suggest that *Olympia* can be seen as a direct deconstruction of the fetishized prostitute as represented in Emma Bovary (see my "*Madame Bovary* and the Genealogy of Dominant Modernism.")

2. Manet takes examples from other texts as well, including Velazquez's *Rokeby Venus,* Van Eyck's *Anolfini Marriage,* and Poussin's Louvre *Self-Portrait.*

3. For a discussion of Emma Bovary's role as prostitute, see Smith, "*Madame Bovary....*"

4. Armstrong made the point during discussion following this paper's presentation at The 21st International Conference of the Joseph Conrad Society (UK) with the Henry James Society of America, University of Kent, Canterbury, England, July 1995.

5. Mulvey's early development of a theory of the gaze has been taken to task as essentialist and indeed Mulvey has since revised her position on the matter. But the analysis put forward in "Visual Pleasure and Narrative Cinema" should not be entirely abandoned. It pertains to the present discussion precisely because up until *Olympia* the representation of the female nude generally if not universally constructed males as "the active controllers of the look."

WORKS CITED

Baudelaire Charles. *Les fleurs du mal,* trans. Richard Howard. Boston: David Godine, 1982.
Bernheimer Charles. "The Uncanny Lure of Manet's *Olympia,*" in *Seduction and Theory,* ed. Dianne Hunter. Urbana: U. of Illinois P., 1989, 13-27.
Bowie Malcolm. *Lacan.* London: Fontana, 1991.
Clark T. J. *The Painting of Modern Life: Paris and the Art of Manet and His Followers.* Princeton: Princeton U. P., 1984.
Flaubert Gustave. *Madame Bovary,* trans. Alan Russell. London: Penguin Books, 1950.
Foucault Michael. *The Order of Things.* New York: Vintage Books, 1973.
Frank Joseph. "Spatial Form in Modern Literature," *The Sewanee Review* (Spring, Summer, Autumn) 1945; reprinted in *Criticism,* ed. Mark Schorer et. al. New York: Harcourt, Brace, 1958, 379-92.
Freud Sigmund. *From the History of an Infantile Neurosis. The Standard Edition,* XVII, ed. James Strachey. London: Hogarth Press, 1955.
Greenberg Clement. "Modernist Painting," *Art and Literature,* 4 (Spring 1963); reprinted in *Postmodern Perspectives,* ed. Howard Risatti. Englewood Cliffs: Prentice Hall, 1990, 12-19.
James Henry. *The Ambassadors,* ed. S. P. Rosenbaum. New York: Norton, 1964.
Lacan Jacques, *Ecrits,* trans. Alan Sheridan. New York: W. W. Norton, 1977.
Lethbridge Robert. "Manet's Textual Frames," in *Artistic Relations,* eds. Peter Collier and Robert Lethbridge. New Haven: Yale U. P., 1994, 144-58.
Lubbock Percy. *The Craft of Fiction.* New York: Viking Press, 1957.
Mathiessen F. O. *Henry James: The Major Phase.* Oxford: Oxford U. P., 1944.
Mitchell W. J. T. *Iconology: Image, Text, Ideology.* Chicago: U. of Chicago P., 1986.
Mulvey Laura. "Visual Pleasure and Narrative Cinema," in *Art After Modernism: Rethinking Representation,* ed. Brian Wallace. New York: The Museum of Contemporary Art, 1984, 361-74; reprinted from *Screen,* 16: 3 (1975), 16-18.
Owens Craig. "The Discourse of Others: Feminists and Post-Modernism," in *The Anti-Aesthetic,* ed. Forster. Seattle: Bay Press, 1983.
Silverman Kaja. *Male Subjectivity at the Margins.* New York: Routledge, 1992.
Silverman Kaja. "Too Early/Too Late: Subjectivity and the Primal Scene in Henry James," *Novel: A Forum on Fiction,* 21 (1988), 147-72.

Smith-Rosenberg Carroll. "The Body Politic," in *Coming to Terms,* ed. Elizabeth Weed. New York: Routledge, 1985, 101-21.

Smith George. "*Madame Bovary* and the Genealogy of Dominant Modernism," *Genre,* 27 (1995), 212-42.

Smith George. "James, Degas, and the Emersonian Gaze," *Novel: A Forum on Fiction,* 25 (1992), 360-87.

Suleiman Susan Rubin. *Subversive Intent.* Cambridge, MA: Harvard U. P., 1990.

The Art of the Novel, ed. R. P. Blackmur. New York: W. W. Norton, 1964.

Velazquez, Diego Rodriguez. Las Meninas. Museo del Prado, Madrid, Spain.

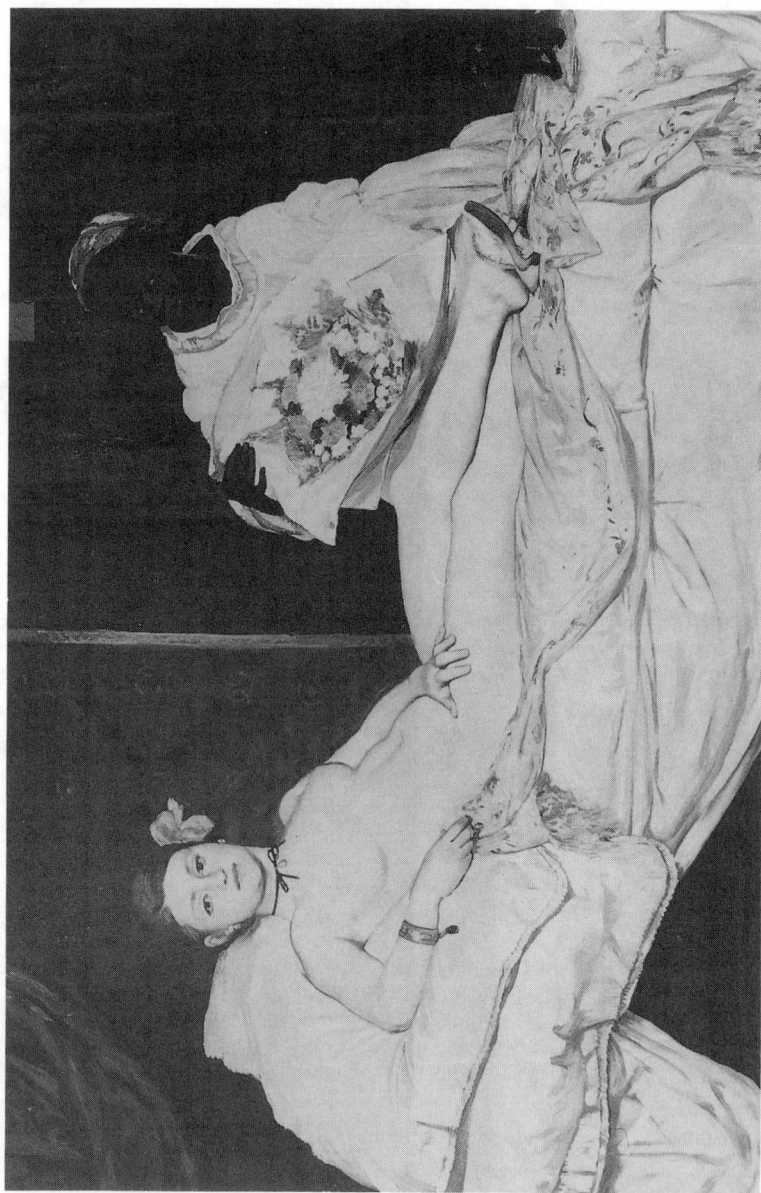

Manet, Edouard. Olympia, 1863. Musee d'Orsay, Paris, France.

INDEX OF NAMES

343

Ford F. M. (Hueffer F. M.) – 62, 79, 189, 190, 207, 216, 263, 264, 267
Forster – 340
Fothergill A. – 113
Foucault M. – 273, 275, 331, 333, 340
Fowler V. C. – 178, 184
France A. – 196, 215, 216
Frank J. – 327, 328, 340
Franklin H. B. – 241, 243
Fraser G. – 257
Frazer J. G. – 217, 218
Freccero Y. – 242
Frederic H. – 195
Freedman J. – 181, 184
Freud S. – 151-153, 158, 160, 170, 217, 218, 275, 331, 333-335, 337, 338, 340
Friedman A. – 102, 112

Galsworthy J. – 25, 26, 167
Gard R. – 307, 325
Garnett E. – 87, 111
Genettes R. des – 326
Gérome – 313
Gervais D. – 325
Gide A. – 235
Giles – 274
Gillon A. – 257
Girard R. – 217-223, 229-232, 236, 241-244
Goetz P. W. – 258
Goldman E. – 300
Gorky M. – 283
Gosse E. – 318
Graham R. B. Cunninghame – 35, 36, 110, 205-207, 261
Graham W. – 292, 301, 308
Gramsci A. – 282, 307
Graver L. – 143, 166, 169
Greenberg C. – 327-329, 340
Greene G. – 181, 182, 184
Gregory P. – 241
Griffin S. M. – 61, 62, 176, 184
Griffith S. – 178
Grossberg L. – 63
Grover P. – 325

Guerard A. J. – 257, 258
Guizot F. – 277

Habegger A. – 95, 96, 184
Habermas J. – 242
Haggard H. Rider – 266
Haight G. S. – 111
Halperin J. – 68, 80
Halperin M. – 311
Halsted J. B. – 24
Hamilton C. Vanderveer – 145
Hampson R. – 123, 145, 194, 213, 215, 216, 259
Hardy T. – 8
Harrison – 274
Hawthorn J. – 157, 166, 167
Hawthorne N. – 180, 183
Hay E. Knapp – 3, 23, 24
Hays H. R. – 325
Hegel G. W. F. – 218
Heidegger M. – 333
Henley W. E. – 189, 205
Hitchcock A. – 182
Hocks R. – 171, 176, 184
Holland L. – 176, 184
Holliday D. – 181
Hollywood P. – 277
Holquist M. – 215
Holzer J. – 339
Hopkins G. M. – 120
Horne P. – 143, 313
Howe I. – 3, 4, 24, 290, 291, 306-308
Hugo V. – 3
Humphries R. – 258
Hunter D. – 340
Hyam R. – 264, 274

Ingersoll E. G. – 146
Ingram A. – 96, 148, 166, 167, 170
Ingres J. A. D. – 333
Iser W. – 41, 61, 62

James H. (senior) – 92, 93, 95
James R. – 94, 95

346   Index of Names